European League Football 1948-1949

by Eric Hayton

ISBN 978-0-9548549-3-5

Published by Rose Villa Publications 2009

Printed by 4edge Ltd, Hockley, Essex

© Rose Villa Publications

Dedication

Thanks to Hans-Eirik Jonassen from Norway for providing additional information and some missing results from Scandinavian and other nations.

Post War European Football

Welcome to the third volume in a season-by-season series of books dedicated to the beauty and preservation of league football in Europe.

Since the first European annual was produced by Mike Hammond in the late 1980's, there are a large number of years post WWII where those annuals have never existed. These cannot be as detailed as those massive volumes, but it is a starting point. As well as working forwards to the 80's, it is intended to work backwards too – at least to the early 30's when professionalism began to be accepted on mainland Europe.

The RSSSF has done and continues to do a fantastic job in accumulating these records, not just for Europe, but for the world. Their work will continue for many years, as there are still many gaps.

For all you statisticians out there I hope these books will be interesting and maybe inspire even more research into the history of the sport.

Just as this volume goes to press, the cover picture of FA Cup winners Wolverhampton Wanderers becomes even more appropriate as the Wolves win The Championship ahead of local rivals Birmingham City, 20 years after their last title and 60 years almost to the day they won the cup. And as a lifelong fan, congratulations to Mick McCarthy and the team are well earned for doing it in style.

1948-1949

No National finals were held in Turkey this year because of the Olympic Games. Many Iron Curtain countries began re-organisation of their sports clubs – many name changes in the pipeline. Internationally the Latin Cup began, featuring the champions of France, Italy, Portugal and Spain.

Nations

There were far less countries after the war than there are now, following the break up of the USSR and Yugoslavia and the splitting of Czechoslovakia.

Even so, by the 1960's around 32 countries were entering the European Cup, sometimes more, sometimes less depending on the politics of the time, and of course Wales only entered the Cup Winners Cup as their best teams played in England (and still do).

Seasons

There are two different views on when the season begins and ends. Many in colder climes – to the north and east of Europe – seasons begin in spring and ends in autumn. To the south and west it is usually the season we are used to in the British Isles – autumn to spring. Some have a long winter break.

Some of those in the first category have moved backwards and forwards between the two systems, which has proved awkward for qualifications for main European tournaments (Champions Cup/League, Cup Winners Cup, Fairs/UEFA Cups) as these are also run on the western season.

In the end the extremes of weather have won through, you simply cannot play when temperatures remain below freezing for months on end.

Therefore we have two different systems running. This volume will deal with the 1948 and the 1948-1949 season. Future volumes will keep the same format so that when the Euro competitions begin in earnest in 1955 it is clear who are the champions that qualified. Of course since the Champions Cup became the Champions League and non-champions were allowed to compete this is not so important, nevertheless it will make it a little more obvious those teams that did qualify.

Consistency

Where possible not just the top level, but also second or even third level, results will be included here, as well as national knockout cups. In many countries the knockout cups were not taken as seriously as the FA Cup – and some didn't have one every season (or at all until the European Cup Winners' Cup began).

In all cases for consistency's sake, regardless of the official name of the league (Premier division, premiership, Eredivisie or whatever), the top division will always be named Division One, the second Division Two and so on, if necessary with a geographical note (eg Division 2 East in the USSR).

As well, the Italian, Spanish, French leagues will have their own nomenclature, ie Serie A etc, as these are well known.

Where there is no national league, only a knockout tournament to decide the champion, just the final stages are included, with tables where known for the regional events.

Three exceptions - first Germany, as one of the major football playing nations I have included their regional league results as well as these have been well-researched. This means that there are nearly 200 clubs results included in some seasons, the differential standard well below top English amateur levels, hence many matches are very one-sided as you will see from the scores.

Secondly USSR, which had so many republics playing in one league, eg Ukraine, Georgia, that there would be no record of many of those now independent nations without going down to regional results. Third Netherlands, still amateur until the mid 50s, but soon to be a major force through the 70s.

For a few countries at least so far I have been unable to research reliable results – tables for sure, but not the individual match scores.

Errors & Omissions

There will undoubtedly be some errors in this volume – for these I apologise unreservedly. But if you do find them, it would be much appreciated if you would let me know so that I can pass on the information to those football fans and stattos that have bought this book.

Equally there is missing data – if you can help with this too I would be most grateful.

You can email editor@gotenpin.clara.net

Eric Hayton
May 20th 2009

Abbreviations

These abbreviations – all fairly standard to the English game – will apply.
Pld – Matches played
W – matches won
D – matches drawn
L - matches lost.
F – goals for
A – goals against
GA – goal average (F/A)
GD – goal difference (F-A)
Pts – total points
Agg – aggregate score (usually two legs added together)
w-o walkover shown in scores (winner = w, loser o)
*- an asterisk at any point will usually refer to a match result altered at a later date and a reference note will be added at suitable point in the text.

Dates

Leagues where match dates (or original match round dates) are known will show matches down the left column to the halfway point of the season and then recommence in the right column beginning underneath the league table, unless otherwise noted.

Points

Most league systems in early post war used 2 pts for win, 1 pt for draw, zero for loss.
However some (Greece) used 3 for a win, 2 draw, 1 loss and zero for no show!
In addition in later years, some leagues attempted to reduce the number of draws (ie USSR) by setting a maximum number and one that was exceeded no points were awarded for a draw.
Eventually leagues standardised on 3 pts for a win, 1 for a draw, zero for loss.
These and other variations are noted where appropriate.
In the Stats section in later issues of this series one standard system will be used.

Positions

Again there are some variations between leagues – most began with goal average (GA) as the deciding factor for tied positions. A few used goal difference (GD).
However some used play-off games if points are tied on points and a promotion or relegation issue (later European qualification as well) would be affected.
Appropriate notes will be made the text.

Names

Consistency is difficult to achieve – where possible I have tried to use the real name of the club. However this is not so simple, particularly with accents etc. So most are anglicised.
Regardless, in the league tables I have tried to use their full name, in the results list some have been shortened to fit the column width available (including the mighty Wolverhampton Wanderers, shortened to Wolves).

League Index

Page	Country	Division	Clubs	Page	Country	Division	Clubs
8	Albania	1	9	111	Northern Ireland	1	12
10	Austria	1	10	113	Norway	1	16
12	Belgium	1	16	116	Poland	1	14
15	Bulgaria	KO	16	118	Poland	2F	5
17	Cyprus	1	5	119	Poland	2G1	4
19	Czechoslovakia	1	11	119	Poland	2G2	4
21	Denmark	1	10	120	Poland	2G3	4
22	Denmark	2	10	120	Poland	2G4	4
23	Denmark	3	10	120	Poland	2G5	4
25	England	1	22	122	Portugal	1	14
31	England	2	22	125	Romania	1	14
37	England	3S	22	128	Scotland	1	16
43	England	3N	22	131	Scotland	2	16
49	Finland	1	16	135	Spain	1	14
51	France	1	18	137	Spain	2	14
56	France	2	20	140	Sweden	1	12
61	Germany - East	KO	10	142	Switzerland	1	14
62	Germany - West	KO	8	144	Turkey	NA	NA
63	Germany - West	1N	12	145	USSR	1	14
65	Germany - West	1W	13	149	USSR	2Final	6
67	Germany - West	1SWn	13	149	USSR	2C	15
69	Germany - West	1SWs	12	152	USSR	2R1	14
71	Germany - West	1S	16	154	USSR	2R2	13
74	Germany - West	1Ber	12	157	USSR	2UkrF	4
76	Greece	1	23	157	USSR	2UkrGA	8
78	Hungary	1	16	157	USSR	2UkrGB	8
81	Iceland	1	5	159	USSR	2S	10
81	Israel	NA	NA	160	USSR	2ME	9
82	Rep Ireland	1	10	161	Yugoslavia	1	10
86	Italy	1	20	162	Wales	NA	NA
91	Italy	2	18				
97	Luxembourg	1	12				
99	Malta	1	8				
100	Netherlands	F	6				
100	Netherlands	W1	11				
102	Netherlands	W2	11				
104	Netherlands	N	11				
105	Netherlands	E	11				
107	Netherlands	S1	11				
108	Netherlands	S2	11				

Cup Index

Page	Country	Competition
	International	
163	Spain	Latin cup
177	Ireland	All-Ireland Inter-City
	Domestic	
164	Austria	Knockout Cup
168	Bulgaria	Soviet Army Cup
169	Cyprus	Knockout Cup
170	England	FA Cup
174	France	Knockout Cup
175	Greece	Knockout Cup
176	Republic of Ireland	FAI Cup
177	Republic of Ireland	Leinster Cup
177	Republic of Ireland	Munster Cup
177	Republic of Ireland	President's Cup
178	Luxembourg	Knockout Cup
179	Malta	FA Trophy
179	Netherlands	Knockout Cup
180	Northern Ireland	Knockout Cup
181	Norway	Knockout Cup
182	Portugal	Knockout Cup
183	Scotland	Scottish FA Cup
184	Scotland	League Cup
188	Spain	Knockout Cup
190	Sweden	Knockout Cup
191	Switzerland	Knockout Cup
194	USSR	Knockout Cup
195	Wales	Welsh Cup
196	Yugoslavia	Knockout Cup

Additions, Errors & Omissions

Page	Country	Competition	Clubs
197	Iceland	1946 & 1947 League	6

Albania

Once again the league switched to a two-group format. In the past play-offs have been used for ties – this time Vllaznia lost the Group A title on GA, having beaten them 4-1 at home and lost 0-1 away. Partizani then thrashed Flamurtari in the final.

Championship play-off
Partizani Tirane - Flamurtari Vlore   6 - 2

Group A	Pld	W	D	L	F	A	GA	Pts
1 Partizani Tirane	10	8	1	1	34	8	4.25	17
2 Vllaznia Shkoder	10	8	1	1	26	7	3.71	17
3 17 Nentori Tirane	9	4	2	3	9	9	1.00	10
4 Lokomotiva Durres	9	3	2	4	12	16	0.75	8
5 Besa Kavaje	9	0	1	8	7	33	0.21	1
6 Skenderbeu Korce	7	0	1	6	3	18	0.17	1

Group B	Pld	W	D	L	F	A	GA	Pts
1 Flamurtari Vlore	14	8	4	2	47	19	2.47	20
2 Labinoti Elbasan	14	7	5	2	34	15	2.27	19
3 Apolonia Fier	14	7	5	2	31	20	1.55	19
4 Luftetari Gjirokaster	14	6	4	4	31	23	1.35	16
5 Erzeni Shijak	14	5	5	4	23	25	0.92	15
6 Traktori Lushnje	14	4	2	8	22	34	0.65	10
7 Tomori Berat	14	3	3	8	18	32	0.56	9
8 Spartaku Kucove	14	1	2	11	17	55	0.31	4

Group A
Partizani Tirane	1 - 0	Vllaznia Shkoder
Partizani Tirane	4 - 1	17 Nentori Tirane
Partizani Tirane	9 - 0	Lokomotiva Durres
Partizani Tirane	7 - 0	Skenderbeu Korce
Partizani Tirane	6 - 1	Besa Kavaje
Vllaznia Shkoder	4 - 1	Partizani Tirane
Vllaznia Shkoder	1 - 0	17 Nentori Tirane
Vllaznia Shkoder	2 - 0	Lokomotiva Durres
Vllaznia Shkoder	4 - 1	Skenderbeu Korce
Lokomotiva Durres	1 - 1	Partizani Tirane
Lokomotiva Durres	1 - 2	Vllaznia Shkoder
Lokomotiva Durres	0 - 0	17 Nentori Tirane
Lokomotiva Durres	1 - 0	Skenderbeu Korce
Lokomotiva Durres	6 - 1	Besa Kavaje
Skenderbeu Korce	0 - 2	Partizani Tirane
Skenderbeu Korce	1 - 2	Vllaznia Shkoder
Skenderbeu Korce	o - o	17 Nentori Tirane
Skenderbeu Korce	o - o	Lokomotiva Durres

Vllaznia Shkoder	6	-	0	Besa Kavaje	Skenderbeu Korce	o - o	Besa Kavaje
17 Nentori Tirane	1	-	2	Partizani Tirane	Besa Kavaje	0 - 1	Partizani Tirane
17 Nentori Tirane	0	-	0	Vllaznia Shkoder	Besa Kavaje	2 - 5	Vllaznia Shkoder
17 Nentori Tirane	1	-	0	Lokomotiva Durres	Besa Kavaje	1 - 2	17 Nentori Tirane
17 Nentori Tirane	1	-	0	Skenderbeu Korce	Besa Kavaje	0 - 3	Lokomotiva Durres
17 Nentori Tirane	3	-	1	Besa Kavaje	Besa Kavaje	1 - 1	Skenderbeu Korce

Group B

Flamurtari Vlore	1 - 1	Labinoti Elbasan	Erzeni Shijak	1 - 4	Flamurtari Vlore
Flamurtari Vlore	6 - 2	Apolonia Fier	Erzeni Shijak	2 - 0	Labinoti Elbasan
Flamurtari Vlore	5 - 0	Luftetari Gjirokaster	Erzeni Shijak	0 - 0	Apolonia Fier
Flamurtari Vlore	5 - 1	Erzeni Shijak	Erzeni Shijak	2 - 2	Luftetari Gjirokaster
Flamurtari Vlore	5 - 1	Traktori Lushnje	Erzeni Shijak	0 - 0	Traktori Lushnje
Flamurtari Vlore	5 - 3	Tomori Berat	Erzeni Shijak	5 - 1	Tomori Berat
Flamurtari Vlore	9 - 0	Spartaku Kucove	Erzeni Shijak	4 - 2	Spartaku Kucove
Labinoti Elbasan	1 - 0	Flamurtari Vlore	Traktori Lushnje	2 - 2	Flamurtari Vlore
Labinoti Elbasan	3 - 1	Apolonia Fier	Traktori Lushnje	0 - 1	Labinoti Elbasan
Labinoti Elbasan	2 - 2	Luftetari Gjirokaster	Traktori Lushnje	2 - 4	Apolonia Fier
Labinoti Elbasan	5 - 0	Erzeni Shijak	Traktori Lushnje	1 - 3	Luftetari Gjirokaster
Labinoti Elbasan	6 - 1	Traktori Lushnje	Traktori Lushnje	2 - 0	Erzeni Shijak
Labinoti Elbasan	3 - 3	Tomori Berat	Traktori Lushnje	2 - 1	Tomori Berat
Labinoti Elbasan	6 - 0	Spartaku Kucove	Traktori Lushnje	5 - 2	Spartaku Kucove
Apolonia Fier	2 - 2	Flamurtari Vlore	Tomori Berat	0 - 0	Flamurtari Vlore
Apolonia Fier	1 - 1	Labinoti Elbasan	Tomori Berat	2 - 0	Labinoti Elbasan
Apolonia Fier	4 - 0	Luftetari Gjirokaster	Tomori Berat	1 - 2	Apolonia Fier
Apolonia Fier	1 - 1	Erzeni Shijak	Tomori Berat	0 - 2	Luftetari Gjirokaster
Apolonia Fier	4 - 1	Traktori Lushnje	Tomori Berat	0 - 2	Erzeni Shijak
Apolonia Fier	4 - 0	Tomori Berat	Tomori Berat	2 - 1	Traktori Lushnje
Apolonia Fier	2 - 0	Spartaku Kucove	Tomori Berat	3 - 1	Spartaku Kucove
Luftetari Gjirokaster	4 - 1	Flamurtari Vlore	Spartaku Kucove	1 - 2	Flamurtari Vlore
Luftetari Gjirokaster	1 - 1	Labinoti Elbasan	Spartaku Kucove	1 - 4	Labinoti Elbasan
Luftetari Gjirokaster	0 - 1	Apolonia Fier	Spartaku Kucove	3 - 3	Apolonia Fier
Luftetari Gjirokaster	2 - 2	Erzeni Shijak	Spartaku Kucove	3 - 2	Luftetari Gjirokaster
Luftetari Gjirokaster	3 - 1	Traktori Lushnje	Spartaku Kucove	1 - 3	Erzeni Shijak
Luftetari Gjirokaster	3 - 0	Tomori Berat	Spartaku Kucove	1 - 3	Traktori Lushnje
Luftetari Gjirokaster	7 - 0	Spartaku Kucove	Spartaku Kucove	2 - 2	Tomori Berat

Austria

The title race came down to Austria's home match with Rapid and an away fixture with bottom club Hochstadt as Rapid had a 2 point lead and a slightly better GA. Austria duly bagged a 5-3 victory, but the needed a point at Hochstadt, so long as it was not a 5-5 draw! They crushed them 9-2, a convincing way to take the title away from the holders. And they went on to do the double by beating Vorwarts Steyr 5-2 in the cup final.

Good news for the rest of Austria, clubs from outside Vienna would compete in league and cup from next season.

		Pld	W	D	L	F	A	GA	Pts
1	Austria Wien	18	13	1	4	65	27	2.41	27
2	Rapid Wien	18	11	3	4	61	29	2.10	25
3	Admira Wien	18	11	2	5	69	33	2.09	24
4	Wacker Wien	18	10	3	5	35	34	1.03	23
5	FC Wien	18	9	3	6	35	33	1.06	21
6	First Vienna FC	18	8	3	7	44	32	1.38	19
7	Sportclub Wien	18	8	3	7	35	34	1.03	19
8	Floridsdorfer AC	18	6	2	10	37	46	0.80	14
9	Rapid Oberlaa	18	1	2	15	16	64	0.25	4
10	Rasenspieler Hochstadt	18	1	2	15	14	79	0.18	4

August 28, 1948
Rapid Wien 1 - 1 Wacker Wien
August 29, 1948
Admira Wien 3 - 2 First Vienna FC
Austria Wien 2 - 1 FC Wien
Ras. Hochstadt 0 - 2 Floridsdorfer AC
September 1, 1948
Sportclub Wien 1 - 1 Rapid Oberlaa
September 4, 1948
Rapid Oberlaa 0 - 2 Austria Wien
September 5, 1948
FC Wien 2 - 0 Ras. Hochstadt
First Vienna FC 5 - 1 Rapid Wien
Floridsdorfer AC 2 - 3 Admira Wien
Wacker Wien 0 - 2 Sportclub Wien
September 8, 1948
Wacker Wien 4 - 0 Ras. Hochstadt
September 11, 1948
Ras. Hochstadt 3 - 2 Rapid Oberlaa
Sportclub Wien 3 - 0 FC Wien
September 12, 1948
Admira Wien 1 - 2 Wacker Wien

February 26, 1949
First Vienna FC 1 - 1 Admira Wien
Rapid Oberlaa 1 - 2 Sportclub Wien
February 27, 1949
FC Wien 3 - 0 Austria Wien
Floridsdorfer AC 2 - 0 Ras. Hochstadt
Wacker Wien 1 - 2 Rapid Wien
March 5, 1949
Ras. Hochstadt 0 - 2 FC Wien
Sportclub Wien 2 - 3 Wacker Wien
March 6, 1949
Admira Wien 8 - 4 Floridsdorfer AC
Austria Wien 4 - 0 Rapid Oberlaa
March 7, 1949
Rapid Wien 2 - 1 First Vienna FC
March 12, 1949
FC Wien 3 - 1 Sportclub Wien
Rapid Oberlaa 3 - 3 Ras. Hochstadt
March 13, 1949
First Vienna FC 2 - 1 Austria Wien
Floridsdorfer AC 2 - 8 Rapid Wien
Wacker Wien 3 - 1 Admira Wien

Austria Wien	6	-	2	First Vienna FC	March 26, 1949			
Rapid Wien	2	-	0	Floridsdorfer AC	Ras. Hochstadt	0	-	3	Wacker Wien

Austria Wien 6 - 2 First Vienna FC
Rapid Wien 2 - 0 Floridsdorfer AC

September 18, 1948
Rapid Oberlaa 1 - 5 Rapid Wien

September 19, 1948
FC Wien 3 - 2 Admira Wien
First Vienna FC 2 - 4 Sportclub Wien
Floridsdorfer AC 2 - 4 Austria Wien

September 25, 1948
FC Wien 2 - 2 Floridsdorfer AC

September 26, 1948
Austria Wien 1 - 1 Admira Wien
Rapid Wien 1 - 1 Sportclub Wien
Ras. Hochstadt 0 - 4 First Vienna FC
Wacker Wien 4 - 3 Rapid Oberlaa

October 9, 1948
Admira Wien 5 - 1 Ras. Hochstadt
Rapid Oberlaa 2 - 1 Floridsdorfer AC

October 10, 1948
First Vienna FC 1 - 2 Wacker Wien
Rapid Wien 5 - 1 FC Wien
Sportclub Wien 1 - 0 Austria Wien

October 16, 1948
First Vienna FC 4 - 2 Rapid Oberlaa
Floridsdorfer AC 4 - 3 Sportclub Wien

October 17, 1948
Admira Wien 3 - 2 Rapid Wien
Austria Wien 10 - 2 Ras. Hochstadt

October 23, 1948
Rapid Oberlaa 1 - 7 Admira Wien
Sportclub Wien 4 - 0 Ras. Hochstadt

October 24, 1948
First Vienna FC 1 - 2 FC Wien
Rapid Wien 1 - 2 Austria Wien
Wacker Wien 3 - 3 Floridsdorfer AC

November 6, 1948
Floridsdorfer AC 2 - 3 First Vienna FC
Ras. Hochstadt 2 - 2 Rapid Wien

November 7, 1948
Admira Wien 8 - 1 Sportclub Wien
Austria Wien 0 - 1 Wacker Wien
FC Wien 6 - 0 Rapid Oberlaa

November 28, 1948
FC Wien 1 - 1 Wacker Wien

March 26, 1949
Ras. Hochstadt 0 - 3 Wacker Wien
Sportclub Wien 1 - 1 First Vienna FC

March 27, 1949
Admira Wien 3 - 1 FC Wien
Austria Wien 1 - 0 Floridsdorfer AC
Rapid Wien 4 - 0 Rapid Oberlaa

April 9, 1949
Floridsdorfer AC 4 - 0 FC Wien
Rapid Oberlaa 0 - 2 Wacker Wien

April 10, 1949
Admira Wien 1 - 5 Austria Wien
First Vienna FC 7 - 0 Ras. Hochstadt
Sportclub Wien 1 - 3 Rapid Wien

April 23, 1949
Austria Wien 3 - 2 Sportclub Wien
Ras. Hochstadt 0 - 8 Admira Wien

April 24, 1949
FC Wien 1 - 6 Rapid Wien
Floridsdorfer AC 2 - 0 Rapid Oberlaa
Wacker Wien 1 - 0 First Vienna FC

April 28, 1949
Rapid Wien 4 - 1 Admira Wien

May 14, 1949
Rapid Wien 9 - 1 Ras. Hochstadt
Sportclub Wien 0 - 4 Admira Wien

May 15, 1949
First Vienna FC 2 - 1 Floridsdorfer AC
Wacker Wien 3 - 10 Austria Wien

May 25, 1949
Sportclub Wien 4 - 0 Floridsdorfer AC

May 26, 1949
Rapid Oberlaa 0 - 2 FC Wien

May 28, 1949
FC Wien 3 - 3 First Vienna FC
Floridsdorfer AC 4 - 1 Wacker Wien

May 29, 1949
Admira Wien 9 - 0 Rapid Oberlaa
Austria Wien 5 - 3 Rapid Wien
Ras. Hochstadt 0 - 2 Sportclub Wien

June 1, 1949
Ras. Hochstadt 2 - 9 Austria Wien

June 11, 1949
Rapid Oberlaa 0 - 3 First Vienna FC
Wacker Wien 0 - 3 FC Wien

Belgium

Anderlecht regained the championship ahead of Berchem, while champions KV faded to mid table. Boom and Union St Gilloise are relegated - Stade Leuven and Club Brugge KV are promoted.

	Team	Pld	W	D	L	F	A	GA	Pts
1	Anderlecht RSC	30	20	1	9	72	45	1.60	41
2	Berchem Sport	30	16	6	8	56	38	1.47	38
3	Standard Liege	30	17	4	9	57	46	1.24	38
4	Charleroi RSC	30	15	6	9	70	47	1.49	36
5	RC Mechelen	30	13	8	9	57	49	1.16	34
6	Beerschot VAC	30	15	3	12	53	46	1.15	33
7	KV Mechelen	30	10	12	8	52	52	1.00	32
8	Liege FC	30	14	2	14	71	52	1.37	30
9	Antwerp FC	30	10	7	13	47	51	0.92	27
10	Racing Club Brussel	30	10	7	13	56	71	0.79	27
11	Lyra TSV	30	9	8	13	45	67	0.67	26
12	AA Gent	30	8	9	13	50	56	0.89	25
13	Tilleur FC	30	8	9	13	34	46	0.74	25
14	Olympic Charleroi	30	9	7	14	36	49	0.73	25
15	Boom KFC	30	7	9	14	40	60	0.67	23
16	Union St Gilloise	30	8	4	18	49	70	0.70	20

AA Gent	0 - 2	Anderlecht RSC	Liege FC	2 - 2	AA Gent
AA Gent	4 - 2	Antwerp FC	Liege FC	4 - 1	Anderlecht RSC
AA Gent	2 - 5	Beerschot VAC	Liege FC	4 - 0	Antwerp FC
AA Gent	0 - 2	Berchem Sport	Liege FC	2 - 0	Beerschot VAC
AA Gent	2 - 2	Boom KFC	Liege FC	2 - 3	Berchem Sport
AA Gent	1 - 4	Charleroi RSC	Liege FC	6 - 0	Boom KFC
AA Gent	0 - 0	KV Mechelen	Liege FC	4 - 1	Charleroi RSC
AA Gent	3 - 2	Liege FC	Liege FC	4 - 1	KV Mechelen
AA Gent	5 - 1	Lyra TSV	Liege FC	6 - 0	Lyra TSV
AA Gent	1 - 1	Olympic Charleroi	Liege FC	4 - 0	Olympic Charleroi
AA Gent	3 - 0	Racing Club Brussel	Liege FC	6 - 1	Racing Club Brussel
AA Gent	0 - 3	RC Mechelen	Liege FC	3 - 1	RC Mechelen
AA Gent	3 - 0	Standard Liege	Liege FC	2 - 1	Standard Liege
AA Gent	1 - 1	Tilleur FC	Liege FC	2 - 2	Tilleur FC
AA Gent	4 - 1	Union St Gilloise	Liege FC	1 - 0	Union St Gilloise
Anderlecht RSC	2 - 0	AA Gent	Lyra TSV	1 - 0	AA Gent
Anderlecht RSC	3 - 1	Antwerp FC	Lyra TSV	1 - 5	Anderlecht RSC
Anderlecht RSC	2 - 1	Beerschot VAC	Lyra TSV	2 - 5	Antwerp FC

Anderlecht RSC	1 - 1	Berchem Sport	Lyra TSV	2 - 0	Beerschot VAC
Anderlecht RSC	3 - 2	Boom KFC	Lyra TSV	3 - 1	Berchem Sport
Anderlecht RSC	2 - 1	Charleroi RSC	Lyra TSV	1 - 0	Boom KFC
Anderlecht RSC	5 - 0	KV Mechelen	Lyra TSV	2 - 2	Charleroi RSC
Anderlecht RSC	3 - 2	Liege FC	Lyra TSV	1 - 4	KV Mechelen
Anderlecht RSC	3 - 2	Lyra TSV	Lyra TSV	4 - 2	Liege FC
Anderlecht RSC	1 - 0	Olympic Charleroi	Lyra TSV	0 - 1	Olympic Charleroi
Anderlecht RSC	2 - 0	Racing Club Brussel	Lyra TSV	3 - 1	Racing Club Brussel
Anderlecht RSC	5 - 2	RC Mechelen	Lyra TSV	1 - 1	RC Mechelen
Anderlecht RSC	6 - 3	Standard Liege	Lyra TSV	1 - 6	Standard Liege
Anderlecht RSC	0 - 1	Tilleur FC	Lyra TSV	3 - 3	Tilleur FC
Anderlecht RSC	2 - 1	Union St Gilloise	Lyra TSV	1 - 0	Union St Gilloise
Antwerp FC	3 - 0	AA Gent	Olympic Charleroi	0 - 0	AA Gent
Antwerp FC	2 - 1	Anderlecht RSC	Olympic Charleroi	1 - 3	Anderlecht RSC
Antwerp FC	1 - 1	Beerschot VAC	Olympic Charleroi	2 - 2	Antwerp FC
Antwerp FC	1 - 2	Berchem Sport	Olympic Charleroi	1 - 2	Beerschot VAC
Antwerp FC	5 - 0	Boom KFC	Olympic Charleroi	2 - 3	Berchem Sport
Antwerp FC	2 - 2	Charleroi RSC	Olympic Charleroi	1 - 0	Boom KFC
Antwerp FC	1 - 1	KV Mechelen	Olympic Charleroi	0 - 2	Charleroi RSC
Antwerp FC	0 - 2	Liege FC	Olympic Charleroi	2 - 2	KV Mechelen
Antwerp FC	2 - 3	Lyra TSV	Olympic Charleroi	2 - 1	Liege FC
Antwerp FC	1 - 0	Olympic Charleroi	Olympic Charleroi	2 - 0	Lyra TSV
Antwerp FC	3 - 2	Racing Club Brussel	Olympic Charleroi	5 - 1	Racing Club Brussel
Antwerp FC	2 - 3	RC Mechelen	Olympic Charleroi	3 - 1	RC Mechelen
Antwerp FC	1 - 0	Standard Liege	Olympic Charleroi	1 - 5	Standard Liege
Antwerp FC	0 - 0	Tilleur FC	Olympic Charleroi	1 - 1	Tilleur FC
Antwerp FC	2 - 0	Union St Gilloise	Olympic Charleroi	3 - 3	Union St Gilloise
Beerschot VAC	1 - 4	AA Gent	Racing Club Brussel	3 - 1	AA Gent
Beerschot VAC	2 - 1	Anderlecht RSC	Racing Club Brussel	0 - 2	Anderlecht RSC
Beerschot VAC	2 - 0	Antwerp FC	Racing Club Brussel	3 - 0	Antwerp FC
Beerschot VAC	2 - 1	Berchem Sport	Racing Club Brussel	0 - 5	Beerschot VAC
Beerschot VAC	3 - 0	Boom KFC	Racing Club Brussel	2 - 2	Berchem Sport
Beerschot VAC	1 - 4	Charleroi RSC	Racing Club Brussel	2 - 2	Boom KFC
Beerschot VAC	3 - 0	KV Mechelen	Racing Club Brussel	3 - 3	Charleroi RSC
Beerschot VAC	3 - 1	Liege FC	Racing Club Brussel	1 - 1	KV Mechelen
Beerschot VAC	3 - 2	Lyra TSV	Racing Club Brussel	6 - 0	Liege FC
Beerschot VAC	2 - 1	Olympic Charleroi	Racing Club Brussel	1 - 2	Lyra TSV
Beerschot VAC	2 - 3	Racing Club Brussel	Racing Club Brussel	1 - 0	Olympic Charleroi
Beerschot VAC	2 - 2	RC Mechelen	Racing Club Brussel	3 - 1	RC Mechelen
Beerschot VAC	0 - 2	Standard Liege	Racing Club Brussel	2 - 1	Standard Liege
Beerschot VAC	2 - 2	Tilleur FC	Racing Club Brussel	6 - 3	Tilleur FC
Beerschot VAC	2 - 1	Union St Gilloise	Racing Club Brussel	3 - 2	Union St Gilloise
Berchem Sport	1 - 1	AA Gent	RC Mechelen	1 - 1	AA Gent
Berchem Sport	1 - 0	Anderlecht RSC	RC Mechelen	4 - 2	Anderlecht RSC
Berchem Sport	1 - 2	Antwerp FC	RC Mechelen	1 - 0	Antwerp FC
Berchem Sport	3 - 1	Beerschot VAC	RC Mechelen	3 - 1	Beerschot VAC
Berchem Sport	1 - 3	Boom KFC	RC Mechelen	0 - 1	Berchem Sport
Berchem Sport	1 - 2	Charleroi RSC	RC Mechelen	2 - 0	Boom KFC
Berchem Sport	1 - 1	KV Mechelen	RC Mechelen	2 - 3	Charleroi RSC
Berchem Sport	1 - 3	Liege FC	RC Mechelen	1 - 4	KV Mechelen
Berchem Sport	4 - 1	Lyra TSV	RC Mechelen	2 - 0	Liege FC
Berchem Sport	3 - 0	Olympic Charleroi	RC Mechelen	1 - 1	Lyra TSV

Berchem Sport	4	-	0	Racing Club Brussel	RC Mechelen	0	-	0	Olympic Charleroi
Berchem Sport	3	-	2	RC Mechelen	RC Mechelen	1	-	1	Racing Club Brussel
Berchem Sport	2	-	3	Standard Liege	RC Mechelen	5	-	0	Standard Liege
Berchem Sport	0	-	0	Tilleur FC	RC Mechelen	2	-	0	Tilleur FC
Berchem Sport	4	-	1	Union St Gilloise	RC Mechelen	3	-	1	Union St Gilloise
Boom KFC	1	-	1	AA Gent	Standard Liege	4	-	2	AA Gent
Boom KFC	0	-	3	Anderlecht RSC	Standard Liege	1	-	0	Anderlecht RSC
Boom KFC	1	-	1	Antwerp FC	Standard Liege	1	-	0	Antwerp FC
Boom KFC	0	-	3	Beerschot VAC	Standard Liege	1	-	0	Beerschot VAC
Boom KFC	1	-	0	Berchem Sport	Standard Liege	0	-	3	Berchem Sport
Boom KFC	2	-	2	Charleroi RSC	Standard Liege	2	-	0	Boom KFC
Boom KFC	2	-	2	KV Mechelen	Standard Liege	1	-	2	Charleroi RSC
Boom KFC	4	-	2	Liege FC	Standard Liege	2	-	2	KV Mechelen
Boom KFC	2	-	2	Lyra TSV	Standard Liege	3	-	1	Liege FC
Boom KFC	5	-	1	Olympic Charleroi	Standard Liege	2	-	1	Lyra TSV
Boom KFC	3	-	3	Racing Club Brussel	Standard Liege	2	-	0	Olympic Charleroi
Boom KFC	1	-	1	RC Mechelen	Standard Liege	2	-	0	Racing Club Brussel
Boom KFC	0	-	1	Standard Liege	Standard Liege	2	-	2	RC Mechelen
Boom KFC	5	-	1	Tilleur FC	Standard Liege	1	-	0	Tilleur FC
Boom KFC	3	-	1	Union St Gilloise	Standard Liege	2	-	2	Union St Gilloise
Charleroi RSC	4	-	1	AA Gent	Tilleur FC	0	-	4	AA Gent
Charleroi RSC	4	-	5	Anderlecht RSC	Tilleur FC	2	-	5	Anderlecht RSC
Charleroi RSC	3	-	0	Antwerp FC	Tilleur FC	3	-	1	Antwerp FC
Charleroi RSC	0	-	2	Beerschot VAC	Tilleur FC	1	-	0	Beerschot VAC
Charleroi RSC	0	-	1	Berchem Sport	Tilleur FC	0	-	1	Berchem Sport
Charleroi RSC	4	-	0	Boom KFC	Tilleur FC	0	-	1	Boom KFC
Charleroi RSC	1	-	0	KV Mechelen	Tilleur FC	3	-	2	Charleroi RSC
Charleroi RSC	3	-	1	Liege FC	Tilleur FC	0	-	0	KV Mechelen
Charleroi RSC	0	-	0	Lyra TSV	Tilleur FC	1	-	0	Liege FC
Charleroi RSC	1	-	3	Olympic Charleroi	Tilleur FC	1	-	0	Lyra TSV
Charleroi RSC	3	-	1	Racing Club Brussel	Tilleur FC	0	-	1	Olympic Charleroi
Charleroi RSC	7	-	1	RC Mechelen	Tilleur FC	4	-	1	Racing Club Brussel
Charleroi RSC	2	-	3	Standard Liege	Tilleur FC	0	-	1	RC Mechelen
Charleroi RSC	1	-	0	Tilleur FC	Tilleur FC	1	-	1	Standard Liege
Charleroi RSC	6	-	1	Union St Gilloise	Tilleur FC	0	-	1	Union St Gilloise
KV Mechelen	3	-	1	AA Gent	Union St Gilloise	4	-	3	AA Gent
KV Mechelen	4	-	1	Anderlecht RSC	Union St Gilloise	2	-	1	Anderlecht RSC
KV Mechelen	1	-	4	Antwerp FC	Union St Gilloise	3	-	3	Antwerp FC
KV Mechelen	3	-	0	Beerschot VAC	Union St Gilloise	1	-	2	Beerschot VAC
KV Mechelen	2	-	2	Berchem Sport	Union St Gilloise	2	-	3	Berchem Sport
KV Mechelen	2	-	0	Boom KFC	Union St Gilloise	2	-	0	Boom KFC
KV Mechelen	1	-	1	Charleroi RSC	Union St Gilloise	3	-	0	Charleroi RSC
KV Mechelen	3	-	2	Liege FC	Union St Gilloise	4	-	3	KV Mechelen
KV Mechelen	2	-	2	Lyra TSV	Union St Gilloise	1	-	0	Liege FC
KV Mechelen	0	-	2	Olympic Charleroi	Union St Gilloise	2	-	2	Lyra TSV
KV Mechelen	3	-	3	Racing Club Brussel	Union St Gilloise	2	-	0	Olympic Charleroi
KV Mechelen	0	-	3	RC Mechelen	Union St Gilloise	2	-	3	Racing Club Brussel
KV Mechelen	2	-	1	Standard Liege	Union St Gilloise	2	-	5	RC Mechelen
KV Mechelen	3	-	1	Tilleur FC	Union St Gilloise	3	-	4	Standard Liege
KV Mechelen	2	-	1	Union St Gilloise	Union St Gilloise	0	-	3	Tilleur FC

Bulgaria

The first league style competition post war was won unbeaten by Levski Sofia, leaving army club CSKA trailing 9 points behind. To add insult to injury they also beat CSKA 2-1 in the Soviet Army cup final.

		Pld	W	D	L	F	A	GA	Pts
1	Levski Sofia	18	15	3	0	44	8	5.50	33
2	CSKA Sofia	18	10	4	4	28	15	1.87	24
3	Lokomotiv Sofia	18	8	5	5	25	17	1.47	21
4	Slavia Sofia	18	9	3	6	29	20	1.45	21
5	Spartak Sofia	18	8	5	5	23	18	1.28	21
6	Cherno more Varna	18	9	3	6	30	25	1.20	21
7	Lokomotiv Plovdiv	18	4	8	6	16	21	0.76	16
8	Marek Dupnitsa	18	2	4	12	16	42	0.38	8
9	Benkovski Vidin	18	2	4	12	13	35	0.37	8
10	Botev Burgas	18	2	3	13	15	38	0.39	7

Levski Sofia	1 - 0	CDNA Sofia	Cherno more Varna	2 - 4	Levski Sofia
Levski Sofia	1 - 0	Lokomotiv Sofia	Cherno more Varna	1 - 3	CDNA Sofia
Levski Sofia	1 - 1	Slavia Sofia	Cherno more Varna	0 - 1	Lokomotiv Sofia
Levski Sofia	3 - 0	Spartak Sofia	Cherno more Varna	3 - 1	Slavia Sofia
Levski Sofia	3 - 2	Cherno more Varna	Cherno more Varna	3 - 1	Spartak Sofia
Levski Sofia	1 - 0	Lokomotiv Plovdiv	Cherno more Varna	1 - 1	Lokomotiv Plovdiv
Levski Sofia	6 - 0	Marek Dupnitsa	Cherno more Varna	3 - 2	Marek Dupnitsa
Levski Sofia	5 - 0	Benkovski Vidin	Cherno more Varna	2 - 2	Benkovski Vidin
Levski Sofia	5 - 1	Botev Burgas	Cherno more Varna	4 - 2	Botev Burgas
CDNA Sofia	0 - 0	Levski Sofia	Lokomotiv Plovdiv	0 - 1	Levski Sofia
CDNA Sofia	2 - 2	Lokomotiv Sofia	Lokomotiv Plovdiv	0 - 1	CDNA Sofia
CDNA Sofia	1 - 4	Slavia Sofia	Lokomotiv Plovdiv	0 - 0	Lokomotiv Sofia
CDNA Sofia	1 - 1	Spartak Sofia	Lokomotiv Plovdiv	0 - 0	Slavia Sofia
CDNA Sofia	0 - 2	Cherno more Varna	Lokomotiv Plovdiv	2 - 5	Spartak Sofia
CDNA Sofia	5 - 0	Lokomotiv Plovdiv	Lokomotiv Plovdiv	1 - 0	Cherno more Varna
CDNA Sofia	1 - 0	Marek Dupnitsa	Lokomotiv Plovdiv	2 - 2	Marek Dupnitsa
CDNA Sofia	2 - 0	Benkovski Vidin	Lokomotiv Plovdiv	0 - 0	Benkovski Vidin
CDNA Sofia	2 - 0	Botev Burgas	Lokomotiv Plovdiv	1 - 1	Botev Burgas
Lokomotiv Sofia	0 - 4	Levski Sofia	Marek Dupnitsa	1 - 3	Levski Sofia
Lokomotiv Sofia	2 - 3	CDNA Sofia	Marek Dupnitsa	0 - 0	CDNA Sofia
Lokomotiv Sofia	2 - 0	Slavia Sofia	Marek Dupnitsa	0 - 4	Lokomotiv Sofia
Lokomotiv Sofia	0 - 0	Spartak Sofia	Marek Dupnitsa	3 - 4	Slavia Sofia
Lokomotiv Sofia	0 - 1	Cherno more Varna	Marek Dupnitsa	1 - 2	Spartak Sofia
Lokomotiv Sofia	0 - 1	Lokomotiv Plovdiv	Marek Dupnitsa	1 - 1	Cherno more Varna
Lokomotiv Sofia	3 - 0	Marek Dupnitsa	Marek Dupnitsa	2 - 2	Lokomotiv Plovdiv
Lokomotiv Sofia	2 - 2	Benkovski Vidin	Marek Dupnitsa	0 - 4	Benkovski Vidin
Lokomotiv Sofia	2 - 0	Botev Burgas	Marek Dupnitsa	1 - 2	Botev Burgas

Slavia Sofia	0	-	1	Levski Sofia	Benkovski Vidin	0	-	3	Levski Sofia
Slavia Sofia	0	-	1	CDNA Sofia	Benkovski Vidin	0	-	4	CDNA Sofia
Slavia Sofia	2	-	3	Lokomotiv Sofia	Benkovski Vidin	0	-	2	Lokomotiv Sofia
Slavia Sofia	1	-	0	Spartak Sofia	Benkovski Vidin	1	-	4	Slavia Sofia
Slavia Sofia	0	-	1	Cherno more Varna	Benkovski Vidin	0	-	3	Spartak Sofia
Slavia Sofia	1	-	0	Lokomotiv Plovdiv	Benkovski Vidin	1	-	2	Cherno more Varna
Slavia Sofia	3	-	0	Marek Dupnitsa	Benkovski Vidin	1	-	1	Lokomotiv Plovdiv
Slavia Sofia	1	-	0	Benkovski Vidin	Benkovski Vidin	0	-	1	Marek Dupnitsa
Slavia Sofia	3	-	2	Botev Burgas	Benkovski Vidin	1	-	0	Botev Burgas
Spartak Sofia	1	-	1	Levski Sofia	Botev Burgas	0	-	1	Levski Sofia
Spartak Sofia	1	-	0	CDNA Sofia	Botev Burgas	1	-	2	CDNA Sofia
Spartak Sofia	0	-	1	Lokomotiv Sofia	Botev Burgas	1	-	1	Lokomotiv Sofia
Spartak Sofia	1	-	1	Slavia Sofia	Botev Burgas	0	-	3	Slavia Sofia
Spartak Sofia	1	-	0	Cherno more Varna	Botev Burgas	1	-	3	Spartak Sofia
Spartak Sofia	0	-	2	Lokomotiv Plovdiv	Botev Burgas	1	-	2	Cherno more Varna
Spartak Sofia	2	-	0	Marek Dupnitsa	Botev Burgas	0	-	3	Lokomotiv Plovdiv
Spartak Sofia	1	-	0	Benkovski Vidin	Botev Burgas	0	-	2	Marek Dupnitsa
Spartak Sofia	1	-	1	Botev Burgas	Botev Burgas	2	-	1	Benkovski Vidin

Cyprus

Politics and the Greek civil war, caused chaos in Cypriot football. New clubs formed as clubs and players took different sides and a second association was formed. This split was not resolved until 1953. Only APOEL played all their matches (and won the lot), the other teams played one round plus the extra game against APOEL. The official table looks nothing like the games played, other games appear to have been awarded to one club or another with differing scores! Both tables are reproduced here.

Official	Pld	W	D	L	F	A	GA	Pts
1 APOEL Nicosia	14	14	0	0	51	20	2.55	28
2 Anorthosis Famagusta	14	10	1	3	58	26	2.23	21
3 Pezoporikos Larnaca	14	9	1	4	42	40	1.05	19
4 AEL Limassol	14	5	5	4	31	25	1.24	15
5 EPA Larnaca	14	4	1	9	25	36	0.69	9
6 AIMA	14	2	5	7	32	36	0.89	9
7 Olympiakos Nicosia	14	2	2	10	22	41	0.54	6
8 Chetin Kaya	14	2	1	11	21	58	0.36	5

Matches Played	Pld	W	D	L	F	A	GA	Pts
1 APOEL Nicosia	14	14	0	0	51	20	2.55	28
2 Anorthosis Famagusta	8	5	1	2	23	16	1.44	11
3 Pezoporikos Larnaca	8	4	2	2	24	22	1.09	10
4 AEL Limassol	8	1	3	4	15	16	0.94	5
5 EPA Larnaca	8	3	0	5	17	27	0.63	6
6 AIMA	8	1	2	5	18	22	0.82	4
7 Olympiakos Nicosia	8	1	1	6	12	23	0.52	3
8 Chetin Kaya	8	1	1	6	17	31	0.55	3

AEL Limassol	1 - 2	Anorthosis Famagusta
AEL Limassol	1 - 3	APOEL Nicosia
AEL Limassol	1 - 1	Olympiakos Nicosia
AEL Limassol	2 - 2	Pezoporikos Larnaca
AEL Limassol	6 - 2	Chetin Kaya
Anorthosis Famagusta	0 - 2	APOEL Nicosia
Anorthosis Famagusta	3 - 2	AIMA
Anorthosis Famagusta	8 - 2	EPA Larnaca
Anorthosis Famagusta	2 - 1	Olympiakos Nicosia
APOEL Nicosia	3 - 2	AEL Limassol
APOEL Nicosia	2 - 0	Anorthosis Famagusta
AIMA	1 - 1	AEL Limassol
AIMA	2 - 3	APOEL Nicosia
AIMA	4 - 1	EPA Larnaca
AIMA	3 - 5	Olympiakos Nicosia
AIMA	3 - 4	Pezoporikos Larnaca
EPA Larnaca	2 - 1	AEL Limassol
EPA Larnaca	1 - 3	APOEL Nicosia
EPA Larnaca	4 - 1	Olympiakos Nicosia
EPA Larnaca	1 - 3	Pezoporikos Larnaca
EPA Larnaca	4 - 3	Chetin Kaya
Olympiakos Nicosia	1 - 5	APOEL Nicosia

APOEL Nicosia	3 - 1	AIMA	Pezoporikos Larnaca	4 - 4	Anorthosis Famagusta
APOEL Nicosia	4 - 2	EPA Larnaca	Pezoporikos Larnaca	3 - 5	APOEL Nicosia
APOEL Nicosia	2 - 0	Olympiakos Nicosia	Pezoporikos Larnaca	3 - 1	Olympiakos Nicosia
APOEL Nicosia	5 - 3	Pezoporikos Larnaca	Pezoporikos Larnaca	2 - 1	Chetin Kaya
APOEL Nicosia	4 - 2	Chetin Kaya	Chetin Kaya	2 - 4	Anorthosis Famagusta
			Chetin Kaya	2 - 7	APOEL Nicosia
			Chetin Kaya	2 - 2	AIMA
			Chetin Kaya	3 - 2	Olympiakos Nicosia

Czechoslovakia

There was a huge re-organisation in Czech football. Only half a season was played in autumn 1948 as the season was changed to a spring to autumn schedule. In addition clubs were being re-organised and names changed into a Soviet style format. More on this in the next edition.

		Pld	W	D	L	F	A	GA	Pts
1	Slavia Praha	13	8	2	3	71	33	2.15	18
2	Viktoria Plzen	13	8	2	3	37	22	1.68	18
3	Sparta Praha	13	8	1	4	42	22	1.91	17
4	Bohemians Praha	13	6	5	2	37	24	1.54	17
5	Slovena Zilina	13	7	3	3	25	24	1.04	17
6	Trnava TSS	13	5	4	4	25	24	1.04	14
7	Jednota Kosice	13	5	3	5	23	24	0.96	13
8	Praha ATK	13	5	2	6	20	27	0.74	12
9	Teplice SK	13	4	3	6	27	27	1.00	11
10	Bratislava SK	13	4	3	6	20	22	0.91	11
11	Slezska Ostrava SK	13	4	3	6	23	35	0.66	11
12	Kladno SONP	13	3	2	8	32	42	0.76	8
13	Zidenice SK	13	3	2	8	21	43	0.49	8
14	Povazska Bystrica	13	3	1	9	23	57	0.40	7

Slavia Praha	4 - 0 Sparta Praha	Praha ATK	0 - 4 Sparta Praha
Slavia Praha	1 - 2 Slovena Zilina	Praha ATK	0 - 1 Slovena Zilina
Slavia Praha	5 - 2 Jednota Kosice	Praha ATK	0 - 1 Trnava TSS
Slavia Praha	8 - 2 Praha ATK	Praha ATK	5 - 1 Kladno SONP
Slavia Praha	3 - 2 Teplice SK	Praha ATK	2 - 1 Zidenice SK
Slavia Praha	5 - 2 Slezska Ostrava SK	Teplice SK	2 - 5 Viktoria Plzen
Slavia Praha	11 - 2 Kladno SONP	Teplice SK	2 - 2 Bohemians Praha
Slavia Praha	12 - 1 Povazska Bystrica	Teplice SK	2 - 0 Praha ATK
Viktoria Plzen	4 - 3 Slavia Praha	Teplice SK	1 - 1 Bratislava SK
Viktoria Plzen	4 - 1 Bohemians Praha	Teplice SK	5 - 0 Slezska Ostrava SK
Viktoria Plzen	0 - 0 Trnava TSS	Teplice SK	2 - 3 Povazska Bystrica
Viktoria Plzen	2 - 1 Jednota Kosice	Bratislava SK	5 - 4 Slavia Praha
Viktoria Plzen	2 - 3 Praha ATK	Bratislava SK	2 - 3 Slovena Zilina
Viktoria Plzen	0 - 1 Bratislava SK	Bratislava SK	0 - 1 Trnava TSS
Viktoria Plzen	3 - 0 Kladno SONP	Bratislava SK	1 - 2 Praha ATK
Viktoria Plzen	9 - 1 Zidenice SK	Bratislava SK	3 - 0 Kladno SONP
Sparta Praha	5 - 0 Viktoria Plzen	Bratislava SK	3 - 1 Zidenice SK
Sparta Praha	4 - 2 Bohemians Praha	Slezska Ostrava SK	1 - 3 Viktoria Plzen

Sparta Praha	6	-	2	Teplice SK	Slezska Ostrava SK	2	-	3	Bohemians Praha
Sparta Praha	2	-	2	Bratislava SK	Slezska Ostrava SK	3	-	1	Trnava TSS
Sparta Praha	4	-	1	Slezska Ostrava SK	Slezska Ostrava SK	2	-	2	Jednota Kosice
Sparta Praha	8	-	2	Povazska Bystrica	Slezska Ostrava SK	1	-	4	Praha ATK
Bohemians Praha	4	-	4	Slavia Praha	Slezska Ostrava SK	2	-	1	Bratislava SK
Bohemians Praha	4	-	1	Trnava TSS	Slezska Ostrava SK	2	-	2	Zidenice SK
Bohemians Praha	2	-	2	Jednota Kosice	Kladno SONP	3	-	5	Sparta Praha
Bohemians Praha	3	-	0	Praha ATK	Kladno SONP	1	-	3	Bohemians Praha
Bohemians Praha	0	-	0	Bratislava SK	Kladno SONP	8	-	1	Slovena Zilina
Bohemians Praha	5	-	0	Zidenice SK	Kladno SONP	3	-	1	Jednota Kosice
Slovena Zilina	3	-	3	Viktoria Plzen	Kladno SONP	1	-	3	Teplice SK
Slovena Zilina	1	-	0	Sparta Praha	Kladno SONP	2	-	2	Slezska Ostrava SK
Slovena Zilina	2	-	2	Bohemians Praha	Kladno SONP	8	-	1	Povazska Bystrica
Slovena Zilina	3	-	0	Jednota Kosice	Zidenice SK	3	-	7	Slavia Praha
Slovena Zilina	2	-	1	Teplice SK	Zidenice SK	1	-	0	Sparta Praha
Slovena Zilina	1	-	2	Slezska Ostrava SK	Zidenice SK	2	-	1	Slovena Zilina
Slovena Zilina	3	-	1	Povazska Bystrica	Zidenice SK	2	-	4	Trnava TSS
Trnava TSS	4	-	4	Slavia Praha	Zidenice SK	1	-	1	Teplice SK
Trnava TSS	1	-	3	Sparta Praha	Zidenice SK	3	-	2	Kladno SONP
Trnava TSS	2	-	2	Slovena Zilina	Povazska Bystrica	1	-	2	Viktoria Plzen
Trnava TSS	1	-	3	Teplice SK	Povazska Bystrica	2	-	6	Bohemians Praha
Trnava TSS	1	-	1	Kladno SONP	Povazska Bystrica	1	-	1	Praha ATK
Trnava TSS	6	-	1	Povazska Bystrica	Povazska Bystrica	3	-	1	Bratislava SK
Jednota Kosice	3	-	1	Sparta Praha	Povazska Bystrica	2	-	3	Slezska Ostrava SK
Jednota Kosice	1	-	2	Trnava TSS	Povazska Bystrica	4	-	3	Zidenice SK
Jednota Kosice	1	-	1	Praha ATK					
Jednota Kosice	2	-	1	Teplice SK					
Jednota Kosice	3	-	0	Bratislava SK					
Jednota Kosice	3	-	1	Zidenice SK					
Jednota Kosice	2	-	1	Povazska Bystrica					

Denmark

KB retained their title with a larger margin than last year, AB still runners-up. Promoted 1909 were sent straight back to Div 2, to be replaced by Esbjerg. Unbeaten Skovshoved took the div 3 title and Bronshoj go down,

	Division 1	Pld	W	D	L	F	A	GA	Pts
1	KB Kopenhavn	18	12	3	3	37	17	2.18	27
2	Akademisk Kobenhavn	18	9	4	5	46	32	1.44	22
3	Aarhus GF	18	8	3	7	36	31	1.16	19
4	Koge BK	18	8	3	7	37	34	1.09	19
5	Odense BK	18	9	1	8	49	51	0.96	19
6	1903 Kobenhavn	18	7	4	7	32	29	1.10	18
7	Oesterbro BK	18	7	4	7	34	39	0.87	18
8	BK Frem Kobenhavn	18	8	1	9	32	35	0.91	17
9	1893 Kobenhavn	18	3	6	9	20	31	0.65	12
10	1909 Odense	18	3	3	12	18	42	0.43	9

Akademisk Kobenhavn	3 - 1	1893 Kobenhavn
Akademisk Kobenhavn	3 - 2	BK Frem Kobenhavn
Akademisk Kobenhavn	1 - 1	KB Kopenhavn
Akademisk Kobenhavn	2 - 0	1903 Kobenhavn
Akademisk Kobenhavn	0 - 0	Oesterbro BK
Akademisk Kobenhavn	4 - 0	1909 Odense
Akademisk Kobenhavn	2 - 3	Odense BK
Akademisk Kobenhavn	5 - 1	Aarhus GF
Akademisk Kobenhavn	0 - 4	Koge BK
1893 Kobenhavn	1 - 4	Akademisk Kobenhavn
1893 Kobenhavn	2 - 1	BK Frem Kobenhavn
1893 Kobenhavn	0 - 1	KB Kopenhavn
1893 Kobenhavn	0 - 0	1903 Kobenhavn
1893 Kobenhavn	1 - 1	Oesterbro BK
1893 Kobenhavn	0 - 1	1909 Odense
1893 Kobenhavn	1 - 2	Odense BK
1893 Kobenhavn	2 - 2	Aarhus GF
1893 Kobenhavn	1 - 4	Koge BK
BK Frem Kobenhavn	3 - 1	Akademisk Kobenhavn
BK Frem Kobenhavn	2 - 0	1893 Kobenhavn
BK Frem Kobenhavn	1 - 3	KB Kopenhavn
BK Frem Kobenhavn	0 - 2	1903 Kobenhavn
BK Frem Kobenhavn	1 - 4	Oesterbro BK
BK Frem Kobenhavn	2 - 2	1909 Odense
BK Frem Kobenhavn	1 - 4	Odense BK
Oesterbro BK	2 - 8	Akademisk Kobenhavn
Oesterbro BK	1 - 1	1893 Kobenhavn
Oesterbro BK	1 - 3	BK Frem Kobenhavn
Oesterbro BK	1 - 3	KB Kopenhavn
Oesterbro BK	3 - 1	1903 Kobenhavn
Oesterbro BK	2 - 1	1909 Odense
Oesterbro BK	5 - 3	Odense BK
Oesterbro BK	3 - 2	Aarhus GF
Oesterbro BK	2 - 2	Koge BK
1909 Odense	1 - 3	Akademisk Kobenhavn
1909 Odense	3 - 1	1893 Kobenhavn
1909 Odense	1 - 2	BK Frem Kobenhavn
1909 Odense	0 - 2	KB Kopenhavn
1909 Odense	2 - 2	1903 Kobenhavn
1909 Odense	0 - 3	Oesterbro BK
1909 Odense	0 - 4	Odense BK
1909 Odense	2 - 1	Aarhus GF
1909 Odense	1 - 4	Koge BK
Odense BK	5 - 6	Akademisk Kobenhavn
Odense BK	3 - 2	1893 Kobenhavn
Odense BK	1 - 3	BK Frem Kobenhavn
Odense BK	2 - 6	KB Kopenhavn
Odense BK	3 - 3	1903 Kobenhavn
Odense BK	4 - 2	Oesterbro BK
Odense BK	3 - 2	1909 Odense

BK Frem Kobenhavn	4 -	0 Aarhus GF		Odense BK	3 -	1 Aarhus GF
BK Frem Kobenhavn	3 -	1 Koge BK		Odense BK	3 -	2 Koge BK
KB Kopenhavn	2 -	2 Akademisk Kobenhavn		Aarhus GF	0 -	0 Akademisk Kobenhavn
KB Kopenhavn	0 -	0 1893 Kobenhavn		Aarhus GF	1 -	1 1893 Kobenhavn
KB Kopenhavn	3 -	0 BK Frem Kobenhavn		Aarhus GF	2 -	0 BK Frem Kobenhavn
KB Kopenhavn	2 -	1 1903 Kobenhavn		Aarhus GF	1 -	0 KB Kopenhavn
KB Kopenhavn	2 -	1 Oesterbro BK		Aarhus GF	1 -	2 1903 Kobenhavn
KB Kopenhavn	2 -	1 1909 Odense		Aarhus GF	5 -	1 Oesterbro BK
KB Kopenhavn	3 -	2 Odense BK		Aarhus GF	3 -	1 1909 Odense
KB Kopenhavn	2 -	0 Aarhus GF		Aarhus GF	3 -	1 Odense BK
KB Kopenhavn	3 -	0 Koge BK		Aarhus GF	6 -	1 Koge BK
1903 Kobenhavn	3 -	1 Akademisk Kobenhavn		Koge BK	3 -	1 Akademisk Kobenhavn
1903 Kobenhavn	1 -	4 1893 Kobenhavn		Koge BK	1 -	2 1893 Kobenhavn
1903 Kobenhavn	3 -	0 BK Frem Kobenhavn		Koge BK	2 -	4 BK Frem Kobenhavn
1903 Kobenhavn	2 -	1 KB Kopenhavn		Koge BK	2 -	1 KB Kopenhavn
1903 Kobenhavn	0 -	1 Oesterbro BK		Koge BK	2 -	1 1903 Kobenhavn
1903 Kobenhavn	4 -	0 1909 Odense		Koge BK	2 -	1 Oesterbro BK
1903 Kobenhavn	4 -	3 Odense BK		Koge BK	0 -	0 1909 Odense
1903 Kobenhavn	2 -	3 Aarhus GF		Koge BK	5 -	0 Odense BK
1903 Kobenhavn	1 -	1 Koge BK		Koge BK	1 -	4 Aarhus GF

	Division 2	Pld	W	D	L	F	A	GA	Pts
1	Esbjerg	18	12	4	2	48	20	2.40	28
2	Fremad Amager	18	9	5	4	35	28	1.25	23
3	Randers Freja	18	8	4	6	37	27	1.37	20
4	Aalborg	18	7	5	6	30	19	1.58	19
5	KFUM Kobenhavn	18	8	3	7	42	42	1.00	19
6	Helsingor	18	9	1	8	35	36	0.97	19
7	Naestved	18	8	1	9	25	30	0.83	17
8	Aalborg Chang	18	4	5	9	26	38	0.68	13
9	Hellerup IK	18	6	1	11	23	39	0.59	13
10	Bronshoj	18	2	5	11	19	41	0.46	9

Esbjerg	3 -	1 Fremad Amager		Helsingor	0 -	6 Esbjerg
Esbjerg	2 -	0 Randers Freja		Helsingor	3 -	0 Fremad Amager
Esbjerg	1 -	1 Aalborg		Helsingor	2 -	1 Randers Freja
Esbjerg	6 -	2 KFUM Kobenhavn		Helsingor	2 -	3 Aalborg
Esbjerg	4 -	1 Helsingor		Helsingor	4 -	1 KFUM Kobenhavn
Esbjerg	4 -	2 Naestved		Helsingor	0 -	3 Naestved
Esbjerg	2 -	0 Aalborg Chang		Helsingor	0 -	1 Aalborg Chang
Esbjerg	5 -	3 Hellerup IK		Helsingor	3 -	0 Hellerup IK
Esbjerg	0 -	0 Bronshoj		Helsingor	5 -	4 Bronshoj
Fremad Amager	4 -	3 Esbjerg		Naestved	0 -	1 Esbjerg

Fremad Amager	1 -	1	Randers Freja	Naestved	3 -	1	Fremad Amager
Fremad Amager	1 -	1	Aalborg	Naestved	1 -	2	Randers Freja
Fremad Amager	2 -	0	KFUM Kobenhavn	Naestved	2 -	1	Aalborg
Fremad Amager	2 -	3	Helsingor	Naestved	1 -	1	KFUM Kobenhavn
Fremad Amager	1 -	0	Naestved	Naestved	0 -	4	Helsingor
Fremad Amager	0 -	0	Aalborg Chang	Naestved	3 -	2	Aalborg Chang
Fremad Amager	1 -	0	Hellerup IK	Naestved	3 -	0	Hellerup IK
Fremad Amager	3 -	2	Bronshoj	Naestved	2 -	0	Bronshoj
Randers Freja	0 -	0	Esbjerg	Aalborg Chang	0 -	4	Esbjerg
Randers Freja	3 -	3	Fremad Amager	Aalborg Chang	1 -	3	Fremad Amager
Randers Freja	0 -	0	Aalborg	Aalborg Chang	1 -	2	Randers Freja
Randers Freja	2 -	4	KFUM Kobenhavn	Aalborg Chang	0 -	0	Aalborg
Randers Freja	0 -	3	Helsingor	Aalborg Chang	1 -	2	KFUM Kobenhavn
Randers Freja	6 -	1	Naestved	Aalborg Chang	1 -	1	Helsingor
Randers Freja	4 -	2	Aalborg Chang	Aalborg Chang	2 -	1	Naestved
Randers Freja	3 -	1	Hellerup IK	Aalborg Chang	1 -	3	Hellerup IK
Randers Freja	2 -	0	Bronshoj	Aalborg Chang	3 -	3	Bronshoj
Aalborg	1 -	1	Esbjerg	Hellerup IK	2 -	1	Esbjerg
Aalborg	1 -	3	Fremad Amager	Hellerup IK	2 -	5	Fremad Amager
Aalborg	1 -	2	Randers Freja	Hellerup IK	1 -	0	Randers Freja
Aalborg	5 -	0	KFUM Kobenhavn	Hellerup IK	0 -	1	Aalborg
Aalborg	3 -	0	Helsingor	Hellerup IK	4 -	3	KFUM Kobenhavn
Aalborg	3 -	0	Naestved	Hellerup IK	0 -	1	Helsingor
Aalborg	3 -	1	Aalborg Chang	Hellerup IK	0 -	1	Naestved
Aalborg	1 -	2	Hellerup IK	Hellerup IK	2 -	4	Aalborg Chang
Aalborg	5 -	0	Bronshoj	Hellerup IK	1 -	0	Bronshoj
KFUM Kobenhavn	3 -	4	Esbjerg	Bronshoj	0 -	1	Esbjerg
KFUM Kobenhavn	1 -	1	Fremad Amager	Bronshoj	1 -	3	Fremad Amager
KFUM Kobenhavn	4 -	2	Randers Freja	Bronshoj	0 -	7	Randers Freja
KFUM Kobenhavn	3 -	0	Aalborg	Bronshoj	1 -	0	Aalborg
KFUM Kobenhavn	5 -	3	Helsingor	Bronshoj	1 -	3	KFUM Kobenhavn
KFUM Kobenhavn	2 -	1	Naestved	Bronshoj	2 -	0	Helsingor
KFUM Kobenhavn	2 -	3	Aalborg Chang	Bronshoj	0 -	1	Naestved
KFUM Kobenhavn	5 -	1	Hellerup IK	Bronshoj	3 -	3	Aalborg Chang
KFUM Kobenhavn	1 -	1	Bronshoj	Bronshoj	1 -	1	Hellerup IK

	Division 3	Pld	W	D	L	F	A	GA	Pts
1	Skovshoved	18	12	6	0	61	25	2.44	30
2	Horsens	18	12	1	5	42	35	1.20	25
3	1913 Kobenhavn	18	9	4	5	43	33	1.30	22
4	Vejle BK	18	7	4	7	34	33	1.03	18
5	Korsor BK	18	6	3	9	40	43	0.93	15
6	Viking Ronne	18	7	1	10	34	41	0.83	15
7	Nakskov	18	6	3	9	29	35	0.83	15
8	Nykobing Falster 1901	18	6	3	9	30	37	0.81	15
9	Vejen	18	7	0	11	31	43	0.72	14
10	Odense KFUM	18	5	1	12	38	57	0.67	11

Skovshoved	8	-	1	Horsens	Viking Ronne	1	-	2	Skovshoved
Skovshoved	3	-	3	1913 Kobenhavn	Viking Ronne	2	-	4	Horsens
Skovshoved	0	-	0	Vejle BK	Viking Ronne	1	-	2	1913 Kobenhavn
Skovshoved	5	-	3	Korsor BK	Viking Ronne	3	-	1	Vejle BK
Skovshoved	4	-	0	Viking Ronne	Viking Ronne	2	-	1	Korsor BK
Skovshoved	6	-	1	Nakskov	Viking Ronne	1	-	1	Nakskov
Skovshoved	4	-	2	Nykobing 1901	Viking Ronne	3	-	1	Nykobing 1901
Skovshoved	3	-	1	Vejen	Viking Ronne	3	-	0	Vejen
Skovshoved	1	-	0	Odense KFUM	Viking Ronne	5	-	1	Odense KFUM
Horsens	0	-	3	Skovshoved	Nakskov	2	-	4	Skovshoved
Horsens	1	-	1	1913 Kobenhavn	Nakskov	1	-	2	Horsens
Horsens	2	-	1	Vejle BK	Nakskov	3	-	1	1913 Kobenhavn
Horsens	1	-	3	Korsor BK	Nakskov	3	-	0	Vejle BK
Horsens	1	-	2	Viking Ronne	Nakskov	1	-	3	Korsor BK
Horsens	1	-	0	Nakskov	Nakskov	3	-	1	Viking Ronne
Horsens	7	-	0	Nykobing 1901	Nakskov	2	-	0	Nykobing 1901
Horsens	2	-	1	Vejen	Nakskov	2	-	0	Vejen
Horsens	2	-	1	Odense KFUM	Nakskov	3	-	0	Odense KFUM
1913 Kobenhavn	2	-	2	Skovshoved	Nykobing 1901	1	-	1	Skovshoved
1913 Kobenhavn	2	-	5	Horsens	Nykobing 1901	1	-	2	Horsens
1913 Kobenhavn	0	-	1	Vejle BK	Nykobing 1901	0	-	2	1913 Kobenhavn
1913 Kobenhavn	5	-	3	Korsor BK	Nykobing 1901	2	-	0	Vejle BK
1913 Kobenhavn	4	-	1	Viking Ronne	Nykobing 1901	2	-	2	Korsor BK
1913 Kobenhavn	2	-	2	Nakskov	Nykobing 1901	2	-	1	Viking Ronne
1913 Kobenhavn	4	-	2	Nykobing 1901	Nykobing 1901	4	-	0	Nakskov
1913 Kobenhavn	3	-	0	Vejen	Nykobing 1901	4	-	0	Vejen
1913 Kobenhavn	3	-	1	Odense KFUM	Nykobing 1901	4	-	2	Odense KFUM
Vejle BK	4	-	4	Skovshoved	Vejen	2	-	4	Skovshoved
Vejle BK	1	-	5	Horsens	Vejen	2	-	3	Horsens
Vejle BK	4	-	2	1913 Kobenhavn	Vejen	3	-	2	1913 Kobenhavn
Vejle BK	2	-	0	Korsor BK	Vejen	0	-	4	Vejle BK
Vejle BK	5	-	2	Viking Ronne	Vejen	7	-	1	Korsor BK
Vejle BK	1	-	1	Nakskov	Vejen	1	-	0	Viking Ronne
Vejle BK	2	-	1	Nykobing 1901	Vejen	4	-	1	Nakskov
Vejle BK	0	-	1	Vejen	Vejen	0	-	1	Nykobing 1901
Vejle BK	3	-	1	Odense KFUM	Vejen	3	-	1	Odense KFUM
Korsor BK	0	-	0	Skovshoved	Odense KFUM	2	-	7	Skovshoved
Korsor BK	1	-	2	Horsens	Odense KFUM	5	-	1	Horsens
Korsor BK	1	-	2	1913 Kobenhavn	Odense KFUM	0	-	3	1913 Kobenhavn
Korsor BK	3	-	3	Vejle BK	Odense KFUM	3	-	2	Vejle BK
Korsor BK	3	-	4	Viking Ronne	Odense KFUM	2	-	8	Korsor BK
Korsor BK	3	-	2	Nakskov	Odense KFUM	5	-	2	Viking Ronne
Korsor BK	2	-	0	Nykobing 1901	Odense KFUM	2	-	1	Nakskov
Korsor BK	1	-	2	Vejen	Odense KFUM	3	-	3	Nykobing 1901
Korsor BK	2	-	1	Odense KFUM	Odense KFUM	8	-	4	Vejen

England

Pompey had their first title sewn up long before two defeats at Arsenal & Man Utd finished their season. At the bottom however it went to the wire – Huddersfield bagged two home wins in three days to squeak past Preston & Sheff Utd.

In Div 2, Southampton could have put more pressure on WBA with a win on April 23rd, but a draw followed by a 0-1 loss at Chesterfield put Fulham and WBA up to the top flight. Hull City and Swansea will join Div 2, while Forest and Lincoln go down to the regional divisions.

The Wolves beat Leicester 3-1 in the FA Cup Final.

	Division 1	Pld	W	D	L	F	A	GA	Pts
1	Portsmouth	42	25	8	9	84	42	2.00	58
2	Liverpool	42	21	11	10	77	44	1.75	53
3	Derby County	42	22	9	11	74	55	1.35	53
4	Newcastle United	42	20	12	10	70	56	1.25	52
5	Arsenal	42	18	13	11	74	44	1.68	49
6	Wolverhampton Wanderers	42	17	12	13	79	66	1.20	46
7	Manchester City	42	15	15	12	47	51	0.92	45
8	Sunderland	42	13	17	12	49	58	0.84	43
9	Arsenal	42	15	12	15	63	67	0.94	42
10	Aston Villa	42	16	10	16	60	76	0.79	42
11	Manchester City	42	16	9	17	66	68	0.97	41
12	Liverpool	42	13	14	15	53	43	1.23	40
13	Aston Villa	42	12	14	16	69	68	1.01	38
14	Bolton Wanderers	42	14	10	18	59	68	0.87	38
15	Burnley	42	12	14	16	43	50	0.86	38
16	Blackpool	42	11	16	15	54	67	0.81	38
17	Birmingham City	42	11	15	16	36	38	0.95	37
18	Everton	42	13	11	18	41	63	0.65	37
19	Middlesbrough	42	11	12	19	46	57	0.81	34
20	Huddersfield Town	42	12	10	20	40	69	0.58	34
21	Preston North End	42	11	11	20	62	75	0.83	33
22	Sheffield United	42	11	11	20	57	78	0.73	33

August 21, 1948

Aston Villa	2 - 1	Liverpool
Burnley	1 - 0	Manchester City
Chelsea	1 - 0	Middlesbrough
Everton	3 - 3	Newcastle United
Huddersfield Town	1 - 1	Arsenal
Manchester United	1 - 2	Derby County

December 18, 1948

Arsenal	3 - 0	Huddersfield Town
Birmingham City	0 - 1	Wolves
Blackpool	0 - 3	Sheffield United
Bolton Wanderers	4 - 1	Sunderland
Charlton Athletic	4 - 1	Stoke City
Derby County	1 - 3	Manchester United

Preston North End	2	-	2	Portsmouth	Liverpool	1 - 1	Aston Villa
Sheffield United	3	-	2	Blackpool	Manchester City	2 - 2	Burnley
Stoke City	2	-	2	Charlton Athletic	Middlesbrough	1 - 1	Chelsea
Sunderland	2	-	0	Bolton Wanderers	Newcastle United	1 - 0	Everton
Wolves	2	-	2	Birmingham City	Portsmouth	3 - 1	Preston North End

August 23, 1948
Blackpool 0 - 3 Manchester United

December 25, 1948
Arsenal 3 - 3 Derby County

August 25, 1948

Arsenal	3	-	0	Stoke City	Birmingham City	2 - 0	Newcastle United
Birmingham City	0	-	0	Middlesbrough	Blackpool	0 - 0	Huddersfield Town
Bolton Wanderers	3	-	0	Aston Villa	Burnley	1 - 3	Stoke City
Charlton Athletic	3	-	1	Burnley	Charlton Athletic	0 - 0	Preston North End
Derby County	4	-	1	Huddersfield Town	Chelsea	1 - 2	Portsmouth
Liverpool	3	-	3	Sheffield United	Everton	0 - 0	Manchester City
Manchester City	3	-	2	Preston North End	Manchester United	0 - 0	Liverpool
Newcastle United	2	-	2	Chelsea	Sheffield United	1 - 1	Bolton Wanderers
Portsmouth	4	-	0	Everton	Sunderland	1 - 0	Middlesbrough
Wolves	0	-	1	Sunderland	Wolves	4 - 0	Aston Villa

August 28, 1948

December 26, 1948

Arsenal	0	-	1	Manchester United	Aston Villa	5 - 1	Wolves
Birmingham City	1	-	0	Chelsea	Bolton Wanderers	6 - 1	Sheffield United
Blackpool	1	-	0	Aston Villa	Derby County	2 - 1	Arsenal
Bolton Wanderers	0	-	5	Wolves	Huddersfield Town	1 - 0	Blackpool
Charlton Athletic	3	-	1	Huddersfield Town	Liverpool	0 - 2	Manchester United
Derby County	2	-	1	Sheffield United	Manchester City	0 - 0	Everton
Liverpool	4	-	0	Sunderland	Middlesbrough	0 - 0	Sunderland
Manchester City	0	-	0	Stoke City	Newcastle United	1 - 0	Birmingham City
Middlesbrough	1	-	0	Everton	Portsmouth	5 - 2	Chelsea
Newcastle United	2	-	5	Preston North End	Preston North End	2 - 3	Charlton Athletic
Portsmouth	1	-	0	Burnley	Stoke City	2 - 1	Burnley

August 30, 1948

January 1, 1949

Aston Villa	2	-	4	Bolton Wanderers	Aston Villa	2 - 5	Blackpool
Sheffield United	1	-	2	Liverpool	Burnley	2 - 1	Portsmouth
Stoke City	1	-	0	Arsenal	Chelsea	2 - 0	Birmingham City

August 31, 1948
Burnley	0	-	0	Charlton Athletic	Everton	3 - 1	Middlesbrough

September 1, 1948

					Huddersfield Town	1 - 2	Charlton Athletic
Chelsea	2	-	3	Newcastle United	Manchester United	2 - 0	Arsenal
Everton	0	-	5	Portsmouth	Preston North End	2 - 1	Newcastle United
Huddersfield Town	1	-	1	Derby County	Sheffield United	3 - 1	Derby County
Manchester United	3	-	4	Blackpool	Stoke City	2 - 3	Manchester City
Middlesbrough	1	-	1	Birmingham City	Sunderland	0 - 2	Liverpool
Preston North End	1	-	3	Manchester City	Wolves	2 - 0	Bolton Wanderers
Sunderland	3	-	3	Wolves			

September 4, 1948

January 15, 1949

Aston Villa	1	-	1	Derby County	Arsenal	5 - 3	Sheffield United
Burnley	0	-	3	Newcastle United	Blackpool	3 - 3	Sunderland
Charlton Athletic	3	-	2	Manchester City	Manchester City	0 - 1	Charlton Athletic
Chelsea	2	-	2	Bolton Wanderers	Middlesbrough	1 - 0	Preston North End
Everton	0	-	5	Birmingham City	Newcastle United	1 - 1	Burnley
Manchester United	4	-	1	Huddersfield Town	Portsmouth	1 - 0	Stoke City
Preston North End	6	-	1	Middlesbrough			

January 22, 1949

					Aston Villa	1 - 0	Arsenal
					Bolton Wanderers	0 - 3	Liverpool
					Burnley	0 - 0	Middlesbrough

26

Sheffield United	1	-	1	Arsenal	Charlton Athletic	0 - 1	Portsmouth
Stoke City	0	-	1	Portsmouth	Everton	2 - 1	Chelsea
Sunderland	2	-	2	Blackpool	Manchester United	0 - 0	Manchester City
Wolves	0	-	0	Liverpool	Preston North End	0 - 0	Birmingham City

September 6, 1948

					Sheffield United	0 - 0	Huddersfield Town
Blackpool	1	-	1	Derby County	Stoke City	1 - 1	Newcastle United
Bolton Wanderers	1	-	2	Huddersfield Town	Sunderland	2 - 1	Derby County
Burnley	1	-	0	Preston North End	Wolves	2 - 1	Blackpool
Sheffield United	2	-	5	Sunderland			

February 5, 1949

September 8, 1948

Arsenal	1	-	1	Liverpool	Arsenal	5 - 0	Sunderland
Charlton Athletic	1	-	1	Chelsea	Birmingham City	0 - 0	Burnley
Everton	2	-	1	Stoke City	Chelsea	5 - 3	Preston North End
Manchester City	1	-	0	Birmingham City	Derby County	3 - 2	Wolves
Newcastle United	2	-	1	Aston Villa	Liverpool	0 - 0	Everton
Portsmouth	1	-	0	Middlesbrough	Newcastle United	2 - 0	Charlton Athletic
Wolves	3	-	2	Manchester United	Portsmouth	3 - 1	Manchester City

September 11, 1948

February 12, 1949

					Birmingham City	0 - 0	Everton
Arsenal	3	-	1	Aston Villa	Blackpool	1 - 0	Bolton Wanderers
Birmingham City	1	-	0	Preston North End	Huddersfield Town	0 - 1	Aston Villa
Blackpool	1	-	3	Wolves			

February 19, 1949

Chelsea	6	-	0	Everton	Aston Villa	2 - 1	Manchester United
Derby County	2	-	2	Sunderland	Bolton Wanderers	4 - 0	Derby County
Huddersfield Town	0	-	0	Sheffield United	Burnley	3 - 0	Chelsea
Liverpool	0	-	1	Bolton Wanderers	Charlton Athletic	2 - 0	Middlesbrough
Manchester City	0	-	0	Manchester United	Liverpool	1 - 1	Blackpool
Middlesbrough	4	-	1	Burnley	Manchester City	1 - 0	Newcastle United
Newcastle United	2	-	2	Stoke City	Preston North End	3 - 1	Everton
Portsmouth	3	-	1	Charlton Athletic	Sheffield United	3 - 1	Portsmouth

September 13, 1948

					Stoke City	2 - 1	Birmingham City
Aston Villa	2	-	4	Newcastle United	Sunderland	0 - 1	Huddersfield Town
Stoke City	1	-	0	Everton	Wolves	1 - 3	Arsenal

September 15, 1948

February 26, 1949

Birmingham City	4	-	1	Manchester City	Arsenal	5 - 0	Bolton Wanderers
Derby County	3	-	1	Blackpool	Birmingham City	1 - 0	Charlton Athletic
Huddersfield Town	0	-	2	Bolton Wanderers	Blackpool	2 - 2	Preston North End
Liverpool	0	-	1	Arsenal	Chelsea	2 - 2	Stoke City
Manchester United	2	-	0	Wolves	Everton	2 - 1	Burnley
Middlesbrough	1	-	1	Portsmouth	Middlesbrough	0 - 1	Manchester City
Preston North End	0	-	3	Burnley	Sheffield United	0 - 1	Aston Villa
Sunderland	2	-	0	Sheffield United			

March 5, 1949

September 16, 1948

					Birmingham City	0 - 0	Bolton Wanderers
Chelsea	2	-	2	Charlton Athletic	Burnley	1 - 1	Arsenal

September 18, 1948

					Charlton Athletic	2 - 3	Manchester United
Aston Villa	3	-	3	Huddersfield Town	Chelsea	2 - 1	Liverpool
Bolton Wanderers	2	-	2	Blackpool	Everton	5 - 0	Blackpool
Burnley	2	-	2	Birmingham City	Manchester City	1 - 0	Sheffield United
Charlton Athletic	0	-	0	Newcastle United	Middlesbrough	4 - 4	Wolves
Everton	1	-	1	Liverpool	Newcastle United	2 - 1	Sunderland
Manchester City	1	-	1	Portsmouth	Portsmouth	3 - 0	Aston Villa
Preston North End	3	-	2	Chelsea	Preston North End	0 - 0	Derby County
Sheffield United	2	-	2	Manchester United	Stoke City	1 - 3	Huddersfield Town

Stoke City	3 - 0	Middlesbrough	
Sunderland	1 - 1	Arsenal	
Wolves	2 - 2	Derby County	

September 25, 1948

Arsenal	3 - 1	Wolves
Birmingham City	2 - 1	Stoke City
Blackpool	1 - 0	Liverpool
Chelsea	1 - 0	Burnley
Derby County	1 - 0	Bolton Wanderers
Everton	4 - 1	Preston North End
Huddersfield Town	2 - 0	Sunderland
Manchester United	3 - 1	Aston Villa
Middlesbrough	2 - 4	Charlton Athletic
Newcastle United	0 - 0	Manchester City
Portsmouth	3 - 0	Sheffield United

October 2, 1948

Aston Villa	4 - 3	Sheffield United
Bolton Wanderers	1 - 0	Arsenal
Burnley	1 - 0	Everton
Charlton Athletic	1 - 1	Birmingham City
Liverpool	0 - 0	Derby County
Manchester City	1 - 0	Middlesbrough
Portsmouth	1 - 0	Newcastle United
Preston North End	1 - 3	Blackpool
Stoke City	4 - 3	Chelsea
Sunderland	2 - 1	Manchester United
Wolves	7 - 1	Huddersfield Town

October 9, 1948

Arsenal	3 - 1	Burnley
Aston Villa	1 - 1	Portsmouth
Blackpool	3 - 0	Everton
Bolton Wanderers	0 - 0	Birmingham City
Derby County	1 - 0	Preston North End
Huddersfield Town	1 - 3	Stoke City
Liverpool	1 - 1	Chelsea
Manchester United	1 - 1	Charlton Athletic
Sheffield United	0 - 2	Manchester City
Sunderland	1 - 1	Newcastle United
Wolves	0 - 3	Middlesbrough

October 16, 1948

Birmingham City	0 - 1	Liverpool
Burnley	1 - 2	Huddersfield Town
Charlton Athletic	2 - 1	Sheffield United
Chelsea	3 - 3	Blackpool
Everton	0 - 1	Derby County
Manchester City	4 - 1	Aston Villa
Middlesbrough	5 - 0	Bolton Wanderers
Newcastle United	3 - 1	Wolves
Portsmouth	3 - 0	Sunderland
Preston North End	1 - 1	Arsenal
Stoke City	2 - 1	Manchester United

October 23, 1948

March 12, 1949

Arsenal	0 - 0	Preston North End
Aston Villa	1 - 0	Manchester City
Blackpool	2 - 1	Chelsea
Bolton Wanderers	4 - 1	Middlesbrough
Derby County	3 - 2	Everton
Huddersfield Town	1 - 0	Burnley
Liverpool	1 - 0	Birmingham City
Manchester United	3 - 0	Stoke City
Sheffield United	2 - 0	Charlton Athletic
Sunderland	1 - 4	Portsmouth
Wolves	3 - 0	Newcastle United

March 19, 1949

Birmingham City	1 - 0	Manchester United
Burnley	0 - 0	Wolves
Charlton Athletic	2 - 1	Liverpool
Chelsea	1 - 0	Sheffield United
Everton	1 - 3	Aston Villa
Manchester City	1 - 1	Blackpool
Middlesbrough	1 - 0	Huddersfield Town
Newcastle United	3 - 2	Arsenal
Portsmouth	1 - 0	Derby County
Preston North End	1 - 3	Sunderland
Stoke City	4 - 0	Bolton Wanderers

March 26, 1949

Aston Villa	1 - 1	Chelsea
Blackpool	0 - 1	Charlton Athletic
Bolton Wanderers	0 - 1	Burnley
Derby County	2 - 0	Manchester City
Huddersfield Town	0 - 2	Newcastle United
Liverpool	4 - 0	Stoke City
Sheffield United	4 - 0	Birmingham City
Sunderland	1 - 1	Everton

April 2, 1949

Birmingham City	1 - 1	Arsenal
Bolton Wanderers	1 - 2	Portsmouth
Burnley	1 - 1	Aston Villa
Charlton Athletic	3 - 1	Everton
Chelsea	5 - 0	Huddersfield Town
Manchester City	1 - 0	Bolton Wanderers
Middlesbrough	1 - 0	Derby County
Newcastle United	3 - 1	Blackpool
Portsmouth	3 - 2	Liverpool
Preston North End	4 - 1	Sheffield United
Stoke City	0 - 0	Sunderland

April 6, 1949

Huddersfield Town	2 - 1	Manchester United
Liverpool	0 - 0	Wolves
Newcastle United	0 - 5	Portsmouth

April 9, 1949

Arsenal	1 - 1	Middlesbrough
Aston Villa	2 - 0	Preston North End

Arsenal	5	-	0	Everton	Blackpool	1 - 0	Portsmouth
Aston Villa	4	-	3	Charlton Athletic	Bolton Wanderers	2 - 2	Charlton Athletic
Blackpool	1	-	0	Birmingham City	Derby County	2 - 4	Newcastle United
Bolton Wanderers	1	-	5	Newcastle United	Huddersfield Town	0 - 0	Birmingham City
Derby County	2	-	1	Chelsea	Liverpool	0 - 1	Manchester City
Huddersfield Town	0	-	2	Preston North End	Manchester United	1 - 1	Chelsea
Liverpool	4	-	0	Middlesbrough	Sheffield United	1 - 1	Everton
Manchester United	1	-	1	Burnley	Sunderland	0 - 0	Burnley
Sheffield United	2	-	2	Stoke City	Wolves	3 - 1	Stoke City
Sunderland	3	-	0	Manchester City			
Wolves	3	-	0	Portsmouth			

October 30, 1948
April 13, 1949

					Charlton Athletic	2 - 3	Wolves

April 15, 1949

Birmingham City	0	-	1	Derby County	Blackpool	1 - 1	Arsenal
Burnley	2	-	0	Sheffield United	Bolton Wanderers	0 - 1	Manchester United
Charlton Athletic	4	-	0	Sunderland	Burnley	3 - 1	Derby County
Chelsea	0	-	1	Arsenal	Liverpool	0 - 1	Huddersfield Town
Everton	2	-	0	Huddersfield Town	Manchester City	1 - 0	Chelsea
Manchester City	3	-	3	Wolves	Newcastle United	1 - 0	Middlesbrough
Middlesbrough	1	-	0	Blackpool	Portsmouth	3 - 1	Birmingham City
Newcastle United	1	-	0	Liverpool	Preston North End	2 - 1	Stoke City
Portsmouth	0	-	0	Bolton Wanderers	Sunderland	0 - 0	Aston Villa
Preston North End	1	-	6	Manchester United			
Stoke City	4	-	2	Aston Villa			

November 6, 1948
April 16, 1949

Arsenal	2	-	0	Birmingham City	Birmingham City	1 - 1	Blackpool
Aston Villa	3	-	1	Burnley	Burnley	0 - 2	Manchester United
Blackpool	1	-	3	Newcastle United	Charlton Athletic	0 - 2	Aston Villa
Bolton Wanderers	5	-	1	Manchester City	Chelsea	0 - 3	Derby County
Derby County	2	-	0	Middlesbrough	Everton	0 - 0	Arsenal
Huddersfield Town	3	-	4	Chelsea	Manchester City	1 - 1	Sunderland
Liverpool	3	-	1	Portsmouth	Middlesbrough	0 - 1	Liverpool
Manchester United	2	-	0	Everton	Newcastle United	1 - 1	Bolton Wanderers
Sheffield United	3	-	2	Preston North End	Portsmouth	5 - 0	Wolves
Sunderland	1	-	1	Stoke City	Preston North End	2 - 0	Huddersfield Town
Wolves	2	-	0	Charlton Athletic	Stoke City	0 - 1	Sheffield United

November 13, 1948
April 18, 1949

Birmingham City	1	-	0	Huddersfield Town	Arsenal	2 - 0	Blackpool
Burnley	3	-	1	Sunderland	Birmingham City	3 - 0	Portsmouth
Charlton Athletic	1	-	4	Bolton Wanderers	Chelsea	1 - 1	Manchester City
Chelsea	1	-	1	Manchester United	Derby County	2 - 0	Burnley
Everton	2	-	1	Sheffield United	Everton	1 - 1	Charlton Athletic
Manchester City	2	-	4	Liverpool	Huddersfield Town	0 - 4	Liverpool
Middlesbrough	0	-	1	Arsenal	Manchester United	3 - 0	Bolton Wanderers
Newcastle United	3	-	0	Derby County	Middlesbrough	3 - 2	Newcastle United
Portsmouth	1	-	1	Blackpool	Sheffield United	1 - 1	Wolves
Preston North End	0	-	1	Aston Villa	Stoke City	2 - 0	Preston North End
Stoke City	2	-	1	Wolves			

November 20, 1948
April 19, 1949

Arsenal	0	-	1	Newcastle United	Aston Villa	1 - 1	Sunderland
Aston Villa	0	-	1	Everton	Wolves	6 - 0	Sheffield United

April 21, 1949

Blackpool	1	-	1	Manchester City	Manchester United	1 - 2	Sunderland
Bolton Wanderers	2	-	1	Stoke City			

April 23, 1949

					Arsenal	1 - 2	Chelsea
					Aston Villa	2 - 1	Stoke City

Derby County	1	-	0 Portsmouth	Blackpool	1	-	1 Middlesbrough
Huddersfield Town	0	-	0 Middlesbrough	Derby County	1	-	0 Birmingham City
Liverpool	1	-	1 Charlton Athletic	Huddersfield Town	1	-	1 Everton
Manchester United	3	-	0 Birmingham City	Liverpool	1	-	1 Newcastle United
Sheffield United	2	-	1 Chelsea	Manchester United	2	-	2 Preston North End
Sunderland	0	-	0 Preston North End	Sheffield United	0	-	0 Burnley
Wolves	3	-	0 Burnley	Sunderland	1	-	0 Charlton Athletic
				Wolves	1	-	1 Manchester City

November 27, 1948

April 27, 1949

Birmingham City	1	-	2 Sheffield United	Derby County	2	-	2 Aston Villa
Burnley	3	-	0 Bolton Wanderers	Everton	2	-	0 Manchester United
Charlton Athletic	0	-	0 Blackpool	Manchester City	0	-	3 Arsenal
Chelsea	2	-	1 Aston Villa	Middlesbrough	1	-	1 Stoke City
Everton	1	-	0 Sunderland				

April 30, 1949

Manchester City	2	-	1 Derby County	Birmingham City	0	-	1 Aston Villa
Middlesbrough	1	-	4 Manchester United	Burnley	0	-	2 Liverpool
Newcastle United	2	-	4 Huddersfield Town	Charlton Athletic	1	-	5 Derby County
Portsmouth	4	-	1 Arsenal	Chelsea	0	-	1 Sunderland
Preston North End	1	-	1 Wolves	Middlesbrough	3	-	1 Sheffield United
Stoke City	3	-	0 Liverpool	Newcastle United	0	-	1 Manchester United
				Portsmouth	2	-	0 Huddersfield Town
				Preston North End	1	-	1 Bolton Wanderers
				Stoke City	3	-	2 Blackpool

December 4, 1948

May 2, 1949

Arsenal	1	-	1 Manchester City	Manchester United	1	-	0 Middlesbrough
Aston Villa	0	-	3 Birmingham City	Wolves	2	-	1 Preston North End
Blackpool	2	-	1 Stoke City				

May 4, 1949

Bolton Wanderers	5	-	3 Preston North End	Arsenal	3	-	2 Portsmouth
Derby County	5	-	1 Charlton Athletic	Bolton Wanderers	1	-	1 Chelsea
Huddersfield Town	0	-	0 Portsmouth	Derby County	3	-	0 Liverpool
Liverpool	1	-	1 Burnley	Everton	1	-	0 Wolves
Manchester United	1	-	1 Newcastle United	Manchester United	3	-	2 Sheffield United
Sheffield United	1	-	0 Middlesbrough				

May 5, 1949

Sunderland	3	-	0 Chelsea	Huddersfield Town	4	-	0 Wolves
Wolves	1	-	0 Everton				

May 7, 1949

December 11, 1948

Birmingham City	0	-	0 Sunderland	Arsenal	2	-	0 Charlton Athletic
Burnley	2	-	0 Blackpool	Aston Villa	1	-	1 Middlesbrough
Charlton Athletic	4	-	3 Arsenal	Blackpool	1	-	1 Burnley
Chelsea	4	-	1 Wolves	Bolton Wanderers	1	-	0 Everton
Everton	1	-	0 Bolton Wanderers	Derby County	4	-	1 Stoke City
Manchester City	3	-	1 Huddersfield Town	Huddersfield Town	1	-	0 Manchester City
Middlesbrough	6	-	0 Aston Villa	Liverpool	0	-	2 Preston North End
Newcastle United	3	-	2 Sheffield United	Manchester United	3	-	2 Portsmouth
Portsmouth	2	-	2 Manchester United	Sheffield United	0	-	0 Newcastle United
Preston North End	3	-	2 Liverpool	Sunderland	1	-	1 Birmingham City
Stoke City	4	-	2 Derby County	Wolves	1	-	1 Chelsea

	Division 2	Pld	W	D	L	F	A	GA	Pts
1	Fulham	42	24	9	9	77	37	2.08	57
2	West Bromwich Albion	42	24	8	10	69	39	1.77	56
3	Southampton	42	23	9	10	69	36	1.92	55
4	Cardiff City	42	19	13	10	62	47	1.32	51
5	Tottenham Hotspur	42	17	16	9	72	44	1.64	50
6	Chesterfield	42	15	17	10	51	45	1.13	47
7	West Ham United	42	18	10	14	56	58	0.97	46
8	Sheffield Wednesday	42	15	13	14	63	56	1.13	43
9	Barnsley	42	14	12	16	62	61	1.02	40
10	Luton Town	42	14	12	16	55	57	0.96	40
11	Grimsby Town	42	15	10	17	72	76	0.95	40
12	Bury	42	17	6	19	67	76	0.88	40
13	Queens Park Rangers	42	14	11	17	44	62	0.71	39
14	Blackburn Rovers	42	15	8	19	53	63	0.84	38
15	Leeds United	42	12	13	17	55	63	0.87	37
16	Coventry City	42	15	7	20	55	64	0.86	37
17	Bradford Park Avenue	42	13	11	18	65	78	0.83	37
18	Brentford	42	11	14	17	42	53	0.79	36
19	Leicester City	42	10	16	16	62	79	0.78	36
20	Plymouth Argyle	42	12	12	18	49	64	0.77	36
21	Nottingham Forest	42	14	7	21	50	54	0.93	35
22	Lincoln City	42	8	12	22	53	91	0.58	28

August 21, 1948

Barnsley	0 - 0	Plymouth Argyle
Bradford PA	3 - 0	Cardiff City
Brentford	2 - 2	Coventry City
Bury	2 - 2	Chesterfield
Grimsby Town	2 - 3	Fulham
Leicester City	6 - 2	Leeds United
Luton Town	0 - 0	QPR
Nottingham Forest	0 - 1	West Bromwich
Southampton	3 - 0	Blackburn Rovers
Tottenham H	3 - 2	Sheffield Weds
West Ham United	2 - 2	Lincoln City

August 23, 1948

Blackburn Rovers	2 - 3	Bradford PA
Cardiff City	3 - 3	Luton Town
Coventry City	2 - 0	Tottenham H
Sheffield Weds	3 - 0	West Ham United

December 25, 1948

Blackburn Rovers	2 - 0	QPR
Bradford PA	1 - 1	Fulham
Brentford	1 - 1	Cardiff City
Bury	0 - 2	Coventry City
Grimsby Town	3 - 0	Barnsley
Leicester City	1 - 2	Tottenham H
Lincoln City	2 - 2	Chesterfield
Luton Town	3 - 1	Plymouth Argyle
Nottingham Forest	2 - 1	Southampton
West Bromwich	1 - 0	Sheffield Weds
West Ham United	3 - 2	Leeds United

December 26, 1948

Barnsley	2 - 1	Grimsby Town
Cardiff City	2 - 0	Brentford
Chesterfield	3 - 1	Lincoln City
Coventry City	2 - 1	Bury

August 24, 1948
Grimsby Town	1	-	2	Nottingham Forest

August 25, 1948
Fulham	1	-	1	Barnsley
Leeds United	0	-	0	Brentford
Lincoln City	1	-	1	Bury
Plymouth Argyle	1	-	2	Southampton
West Bromwich	0	-	0	Chesterfield

August 26, 1948
QPR	4	-	1	Leicester City

August 28, 1948
Blackburn Rovers	5	-	3	Barnsley
Cardiff City	2	-	1	Southampton
Chesterfield	0	-	0	West Ham United
Coventry City	1	-	2	Leicester City
Fulham	4	-	0	Nottingham Forest
Leeds United	2	-	0	Luton Town
Lincoln City	0	-	0	Tottenham H
Plymouth Argyle	0	-	2	Grimsby Town
QPR	1	-	0	Bradford PA
Sheffield Weds	0	-	0	Brentford
West Bromwich	2	-	3	Bury

August 30, 1948
Leicester City	2	-	3	QPR
Luton Town	3	-	0	Cardiff City
Tottenham H	4	-	0	Coventry City
West Ham United	2	-	2	Sheffield Weds

September 1, 1948
Barnsley	1	-	1	Fulham
Bradford PA	2	-	0	Blackburn Rovers
Brentford	1	-	3	Leeds United
Bury	3	-	1	Lincoln City
Chesterfield	0	-	0	West Bromwich
Nottingham Forest	0	-	0	Grimsby Town
Southampton	2	-	0	Plymouth Argyle

September 4, 1948
Barnsley	1	-	1	Cardiff City
Bradford PA	4	-	1	Luton Town
Brentford	2	-	1	Lincoln City
Bury	2	-	0	Fulham
Grimsby Town	1	-	2	Blackburn Rovers
Leeds United	4	-	1	Coventry City
Leicester City	2	-	2	Sheffield Weds
Nottingham Forest	1	-	0	Plymouth Argyle
Southampton	3	-	0	QPR
Tottenham H	4	-	0	Chesterfield
West Ham United	1	-	0	West Bromwich

September 6, 1948
Coventry City	1	-	0	West Ham United
Leicester City	0	-	0	Brentford
Luton Town	2	-	0	Blackburn Rovers

September 8, 1948
Fulham	2	-	0	Bradford PA
Leeds United	1	-	3	West Ham United
Plymouth Argyle	1	-	1	Luton Town
QPR	4	-	2	Blackburn Rovers
Sheffield Weds	2	-	1	West Bromwich
Southampton	2	-	1	Nottingham Forest
Tottenham H	1	-	1	Leicester City

January 1, 1949
Barnsley	1	-	1	Blackburn Rovers
Bradford PA	0	-	0	QPR
Brentford	2	-	1	Sheffield Weds
Bury	4	-	0	West Bromwich
Grimsby Town	2	-	2	Plymouth Argyle
Leicester City	3	-	1	Coventry City
Luton Town	0	-	0	Leeds United
Nottingham Forest	0	-	2	Fulham
Southampton	2	-	0	Cardiff City
Tottenham H	1	-	2	Lincoln City
West Ham United	1	-	2	Chesterfield

January 15, 1949
Blackburn Rovers	3	-	3	Grimsby Town
Cardiff City	0	-	3	Barnsley
Chesterfield	1	-	0	Tottenham H
Coventry City	4	-	1	Leeds United
Fulham	7	-	2	Bury
Lincoln City	3	-	1	Brentford
Luton Town	0	-	1	Bradford PA
West Bromwich	2	-	1	West Ham United

January 22, 1949
Barnsley	4	-	0	QPR
Bradford PA	2	-	1	Coventry City
Brentford	1	-	1	Chesterfield
Fulham	6	-	1	Plymouth Argyle
Grimsby Town	2	-	2	Cardiff City
Leeds United	1	-	1	Sheffield Weds
Leicester City	5	-	3	Lincoln City
Nottingham Forest	1	-	0	Blackburn Rovers
Southampton	1	-	1	Luton Town
Tottenham H	2	-	0	West Bromwich
West Ham United	2	-	1	Bury

January 29, 1949
Leeds United	1	-	0	Blackburn Rovers
Plymouth Argyle	1	-	0	Nottingham Forest
QPR	1	-	3	Southampton

February 5, 1949
Blackburn Rovers	1	-	0	Fulham
Bury	1	-	1	Tottenham H
Cardiff City	1	-	0	Nottingham Forest
Chesterfield	1	-	1	Leicester City
Lincoln City	0	-	0	Leeds United
Luton Town	1	-	0	Barnsley
Plymouth Argyle	2	-	0	West Ham United

Barnsley	4	-	0	Nottingham Forest	QPR	1	-	2	Grimsby Town
Bury	2	-	1	Sheffield Weds	Sheffield Weds	2	-	1	Coventry City
Chesterfield	0	-	3	Grimsby Town	West Bromwich	2	-	0	Brentford
Fulham	1	-	0	Southampton			February 12, 1949		
Leeds United	0	-	0	Tottenham H	Leeds United	0	-	1	Bury
Plymouth Argyle	3	-	0	Bradford PA	Southampton	4	-	0	Lincoln City
West Bromwich	5	-	0	Lincoln City	Tottenham H	2	-	1	Nottingham Forest
		September 9, 1948			West Ham United	1	-	0	Grimsby Town
QPR	0	-	0	Cardiff City			February 19, 1949		
		September 11, 1948			Barnsley	0	-	0	Bradford PA
Blackburn Rovers	2	-	1	Nottingham Forest	Brentford	8	-	2	Bury
Bury	2	-	0	West Ham United	Coventry City	1	-	0	Lincoln City
Cardiff City	3	-	0	Grimsby Town	Fulham	4	-	0	Cardiff City
Chesterfield	0	-	1	Brentford	Leeds United	1	-	0	Chesterfield
Coventry City	2	-	0	Bradford PA	Nottingham Forest	0	-	0	QPR
Lincoln City	2	-	0	Leicester City	Plymouth Argyle	3	-	0	Blackburn Rovers
Luton Town	1	-	1	Southampton	Southampton	1	-	0	Sheffield Weds
Plymouth Argyle	3	-	1	Fulham	Tottenham H	1	-	1	West Ham United
QPR	2	-	2	Barnsley			February 26, 1949		
Sheffield Weds	3	-	1	Leeds United	Blackburn Rovers	1	-	1	Tottenham H
West Bromwich	2	-	2	Tottenham H	Bradford PA	0	-	1	Grimsby Town
		September 13, 1948			Cardiff City	1	-	0	Plymouth Argyle
Cardiff City	3	-	0	QPR	Chesterfield	0	-	0	Coventry City
Sheffield Weds	1	-	2	Bury	Lincoln City	3	-	1	Sheffield Weds
Tottenham H	2	-	2	Leeds United	Luton Town	4	-	3	Nottingham Forest
West Ham United	2	-	2	Coventry City	QPR	1	-	0	Fulham
		September 14, 1948			Southampton	3	-	0	Barnsley
Grimsby Town	3	-	3	Chesterfield			March 5, 1949		
		September 15, 1948			Brentford	0	-	3	QPR
Bradford PA	2	-	2	Plymouth Argyle	Chesterfield	2	-	1	Nottingham Forest
Brentford	1	-	2	Leicester City	Coventry City	2	-	2	Southampton
Lincoln City	0	-	3	West Bromwich	Leeds United	4	-	2	Bradford PA
Nottingham Forest	0	-	1	Barnsley	Leicester City	1	-	1	Luton Town
Southampton	3	-	0	Fulham	Lincoln City	2	-	3	Grimsby Town
		September 18, 1948			Sheffield Weds	1	-	1	Barnsley
Barnsley	1	-	2	Luton Town	Tottenham H	0	-	1	Cardiff City
Brentford	0	-	0	West Bromwich	West Bromwich	1	-	2	Fulham
Coventry City	3	-	4	Sheffield Weds	West Ham United	2	-	1	Blackburn Rovers
Fulham	1	-	1	Blackburn Rovers			March 12, 1949		
Grimsby Town	4	-	1	QPR	Barnsley	1	-	1	Coventry City
Leeds United	3	-	1	Lincoln City	Blackburn Rovers	1	-	2	Bury
Leicester City	2	-	2	Chesterfield	Bradford PA	3	-	3	Leicester City
Nottingham Forest	0	-	0	Cardiff City	Cardiff City	4	-	0	West Ham United
Southampton	2	-	2	Bradford PA	Fulham	2	-	1	Chesterfield
Tottenham H	3	-	1	Bury	Grimsby Town	2	-	0	Sheffield Weds
West Ham United	3	-	0	Plymouth Argyle	Luton Town	2	-	1	Brentford
		September 20, 1948			Nottingham Forest	1	-	1	Lincoln City
Blackburn Rovers	4	-	1	Luton Town	Plymouth Argyle	1	-	2	West Bromwich
		September 25, 1948			QPR	0	-	0	Tottenham H
Blackburn Rovers	2	-	1	Plymouth Argyle	Southampton	2	-	1	Leeds United
Bradford PA	0	-	2	Barnsley			March 19, 1949		
Bury	1	-	2	Brentford	Brentford	1	-	0	Bradford PA

Cardiff City	2	-	1	Fulham	Bury	0	-	3 Cardiff City
Chesterfield	3	-	1	Leeds United	Chesterfield	0	-	0 Plymouth Argyle
Lincoln City	1	-	0	Coventry City	Coventry City	4	-	1 Grimsby Town
Luton Town	1	-	1	Grimsby Town	Leeds United	4	-	1 Barnsley
QPR	2	-	1	Nottingham Forest	Leicester City	1	-	3 Southampton
Sheffield Weds	2	-	0	Southampton	Lincoln City	0	-	3 Fulham
West Bromwich	2	-	1	Leicester City	Sheffield Weds	2	-	1 Nottingham Forest
West Ham United	1	-	0	Tottenham H	Tottenham H	2	-	1 Luton Town

October 2, 1948

West Bromwich 2 - 1 Blackburn Rovers
West Ham United 2 - 0 QPR

Barnsley	3	-	0	Southampton				
Brentford	0	-	0	West Ham United				

March 26, 1949

Coventry City	0	-	2	Chesterfield	Blackburn Rovers	0	-	2 Chesterfield
Fulham	5	-	0	QPR	Bradford PA	1	-	1 Tottenham H
Grimsby Town	0	-	3	Bradford PA	Cardiff City	2	-	2 West Bromwich
Leeds United	1	-	3	West Bromwich	Fulham	1	-	1 Sheffield Weds
Leicester City	3	-	2	Bury	Grimsby Town	5	-	1 Leeds United
Nottingham Forest	2	-	0	Luton Town	Luton Town	0	-	1 West Ham United
Plymouth Argyle	0	-	1	Cardiff City	Nottingham Forest	3	-	0 Coventry City
Sheffield Weds	2	-	2	Lincoln City	Plymouth Argyle	0	-	0 Lincoln City
Tottenham H	4	-	0	Blackburn Rovers	QPR	3	-	1 Bury
					Southampton	2	-	0 Brentford

October 4, 1948

April 2, 1949

Barnsley	2	-	0	West Bromwich	Brentford	0	-	0 Barnsley

October 9, 1948

					Bury	3	-	1 Luton Town
Barnsley	4	-	0	Sheffield Weds	Chesterfield	0	-	2 Cardiff City
Blackburn Rovers	0	-	0	West Ham United	Coventry City	1	-	0 Fulham
Bradford PA	1	-	1	Leeds United	Leeds United	1	-	0 Nottingham Forest
Cardiff City	0	-	1	Tottenham H	Leicester City	1	-	1 Grimsby Town
Fulham	1	-	2	West Bromwich	Lincoln City	3	-	0 Blackburn Rovers
Grimsby Town	2	-	2	Lincoln City	Sheffield Weds	2	-	1 Plymouth Argyle
Luton Town	1	-	1	Leicester City	Tottenham H	0	-	1 Southampton
Nottingham Forest	0	-	1	Chesterfield	West Bromwich	1	-	1 QPR
Plymouth Argyle	1	-	0	Bury	West Ham United	4	-	1 Bradford PA
QPR	2	-	0	Brentford				
Southampton	5	-	2	Coventry City				

April 4, 1949

					Bradford PA	2	-	0 Southampton
					Cardiff City	2	-	1 Bury

October 16, 1948

April 6, 1949

Brentford	2	-	0	Luton Town	Barnsley	3	-	1 Leicester City
Bury	3	-	1	Blackburn Rovers	Brentford	0	-	0 Fulham
Chesterfield	0	-	1	Fulham	West Bromwich	1	-	0 Leeds United
Coventry City	4	-	0	Barnsley				
Leeds United	1	-	1	Southampton				

April 9, 1949

Leicester City	2	-	2	Bradford PA	Barnsley	4	-	1 Tottenham H
Lincoln City	1	-	3	Nottingham Forest	Blackburn Rovers	2	-	1 Sheffield Weds
Sheffield Weds	4	-	1	Grimsby Town	Bradford PA	4	-	1 Bury
Tottenham H	1	-	0	QPR	Cardiff City	3	-	1 Lincoln City
West Bromwich	3	-	0	Plymouth Argyle	Fulham	1	-	0 Leeds United
West Ham United	3	-	1	Cardiff City	Grimsby Town	3	-	0 Brentford

October 23, 1948

					Luton Town	0	-	1 West Bromwich
Barnsley	1	-	1	Leeds United	Nottingham Forest	2	-	1 Leicester City
Blackburn Rovers	0	-	0	West Bromwich	Plymouth Argyle	2	-	3 Coventry City
Bradford PA	3	-	1	Brentford	QPR	1	-	1 Chesterfield
Fulham	2	-	1	Lincoln City	Southampton	0	-	1 West Ham United
Grimsby Town	4	-	1	Coventry City				

Luton Town	1	-	1	Tottenham H	April 11, 1949			
Nottingham Forest	1	-	2	Sheffield Weds	Sheffield Weds	0	- 1	Leicester City
Plymouth Argyle	2	-	2	Chesterfield	April 15, 1949			
QPR	2	-	1	West Ham United	Blackburn Rovers	2	- 1	Cardiff City
Southampton	6	-	0	Leicester City	Chesterfield	1	- 1	Sheffield Weds
October 30, 1948					Fulham	4	- 1	Luton Town
Brentford	0	-	0	Southampton	Grimsby Town	0	- 1	Southampton
Bury	0	-	0	QPR	Lincoln City	0	- 1	Barnsley
Chesterfield	0	-	0	Blackburn Rovers	Nottingham Forest	2	- 0	Bradford PA
Coventry City	1	-	2	Nottingham Forest	QPR	2	- 1	Plymouth Argyle
Leeds United	6	-	3	Grimsby Town	Tottenham H	2	- 0	Brentford
Leicester City	1	-	1	Barnsley	West Ham United	4	- 1	Leicester City
Lincoln City	1	-	2	Plymouth Argyle	April 16, 1949			
Sheffield Weds	1	-	2	Fulham	Brentford	2	- 1	Nottingham Forest
Tottenham H	5	-	1	Bradford PA	Bury	1	- 0	Southampton
West Bromwich	2	-	0	Cardiff City	Chesterfield	1	- 0	Luton Town
West Ham United	0	-	1	Luton Town	Coventry City	0	- 1	Blackburn Rovers
November 6, 1948					Leeds United	1	- 0	Plymouth Argyle
Barnsley	1	-	2	Brentford	Leicester City	0	- 3	Fulham
Blackburn Rovers	7	-	1	Lincoln City	Lincoln City	0	- 0	QPR
Bradford PA	2	-	3	West Ham United	Sheffield Weds	1	- 1	Cardiff City
Cardiff City	3	-	4	Chesterfield	Tottenham H	5	- 2	Grimsby Town
Fulham	1	-	0	Coventry City	West Bromwich	7	- 1	Bradford PA
Grimsby Town	1	-	0	Leicester City	West Ham United	2	- 0	Barnsley
Luton Town	1	-	0	Bury	April 18, 1949			
Nottingham Forest	0	-	0	Leeds United	Barnsley	2	- 0	Lincoln City
Plymouth Argyle	3	-	2	Sheffield Weds	Bradford PA	1	- 2	Nottingham Forest
QPR	0	-	2	West Bromwich	Brentford	1	- 1	Tottenham H
Southampton	3	-	1	Tottenham H	Bury	3	- 1	Leeds United
November 13, 1948					Cardiff City	1	- 0	Blackburn Rovers
Brentford	2	-	0	Grimsby Town	Leicester City	1	- 1	West Ham United
Bury	2	-	1	Bradford PA	Luton Town	1	- 3	Fulham
Chesterfield	2	-	1	QPR	Plymouth Argyle	3	- 1	QPR
Coventry City	1	-	1	Plymouth Argyle	Southampton	0	- 0	Grimsby Town
Leeds United	1	-	1	Fulham	West Bromwich	1	- 0	Coventry City
Leicester City	4	-	2	Nottingham Forest	April 19, 1949			
Lincoln City	0	-	0	Cardiff City	Coventry City	1	- 0	West Bromwich
Sheffield Weds	3	-	0	Blackburn Rovers	Sheffield Weds	0	- 0	Chesterfield
Tottenham H	4	-	1	Barnsley	April 21, 1949			
West Bromwich	2	-	1	Luton Town	Leicester City	3	- 1	Blackburn Rovers
West Ham United	1	-	1	Southampton	April 23, 1949			
November 20, 1948					Barnsley	3	- 2	Bury
Barnsley	2	-	3	West Ham United	Blackburn Rovers	0	- 0	Leeds United
Blackburn Rovers	2	-	0	Coventry City	Bradford PA	1	- 1	Chesterfield
Bradford PA	4	-	1	West Bromwich	Cardiff City	3	- 0	Coventry City
Cardiff City	1	-	1	Sheffield Weds	Fulham	2	- 1	Brentford
Fulham	1	-	0	Leicester City	Grimsby Town	3	- 0	West Ham United
Grimsby Town	1	-	1	Tottenham H	Luton Town	6	- 0	Lincoln City
Luton Town	1	-	0	Chesterfield	Nottingham Forest	2	- 2	Tottenham H
Nottingham Forest	1	-	2	Brentford	Plymouth Argyle	1	- 1	Leicester City
Plymouth Argyle	2	-	1	Leeds United	QPR	1	- 3	Sheffield Weds
QPR	2	-	0	Lincoln City	Southampton	1	- 1	West Bromwich

Southampton	2	-	0	Bury

November 27, 1948

Bury	4	-	2	Barnsley
Chesterfield	2	-	3	Bradford PA
Coventry City	0	-	1	Cardiff City
Leicester City	1	-	1	Plymouth Argyle
Lincoln City	4	-	4	Luton Town
Sheffield Weds	2	-	0	QPR
West Bromwich	2	-	0	Southampton

December 4, 1948

Blackburn Rovers	2	-	0	Leicester City
Cardiff City	2	-	1	Leeds United
Fulham	1	-	1	Tottenham H
Grimsby Town	2	-	3	Bury
Lincoln City	3	-	6	Bradford PA
Luton Town	2	-	1	Sheffield Weds
Nottingham Forest	3	-	0	West Ham United
Plymouth Argyle	1	-	0	Brentford
QPR	0	-	3	Coventry City
Southampton	1	-	0	Chesterfield

December 11, 1948

Brentford	0	-	1	Blackburn Rovers
Bury	1	-	1	Nottingham Forest
Chesterfield	3	-	2	Barnsley
Coventry City	2	-	0	Luton Town
Leeds United	1	-	2	QPR
Leicester City	2	-	2	Cardiff City
Lincoln City	1	-	2	Southampton
Sheffield Weds	2	-	1	Bradford PA
Tottenham H	3	-	0	Plymouth Argyle
West Bromwich	5	-	2	Grimsby Town
West Ham United	1	-	0	Fulham

December 18, 1948

Blackburn Rovers	1	-	2	Southampton
Cardiff City	6	-	1	Bradford PA
Chesterfield	4	-	0	Bury
Coventry City	2	-	1	Brentford
Fulham	3	-	1	Grimsby Town
Leeds United	3	-	1	Leicester City
Lincoln City	4	-	3	West Ham United
Plymouth Argyle	3	-	1	Barnsley
QPR	0	-	3	Luton Town
Sheffield Weds	3	-	1	Tottenham H
West Bromwich	2	-	1	Nottingham Forest

April 25, 1949

West Ham United	1	-	1	Brentford

April 27, 1949

Bury	1	-	1	Plymouth Argyle

April 30, 1949

Brentford	2	-	2	Plymouth Argyle
Bury	5	-	1	Grimsby Town
Chesterfield	1	-	0	Southampton
Coventry City	1	-	1	QPR
Leeds United	0	-	0	Cardiff City
Sheffield Weds	0	-	0	Luton Town
Tottenham H	1	-	1	Fulham
West Bromwich	2	-	0	Barnsley
West Ham United	0	-	5	Nottingham Forest

May 3, 1949

Grimsby Town	2	-	1	Luton Town

May 4, 1949

Bradford PA	0	-	3	Lincoln City
Bury	1	-	2	Leicester City

May 5, 1949

Leicester City	0	-	3	West Bromwich

May 7, 1949

Barnsley	0	-	1	Chesterfield
Blackburn Rovers	2	-	1	Brentford
Bradford PA	1	-	1	Sheffield Weds
Cardiff City	1	-	1	Leicester City
Fulham	2	-	0	West Ham United
Grimsby Town	1	-	0	West Bromwich
Luton Town	2	-	0	Coventry City
Nottingham Forest	1	-	0	Bury
Plymouth Argyle	0	-	5	Tottenham H
QPR	2	-	0	Leeds United

	Division 3 North	Pld	W	D	L	F	A	GA	Pts
1	Hull City	42	27	11	4	93	28	3.32	65
2	Rotherham United	42	28	6	8	90	46	1.96	62
3	Doncaster Rovers	42	20	10	12	53	40	1.33	50
4	Darlington	42	20	6	16	83	74	1.12	46
5	Gateshead	42	16	13	13	69	58	1.19	45
6	Oldham Athletic	42	18	9	15	75	67	1.12	45
7	Rochdale	42	18	9	15	55	53	1.04	45
8	Stockport County	42	16	11	15	61	56	1.09	43
9	Wrexham	42	17	9	16	56	62	0.90	43
10	Mansfield Town	42	14	14	14	52	48	1.08	42
11	Tranmere Rovers	42	13	15	14	46	57	0.81	41
12	Crewe Alexandra	42	16	9	17	52	74	0.70	41
13	Barrow	42	14	12	16	41	48	0.85	40
14	York City	42	15	9	18	74	74	1.00	39
15	Carlisle United	42	14	11	17	60	77	0.78	39
16	Hartlepool United	42	14	10	18	45	58	0.78	38
17	New Brighton	42	14	8	20	46	58	0.79	36
18	Chester City	42	11	13	18	57	56	1.02	35
19	Halifax Town	42	12	11	19	45	62	0.73	35
20	Accrington Stanley	42	12	10	20	55	64	0.86	34
21	Southport	42	11	9	22	45	64	0.70	31
22	Bradford City	42	10	9	23	48	77	0.62	29

August 21, 1948

Barrow	0	-	0	Bradford City
Carlisle United	2	-	1	Chester City
Darlington	3	-	0	Accrington Stanley
Gateshead	3	-	0	New Brighton
Hartlepool United	6	-	1	Rochdale
Mansfield Town	2	-	2	Doncaster Rovers
Oldham Athletic	1	-	3	Rotherham United
Stockport County	0	-	0	Southport
Tranmere Rovers	1	-	2	Hull City
Wrexham	2	-	1	Halifax Town
York City	1	-	3	Crewe Alexandra

August 23, 1948

| Halifax Town | 1 | - | 0 | Barrow |
| Southport | 0 | - | 2 | York City |

August 24, 1948

| Rochdale | 3 | - | 0 | Gateshead |

January 1, 1949

Barrow	3	-	1	Doncaster Rovers
Carlisle United	4	-	2	Southport
Darlington	6	-	1	Rochdale
Gateshead	2	-	1	Chester City
Hartlepool United	3	-	1	New Brighton
Mansfield Town	1	-	1	Hull City
Oldham Athletic	4	-	3	Accrington Stanley
Stockport County	4	-	0	Crewe Alexandra
Tranmere Rovers	2	-	1	Rotherham United
Wrexham	5	-	0	Bradford City
York City	2	-	2	Halifax Town

January 8, 1949

Bradford City	0	-	2	Barrow
Hartlepool United	1	-	0	Accrington Stanley
Wrexham	1	-	0	Chester City
York City	2	-	3	Doncaster Rovers

August 25, 1948
Accrington Stanley	2	-	3	Rotherham United
Bradford City	1	-	0	Mansfield Town
Chester City	2	-	0	Stockport County
Crewe Alexandra	1	-	0	Wrexham
Darlington	2	-	0	Hartlepool United
New Brighton	2	-	0	Carlisle United

August 26, 1948
Doncaster Rovers	2	-	0	Tranmere Rovers
Hull City	6	-	0	Oldham Athletic

August 28, 1948
Accrington Stanley	1	-	1	Oldham Athletic
Bradford City	1	-	2	Wrexham
Chester City	1	-	1	Gateshead
Crewe Alexandra	3	-	3	Stockport County
Doncaster Rovers	0	-	0	Barrow
Halifax Town	1	-	2	York City
Hull City	4	-	0	Mansfield Town
New Brighton	1	-	1	Hartlepool United
Rochdale	3	-	4	Darlington
Rotherham United	7	-	0	Tranmere Rovers
Southport	2	-	2	Carlisle United

August 30, 1948
Gateshead	2	-	1	Rochdale
Hartlepool United	0	-	1	Darlington
Mansfield Town	1	-	0	Bradford City
Rotherham United	1	-	0	Accrington Stanley
York City	1	-	3	Southport

August 31, 1948
Barrow	0	-	0	Halifax Town
Tranmere Rovers	2	-	0	Doncaster Rovers

September 1, 1948
Stockport County	1	-	1	Chester City
Wrexham	2	-	2	Crewe Alexandra

September 2, 1948
Carlisle United	2	-	2	New Brighton

September 4, 1948
Barrow	1	-	2	Hull City
Carlisle United	6	-	2	Crewe Alexandra
Darlington	0	-	2	New Brighton
Gateshead	2	-	2	Southport
Halifax Town	1	-	1	Bradford City
Hartlepool United	2	-	1	Chester City
Mansfield Town	1	-	2	Rotherham United
Oldham Athletic	0	-	1	Rochdale
Stockport County	1	-	1	York City
Tranmere Rovers	2	-	2	Accrington Stanley
Wrexham	2	-	0	Doncaster Rovers

September 6, 1948
Crewe Alexandra	1	-	0	Southport
Doncaster Rovers	3	-	0	Oldham Athletic
Mansfield Town	2	-	1	Halifax Town

January 15, 1949
Accrington Stanley	0	-	2	Tranmere Rovers
Bradford City	2	-	1	Halifax Town
Chester City	0	-	0	Hartlepool United
Crewe Alexandra	3	-	0	Carlisle United
Doncaster Rovers	4	-	2	Wrexham
Hull City	3	-	0	Barrow
New Brighton	1	-	0	Darlington
Rochdale	1	-	2	Oldham Athletic
Rotherham United	1	-	0	Mansfield Town
Southport	0	-	3	Gateshead
York City	4	-	0	Stockport County

January 22, 1949
Barrow	0	-	2	Rotherham United
Carlisle United	3	-	3	York City
Darlington	3	-	3	Chester City
Doncaster Rovers	1	-	2	Halifax Town
Gateshead	4	-	1	Crewe Alexandra
Hartlepool United	2	-	2	Southport
Mansfield Town	2	-	0	Accrington Stanley
Rochdale	1	-	1	New Brighton
Stockport County	5	-	2	Bradford City
Tranmere Rovers	1	-	1	Oldham Athletic
Wrexham	0	-	2	Hull City

January 29, 1949
Accrington Stanley	2	-	1	Carlisle United
Barrow	0	-	1	Rochdale
Bradford City	4	-	2	Southport
Crewe Alexandra	2	-	0	York City
Halifax Town	1	-	2	Chester City
Mansfield Town	2	-	2	Darlington
Tranmere Rovers	0	-	2	Hartlepool United
Wrexham	2	-	1	New Brighton

February 5, 1949
Accrington Stanley	1	-	1	Barrow
Chester City	2	-	1	Rochdale
Crewe Alexandra	3	-	0	Hartlepool United
Doncaster Rovers	2	-	0	Bradford City
Hull City	6	-	0	Halifax Town
New Brighton	2	-	1	Tranmere Rovers
Oldham Athletic	4	-	0	Mansfield Town
Rotherham United	1	-	3	Wrexham
Southport	1	-	3	Darlington
Stockport County	2	-	0	Carlisle United
York City	0	-	1	Gateshead

February 12, 1949
Barrow	1	-	1	Chester City
Bradford City	2	-	2	York City
Halifax Town	0	-	0	Crewe Alexandra
Mansfield Town	2	-	0	New Brighton
Oldham Athletic	7	-	1	Darlington
Rotherham United	2	-	1	Stockport County

Rotherham United	2	-	1	Hartlepool United	Tranmere Rovers	0	-	0 Rochdale
September 7, 1948					Wrexham	2	-	0 Southport
Barrow	1	-	1	Wrexham	February 19, 1949			
Rochdale	1	-	0	Carlisle United	Barrow	2	-	1 Oldham Athletic
September 8, 1948					Bradford City	4	-	2 Hull City
Bradford City	1	-	3	Tranmere Rovers	Carlisle United	3	-	0 Doncaster Rovers
Chester City	4	-	1	York City	Darlington	4	-	1 Crewe Alexandra
Darlington	1	-	3	Gateshead	Gateshead	0	-	1 Stockport County
New Brighton	0	-	2	Stockport County	Halifax Town	2	-	0 Rotherham United
September 9, 1948					Hartlepool United	2	-	3 York City
Hull City	3	-	1	Accrington Stanley	Mansfield Town	0	-	0 Tranmere Rovers
September 11, 1948					New Brighton	1	-	1 Chester City
Accrington Stanley	1	-	1	Mansfield Town	Rochdale	1	-	0 Southport
Bradford City	1	-	1	Stockport County	Wrexham	1	-	0 Accrington Stanley
Chester City	1	-	2	Darlington	February 26, 1949			
Crewe Alexandra	2	-	1	Gateshead	Accrington Stanley	1	-	0 Halifax Town
Halifax Town	1	-	0	Doncaster Rovers	Carlisle United	2	-	1 Gateshead
Hull City	3	-	0	Wrexham	Chester City	1	-	1 Mansfield Town
New Brighton	1	-	2	Rochdale	Crewe Alexandra	1	-	2 Rochdale
Oldham Athletic	0	-	2	Tranmere Rovers	Oldham Athletic	1	-	1 Wrexham
Rotherham United	2	-	2	Barrow	Rotherham United	2	-	0 Bradford City
Southport	1	-	2	Hartlepool United	Southport	0	-	1 New Brighton
York City	6	-	0	Carlisle United	Stockport County	4	-	0 Hartlepool United
September 13, 1948					Tranmere Rovers	2	-	0 Barrow
Gateshead	1	-	3	Darlington	York City	2	-	5 Darlington
Halifax Town	2	-	2	Mansfield Town	March 5, 1949			
Hartlepool United	1	-	4	Rotherham United	Bradford City	1	-	2 Carlisle United
York City	2	-	0	Chester City	Doncaster Rovers	2	-	1 Gateshead
September 14, 1948					Halifax Town	0	-	1 Stockport County
Oldham Athletic	0	-	2	Doncaster Rovers	Hull City	2	-	0 Hartlepool United
Southport	0	-	0	Crewe Alexandra	Mansfield Town	1	-	1 Southport
Tranmere Rovers	1	-	0	Bradford City	Oldham Athletic	4	-	2 New Brighton
September 15, 1948					Rotherham United	4	-	3 Darlington
Stockport County	1	-	0	New Brighton	Wrexham	3	-	3 York City
Wrexham	1	-	0	Barrow	March 12, 1949			
September 16, 1948					Carlisle United	0	-	0 Halifax Town
Carlisle United	1	-	1	Rochdale	Chester City	2	-	2 Oldham Athletic
September 18, 1948					Crewe Alexandra	3	-	1 Mansfield Town
Barrow	0	-	0	Accrington Stanley	Darlington	0	-	1 Hull City
Bradford City	0	-	1	Doncaster Rovers	Gateshead	6	-	2 Bradford City
Carlisle United	2	-	1	Stockport County	Hartlepool United	2	-	1 Doncaster Rovers
Darlington	0	-	1	Southport	New Brighton	1	-	3 Accrington Stanley
Gateshead	1	-	1	York City	Rochdale	2	-	0 Rotherham United
Halifax Town	2	-	4	Hull City	Southport	2	-	3 Tranmere Rovers
Hartlepool United	4	-	1	Crewe Alexandra	Stockport County	1	-	0 Wrexham
Mansfield Town	3	-	2	Oldham Athletic	York City	2	-	0 Barrow
Rochdale	3	-	1	Chester City	March 19, 1949			
Tranmere Rovers	0	-	1	New Brighton	Accrington Stanley	3	-	1 Chester City
Wrexham	0	-	4	Rotherham United	Barrow	2	-	1 Stockport County
September 23, 1948					Bradford City	0	-	0 Hartlepool United
Doncaster Rovers	0	-	1	Crewe Alexandra	Doncaster Rovers	1	-	1 Darlington
September 25, 1948					Halifax Town	2	-	2 Gateshead

Accrington Stanley	0	-	1	Wrexham	Hull City	1	-	1	Rochdale
Chester City	2	-	0	New Brighton	Mansfield Town	3	-	0	York City
Crewe Alexandra	3	-	1	Darlington	Oldham Athletic	2	-	1	Southport
Doncaster Rovers	2	-	0	Carlisle United	Rotherham United	1	-	1	New Brighton
Hull City	2	-	0	Bradford City	Tranmere Rovers	2	-	2	Crewe Alexandra
Oldham Athletic	2	-	1	Barrow	Wrexham	4	-	0	Carlisle United
Rotherham United	4	-	0	Halifax Town					

March 23, 1949

Southport	3	-	1	Rochdale	Hull City	3	-	0	Carlisle United

March 26, 1949

Stockport County	3	-	1	Gateshead	Carlisle United	2	-	0	Barrow
Tranmere Rovers	1	-	0	Mansfield Town	Chester City	1	-	1	Rotherham United
York City	4	-	0	Hartlepool United	Crewe Alexandra	0	-	4	Oldham Athletic

September 28, 1948

					Darlington	1	-	5	Bradford City
Accrington Stanley	1	-	2	Hull City	Gateshead	2	-	0	Wrexham

September 30, 1948

					Hartlepool United	0	-	0	Halifax Town
Doncaster Rovers	3	-	1	Stockport County	New Brighton	0	-	0	Hull City

October 2, 1948

					Rochdale	0	-	2	Doncaster Rovers
Barrow	0	-	0	Tranmere Rovers	Southport	3	-	0	Accrington Stanley
Bradford City	1	-	2	Rotherham United	Stockport County	2	-	0	Mansfield Town
Darlington	3	-	1	York City	York City	1	-	0	Tranmere Rovers
Doncaster Rovers	0	-	0	Hull City					

March 30, 1949

Gateshead	3	-	0	Carlisle United	Hull City	2	-	0	Tranmere Rovers
Halifax Town	1	-	0	Accrington Stanley					

April 2, 1949

Hartlepool United	0	-	0	Stockport County	Accrington Stanley	2	-	0	Crewe Alexandra
Mansfield Town	1	-	0	Chester City	Barrow	3	-	0	Gateshead
New Brighton	0	-	1	Southport	Bradford City	1	-	0	Rochdale
Rochdale	3	-	0	Crewe Alexandra	Doncaster Rovers	2	-	1	New Brighton
Wrexham	1	-	1	Oldham Athletic	Halifax Town	0	-	3	Darlington

October 9, 1948

					Hull City	3	-	2	Chester City
Carlisle United	3	-	2	Bradford City	Mansfield Town	2	-	0	Carlisle United
Chester City	2	-	2	Tranmere Rovers	Oldham Athletic	4	-	0	York City
Crewe Alexandra	0	-	1	Barrow	Rotherham United	1	-	0	Southport
Darlington	2	-	0	Rotherham United	Tranmere Rovers	0	-	0	Stockport County
Gateshead	0	-	3	Doncaster Rovers	Wrexham	1	-	0	Hartlepool United
Hartlepool United	0	-	2	Hull City					

April 4, 1949

New Brighton	0	-	1	Oldham Athletic	Rochdale	1	-	0	Mansfield Town
Rochdale	4	-	1	Accrington Stanley	Rotherham United	2	-	1	Oldham Athletic

April 5, 1949

Southport	1	-	1	Mansfield Town	Barrow	1	-	0	Crewe Alexandra

April 6, 1949

Stockport County	3	-	1	Halifax Town	Hull City	2	-	3	York City
York City	5	-	1	Wrexham					

April 9, 1949

October 16, 1948

					Carlisle United	2	-	2	Tranmere Rovers
Accrington Stanley	5	-	1	New Brighton	Chester City	1	-	2	Doncaster Rovers
Barrow	5	-	0	York City	Crewe Alexandra	0	-	3	Rotherham United
Bradford City	1	-	1	Gateshead	Darlington	3	-	1	Wrexham
Doncaster Rovers	0	-	0	Hartlepool United	Gateshead	0	-	0	Mansfield Town
Halifax Town	3	-	4	Carlisle United	Hartlepool United	1	-	0	Barrow
Hull City	0	-	1	Darlington	New Brighton	1	-	0	Bradford City
Mansfield Town	5	-	1	Crewe Alexandra	Rochdale	1	-	0	Halifax Town
Oldham Athletic	2	-	1	Chester City	Southport	0	-	0	Hull City
Rotherham United	3	-	1	Rochdale	Stockport County	1	-	2	Oldham Athletic
Tranmere Rovers	1	-	0	Southport					
Wrexham	0	-	0	Stockport County					

October 23, 1948

Carlisle United	3	-	2	Wrexham	York City	1	-	1 Accrington Stanley
Chester City	3	-	0	Accrington Stanley	April 12, 1949			
Crewe Alexandra	2	-	0	Tranmere Rovers	Oldham Athletic	0	-	0 Gateshead
Darlington	1	-	5	Doncaster Rovers	April 15, 1949			
Gateshead	1	-	2	Halifax Town	Barrow	1	-	0 Mansfield Town
Hartlepool United	1	-	0	Bradford City	Chester City	2	-	0 Southport
New Brighton	0	-	1	Rotherham United	Crewe Alexandra	2	-	1 New Brighton
Rochdale	1	-	1	Hull City	Darlington	1	-	1 Stockport County
Southport	0	-	1	Oldham Athletic	Doncaster Rovers	0	-	0 Rotherham United
Stockport County	1	-	2	Barrow	Hartlepool United	1	-	0 Carlisle United
York City	2	-	1	Mansfield Town	Hull City	2	-	0 Gateshead
October 30, 1948					Oldham Athletic	2	-	2 Halifax Town
Accrington Stanley	3	-	1	Southport	Tranmere Rovers	0	-	2 Wrexham
Barrow	0	-	0	Carlisle United	York City	1	-	1 Rochdale
Bradford City	0	-	2	Darlington	April 16, 1949			
Doncaster Rovers	1	-	0	Rochdale	Accrington Stanley	2	-	1 Stockport County
Halifax Town	2	-	0	Hartlepool United	Barrow	1	-	1 Darlington
Hull City	4	-	1	New Brighton	Bradford City	3	-	2 Chester City
Mansfield Town	4	-	0	Stockport County	Doncaster Rovers	1	-	2 Southport
Oldham Athletic	3	-	2	Crewe Alexandra	Halifax Town	0	-	2 New Brighton
Rotherham United	2	-	1	Chester City	Hull City	5	-	0 Crewe Alexandra
Tranmere Rovers	0	-	0	York City	Mansfield Town	1	-	0 Hartlepool United
Wrexham	1	-	4	Gateshead	Oldham Athletic	1	-	0 Carlisle United
November 6, 1948					Rotherham United	2	-	1 York City
Carlisle United	3	-	1	Mansfield Town	Tranmere Rovers	1	-	1 Gateshead
Chester City	0	-	2	Hull City	Wrexham	2	-	0 Rochdale
Crewe Alexandra	2	-	0	Accrington Stanley	April 18, 1949			
Darlington	2	-	1	Halifax Town	Accrington Stanley	6	-	0 Bradford City
Gateshead	3	-	0	Barrow	Carlisle United	0	-	0 Hartlepool United
Hartlepool United	2	-	2	Wrexham	Gateshead	0	-	2 Hull City
New Brighton	0	-	1	Doncaster Rovers	Halifax Town	3	-	1 Oldham Athletic
Rochdale	1	-	1	Bradford City	Mansfield Town	2	-	0 Barrow
Southport	1	-	3	Rotherham United	New Brighton	2	-	1 Crewe Alexandra
Stockport County	4	-	1	Tranmere Rovers	Rochdale	2	-	0 York City
York City	4	-	0	Oldham Athletic	Rotherham United	2	-	0 Doncaster Rovers
November 13, 1948					Southport	2	-	1 Chester City
Accrington Stanley	2	-	1	York City	Stockport County	2	-	0 Darlington
Barrow	2	-	0	Hartlepool United	Wrexham	0	-	0 Tranmere Rovers
Bradford City	1	-	1	New Brighton	April 19, 1949			
Doncaster Rovers	0	-	0	Chester City	Bradford City	2	-	2 Accrington Stanley
Halifax Town	2	-	1	Rochdale	April 23, 1949			
Hull City	5	-	1	Southport	Carlisle United	4	-	1 Accrington Stanley
Mansfield Town	1	-	1	Gateshead	Chester City	0	-	1 Halifax Town
Oldham Athletic	5	-	2	Stockport County	Crewe Alexandra	0	-	0 Doncaster Rovers
Rotherham United	6	-	1	Crewe Alexandra	Darlington	1	-	2 Mansfield Town
Tranmere Rovers	2	-	1	Carlisle United	Gateshead	2	-	2 Oldham Athletic
Wrexham	4	-	3	Darlington	Hartlepool United	3	-	0 Tranmere Rovers
November 20, 1948					New Brighton	2	-	0 Wrexham
Carlisle United	2	-	0	Oldham Athletic	Rochdale	3	-	0 Barrow
Chester City	3	-	0	Bradford City	Southport	2	-	1 Bradford City
Crewe Alexandra	0	-	0	Hull City	Stockport County	0	-	1 Rotherham United
Darlington	2	-	3	Barrow	York City	1	-	3 Hull City

Gateshead	3	-	3	Tranmere Rovers
Hartlepool United	1	-	1	Mansfield Town
New Brighton	2	-	0	Halifax Town
Rochdale	2	-	1	Wrexham
Southport	0	-	2	Doncaster Rovers
Stockport County	2	-	1	Accrington Stanley
York City	6	-	1	Rotherham United

December 4, 1948

Carlisle United	1	-	8	Rotherham United
Chester City	2	-	0	Wrexham
Darlington	3	-	2	Tranmere Rovers
Gateshead	1	-	1	Accrington Stanley
Hartlepool United	1	-	2	Oldham Athletic
New Brighton	1	-	0	Mansfield Town
Stockport County	0	-	0	Hull City

December 11, 1948

Accrington Stanley	1	-	2	Hartlepool United

December 18, 1948

Accrington Stanley	3	-	2	Darlington
Chester City	2	-	1	Carlisle United
Doncaster Rovers	1	-	1	Mansfield Town
Halifax Town	2	-	0	Wrexham
Rochdale	0	-	1	Hartlepool United
Rotherham United	1	-	0	Gateshead

December 25, 1948

Crewe Alexandra	1	-	0	Chester City
Darlington	2	-	2	Carlisle United
Doncaster Rovers	0	-	0	Accrington Stanley
Gateshead	2	-	1	Hartlepool United
Halifax Town	0	-	1	Tranmere Rovers
Hull City	3	-	2	Rotherham United
New Brighton	3	-	1	York City
Oldham Athletic	1	-	2	Bradford City
Southport	0	-	0	Barrow
Stockport County	2	-	2	Rochdale

December 27, 1948

Accrington Stanley	2	-	0	Doncaster Rovers
Barrow	2	-	1	Southport
Bradford City	2	-	1	Oldham Athletic
Carlisle United	0	-	2	Darlington
Chester City	1	-	1	Crewe Alexandra
Hartlepool United	1	-	3	Gateshead
Mansfield Town	1	-	2	Wrexham
Rochdale	2	-	0	Stockport County
Rotherham United	0	-	0	Hull City
Tranmere Rovers	2	-	2	Halifax Town
York City	2	-	1	New Brighton

April 26, 1949

Oldham Athletic	1	-	1	Hull City
Southport	2	-	3	Halifax Town

April 27, 1949

Accrington Stanley	0	-	0	Rochdale
Crewe Alexandra	2	-	1	Bradford City
New Brighton	3	-	1	Barrow

April 28, 1949

Tranmere Rovers	2	-	1	Darlington

April 30, 1949

Accrington Stanley	1	-	2	Gateshead
Barrow	2	-	1	New Brighton
Bradford City	1	-	2	Crewe Alexandra
Doncaster Rovers	1	-	0	York City
Halifax Town	0	-	1	Southport
Hull City	6	-	1	Stockport County
Mansfield Town	2	-	0	Rochdale
Oldham Athletic	5	-	1	Hartlepool United
Rotherham United	1	-	1	Carlisle United

May 2, 1949

Southport	1	-	0	Stockport County
Tranmere Rovers	1	-	1	Chester City

May 4, 1949

Chester City	4	-	1	Barrow
Hull City	0	-	1	Doncaster Rovers
New Brighton	2	-	2	Gateshead
Wrexham	1	-	1	Mansfield Town

May 7, 1949

Carlisle United	1	-	1	Hull City
Crewe Alexandra	0	-	0	Halifax Town
Darlington	2	-	1	Oldham Athletic
Gateshead	3	-	2	Rotherham United
Rochdale	2	-	1	Tranmere Rovers
Southport	3	-	0	Wrexham
Stockport County	5	-	1	Doncaster Rovers
York City	0	-	2	Bradford City

Division 3 South	Pld	W	D	L	F	A	GA	Pts
1 Swansea City	42	27	8	7	87	34	2.56	62
2 Reading	42	25	5	12	77	50	1.54	55
3 Bournemouth & Boscombe Athletic	42	22	8	12	69	48	1.44	52
4 Swindon Town	42	18	15	9	64	56	1.14	51
5 Bristol Rovers	42	19	10	13	61	51	1.20	48
6 Brighton & HA	42	15	18	9	55	55	1.00	48
7 Ipswich Town	42	18	9	15	78	77	1.01	45
8 Millwall	42	17	11	14	63	64	0.98	45
9 Torquay United	42	17	11	14	65	70	0.93	45
10 Norwich City	42	16	12	14	67	49	1.37	44
11 Notts County	42	19	5	18	102	68	1.50	43
12 Exeter City	42	15	10	17	63	76	0.83	40
13 Port Vale	42	14	11	17	51	54	0.94	39
14 Walsall	42	15	8	19	56	64	0.88	38
15 Newport County	42	14	9	19	68	92	0.74	37
16 Bristol City	42	11	14	17	44	62	0.71	36
17 Watford	42	10	15	17	41	54	0.76	35
18 Southend United	42	9	16	17	41	46	0.89	34
19 Leyton Orient	42	11	12	19	58	80	0.73	34
20 Northampton Town	42	12	9	21	51	62	0.82	33
21 Aldershot	42	11	11	20	48	59	0.81	33
22 Crystal Palace	42	8	11	23	38	76	0.50	27

August 21, 1948

Aldershot	1 - 1	Leyton Orient
Brighton & HA	1 - 1	Swindon Town
Bristol Rovers	1 - 6	Ipswich Town
Exeter City	5 - 1	Northampton Town
Millwall	1 - 1	Port Vale
Newport County	1 - 2	Bournemouth & BA
Norwich City	1 - 2	Walsall
Reading	5 - 1	Crystal Palace
Southend United	1 - 0	Bristol City
Swansea City	2 - 0	Watford
Torquay United	3 - 1	Notts County

August 23, 1948

Port Vale	3 - 0	Reading

August 25, 1948

Bournemouth & BA	1 - 0	Bristol Rovers
Bristol City	1 - 1	Brighton & HA

December 27, 1948

Brighton & HA	2 - 0	Exeter City
Bristol City	1 - 1	Aldershot
Crystal Palace	0 - 1	Newport County
Ipswich Town	3 - 2	Walsall
Leyton Orient	2 - 0	Port Vale
Notts County	2 - 0	Northampton Town
Southend United	2 - 2	Norwich City
Swansea City	2 - 1	Reading
Swindon Town	2 - 0	Millwall
Torquay United	1 - 1	Bournemouth & BA
Watford	0 - 0	Bristol Rovers

January 1, 1949

Aldershot	0 - 1	Port Vale
Brighton & HA	3 - 1	Leyton Orient
Bristol Rovers	3 - 2	Notts County
Millwall	1 - 0	Crystal Palace

Crystal Palace	1	-	1	Swansea City	Newport County	3 - 0	Ipswich Town
Exeter City	0	-	0	Southend United	Northampton Town	3 - 1	Bristol City
Ipswich Town	5	-	1	Torquay United	Norwich City	3 - 0	Exeter City
Norwich City	2	-	1	Northampton Town	Reading	3 - 1	Watford
Swindon Town	3	-	1	Aldershot	Southend United	3 - 4	Swindon Town
Watford	2	-	2	Newport County	Swansea City	2 - 0	Bournemouth & BA
					Torquay United	5 - 1	Walsall

August 26, 1948

Leyton Orient	2	-	2	Millwall			
Notts County	2	-	0	Walsall			

January 8, 1949

Crystal Palace	0 - 1	Reading
Port Vale	3 - 1	Watford

August 28, 1948

Bournemouth & BA	1	-	1	Swansea City
Bristol City	3	-	0	Northampton Town
Crystal Palace	1	-	1	Millwall
Exeter City	4	-	1	Norwich City
Ipswich Town	5	-	1	Newport County
Leyton Orient	0	-	3	Brighton & HA
Notts County	4	-	1	Bristol Rovers
Port Vale	3	-	0	Aldershot
Swindon Town	2	-	1	Southend United
Walsall	1	-	1	Torquay United
Watford	4	-	1	Reading

January 15, 1949

Bournemouth & BA	1 - 3	Reading
Bristol City	1 - 6	Norwich City
Exeter City	2 - 0	Torquay United
Ipswich Town	2 - 0	Swansea City
Leyton Orient	2 - 0	Southend United
Millwall	1 - 1	Aldershot
Notts County	11 - 1	Newport County
Port Vale	3 - 4	Brighton & HA
Swindon Town	2 - 2	Northampton Town
Walsall	0 - 1	Bristol Rovers
Watford	2 - 0	Crystal Palace

August 30, 1948

Bristol Rovers	4	-	0	Bournemouth & BA
Millwall	0	-	0	Leyton Orient

January 22, 1949

Aldershot	0 - 0	Watford
Brighton & HA	1 - 2	Millwall
Bristol Rovers	1 - 0	Torquay United
Crystal Palace	2 - 1	Bournemouth & BA
Exeter City	1 - 1	Bristol City
Newport County	1 - 1	Walsall
Northampton Town	4 - 1	Leyton Orient
Norwich City	0 - 0	Swindon Town
Reading	2 - 1	Ipswich Town
Southend United	0 - 0	Port Vale
Swansea City	3 - 1	Notts County

August 31, 1948

Southend United	0	-	0	Exeter City

September 1, 1948

Aldershot	1	-	2	Swindon Town
Brighton & HA	0	-	0	Bristol City
Reading	1	-	2	Port Vale
Torquay United	1	-	1	Ipswich Town

September 2, 1948

Newport County	1	-	1	Watford
Northampton Town	1	-	0	Norwich City
Swansea City	3	-	0	Crystal Palace
Walsall	3	-	2	Notts County

January 29, 1949

Crystal Palace	2 - 2	Northampton Town
Ipswich Town	2 - 0	Bristol City
Swansea City	3 - 0	Brighton & HA
Watford	1 - 1	Norwich City

September 4, 1948

Aldershot	5	-	0	Millwall
Brighton & HA	1	-	0	Port Vale
Bristol Rovers	3	-	0	Walsall
Crystal Palace	3	-	1	Watford
Newport County	3	-	3	Notts County
Northampton Town	0	-	1	Swindon Town
Norwich City	4	-	0	Bristol City
Reading	4	-	2	Bournemouth & BA
Southend United	2	-	2	Leyton Orient
Swansea City	2	-	0	Ipswich Town
Torquay United	2	-	1	Exeter City

February 5, 1949

Aldershot	1 - 1	Brighton & HA
Bournemouth & BA	2 - 1	Watford
Bristol City	1 - 1	Bristol Rovers
Ipswich Town	3 - 2	Crystal Palace
Leyton Orient	0 - 3	Norwich City
Millwall	1 - 0	Southend United
Notts County	1 - 0	Reading
Port Vale	1 - 0	Northampton Town
Swindon Town	1 - 1	Exeter City
Walsall	2 - 1	Swansea City

September 6, 1948

Port Vale	2	-	0	Swindon Town

September 7, 1948					February 12, 1949				
Southend United	0	-	1	Northampton Town	Bristol Rovers	3	-	1	Exeter City
September 8, 1948					Crystal Palace	1	-	1	Port Vale
Bournemouth & BA	2	-	0	Walsall	Ipswich Town	2	-	2	Brighton & HA
Brighton & HA	1	-	0	Norwich City	Northampton Town	0	-	1	Walsall
Bristol City	0	-	0	Millwall	Notts County	0	-	0	Southend United
Crystal Palace	1	-	0	Bristol Rovers	Reading	3	-	0	Leyton Orient
Exeter City	3	-	3	Aldershot	Torquay United	2	-	1	Norwich City
Reading	4	-	1	Newport County	February 19, 1949				
Watford	1	-	1	Torquay United	Brighton & HA	1	-	6	Bournemouth & BA
September 9, 1948					Bristol City	1	-	3	Swindon Town
Notts County	9	-	2	Ipswich Town	Crystal Palace	1	-	5	Notts County
Swansea City	3	-	1	Leyton Orient	Exeter City	3	-	1	Leyton Orient
September 11, 1948					Newport County	2	-	1	Bristol Rovers
Bournemouth & BA	2	-	0	Crystal Palace	Northampton Town	4	-	0	Millwall
Bristol City	1	-	0	Exeter City	Norwich City	2	-	0	Port Vale
Ipswich Town	3	-	2	Reading	Reading	1	-	0	Walsall
Leyton Orient	0	-	3	Northampton Town	Southend United	1	-	0	Aldershot
Millwall	6	-	2	Brighton & HA	Swansea City	6	-	1	Torquay United
Notts County	1	-	1	Swansea City	Watford	1	-	2	Ipswich Town
Port Vale	0	-	2	Southend United	February 26, 1949				
Swindon Town	3	-	3	Norwich City	Aldershot	3	-	1	Northampton Town
Torquay United	0	-	2	Bristol Rovers	Brighton & HA	1	-	0	Southend United
Walsall	3	-	1	Newport County	Bristol Rovers	1	-	1	Swansea City
Watford	0	-	1	Aldershot	Ipswich Town	1	-	0	Bournemouth & BA
September 13, 1948					Leyton Orient	3	-	1	Bristol City
Bristol Rovers	1	-	0	Crystal Palace	Millwall	1	-	3	Norwich City
Millwall	4	-	1	Bristol City	Notts County	4	-	0	Watford
September 15, 1948					Port Vale	1	-	1	Exeter City
Aldershot	1	-	2	Exeter City	Torquay United	4	-	2	Reading
Ipswich Town	3	-	2	Notts County	Walsall	3	-	1	Crystal Palace
Norwich City	2	-	1	Brighton & HA	March 5, 1949				
Swindon Town	0	-	2	Port Vale	Bournemouth & BA	3	-	2	Southend United
Torquay United	3	-	1	Watford	Bristol Rovers	1	-	1	Swindon Town
September 16, 1948					Crystal Palace	2	-	1	Aldershot
Leyton Orient	3	-	1	Swansea City	Ipswich Town	4	-	2	Northampton Town
Newport County	1	-	1	Reading	Newport County	3	-	2	Leyton Orient
Northampton Town	2	-	2	Southend United	Notts County	2	-	1	Norwich City
Walsall	0	-	0	Bournemouth & BA	Reading	2	-	0	Millwall
September 18, 1948					Swansea City	3	-	1	Port Vale
Brighton & HA	0	-	4	Aldershot	Torquay United	0	-	2	Bristol City
Bristol Rovers	3	-	1	Bristol City	Walsall	4	-	3	Exeter City
Crystal Palace	1	-	1	Ipswich Town	Watford	0	-	0	Brighton & HA
Exeter City	3	-	1	Swindon Town	March 12, 1949				
Newport County	1	-	2	Torquay United	Aldershot	0	-	6	Reading
Northampton Town	2	-	2	Port Vale	Brighton & HA	1	-	1	Crystal Palace
Norwich City	0	-	0	Leyton Orient	Bristol City	2	-	2	Walsall
Reading	1	-	4	Notts County	Exeter City	3	-	1	Notts County
Southend United	2	-	1	Millwall	Leyton Orient	1	-	1	Bristol Rovers
Swansea City	3	-	1	Walsall	Millwall	2	-	0	Swansea City
Watford	0	-	1	Bournemouth & BA	Northampton Town	1	-	0	Bournemouth & BA
September 20, 1948					Norwich City	2	-	0	Ipswich Town

Bristol Rovers	2	-	0	Millwall	Port Vale	1	-	2 Newport County
September 22, 1948					Southend United	0	-	1 Watford
Bournemouth & BA	1	-	0	Exeter City	Swindon Town	1	-	1 Torquay United
September 23, 1948					March 19, 1949			
Notts County	1	-	2	Swindon Town	Bournemouth & BA	3	-	0 Leyton Orient
September 25, 1948					Bristol Rovers	0	-	0 Southend United
Aldershot	1	-	0	Southend United	Crystal Palace	4	-	0 Bristol City
Bournemouth & BA	0	-	1	Brighton & HA	Ipswich Town	4	-	1 Port Vale
Bristol Rovers	3	-	1	Newport County	Newport County	2	-	0 Northampton Town
Ipswich Town	1	-	2	Watford	Notts County	1	-	3 Millwall
Leyton Orient	5	-	2	Exeter City	Reading	2	-	0 Exeter City
Millwall	3	-	2	Northampton Town	Swansea City	2	-	1 Norwich City
Notts County	5	-	1	Crystal Palace	Torquay United	1	-	1 Brighton & HA
Port Vale	0	-	0	Norwich City	Walsall	0	-	0 Aldershot
Swindon Town	2	-	1	Bristol City	Watford	0	-	3 Swindon Town
Torquay United	0	-	4	Swansea City	March 23, 1949			
Walsall	2	-	0	Reading	Torquay United	4	-	0 Newport County
September 29, 1948					March 26, 1949			
Bournemouth & BA	1	-	0	Aldershot	Aldershot	0	-	1 Notts County
Watford	1	-	1	Millwall	Brighton & HA	1	-	2 Walsall
September 30, 1948					Bristol City	0	-	2 Reading
Swansea City	4	-	0	Swindon Town	Exeter City	1	-	1 Swansea City
October 2, 1948					Leyton Orient	1	-	0 Watford
Bournemouth & BA	4	-	2	Ipswich Town	Millwall	0	-	0 Ipswich Town
Bristol City	3	-	0	Leyton Orient	Northampton Town	0	-	1 Bristol Rovers
Crystal Palace	1	-	3	Walsall	Norwich City	0	-	0 Newport County
Exeter City	2	-	1	Port Vale	Port Vale	0	-	2 Bournemouth & BA
Newport County	4	-	1	Swindon Town	Southend United	1	-	1 Torquay United
Northampton Town	2	-	0	Aldershot	Swindon Town	1	-	0 Crystal Palace
Norwich City	1	-	2	Millwall	March 30, 1949			
Reading	4	-	0	Torquay United	Torquay United	0	-	0 Port Vale
Southend United	0	-	0	Brighton & HA	April 2, 1949			
Swansea City	5	-	0	Bristol Rovers	Bournemouth & BA	0	-	0 Bristol City
Watford	1	-	1	Notts County	Bristol Rovers	0	-	2 Aldershot
October 9, 1948					Crystal Palace	1	-	1 Norwich City
Aldershot	3	-	0	Crystal Palace	Ipswich Town	4	-	2 Swindon Town
Brighton & HA	0	-	0	Watford	Newport County	1	-	1 Brighton & HA
Bristol City	0	-	2	Torquay United	Notts County	2	-	1 Leyton Orient
Exeter City	2	-	1	Walsall	Reading	1	-	0 Northampton Town
Leyton Orient	5	-	2	Newport County	Swansea City	2	-	2 Southend United
Millwall	1	-	1	Reading	Torquay United	2	-	1 Millwall
Northampton Town	1	-	1	Ipswich Town	Walsall	1	-	1 Port Vale
Norwich City	3	-	0	Notts County	Watford	0	-	1 Exeter City
Port Vale	0	-	2	Swansea City	April 6, 1949			
Southend United	0	-	0	Bournemouth & BA	Aldershot	2	-	0 Ipswich Town
Swindon Town	1	-	1	Bristol Rovers	Southend United	2	-	0 Walsall
October 16, 1948					Swindon Town	1	-	1 Reading
Bournemouth & BA	5	-	2	Northampton Town	April 7, 1949			
Bristol Rovers	2	-	3	Leyton Orient	Newport County	0	-	2 Bristol City
Crystal Palace	0	-	2	Brighton & HA	April 9, 1949			
Ipswich Town	1	-	2	Norwich City	Aldershot	1	-	3 Torquay United
Newport County	2	-	2	Port Vale	Brighton & HA	2	-	1 Bristol Rovers

Notts County	9	-	0	Exeter City	Bristol City	1	-	1	Watford
Reading	2	-	0	Aldershot	Exeter City	3	-	1	Crystal Palace
Swansea City	2	-	0	Millwall	Leyton Orient	1	-	1	Ipswich Town
Torquay United	3	-	1	Swindon Town	Millwall	2	-	1	Walsall
Walsall	0	-	1	Bristol City	Northampton Town	0	-	1	Swansea City
Watford	0	-	0	Southend United	Norwich City	1	-	2	Reading

October 23, 1948 / Port Vale 1 - 0 Notts County

Aldershot	0	-	1	Walsall	Southend United	0	-	1	Newport County
Brighton & HA	3	-	1	Torquay United	Swindon Town	2	-	2	Bournemouth & BA

April 15, 1949

Bristol City	2	-	0	Crystal Palace					
Exeter City	1	-	2	Reading	Aldershot	4	-	1	Norwich City
Leyton Orient	1	-	2	Bournemouth & BA	Bournemouth & BA	2	-	1	Notts County
Millwall	3	-	2	Notts County	Brighton & HA	0	-	0	Northampton Town
Northampton Town	2	-	1	Newport County	Bristol Rovers	4	-	1	Reading
Norwich City	1	-	0	Swansea City	Leyton Orient	1	-	1	Swindon Town
Port Vale	1	-	2	Ipswich Town	Millwall	2	-	1	Exeter City
Southend United	0	-	1	Bristol Rovers	Newport County	2	-	5	Swansea City
Swindon Town	1	-	0	Watford	Port Vale	4	-	2	Bristol City

October 30, 1948 / Southend United 1 - 1 Ipswich Town

					Watford	2	-	0	Walsall
Bournemouth & BA	2	-	0	Port Vale					

April 16, 1949

Bristol Rovers	1	-	0	Northampton Town	Bournemouth & BA	1	-	2	Norwich City
Crystal Palace	1	-	1	Swindon Town	Bristol Rovers	4	-	1	Port Vale
Ipswich Town	1	-	0	Millwall	Crystal Palace	2	-	1	Southend United
Newport County	4	-	3	Norwich City	Ipswich Town	2	-	2	Exeter City
Notts County	2	-	0	Aldershot	Newport County	1	-	2	Millwall
Reading	2	-	1	Bristol City	Notts County	2	-	1	Bristol City
Swansea City	6	-	0	Exeter City	Reading	6	-	1	Brighton & HA
Torquay United	0	-	3	Southend United	Swansea City	2	-	1	Aldershot
Walsall	0	-	0	Brighton & HA	Torquay United	7	-	1	Leyton Orient
Watford	2	-	1	Leyton Orient	Walsall	0	-	1	Swindon Town

November 6, 1948 / Watford 0 - 1 Northampton Town

April 18, 1949

Aldershot	1	-	5	Bristol Rovers					
Brighton & HA	3	-	2	Newport County	Bristol City	1	-	1	Port Vale
Bristol City	2	-	1	Bournemouth & BA	Crystal Palace	0	-	1	Torquay United
Exeter City	2	-	1	Watford	Exeter City	3	-	0	Millwall
Leyton Orient	3	-	1	Notts County	Ipswich Town	1	-	3	Southend United
Millwall	1	-	3	Torquay United	Northampton Town	1	-	1	Brighton & HA
Northampton Town	1	-	2	Reading	Norwich City	0	-	0	Aldershot
Norwich City	3	-	0	Crystal Palace	Notts County	2	-	3	Bournemouth & BA
Port Vale	0	-	2	Walsall	Reading	1	-	0	Bristol Rovers
Southend United	0	-	0	Swansea City	Swansea City	2	-	1	Newport County
Swindon Town	4	-	0	Ipswich Town	Swindon Town	1	-	1	Leyton Orient

November 13, 1948 / Walsall 0 - 1 Watford

April 19, 1949

Bournemouth & BA	3	-	0	Swindon Town	Torquay United	2	-	0	Crystal Palace
Bristol Rovers	0	-	0	Brighton & HA					

April 23, 1949

Crystal Palace	1	-	1	Exeter City					
Ipswich Town	2	-	2	Leyton Orient	Aldershot	1	-	2	Newport County
Newport County	4	-	2	Southend United	Brighton & HA	0	-	2	Swansea City
Notts County	2	-	1	Port Vale	Bristol City	2	-	0	Ipswich Town
Reading	2	-	1	Norwich City	Exeter City	2	-	3	Bournemouth & BA
Swansea City	1	-	0	Northampton Town	Leyton Orient	1	-	1	Walsall
Torquay United	2	-	2	Aldershot					

Walsall	5	-	6	Millwall	Millwall	1	-	1	Bristol Rovers
Watford	1	-	1	Bristol City	Northampton Town	3	-	2	Crystal Palace

November 20, 1948

					Norwich City	0	-	1	Watford
Aldershot	1	-	2	Swansea City	Port Vale	3	-	1	Torquay United
Brighton & HA	2	-	0	Reading	Southend United	0	-	0	Reading
Bristol City	3	-	1	Notts County	Swindon Town	3	-	0	Notts County
Exeter City	1	-	3	Ipswich Town

April 27, 1949

Leyton Orient	3	-	1	Torquay United	Bristol City	0	-	0	Swansea City
Millwall	3	-	1	Newport County	Reading	2	-	1	Southend United
Northampton Town	1	-	1	Watford

April 28, 1949

Norwich City	1	-	1	Bournemouth & BA	Newport County	0	-	2	Aldershot
Port Vale	2	-	0	Bristol Rovers	Walsall	2	-	3	Leyton Orient
Southend United	0	-	1	Crystal Palace

April 30, 1949

Swindon Town	2	-	1	Walsall	Bournemouth & BA	2	-	0	Millwall

December 4, 1948

					Bristol Rovers	2	-	2	Norwich City
Brighton & HA	3	-	2	Notts County	Crystal Palace	2	-	1	Leyton Orient
Leyton Orient	1	-	1	Crystal Palace	Ipswich Town	4	-	1	Aldershot
Millwall	4	-	0	Bournemouth & BA	Newport County	0	-	2	Exeter City
Northampton Town	0	-	0	Torquay United	Notts County	1	-	1	Brighton & HA
Norwich City	3	-	0	Bristol Rovers	Reading	0	-	0	Swindon Town
Swindon Town	5	-	2	Newport County	Swansea City	2	-	0	Bristol City

December 18, 1948

					Torquay United	3	-	0	Northampton Town
Bournemouth & BA	1	-	2	Newport County	Walsall	0	-	3	Southend United
Bristol City	2	-	1	Southend United	Watford	2	-	1	Port Vale
Ipswich Town	0	-	1	Bristol Rovers

May 4, 1949

Leyton Orient	1	-	2	Aldershot	Exeter City	1	-	2	Newport County
Northampton Town	4	-	0	Exeter City

May 7, 1949

Notts County	5	-	0	Torquay United	Aldershot	0	-	0	Bournemouth & BA
Port Vale	1	-	0	Millwall	Brighton & HA	6	-	1	Ipswich Town
Swindon Town	0	-	0	Brighton & HA	Bristol City	1	-	1	Newport County
Walsall	4	-	1	Norwich City	Exeter City	2	-	1	Bristol Rovers
Watford	4	-	2	Swansea City	Leyton Orient	0	-	1	Reading

December 25, 1948

					Millwall	2	-	2	Watford
Aldershot	0	-	0	Bristol City	Norwich City	0	-	0	Torquay United
Bournemouth & BA	5	-	0	Torquay United	Port Vale	0	-	0	Crystal Palace
Bristol Rovers	3	-	1	Watford	Southend United	3	-	2	Notts County
Exeter City	1	-	1	Brighton & HA	Swindon Town	1	-	0	Swansea City
Millwall	3	-	1	Swindon Town	Walsall	2	-	0	Northampton Town
Newport County	5	-	0	Crystal Palace
Northampton Town	1	-	2	Notts County
Norwich City	3	-	0	Southend United
Port Vale	3	-	0	Leyton Orient
Reading	0	-	2	Swansea City
Walsall	2	-	1	Ipswich Town

Finland

SPL and TUL clubs combined, playing each other once only in the first spring-autumn season. VPS won the title as most of the SPL clubs fared well. They won the championship play-off 3-0. The bottom six are relegated.

Championship play-off VPS Vaasa - TPS Turku 3-0.

		Pld	W	D	L	F	A	GA	Pts
1	VPS Vaasa	15	11	2	2	41	12	3.42	24
2	TPS Turku	15	11	2	2	37	18	2.06	24
3	HPS Helsinki	15	9	3	3	21	13	1.62	21
4	HJK Helsinki	15	6	6	3	32	20	1.60	18
5	VIFK Vaasa	15	7	4	4	30	19	1.58	18
6	KIF/Kiffen Helsinki	15	8	2	5	38	30	1.27	18
7	TuWe Turku	15	6	5	4	20	25	0.80	17
8	TuTo Turku	15	6	4	5	23	22	1.05	16
9	KTP Kotka	15	6	4	5	24	26	0.92	16
10	HIFK Helsinki	15	6	3	6	38	29	1.31	15
11	RTU Rauma	15	4	5	6	32	38	0.84	13
12	Sudet Helsinki	15	4	3	8	29	38	0.76	11
13	Kullervo Helsinki	15	4	1	10	19	30	0.63	9
14	TuKV Turku	15	2	5	8	14	27	0.52	9
15	Kiri Kotka	15	2	2	11	14	41	0.34	6
16	Ponnistus Helsinki	15	1	3	11	12	36	0.33	5

VPS Vaasa	2 - 0	TPS Turku	KTP Kotka	2 - 4	VPS Vaasa
VPS Vaasa	0 - 0	HPS Helsinki	KTP Kotka	0 - 2	HPS Helsinki
VPS Vaasa	2 - 0	KIF/Kiffen Helsinki	KTP Kotka	2 - 2	HJK Helsinki
VPS Vaasa	2 - 0	TuTo Turku	KTP Kotka	1 - 1	TuTo Turku
VPS Vaasa	7 - 2	RTU Rauma	KTP Kotka	5 - 2	RTU Rauma
VPS Vaasa	6 - 1	Kullervo Helsinki	KTP Kotka	3 - 2	Sudet Helsinki
VPS Vaasa	3 - 0	Kiri Kotka	KTP Kotka	2 - 1	Kullervo Helsinki
VPS Vaasa	4 - 2	Ponnistus Helsinki	KTP Kotka	1 - 0	TuKV Turku
TPS Turku	3 - 1	HJK Helsinki	HIFK Helsinki	2 - 3	VPS Vaasa
TPS Turku	2 - 0	TuWe Turku	HIFK Helsinki	1 - 1	HJK Helsinki
TPS Turku	1 - 2	TuTo Turku	HIFK Helsinki	0 - 1	TuWe Turku
TPS Turku	1 - 0	KTP Kotka	HIFK Helsinki	1 - 1	KTP Kotka
TPS Turku	3 - 2	HIFK Helsinki	HIFK Helsinki	3 - 3	RTU Rauma
TPS Turku	3 - 1	RTU Rauma	HIFK Helsinki	2 - 3	Sudet Helsinki
TPS Turku	3 - 2	Sudet Helsinki	RTU Rauma	1 - 1	HPS Helsinki
TPS Turku	2 - 0	Kullervo Helsinki	RTU Rauma	0 - 4	HJK Helsinki

HPS Helsinki	1	-	3	TPS Turku	RTU Rauma	3 - 3	VIFK Vaasa
HPS Helsinki	0	-	1	KIF/Kiffen Helsinki	RTU Rauma	3 - 3	KIF/Kiffen Helsinki
HPS Helsinki	1	-	2	HIFK Helsinki	RTU Rauma	1 - 3	TuWe Turku
HPS Helsinki	3	-	2	TuKV Turku	RTU Rauma	4 - 1	TuTo Turku
HPS Helsinki	2	-	1	Kiri Kotka	RTU Rauma	0 - 1	Kullervo Helsinki
HPS Helsinki	2	-	0	Ponnistus Helsinki	RTU Rauma	5 - 0	Kiri Kotka
HJK Helsinki	1	-	0	VPS Vaasa	RTU Rauma	2 - 0	Ponnistus Helsinki
HJK Helsinki	0	-	1	HPS Helsinki	Sudet Helsinki	0 - 6	VPS Vaasa
HJK Helsinki	2	-	2	TuWe Turku	Sudet Helsinki	1 - 2	HPS Helsinki
HJK Helsinki	2	-	2	Sudet Helsinki	Sudet Helsinki	2 - 3	TuWe Turku
HJK Helsinki	2	-	1	Kullervo Helsinki	Sudet Helsinki	2 - 3	RTU Rauma
HJK Helsinki	1	-	2	TuKV Turku	Sudet Helsinki	6 - 2	TuKV Turku
HJK Helsinki	3	-	0	Kiri Kotka	Sudet Helsinki	3 - 2	Ponnistus Helsinki
VIFK Vaasa	1	-	2	VPS Vaasa	Kullervo Helsinki	1 - 1	HPS Helsinki
VIFK Vaasa	1	-	1	TPS Turku	Kullervo Helsinki	3 - 4	KIF/Kiffen Helsinki
VIFK Vaasa	0	-	1	HPS Helsinki	Kullervo Helsinki	1 - 0	TuTo Turku
VIFK Vaasa	1	-	1	HJK Helsinki	Kullervo Helsinki	1 - 2	HIFK Helsinki
VIFK Vaasa	6	-	0	TuWe Turku	Kullervo Helsinki	1 - 2	Sudet Helsinki
VIFK Vaasa	2	-	1	KTP Kotka	Kullervo Helsinki	0 - 1	TuKV Turku
VIFK Vaasa	7	-	0	HIFK Helsinki	Kullervo Helsinki	3 - 1	Kiri Kotka
VIFK Vaasa	0	-	0	Sudet Helsinki	TuKV Turku	0 - 0	VPS Vaasa
VIFK Vaasa	2	-	1	Kullervo Helsinki	TuKV Turku	1 - 2	TPS Turku
KIF/Kiffen Helsinki	2	-	5	TPS Turku	TuKV Turku	2 - 3	VIFK Vaasa
KIF/Kiffen Helsinki	1	-	4	HJK Helsinki	TuKV Turku	0 - 2	KIF/Kiffen Helsinki
KIF/Kiffen Helsinki	5	-	1	VIFK Vaasa	TuKV Turku	1 - 1	TuWe Turku
KIF/Kiffen Helsinki	5	-	0	KTP Kotka	TuKV Turku	0 - 2	HIFK Helsinki
KIF/Kiffen Helsinki	1	-	5	HIFK Helsinki	TuKV Turku	2 - 2	RTU Rauma
KIF/Kiffen Helsinki	4	-	1	Sudet Helsinki	TuKV Turku	0 - 0	Ponnistus Helsinki
KIF/Kiffen Helsinki	5	-	0	Ponnistus Helsinki	Kiri Kotka	1 - 6	TPS Turku
TuWe Turku	1	-	0	VPS Vaasa	Kiri Kotka	0 - 1	VIFK Vaasa
TuWe Turku	1	-	2	HPS Helsinki	Kiri Kotka	1 - 1	KIF/Kiffen Helsinki
TuWe Turku	0	-	4	KIF/Kiffen Helsinki	Kiri Kotka	0 - 2	TuTo Turku
TuWe Turku	1	-	1	TuTo Turku	Kiri Kotka	0 - 2	KTP Kotka
TuWe Turku	2	-	2	KTP Kotka	Kiri Kotka	1 - 8	HIFK Helsinki
TuWe Turku	4	-	2	Kullervo Helsinki	Kiri Kotka	4 - 2	Sudet Helsinki
TuWe Turku	0	-	0	Kiri Kotka	Kiri Kotka	4 - 1	TuKV Turku
TuWe Turku	1	-	0	Ponnistus Helsinki	Kiri Kotka	1 - 2	Ponnistus Helsinki
TuTo Turku	0	-	2	HPS Helsinki	Ponnistus Helsinki	2 - 2	TPS Turku
TuTo Turku	2	-	6	HJK Helsinki	Ponnistus Helsinki	2 - 2	HJK Helsinki
TuTo Turku	2	-	1	VIFK Vaasa	Ponnistus Helsinki	0 - 1	VIFK Vaasa
TuTo Turku	5	-	0	KIF/Kiffen Helsinki	Ponnistus Helsinki	1 - 2	KTP Kotka
TuTo Turku	3	-	2	HIFK Helsinki	Ponnistus Helsinki	0 - 6	HIFK Helsinki
TuTo Turku	1	-	1	Sudet Helsinki	Ponnistus Helsinki	1 - 2	Kullervo Helsinki
TuTo Turku	0	-	0	TuKV Turku			
TuTo Turku	3	-	0	Ponnistus Helsinki			

France

Lille's win at Nice on the last full day May 29th gave them a one point lead over Reims, but Reims still had one game to play 3 days later at Sete - a win was needed and this they did 2-1. At the bottom double champions Roubaix were in severe danger of relegation. Their final fixture was at home to Cannes and a 4-0 win doomed Cannes. Only one up, one down this season - a tie on points meant 100 goals for Bordeaux would not be enough in Ligue 2 despite Lens scoring 42 goals less, they had a better GA.

	Ligue 1	Pld	W	D	L	F	A	GA	Pts
1	Stade de Reims	34	22	4	8	90	54	1.67	48
2	Olympique SC de Lille Metropole	34	21	5	8	102	40	2.55	47
3	Olympique de Marseille	34	18	6	10	95	58	1.64	42
4	Stade Rennais FC	34	16	9	9	61	49	1.24	41
5	Sochaux-Montbeliard FC	34	16	6	12	74	52	1.42	38
6	Racing Club Paris	34	14	8	12	71	56	1.27	36
7	Nice Olympique	34	13	10	11	60	58	1.03	36
8	St Etienne AS	34	13	9	12	68	72	0.94	35
9	Toulouse FC	34	16	2	16	56	53	1.06	34
10	Red Star Paris	34	10	12	12	59	72	0.82	32
11	Colmar SR	34	12	7	15	61	78	0.78	31
12	SO Montpellier	34	12	5	17	57	71	0.80	29
13	Roubaix-Tourcoing CO	34	11	7	16	55	89	0.62	29
14	Sete FC	34	10	9	15	34	58	0.59	29
15	Nancy-Lorraine FC	34	11	6	17	53	69	0.77	28
16	Metz FC	34	10	6	18	60	79	0.76	26
17	Strasbourg RC	34	10	6	18	40	68	0.59	26
18	Cannes AS	34	10	5	19	42	62	0.68	25

August 22, 1948
Cannes AS 2 - 1 Racing Club Paris
Metz FC 1 - 6 Stade Rennais FC
Oly Marseille 7 - 2 Colmar SR
Red Star Paris 1 - 1 Nice Olympique
Roubaix-Tourcoing 2 - 3 SO Montpellier
Sete FC 1 - 0 Oly Lille
Sochaux-Montbeliard 3 - 0 Toulouse FC
St Etienne AS 2 - 3 Stade de Reims
Strasbourg RC 4 - 2 Nancy-Lorraine FC

August 29, 1948
Colmar SR 3 - 3 Stade de Reims

December 5, 1948
Colmar SR 1 - 1 Oly Marseille
Nancy-Lorraine FC 3 - 3 Strasbourg RC
Nice Olympique 2 - 2 Red Star Paris
Oly Lille 6 - 1 Sete FC
Racing Club Paris 3 - 0 Cannes AS
SO Montpellier 4 - 1 Roubaix-Tourcoing
Stade de Reims 2 - 3 St Etienne AS
Stade Rennais FC 4 - 3 Metz FC
Toulouse FC 3 - 0 Sochaux-Montbeliard

December 19, 1948
Cannes AS 4 - 1 Nancy-Lorraine FC

Nancy-Lorraine FC	1	-	0	Cannes AS	Metz FC	2	-	2	Nice Olympique
Nice Olympique	5	-	2	Metz FC	Racing Club Paris	1	-	1	SO Montpellier
Oly Marseille	4	-	2	Roubaix-Tourcoing	Roubaix-Tourcoing	2	-	10	Oly Marseille
Oly Lille	5	-	0	St Etienne AS	Sete FC	1	-	0	Red Star Paris
Red Star Paris	2	-	2	Sete FC	Sochaux-Montbeliard	3	-	0	Strasbourg RC
SO Montpellier	0	-	4	Racing Club Paris	St Etienne AS	2	-	2	Oly Lille
Strasbourg RC	0	-	3	Sochaux-Montbeliard	Stade de Reims	1	-	2	Colmar SR
Toulouse FC	2	-	1	Stade Rennais FC	Stade Rennais FC	2	-	0	Toulouse FC

September 4, 1948   December 25, 1948

Racing Club Paris	5	-	4	Oly Marseille	Red Star Paris	4	-	1	St Etienne AS
St Etienne AS	2	-	2	Red Star Paris					
Stade Rennais FC	1	-	1	Strasbourg RC					

September 5, 1948   December 26, 1948

Nancy-Lorraine FC	1	-	0	SO Montpellier	Cannes AS	1	-	1	Sochaux-Montbeliard
Nice Olympique	2	-	1	Toulouse FC	Colmar SR	5	-	0	Roubaix-Tourcoing
Roubaix-Tourcoing	3	-	2	Colmar SR	Metz FC	0	-	2	Sete FC
Sete FC	1	-	1	Metz FC	Oly Marseille	3	-	0	Racing Club Paris
Sochaux-Montbeliard	4	-	0	Cannes AS	Oly Lille	2	-	1	Stade de Reims
Stade de Reims	2	-	4	Oly Lille	SO Montpellier	3	-	4	Nancy-Lorraine FC
					Strasbourg RC	3	-	0	Stade Rennais FC
					Toulouse FC	3	-	0	Nice Olympique

September 9, 1948   January 2, 1949

Cannes AS	1	-	1	Stade Rennais FC	Nancy-Lorraine FC	3	-	2	Oly Marseille
Colmar SR	2	-	2	Oly Lille	Nice Olympique	1	-	0	Strasbourg RC
Metz FC	2	-	0	St Etienne AS	Oly Lille	8	-	0	Colmar SR
Oly Marseille	3	-	1	Nancy-Lorraine FC	Racing Club Paris	1	-	1	Roubaix-Tourcoing
Red Star Paris	3	-	5	Stade de Reims	Sete FC	0	-	0	Toulouse FC
Roubaix-Tourcoing	2	-	2	Racing Club Paris	St Etienne AS	3	-	1	Metz FC
SO Montpellier	2	-	1	Sochaux-Montbeliard	Stade de Reims	4	-	0	Red Star Paris
Strasbourg RC	3	-	1	Nice Olympique	Stade Rennais FC	1	-	0	Cannes AS
Toulouse FC	0	-	2	Sete FC					

September 12, 1948   January 16, 1949

Nancy-Lorraine FC	1	-	2	Roubaix-Tourcoing	Cannes AS	1	-	2	Nice Olympique
Nice Olympique	2	-	0	Cannes AS	Metz FC	2	-	3	Stade de Reims
Oly Lille	2	-	1	Red Star Paris	Oly Marseille	3	-	1	Sochaux-Montbeliard
Racing Club Paris	3	-	3	Colmar SR	Red Star Paris	1	-	0	Oly Lille
Sete FC	0	-	1	Strasbourg RC	Roubaix-Tourcoing	3	-	1	Nancy-Lorraine FC
Sochaux-Montbeliard	1	-	1	Oly Marseille	SO Montpellier	2	-	1	Stade Rennais FC
St Etienne AS	4	-	2	Toulouse FC	Strasbourg RC	0	-	0	Sete FC
Stade de Reims	6	-	1	Metz FC	Toulouse FC	5	-	1	St Etienne AS
Stade Rennais FC	3	-	0	SO Montpellier					

September 18, 1948   January 20, 1949

Red Star Paris	2	-	6	Metz FC	Colmar SR	3	-	0	Racing Club Paris

September 19, 1948   January 23, 1949

Nancy-Lorraine FC	1	-	2	Colmar SR	Nancy-Lorraine FC	3	-	1	Racing Club Paris
Nice Olympique	0	-	5	Oly Marseille	Nice Olympique	0	-	0	SO Montpellier
Oly Lille	1	-	1	Toulouse FC	Oly Lille	5	-	0	Metz FC
Sete FC	2	-	1	SO Montpellier	Red Star Paris	5	-	2	Colmar SR
Sochaux-Montbeliard	1	-	2	Racing Club Paris	Sete FC	1	-	0	Cannes AS
St Etienne AS	3	-	1	Cannes AS	Sochaux-Montbeliard	5	-	1	Roubaix-Tourcoing
Stade de Reims	3	-	0	Strasbourg RC	St Etienne AS	5	-	1	Strasbourg RC
Stade Rennais FC	3	-	1	Roubaix-Tourcoing	Stade de Reims	2	-	0	Toulouse FC
					Stade Rennais FC	6	-	1	Oly Marseille

September 23, 1948   February 6, 1949

Cannes AS	0	-	2	Sete FC	Cannes AS	1	-	0	St Etienne AS
					Colmar SR	0	-	2	Nancy-Lorraine FC

Colmar SR	3	-	0	Red Star Paris	Metz FC	2	-	3 Red Star Paris
Metz FC	3	-	1	Oly Lille	Oly Marseille	2	-	2 Nice Olympique
Oly Marseille	1	-	3	Stade Rennais FC	Racing Club Paris	0	-	1 Sochaux-Montbeliard
Racing Club Paris	5	-	1	Nancy-Lorraine FC	Roubaix-Tourcoing	3	-	2 Stade Rennais FC
Roubaix-Tourcoing	5	-	1	Sochaux-Montbeliard	SO Montpellier	1	-	0 Sete FC
SO Montpellier	1	-	1	Nice Olympique	Strasbourg RC	1	-	4 Stade de Reims
Strasbourg RC	1	-	2	St Etienne AS	Toulouse FC	1	-	4 Oly Lille
Toulouse FC	2	-	0	Stade de Reims				

September 26, 1948

February 13, 1949

Cannes AS	1	-	3	Stade de Reims	Metz FC	2	-	0 Colmar SR
Colmar SR	5	-	1	Metz FC	Nice Olympique	4	-	2 Roubaix-Tourcoing
Nancy-Lorraine FC	2	-	2	Sochaux-Montbeliard	Oly Lille	1	-	2 Strasbourg RC
Oly Marseille	3	-	1	Sete FC	Red Star Paris	3	-	1 Toulouse FC
Racing Club Paris	2	-	3	Stade Rennais FC	Sete FC	1	-	1 Oly Marseille
Roubaix-Tourcoing	2	-	1	Nice Olympique	Sochaux-Montbeliard	3	-	2 Nancy-Lorraine FC
SO Montpellier	2	-	2	St Etienne AS	St Etienne AS	0	-	4 SO Montpellier
Strasbourg RC	0	-	6	Oly Lille	Stade de Reims	5	-	2 Cannes AS
Toulouse FC	4	-	1	Red Star Paris	Stade Rennais FC	0	-	0 Racing Club Paris

October 3, 1948

February 20, 1949

Metz FC	2	-	1	Toulouse FC	Cannes AS	1	-	6 Oly Lille
Nice Olympique	3	-	0	Racing Club Paris	Colmar SR	0	-	3 Sochaux-Montbeliard
Oly Lille	2	-	0	Cannes AS	Nancy-Lorraine FC	1	-	2 Stade Rennais FC
Red Star Paris	1	-	1	Strasbourg RC	Oly Marseille	6	-	1 St Etienne AS
Sete FC	0	-	0	Roubaix-Tourcoing	Racing Club Paris	1	-	1 Nice Olympique
Sochaux-Montbeliard	2	-	0	Colmar SR	Roubaix-Tourcoing	2	-	1 Sete FC
St Etienne AS	4	-	1	Oly Marseille	SO Montpellier	0	-	1 Stade de Reims
Stade de Reims	6	-	4	SO Montpellier	Strasbourg RC	3	-	2 Red Star Paris
Stade Rennais FC	4	-	0	Nancy-Lorraine FC	Toulouse FC	1	-	0 Metz FC

October 7, 1948

February 28, 1949

Colmar SR	1	-	1	Cannes AS	Sochaux-Montbeliard	4	-	2 SO Montpellier

March 6, 1949

Nancy-Lorraine FC	0	-	1	Oly Lille	Metz FC	3	-	0 Strasbourg RC
Nice Olympique	4	-	1	Sete FC	Nice Olympique	0	-	0 Nancy-Lorraine FC
Oly Marseille	4	-	0	Toulouse FC	Oly Lille	5	-	0 SO Montpellier
Racing Club Paris	4	-	0	Red Star Paris	Red Star Paris	6	-	3 Cannes AS
Roubaix-Tourcoing	2	-	2	Metz FC	Sete FC	0	-	2 Racing Club Paris
SO Montpellier	2	-	0	Strasbourg RC	St Etienne AS	6	-	0 Roubaix-Tourcoing
Sochaux-Montbeliard	3	-	0	Stade de Reims	Stade de Reims	2	-	0 Oly Marseille
Stade Rennais FC	1	-	3	St Etienne AS	Stade Rennais FC	1	-	0 Sochaux-Montbeliard
					Toulouse FC	7	-	0 Colmar SR

October 10, 1948

March 13, 1949

Cannes AS	3	-	0	SO Montpellier	Cannes AS	1	-	1 Metz FC
Metz FC	1	-	2	Racing Club Paris	Colmar SR	2	-	2 Stade Rennais FC
Oly Lille	3	-	1	Sochaux-Montbeliard	Nancy-Lorraine FC	3	-	0 Sete FC
Red Star Paris	3	-	3	Nancy-Lorraine FC	Oly Marsellle	2	-	1 Oly Lille
Sete FC	3	-	4	Colmar SR	Racing Club Paris	1	-	2 St Etienne AS
St Etienne AS	2	-	0	Nice Olympique	Roubaix-Tourcoing	1	-	5 Stade de Reims
Stade de Reims	4	-	2	Stade Rennais FC	SO Montpellier	6	-	1 Red Star Paris
Strasbourg RC	1	-	2	Oly Marseille	Sochaux-Montbeliard	2	-	0 Nice Olympique
Toulouse FC	2	-	0	Roubaix-Tourcoing	Strasbourg RC	0	-	1 Toulouse FC

October 24, 1948

March 27, 1949

Metz FC	2	-	1	Cannes AS	Metz FC	2	-	2 SO Montpellier
Nice Olympique	5	-	4	Sochaux-Montbeliard	Nice Olympique	8	-	0 Stade Rennais FC
Oly Lille	2	-	2	Oly Marseille				

Red Star Paris	3	-	0	SO Montpellier	Oly Lille	6	-	2	Roubaix-Tourcoing
Sete FC	1	-	0	Nancy-Lorraine FC	Red Star Paris	1	-	0	Oly Marseille
St Etienne AS	3	-	3	Racing Club Paris	Sete FC	3	-	0	Sochaux-Montbeliard
Stade de Reims	1	-	0	Roubaix-Tourcoing	St Etienne AS	4	-	1	Nancy-Lorraine FC
Stade Rennais FC	2	-	0	Colmar SR	Stade de Reims	1	-	0	Racing Club Paris
Toulouse FC	5	-	1	Strasbourg RC	Strasbourg RC	0	-	0	Colmar SR
					Toulouse FC	1	-	0	Cannes AS

October 31, 1948

April 10, 1949

Cannes AS	4	-	1	Red Star Paris	Stade Rennais FC	3	-	1	Sete FC

April 14, 1949

Colmar SR	2	-	0	Toulouse FC	Cannes AS	1	-	1	Strasbourg RC
Nancy-Lorraine FC	1	-	1	Nice Olympique	Nancy-Lorraine FC	0	-	1	Stade de Reims
Oly Marseille	3	-	4	Stade de Reims	Oly Marseille	4	-	2	Metz FC
Racing Club Paris	5	-	1	Sete FC	Racing Club Paris	4	-	3	Oly Lille
Roubaix-Tourcoing	2	-	2	St Etienne AS	Roubaix-Tourcoing	2	-	2	Red Star Paris
SO Montpellier	2	-	1	Oly Lille	SO Montpellier	2	-	1	Toulouse FC
Sochaux-Montbeliard	3	-	1	Stade Rennais FC	Sochaux-Montbeliard	6	-	0	St Etienne AS
Strasbourg RC	2	-	1	Metz FC					

November 7, 1948

April 15, 1949

Metz FC	1	-	4	Oly Marseille	Colmar SR	1	-	2	Nice Olympique

April 17, 1949

Nice Olympique	2	-	0	Colmar SR	Cannes AS	4	-	2	Colmar SR
Oly Lille	2	-	3	Racing Club Paris	Metz FC	3	-	0	Roubaix-Tourcoing
Red Star Paris	1	-	1	Roubaix-Tourcoing	Oly Lille	4	-	0	Nancy-Lorraine FC
Sete FC	0	-	0	Stade Rennais FC	Red Star Paris	1	-	0	Racing Club Paris
St Etienne AS	1	-	1	Sochaux-Montbeliard	Sete FC	3	-	2	Nice Olympique
Stade de Reims	3	-	3	Nancy-Lorraine FC	St Etienne AS	1	-	1	Stade Rennais FC
Strasbourg RC	1	-	0	Cannes AS	Stade de Reims	2	-	2	Sochaux-Montbeliard
Toulouse FC	4	-	1	SO Montpellier	Strasbourg RC	3	-	0	SO Montpellier
					Toulouse FC	2	-	1	Oly Marseille

November 11, 1948

May 1, 1949

Roubaix-Tourcoing	1	-	0	Strasbourg RC	Colmar SR	5	-	1	Sete FC
Sete FC	1	-	1	St Etienne AS	Nancy-Lorraine FC	3	-	1	Red Star Paris

November 14, 1948

Cannes AS	2	-	1	Toulouse FC	Nice Olympique	1	-	0	St Etienne AS
Colmar SR	2	-	1	Strasbourg RC	Oly Marseille	5	-	0	Strasbourg RC
Nancy-Lorraine FC	4	-	2	St Etienne AS	Racing Club Paris	2	-	2	Metz FC
Oly Marseille	1	-	1	Red Star Paris	Roubaix-Tourcoing	3	-	1	Toulouse FC
Racing Club Paris	3	-	1	Stade de Reims	SO Montpellier	1	-	3	Cannes AS
Roubaix-Tourcoing	1	-	4	Oly Lille	Sochaux-Montbeliard	1	-	3	Oly Lille
SO Montpellier	4	-	1	Metz FC	Stade Rennais FC	1	-	0	Stade de Reims
Sochaux-Montbeliard	7	-	0	Sete FC					
Stade Rennais FC	2	-	0	Nice Olympique					

May 14, 1949

					Red Star Paris	2	-	2	Sochaux-Montbeliard

November 21, 1948

May 15, 1949

Colmar SR	1	-	3	SO Montpellier	Cannes AS	1	-	0	Oly Marseille
Nancy-Lorraine FC	2	-	1	Metz FC	Metz FC	2	-	0	Nancy-Lorraine FC
Nice Olympique	2	-	2	Stade de Reims	Oly Lille	3	-	0	Stade Rennais FC
Oly Marseille	1	-	0	Cannes AS	SO Montpellier	0	-	1	Colmar SR
Racing Club Paris	5	-	0	Toulouse FC	St Etienne AS	0	-	0	Sete FC
Sochaux-Montbeliard	0	-	2	Red Star Paris	Stade de Reims	6	-	1	Nice Olympique
Stade Rennais FC	1	-	1	Oly Lille	Strasbourg RC	1	-	2	Roubaix-Tourcoing
					Toulouse FC	2	-	1	Racing Club Paris

November 28, 1948

May 29, 1949

Cannes AS	3	-	0	Roubaix-Tourcoing	Colmar SR	3	-	1	St Etienne AS
Metz FC	4	-	1	Sochaux-Montbeliard					
Oly Lille	4	-	1	Nice Olympique					
Red Star Paris	0	-	0	Stade Rennais FC					

SO Montpellier	1	-	2	Oly Marseille	Nancy-Lorraine FC	2	-	0	Toulouse FC
St Etienne AS	5	-	2	Colmar SR	Nice Olympique	1	-	2	Oly Lille
Stade de Reims	2	-	0	Sete FC	Oly Marseille	6	-	3	SO Montpellier
Strasbourg RC	3	-	1	Racing Club Paris	Racing Club Paris	4	-	2	Strasbourg RC
Toulouse FC	2	-	1	Nancy-Lorraine FC	Roubaix-Tourcoing	4	-	0	Cannes AS
					Sochaux-Montbeliard	2	-	1	Metz FC
					Stade Rennais FC	1	-	1	Red Star Paris

June 1, 1949

Sete FC 1 - 2 Stade de Reims

#	Ligue 2	Pld	W	D	L	F	A	GA	Pts
1	Lens RC	36	21	11	4	65	27	2.41	53
2	Girondins de Bordeaux FC	36	24	5	7	107	49	2.18	53
3	Rouen FC	36	20	11	5	67	37	1.81	51
4	Le Havre AC	36	19	10	7	64	30	2.13	48
5	Nimes Olympique	36	16	10	10	89	51	1.75	42
6	Ales Olympique en Cevennes	36	16	10	10	76	57	1.33	42
7	Besancon Racing Club	36	15	10	11	81	59	1.37	40
8	Nantes Atlantique FC	36	13	12	11	58	53	1.09	38
9	Olympique Lyonnais	36	16	6	14	65	72	0.90	38
10	Angers SCO	36	11	15	10	61	49	1.24	37
11	Monaco AS	36	16	5	15	72	64	1.13	37
12	Stade Beziers Sport	36	13	5	18	58	66	0.88	31
13	Sporting Toulon Var	36	11	9	16	56	72	0.78	31
14	Amiens SC	36	12	5	19	46	70	0.66	29
15	Le Mans UC 72	36	11	6	19	60	92	0.65	28
16	Troyes ESTAC	36	9	7	20	52	90	0.58	25
17	Valenciennes FC	36	8	8	20	38	76	0.50	24
18	Cercle Athletique de Paris Charenton	36	5	10	21	35	82	0.43	20
19	SC Douai	36	5	7	24	36	90	0.40	17

August 22, 1948
Amiens SC   2 - 2 Besancon RC
CA Paris   1 - 1 Rouen FC
Gir Bordeaux   1 - 1 Angers SCO
Le Havre AC   4 - 0 Le Mans UC 72
Lens RC   3 - 0 Monaco AS
Nimes Olympique   1 - 3 Stade Beziers
Oly Lyonnais   1 - 1 Ales Olympique
SC Douai   1 - 2 Troyes ASTS
Valenciennes FC   1 - 1 Sporting Toulon

August 29, 1948
Ales Olympique   2 - 2 Nantes Atlantique
Angers SCO   4 - 0 Valenciennes FC
Besancon RC   0 - 2 Le Havre AC
Le Mans UC 72   3 - 3 Nimes Olympique
Monaco AS   1 - 4 Amiens SC
Rouen FC   4 - 0 Oly Lyonnais
Sporting Toulon   2 - 1 SC Douai
Stade Beziers   2 - 4 Gir Bordeaux
Troyes ESTAC   1 - 2 CA Paris

September 5, 1948

January 2, 1949
Ales Olympique   4 - 0 Stade Beziers
Angers SCO   1 - 1 Rouen FC
Gir Bordeaux   1 - 0 CA Paris
Le Havre AC   1 - 1 Nantes Atlantique
Lens RC   1 - 1 Amiens SC
Monaco AS   2 - 1 Besancon RC
Nimes Olympique   7 - 1 Oly Lyonnais
SC Douai   0 - 0 Valenciennes FC
Troyes ESTAC   4 - 1 Sporting Toulon

January 13, 1949
Le Mans UC 72   0 - 1 Besancon
Lens RC   2 - 1 Nimes Olympique

January 16, 1949
Ales Olympique   0 - 1 Rouen FC
Le Havre AC   4 - 0 Nimes Olympique
Le Mans UC 72   3 - 2 Stade Beziers
Lens RC   2 - 1 Valenciennes FC
Monaco AS   1 - 0 Sporting Toulon
Nantes Atlantique   2 - 0 Amiens SC
SC Douai   3 - 5 Gir Bordeaux

Amiens SC	2	-	0	Stade Beziers	Troyes ESTAC	2	-	1	Angers SCO
Gir Bordeaux	10	-	1	Troyes ESTAC	January 23, 1949			
Le Havre AC	0	-	0	Angers SCO	Amiens SC	1	-	2	Le Havre AC
Lens RC	4	-	1	Le Mans UC 72	Besancon RC	2	-	4	Le Mans UC 72
Nantes Atlantique	4	-	4	Besancon RC	CA Paris	4	-	2	SC Douai
Nimes Olympique	3	-	1	Sporting Toulon	Gir Bordeaux	5	-	0	Nantes Atlantique
Oly Lyonnais	1	-	5	Monaco AS	Nimes Olympique	2	-	2	Lens RC
SC Douai	2	-	2	Ales Olympique	Rouen FC	0	-	0	Troyes ESTAC
Valenciennes FC	0	-	3	Rouen FC	Sporting Toulon	5	-	3	Ales Olympique
September 9, 1948					Stade Beziers	3	-	1	Monaco AS
Ales Olympique	1	-	1	Lens RC	Valenciennes FC	4	-	3	Oly Lyonnais
Angers SCO	1	-	1	SC Douai	February 6, 1949			
Besancon RC	1	-	1	Nimes Olympique	Ales Olympique	1	-	1	Troyes ESTAC
Le Mans UC 72	0	-	3	Gir Bordeaux	Amiens SC	1	-	4	Valenciennes FC
Monaco AS	1	-	2	Le Havre AC	Besancon RC	4	-	1	Sporting Toulon
Rouen FC	0	-	0	Nantes Atlantique	Le Havre AC	0	-	0	CA Paris
Sporting Toulon	3	-	1	CA Paris	Le Mans UC 72	0	-	2	Rouen FC
Stade Beziers	4	-	1	Valenciennes FC	Lens RC	0	-	0	Gir Bordeaux
Troyes ESTAC	1	-	3	Oly Lyonnais	Monaco AS	0	-	0	Angers SCO
September 12, 1948					Nantes Atlantique	1	-	1	Nimes Olympique
Ales Olympique	1	-	1	Valenciennes FC	Oly Lyonnais	3	-	1	SC Douai
Angers SCO	4	-	1	Amiens SC	February 13, 1949			
Besancon RC	2	-	0	Oly Lyonnais	Angers SCO	2	-	2	Ales Olympique
Le Mans UC 72	6	-	2	Nantes Atlantique	CA Paris	0	-	3	Lens RC
Monaco AS	5	-	2	CA Paris	Gir Bordeaux	2	-	0	Oly Lyonnais
Rouen FC	1	-	0	Gir Bordeaux	Nimes Olympique	2	-	0	Amiens SC
Sporting Toulon	1	-	0	Le Havre AC	Rouen FC	4	-	2	Monaco AS
Stade Beziers	1	-	5	Lens RC	SC Douai	2	-	1	Nantes Atlantique
Troyes ESTAC	0	-	3	Nimes Olympique	Sporting Toulon	2	-	1	Le Mans UC 72
September 19, 1948					Stade Beziers	0	-	3	Besancon RC
Amiens SC	2	-	1	Troyes ESTAC	Valenciennes FC	2	-	1	Le Havre AC
CA Paris	1	-	1	Le Mans UC 72	February 20, 1949			
Le Havre AC	0	-	0	Rouen FC	Amiens SC	0	-	3	Gir Bordeaux
Lens RC	2	-	0	Sporting Toulon	Besancon RC	1	-	1	Angers SCO
Nantes Atlantique	1	-	2	Angers SCO	Le Havre AC	4	-	0	SC Douai
Nimes Olympique	3	-	3	Ales Olympique	Le Mans UC 72	1	-	1	Troyes ESTAC
Oly Lyonnais	2	-	0	Stade Beziers	Lens RC	6	-	0	Oly Lyonnais
SC Douai	0	-	4	Besancon RC	Monaco AS	7	-	0	Ales Olympique
Valenciennes FC	1	-	2	Monaco AS	Nantes Atlantique	0	-	0	Valenciennes FC
September 26, 1948					Nimes Olympique	4	-	4	CA Paris
Ales Olympique	2	-	0	Gir Bordeaux	Stade Beziers	1	-	1	Rouen FC
Angers SCO	0	-	0	Lens RC	February 26, 1949			
Besancon RC	3	-	1	CA Paris	Oly Lyonnais	3	-	0	CA Paris
Le Mans UC 72	0	-	2	Oly Lyonnais	March 6, 1949			
Monaco AS	5	-	0	SC Douai	Angers SCO	7	-	2	Le Mans UC 72
Rouen FC	2	-	1	Nimes Olympique	CA Paris	2	-	1	Amiens SC
Sporting Toulon	2	-	1	Amiens SC	Gir Bordeaux	2	-	2	Le Havre AC
Stade Beziers	1	-	1	Nantes Atlantique	Oly Lyonnais	2	-	1	Nantes Atlantique
Troyes ESTAC	1	-	1	Le Havre AC	Rouen FC	2	-	2	Besancon RC
September 30, 1948					SC Douai	2	-	1	Lens RC
Amiens SC	5	-	4	Le Mans UC 72	Sporting Toulon	1	-	0	Stade Beziers
CA Paris	0	-	4	Ales Olympique	Troyes ESTAC	1	-	2	Monaco AS

Gir Bordeaux	4	-	3	Sporting Toulon	Valenciennes FC	2	-	0	Nimes Olympique
Le Havre AC	5	-	0	Stade Beziers	\multicolumn{5}{c}{March 13, 1949}			
Lens RC	2	-	0	Besancon RC	Ales Olympique	6	-	1	Le Mans UC 72
Nantes Atlantique	2	-	1	Monaco AS	Angers SCO	1	-	1	Stade Beziers
Nimes Olympique	0	-	2	Angers SCO	CA Paris	0	-	2	Valenciennes FC
SC Douai	1	-	1	Rouen FC	Gir Bordeaux	4	-	1	Nimes Olympique
Valenciennes FC	2	-	3	Troyes ESTAC	Lens RC	4	-	1	Nantes Atlantique

October 3, 1948

Amiens SC	3	-	1	Rouen FC	Oly Lyonnais	0	-	0	Le Havre AC
CA Paris	1	-	0	Stade Beziers	Rouen FC	2	-	1	Sporting Toulon
Gir Bordeaux	4	-	3	Monaco AS	SC Douai	1	-	0	Amiens SC
Le Havre AC	3	-	1	Ales Olympique	Troyes ESTAC	3	-	2	Besancon RC
Lens RC	3	-	1	Troyes ESTAC					

March 27, 1949

Nantes Atlantique	4	-	1	Sporting Toulon	Amiens SC	0	-	0	Oly Lyonnais
Oly Lyonnais	2	-	3	Angers SCO	Besancon RC	3	-	0	Ales Olympique
SC Douai	3	-	2	Le Mans UC 72	Le Havre AC	3	-	0	Lens RC
Valenciennes FC	1	-	3	Besancon RC	Le Mans UC 72	3	-	2	Monaco AS

October 17, 1948

					Nantes Atlantique	1	-	1	CA Paris
					Nimes Olympique	3	-	2	SC Douai
Angers SCO	2	-	0	Monaco AS	Sporting Toulon	5	-	1	Angers SCO
CA Paris	1	-	1	Le Havre AC	Stade Beziers	6	-	1	Troyes ESTAC
Gir Bordeaux	0	-	0	Lens RC	Valenciennes FC	2	-	1	Gir Bordeaux
Nimes Olympique	1	-	1	Nantes Atlantique					
Rouen FC	6	-	0	Le Mans UC 72					

April 3, 1949

SC Douai	0	-	2	Oly Lyonnais	Sporting Toulon	1	-	1	Valenciennes FC
Sporting Toulon	0	-	0	Besancon RC					
Troyes ESTAC	1	-	1	Ales Olympique					
Valenciennes FC	0	-	1	Amiens SC					

April 10, 1949

					Ales Olympique	4	-	1	Oly Lyonnais
					Angers SCO	1	-	2	Gir Bordeaux
					Besancon RC	5	-	0	Amiens SC
					Le Mans UC 72	2	-	1	Le Havre AC

October 18, 1948

Ales Olympique	3	-	0	Amiens SC	Monaco AS	1	-	2	Lens RC
Angers SCO	0	-	0	CA Paris	Rouen FC	3	-	1	CA Paris
Besancon RC	6	-	1	Gir Bordeaux	Stade Beziers	2	-	4	Nimes Olympique
Le Mans UC 72	3	-	0	Valenciennes FC	Troyes ESTAC	1	-	1	SC Douai
Monaco AS	1	-	1	Nimes Olympique					

April 14, 1949

Rouen FC	3	-	0	Lens RC	CA Paris	1	-	4	Monaco AS
Sporting Toulon	4	-	4	Oly Lyonnais	Nantes Atlantique	4	-	1	Le Mans UC 72
Stade Beziers	3	-	0	SC Douai	Nimes Olympique	7	-	1	Troyes ESTAC
Troyes ESTAC	4	-	2	Nantes Atlantique	Oly Lyonnais	2	-	1	Besancon RC

October 24, 1948

April 15, 1949

Amiens SC	2	-	1	Nimes Olympique	Amiens SC	2	-	0	Angers SCO
Le Havre AC	3	-	0	Valenciennes FC	Gir Bordeaux	2	-	1	Rouen FC
Le Mans UC 72	3	-	3	Sporting Toulon	Le Havre AC	4	-	1	Sporting Toulon
Lens RC	0	-	0	CA Paris	Lens RC	0	-	0	Stade Beziers
Monaco AS	2	-	2	Rouen FC	Valenciennes FC	1	-	3	Ales Olympique
Nantes Atlantique	2	-	1	SC Douai					
Oly Lyonnais	3	-	5	Gir Bordeaux					

October 31, 1948

April 17, 1949

					CA Paris	1	-	3	Sporting Toulon
Amiens SC	3	-	0	SC Douai	Gir Bordeaux	5	-	0	Le Mans UC 72
Besancon RC	1	-	1	Troyes ESTAC	Le Havre AC	3	-	1	Monaco AS
Le Havre AC	2	-	0	Oly Lyonnais	Lens RC	2	-	2	Ales Olympique
Le Mans UC 72	1	-	0	Ales Olympique	Nantes Atlantique	2	-	0	Rouen FC
Nantes Atlantique	0	-	0	Lens RC	Nimes Olympique	4	-	0	Besancon RC
Nimes Olympique	2	-	0	Gir Bordeaux	Oly Lyonnais	2	-	1	Troyes ESTAC
					SC Douai	0	-	1	Angers SCO

Sporting Toulon	3	-	4	Rouen FC	Valenciennes FC	1	-	1 Stade Beziers
Stade Beziers	2	-	1	Angers SCO	April 24, 1949			
Valenciennes FC	1	-	0	CA Paris	Ales Olympique	2	-	0 SC Douai
November 7, 1948					Angers SCO	2	-	3 Le Havre AC
Ales Olympique	4	-	3	Besancon RC	Besancon RC	3	-	4 Nantes Atlantique
Angers SCO	1	-	1	Sporting Toulon	Le Mans UC 72	1	-	3 Lens RC
CA Paris	1	-	3	Nantes Atlantique	Monaco AS	4	-	0 Oly Lyonnais
Gir Bordeaux	2	-	0	Valenciennes FC	Rouen FC	3	-	0 Valenciennes FC
Lens RC	2	-	0	Le Havre AC	Sporting Toulon	0	-	0 Nimes Olympique
Monaco AS	2	-	1	Le Mans UC 72	Stade Beziers	5	-	1 Amiens SC
Oly Lyonnais	7	-	1	Amiens SC	Troyes ESTAC	2	-	4 Gir Bordeaux
SC Douai	1	-	4	Nimes Olympique	May 1, 1949			
Troyes ESTAC	2	-	3	Stade Beziers	Amiens SC	1	-	1 Monaco AS
November 11, 1948					CA Paris	0	-	3 Troyes ESTAC
Amiens SC	0	-	1	Lens RC	Gir Bordeaux	5	-	2 Stade Beziers
Besancon RC	1	-	0	Stade Beziers	Le Havre AC	2	-	0 Besancon RC
Nantes Atlantique	0	-	1	Le Havre AC	Nantes Atlantique	2	-	3 Ales Olympique
Oly Lyonnais	1	-	0	Nimes Olympique	Nimes Olympique	5	-	1 Le Mans UC 72
Rouen FC	1	-	0	Angers SCO	Oly Lyonnais	1	-	1 Rouen FC
Valenciennes FC	0	-	3	SC Douai	SC Douai	1	-	1 Sporting Toulon
November 14, 1948					Valenciennes FC	2	-	2 Angers SCO
Besancon RC	4	-	1	Monaco AS	May 8, 1949			
CA Paris	2	-	3	Gir Bordeaux	Ales Olympique	1	-	3 Nimes Olympique
Sporting Toulon	2	-	1	Troyes ASTS	Angers SCO	0	-	0 Nantes Atlantique
Stade Beziers	1	-	0	Ales Olympique	Besancon RC	7	-	2 SC Douai
November 25, 1948					Le Mans UC 72	2	-	0 CA Paris
Ales Olympique	4	-	0	Angers SCO	Monaco AS	3	-	1 Valenciennes FC
November 28, 1948					Rouen FC	2	-	0 Le Havre AC
Amiens SC	1	-	1	CA Paris	Sporting Toulon	3	-	2 Lens RC
Besancon RC	1	-	1	Rouen FC	Stade Beziers	4	-	2 Oly Lyonnais
Le Havre AC	3	-	3	Gir Bordeaux	Troyes ESTAC	3	-	1 Amiens SC
Le Mans UC 72	2	-	2	Angers SCO	May 15, 1949			
Lens RC	2	-	0	SC Douai	Amiens SC	0	-	2 Ales Olympique
Monaco AS	3	-	0	Troyes ESTAC	CA Paris	0	-	6 Angers SCO
Nantes Atlantique	0	-	0	Oly Lyonnais	Gir Bordeaux	5	-	0 Besancon RC
Nimes Olympique	5	-	0	Valenciennes FC	Lens RC	2	-	0 Rouen FC
Stade Beziers	3	-	0	Sporting Toulon	Nantes Atlantique	5	-	0 Troyes ESTAC
December 5, 1948					Nimes Olympique	4	-	0 Monaco AS
Ales Olympique	0	-	3	Monaco AS	Oly Lyonnais	1	-	0 Sporting Toulon
Angers SCO	2	-	2	Besancon RC	SC Douai	1	-	3 Stade Beziers
CA Paris	1	-	1	Nimes Olympique	Valenciennes FC	1	-	1 Le Mans UC 72
Gir Bordeaux	3	-	0	Amiens SC	May 22, 1949			
Oly Lyonnais	1	-	4	Lens RC	Amiens SC	4	-	1 Sporting Toulon
Rouen FC	1	-	0	Stade Beziers	CA Paris	2	-	3 Besancon RC
SC Douai	1	-	1	Havre AC	Gir Bordeaux	2	-	3 Ales Olympique
Troyes ESTAC	1	-	3	Le Mans UC 72	Le Havre AC	3	-	0 Troyes ESTAC
Valenciennes FC	1	-	0	Nantes Atlantique	Lens RC	1	-	0 Angers SCO
December 19, 1948					Nantes Atlantique	2	-	0 Stade Beziers
Ales Olympique	2	-	1	Sporting Toulon	Nimes Olympique	7	-	0 Rouen FC
Le Havre AC	2	-	0	Amiens SC	Oly Lyonnais	3	-	0 Le Mans UC 72
Monaco AS	2	-	1	Stade Beziers	SC Douai	1	-	2 Monaco AS
Nantes Atlantique	3	-	1	Gir Bordeaux	May 26, 1949			

Oly Lyonnais	3	-	1	Valenciennes FC	Ales Olympique	2	-	0 Le Havre AC
SC Douai	0	-	1	CA Paris	Angers SCO	2	-	5 Oly Lyonnais
Troyes ESTAC	1	-	3	Rouen FC	Besancon RC	6	-	2 Valenciennes FC

December 26, 1948

Le Mans UC 72   2 - 1 SC Douai
Amiens SC   3 - 0 Nantes Atlantique
Monaco AS   0 - 5 Gir Bordeaux
Angers SCO   6 - 1 Troyes ESTAC
Rouen FC   2 - 0 Amiens SC
CA Paris   1 - 4 Oly Lyonnais
Sporting Toulon   0 - 2 Nantes Atlantique
Gir Bordeaux   7 - 0 SC Douai
Stade Beziers   3 - 1 CA Paris
Nimes Olympique   3 - 0 Le Havre AC
Troyes ESTAC   0 - 1 Lens RC
Rouen FC   2 - 1 Ales Olympique

May 29, 1949

Sporting Toulon   2 - 2 Monaco AS
Ales Olympique   6 - 1 CA Paris
Stade Beziers   1 - 4 Le Mans UC 72
Angers SCO   2 - 1 Nimes Olympique
Valenciennes FC   1 - 2 Lens RC
Besancon RC   0 - 0 Lens RC
Le Mans UC 72   1 - 2 Amiens SC
Monaco AS   0 - 2 Nantes Atlantique
Rouen FC   6 - 1 SC Douai
Sporting Toulon   0 - 3 Gir Bordeaux
Stade Beziers   0 - 1 Le Havre AC
Troyes ESTAC   5 - 1 Valenciennes FC

Germany - East

Union Halle won the Meisterschaft, teams once more qualifying through regional leagues. The National league begins next season.

Preliminary Round
    May 8, 1949
Franz Meringue Marga	2 - 0	Schwerin	at Cottbus
Eintracht Stendal	4 - 3	Altenburg-Nord	at Planitz

Quarter Final
    May 26, 1949
Eintracht Stendal	4 - 0	Franz Meringue Marga	at Dessau
Einheit Meerane	3 - 1	Babelsberg	at Brandenburg
Union Halle	2 - 1	Dresden-Friedrichstadt	at Halle

    May 29, 1949
Fortuna Erfurt	10 - 0	Wismar Sud	at Jena

Semi Final
    May 12, 1949
Union Halle	3 - 0	Eintracht Stendal	at Halle
Fortuna Erfurt	4 - 3	Einheit Meerane	at Chemnitz

Final
    June 26, 1949
Union Halle	4 - 1	Fortuna Erfurt	at Dresden

Germany - West

Mannheim were possibly the most surprising champions ever. They were only distant runners-up to Offenbach in the South league, though they did draw both games, and had to face North champions Hamburg in the quarter finals and thrashed them 5-0. Then it was a rematch with Offenbach, which they edged 2-1 before facing free-scoring Dortmund in the final. A 3-2 win in extra time after being 2-1 down, thanks to two goals from Ernst Lottke gave them the title.

Meisterschaft
Qualification Rounds
    May 29, 1949
St Pauli Hamburg   4 - 1 Rot-Weiss Essen   at Braunschweig
    June 5, 1949
St Pauli Hamburg   1 - 1 Bayern Munchen   at Hannover
Replay
    June 6, 1949
St Pauli Hamburg   2 - 0 Bayern Munchen   at Hannover

Quarter Final
    June 12, 1949
Wormatia Worms   2 - 2 Offenbach Kickers   at Kaiserslautern
Mannheim Vfr   5 - 0 Hamburger SV   at Frankfurter
Berliner SV 92   0 - 5 Borussia Dortmund   at Berlin
St Pauli Hamburg   1 - 1 Kaiserslautern 1FC   at Bremer
Replays
    June 19, 1949
Wormatia Worms   0 - 2 Offenbach Kickers   at Karlsruhe
St Pauli Hamburg   1 - 4 Kaiserslautern 1FC   at Dusseldorf

Semi Final
    June 26, 1949
Mannheim Vfr   2 - 1 Offenbach Kickers   at Gelsenkirchen
Kaiserslautern 1FC   0 - 0 Borussia Dortmund   at Munchen
Replay
    July 3, 1949
Kaiserslautern 1FC   1 - 4 Borussia Dortmund   at Koln

3rd Place play-off
Kaiserslautern 1FC   1 - 4 Borussia Dortmund   at Koblenz

Final
    August 8, 1948
Mannheim Vfr   3 - 2 Borussia Dortmund   at Stuttgart

	North	Pld	W	D	L	F	A	GA	Pts
1	Hamburger SV	22	14	4	4	61	31	1.97	32
2	St Pauli Hamburg	22	15	2	5	47	22	2.14	32
3	Osnabruck Vfl	22	14	3	5	61	23	2.65	31
4	Eintracht Braunschweig TSV	22	12	1	9	48	48	1.00	25
5	Bremer SV 06	22	9	4	9	45	53	0.85	22
6	Eimsbuttler TV	22	9	3	10	35	40	0.88	21
7	Lubeck Vfl	22	8	4	10	35	44	0.80	20
8	Werder Bremen	22	8	3	11	49	50	0.98	19
9	Concordia Hamburg	22	6	6	10	44	49	0.90	18
10	Arminia Hannover	22	6	4	12	33	50	0.66	16
11	Gottingen 05	22	5	4	13	35	57	0.61	14
12	Bremerhaven 93	22	7	0	15	28	54	0.52	14

Kiel were excluded after 8 games and effectively relegated because they had fielded and falsified papers for an ineligible player in 47-48 season. Kiel's games are shown below for the record. Hannover 96 would not have been relegated, so have been granted a place for next season.

Championship play-off   May 22, 1949 St Pauli Hamburg   3 -   5 Hamburger SV

St Pauli Hamburg	2 - 1	Hamburger SV	Lubeck Vfl	1 - 0	St Pauli Hamburg
St Pauli Hamburg	2 - 0	Osnabruck Vfl	Lubeck Vfl	1 - 4	Hamburger SV
St Pauli Hamburg	2 - 1	Eint Braunschweig	Lubeck Vfl	0 - 3	Osnabruck Vfl
St Pauli Hamburg	4 - 1	Bremer SV 06	Lubeck Vfl	1 - 2	Eint Braunschweig
St Pauli Hamburg	5 - 1	Eimsbuttler TV	Lubeck Vfl	4 - 3	Bremer SV 06
St Pauli Hamburg	3 - 0	Lubeck Vfl	Lubeck Vfl	1 - 2	Eimsbuttler TV
St Pauli Hamburg	2 - 0	Werder Bremen	Lubeck Vfl	1 - 1	Werder Bremen
St Pauli Hamburg	2 - 0	Concordia Hamburg	Lubeck Vfl	5 - 2	Concordia Hamburg
St Pauli Hamburg	1 - 2	Arminia Hannover	Lubeck Vfl	3 - 1	Arminia Hannover
St Pauli Hamburg	2 - 2	Gottingen 05	Lubeck Vfl	2 - 1	Gottingen 05
St Pauli Hamburg	2 - 1	Bremerhaven 93	Lubeck Vfl	3 - 1	Bremerhaven 93
Hamburger SV	0 - 2	St Pauli Hamburg	Werder Bremen	0 - 4	St Pauli Hamburg
Hamburger SV	1 - 2	Osnabruck Vfl	Werder Bremen	2 - 3	Hamburger SV
Hamburger SV	7 - 2	Eint Braunschweig	Werder Bremen	4 - 3	Osnabruck Vfl
Hamburger SV	4 - 2	Bremer SV 06	Werder Bremen	4 - 2	Eint Braunschweig
Hamburger SV	2 - 1	Eimsbuttler TV	Werder Bremen	0 - 0	Bremer SV 06
Hamburger SV	2 - 2	Lubeck Vfl	Werder Bremen	0 - 3	Eimsbuttler TV
Hamburger SV	5 - 2	Werder Bremen	Werder Bremen	6 - 1	Lubeck Vfl
Hamburger SV	2 - 2	Concordia Hamburg	Werder Bremen	2 - 2	Concordia Hamburg
Hamburger SV	2 - 0	Arminia Hannover	Werder Bremen	3 - 1	Arminia Hannover
Hamburger SV	4 - 1	Gottingen 05	Werder Bremen	6 - 1	Gottingen 05
Hamburger SV	7 - 1	Bremerhaven 93	Werder Bremen	5 - 0	Bremerhaven 93
Osnabruck Vfl	0 - 1	St Pauli Hamburg	Concordia Hamburg	2 - 3	St Pauli Hamburg
Osnabruck Vfl	0 - 1	Hamburger SV	Concordia Hamburg	1 - 1	Hamburger SV
Osnabruck Vfl	2 - 1	Eint Braunschweig	Concordia Hamburg	3 - 3	Osnabruck Vfl

Osnabruck Vfl	7	-	0	Bremer SV 06	Concordia Hamburg	3	-	4	Eint Braunschweig
Osnabruck Vfl	6	-	1	Eimsbuttler TV	Concordia Hamburg	1	-	3	Bremer SV 06
Osnabruck Vfl	1	-	1	Lubeck Vfl	Concordia Hamburg	1	-	2	Eimsbuttler TV
Osnabruck Vfl	5	-	1	Werder Bremen	Concordia Hamburg	0	-	2	Lubeck Vfl
Osnabruck Vfl	5	-	0	Concordia Hamburg	Concordia Hamburg	3	-	2	Werder Bremen
Osnabruck Vfl	2	-	3	Arminia Hannover	Concordia Hamburg	3	-	1	Arminia Hannover
Osnabruck Vfl	4	-	1	Gottingen 05	Concordia Hamburg	5	-	0	Gottingen 05
Osnabruck Vfl	2	-	0	Bremerhaven 93	Concordia Hamburg	3	-	0	Bremerhaven 93
Eint Braunschweig	3	-	1	St Pauli Hamburg	Arminia Hannover	1	-	1	St Pauli Hamburg
Eint Braunschweig	0	-	2	Hamburger SV	Arminia Hannover	1	-	3	Hamburger SV
Eint Braunschweig	0	-	2	Osnabruck Vfl	Arminia Hannover	0	-	5	Osnabruck Vfl
Eint Braunschweig	1	-	5	Bremer SV 06	Arminia Hannover	1	-	2	Eint Braunschweig
Eint Braunschweig	2	-	1	Eimsbuttler TV	Arminia Hannover	1	-	1	Bremer SV 06
Eint Braunschweig	6	-	2	Lubeck Vfl	Arminia Hannover	1	-	3	Eimsbuttler TV
Eint Braunschweig	3	-	2	Werder Bremen	Arminia Hannover	2	-	0	Lubeck Vfl
Eint Braunschweig	3	-	1	Concordia Hamburg	Arminia Hannover	4	-	2	Werder Bremen
Eint Braunschweig	2	-	1	Arminia Hannover	Arminia Hannover	2	-	2	Concordia Hamburg
Eint Braunschweig	2	-	2	Gottingen 05	Arminia Hannover	0	-	4	Gottingen 05
Eint Braunschweig	2	-	1	Bremerhaven 93	Arminia Hannover	2	-	1	Bremerhaven 93
Bremer SV 06	1	-	2	St Pauli Hamburg	Gottingen 05	2	-	0	St Pauli Hamburg
Bremer SV 06	2	-	2	Hamburger SV	Gottingen 05	1	-	4	Hamburger SV
Bremer SV 06	1	-	4	Osnabruck Vfl	Gottingen 05	1	-	2	Osnabruck Vfl
Bremer SV 06	4	-	3	Eint Braunschweig	Gottingen 05	1	-	4	Eint Braunschweig
Bremer SV 06	2	-	4	Eimsbuttler TV	Gottingen 05	3	-	3	Bremer SV 06
Bremer SV 06	2	-	1	Lubeck Vfl	Gottingen 05	3	-	2	Eimsbuttler TV
Bremer SV 06	3	-	2	Werder Bremen	Gottingen 05	1	-	1	Lubeck Vfl
Bremer SV 06	0	-	4	Concordia Hamburg	Gottingen 05	3	-	2	Werder Bremen
Bremer SV 06	5	-	2	Arminia Hannover	Gottingen 05	4	-	1	Concordia Hamburg
Bremer SV 06	2	-	1	Gottingen 05	Gottingen 05	1	-	6	Arminia Hannover
Bremer SV 06	1	-	2	Bremerhaven 93	Gottingen 05	0	-	1	Bremerhaven 93
Eimsbuttler TV	0	-	6	St Pauli Hamburg	Bremerhaven 93	3	-	0	St Pauli Hamburg
Eimsbuttler TV	2	-	1	Hamburger SV	Bremerhaven 93	2	-	3	Hamburger SV
Eimsbuttler TV	0	-	0	Osnabruck Vfl	Bremerhaven 93	1	-	3	Osnabruck Vfl
Eimsbuttler TV	2	-	1	Eint Braunschweig	Bremerhaven 93	1	-	2	Eint Braunschweig
Eimsbuttler TV	0	-	1	Bremer SV 06	Bremerhaven 93	1	-	3	Bremer SV 06
Eimsbuttler TV	0	-	3	Lubeck Vfl	Bremerhaven 93	2	-	1	Eimsbuttler TV
Eimsbuttler TV	0	-	1	Werder Bremen	Bremerhaven 93	1	-	0	Lubeck Vfl
Eimsbuttler TV	1	-	1	Concordia Hamburg	Bremerhaven 93	1	-	2	Werder Bremen
Eimsbuttler TV	1	-	1	Arminia Hannover	Bremerhaven 93	2	-	4	Concordia Hamburg
Eimsbuttler TV	1	-	0	Gottingen 05	Bremerhaven 93	3	-	0	Arminia Hannover
Eimsbuttler TV	7	-	0	Bremerhaven 93	Bremerhaven 93	3	-	2	Gottingen 05
Kieler SV Holstein	0	-	1	St Pauli Hamburg					
Kieler SV Holstein	5	-	1	Eimsbuttler TV					
Kieler SV Holstein	2	-	2	Werder Bremen					
Kieler SV Holstein	5	-	0	Bremerhaven 93					
Eint Braunschweig	0	-	0	Kieler SV Holstein					
Lubeck Vfl	4	-	0	Kieler SV Holstein					
Concordia Hamburg	2	-	2	Kieler SV Holstein					
Gottingen 05	1	-	3	Kieler SV Holstein					

	West	Pld	W	D	L	F	A	GA	Pts
1	Borussia Dortmund	24	17	4	3	79	30	2.63	38
2	Rot Weiss Essen	24	10	10	4	39	22	1.77	30
3	Horst-Emscher STV	24	11	5	8	51	40	1.28	27
4	Preussen Munster	24	9	7	8	33	35	0.94	25
5	Rot-Weiss Oberhausen	24	9	6	9	36	25	1.44	24
6	Hamborn 07 SV	24	10	4	10	40	44	0.91	24
7	Vohwinkel 80 TSG	24	10	3	11	41	45	0.91	23
8	Alemannia Aachen	24	8	7	9	33	39	0.85	23
9	Erkenschwick SpVgg	24	9	3	12	42	53	0.79	21
10	Rhenania Wurselen	24	8	5	11	33	48	0.69	21
11	Fortuna Dusseldorf	24	8	4	12	31	45	0.69	20
12	Schalke 04 Gelsenkirchen	24	6	6	12	33	43	0.77	18
13	Sportfreunde Katernburg	24	7	4	13	29	51	0.57	18

Dortmund were comfortably best in the West, though they did struggle with Essen, who had a good defence but had difficulty scoring in games they dominated, particularly away from home.

Borussia Dortmund	3 - 3 Rot Weiss Essen	Alemannia Aachen	2 - 0 Borussia Dortmund
Borussia Dortmund	2 - 2 Horst-Emscher STV	Alemannia Aachen	1 - 1 Rot Weiss Essen
Borussia Dortmund	3 - 2 Preussen Munster	Alemannia Aachen	3 - 1 Horst-Emscher STV
Borussia Dortmund	1 - 0 R-W Oberhausen	Alemannia Aachen	0 - 0 Preussen Munster
Borussia Dortmund	5 - 0 Hamborn 07 SV	Alemannia Aachen	0 - 0 R-W Oberhausen
Borussia Dortmund	3 - 1 Vohwinkel 80 TSG	Alemannia Aachen	1 - 0 Hamborn 07 SV
Borussia Dortmund	8 - 1 Alemannia Aachen	Alemannia Aachen	4 - 0 Vohwinkel 80 TSG
Borussia Dortmund	4 - 2 Erkenschwick SpVgg	Alemannia Aachen	0 - 1 Erkenschwick SpVgg
Borussia Dortmund	2 - 1 Rhenania Wurselen	Alemannia Aachen	1 - 5 Rhenania Wurselen
Borussia Dortmund	3 - 1 Fortuna Dusseldorf	Alemannia Aachen	0 - 3 Fortuna Dusseldorf
Borussia Dortmund	5 - 2 Schalke 04	Alemannia Aachen	1 - 1 Schalke 04
Borussia Dortmund	8 - 1 Sp Katernburg	Alemannia Aachen	3 - 0 Sp Katernburg
Rot Weiss Essen	5 - 3 Borussia Dortmund	Erkenschwick SpVgg	0 - 4 Borussia Dortmund
Rot Weiss Essen	0 - 0 Horst-Emscher STV	Erkenschwick SpVgg	1 - 1 Rot Weiss Essen
Rot Weiss Essen	1 - 0 Preussen Munster	Erkenschwick SpVgg	2 - 3 Horst-Emscher STV
Rot Weiss Essen	2 - 0 R-W Oberhausen	Erkenschwick SpVgg	3 - 0 Preussen Munster
Rot Weiss Essen	3 - 0 Hamborn 07 SV	Erkenschwick SpVgg	2 - 0 R-W Oberhausen
Rot Weiss Essen	0 - 0 Vohwinkel 80 TSG	Erkenschwick SpVgg	5 - 2 Hamborn 07 SV
Rot Weiss Essen	3 - 1 Alemannia Aachen	Erkenschwick SpVgg	2 - 1 Vohwinkel 80 TSG
Rot Weiss Essen	2 - 2 Erkenschwick SpVgg	Erkenschwick SpVgg	0 - 3 Alemannia Aachen
Rot Weiss Essen	3 - 0 Rhenania Wurselen	Erkenschwick SpVgg	5 - 1 Rhenania Wurselen
Rot Weiss Essen	3 - 0 Fortuna Dusseldorf	Erkenschwick SpVgg	3 - 1 Fortuna Dusseldorf
Rot Weiss Essen	1 - 1 Schalke 04	Erkenschwick SpVgg	0 - 2 Schalke 04
Rot Weiss Essen	1 - 2 Sp Katernburg	Erkenschwick SpVgg	4 - 0 Sp Katernburg
Horst-Emscher STV	0 - 1 Borussia Dortmund	Rhenania Wurselen	0 - 8 Borussia Dortmund
Horst-Emscher STV	0 - 2 Rot Weiss Essen	Rhenania Wurselen	1 - 0 Rot Weiss Essen
Horst-Emscher STV	1 - 3 Preussen Munster	Rhenania Wurselen	1 - 1 Horst-Emscher STV
Horst-Emscher STV	1 - 0 R-W Oberhausen	Rhenania Wurselen	1 - 3 Preussen Munster

Horst-Emscher STV	6 - 1	Hamborn 07 SV		Rhenania Wurselen	0 - 2	R-W Oberhausen
Horst-Emscher STV	2 - 2	Vohwinkel 80 TSG		Rhenania Wurselen	1 - 2	Hamborn 07 SV
Horst-Emscher STV	2 - 2	Alemannia Aachen		Rhenania Wurselen	2 - 1	Vohwinkel 80 TSG
Horst-Emscher STV	6 - 0	Erkenschwick SpVgg		Rhenania Wurselen	3 - 0	Alemannia Aachen
Horst-Emscher STV	6 - 1	Rhenania Wurselen		Rhenania Wurselen	3 - 1	Erkenschwick SpVgg
Horst-Emscher STV	2 - 1	Fortuna Dusseldorf		Rhenania Wurselen	1 - 2	Fortuna Dusseldorf
Horst-Emscher STV	4 - 2	Schalke 04		Rhenania Wurselen	3 - 2	Schalke 04
Horst-Emscher STV	0 - 1	Sp Katernburg		Rhenania Wurselen	2 - 1	Sp Katernburg
Preussen Munster	0 - 4	Borussia Dortmund		Fortuna Dusseldorf	0 - 7	Borussia Dortmund
Preussen Munster	2 - 1	Rot Weiss Essen		Fortuna Dusseldorf	1 - 1	Rot Weiss Essen
Preussen Munster	4 - 0	Horst-Emscher STV		Fortuna Dusseldorf	3 - 2	Horst-Emscher STV
Preussen Munster	0 - 3	R-W Oberhausen		Fortuna Dusseldorf	3 - 4	Preussen Munster
Preussen Munster	1 - 2	Hamborn 07 SV		Fortuna Dusseldorf	1 - 3	R-W Oberhausen
Preussen Munster	0 - 2	Vohwinkel 80 TSG		Fortuna Dusseldorf	3 - 2	Hamborn 07 SV
Preussen Munster	1 - 1	Alemannia Aachen		Fortuna Dusseldorf	2 - 0	Vohwinkel 80 TSG
Preussen Munster	2 - 1	Erkenschwick SpVgg		Fortuna Dusseldorf	2 - 1	Alemannia Aachen
Preussen Munster	2 - 1	Rhenania Wurselen		Fortuna Dusseldorf	0 - 0	Erkenschwick SpVgg
Preussen Munster	1 - 0	Fortuna Dusseldorf		Fortuna Dusseldorf	0 - 0	Rhenania Wurselen
Preussen Munster	0 - 0	Schalke 04		Fortuna Dusseldorf	1 - 3	Schalke 04
Preussen Munster	1 - 1	Sp Katernburg		Fortuna Dusseldorf	3 - 0	Sp Katernburg
R-W Oberhausen	2 - 3	Borussia Dortmund		Schalke 04	0 - 1	Borussia Dortmund
R-W Oberhausen	0 - 0	Rot Weiss Essen		Schalke 04	0 - 2	Rot Weiss Essen
R-W Oberhausen	5 - 0	Horst-Emscher STV		Schalke 04	1 - 4	Horst-Emscher STV
R-W Oberhausen	1 - 1	Preussen Munster		Schalke 04	3 - 3	Preussen Munster
R-W Oberhausen	2 - 1	Hamborn 07 SV		Schalke 04	0 - 0	R-W Oberhausen
R-W Oberhausen	2 - 3	Vohwinkel 80 TSG		Schalke 04	0 - 2	Hamborn 07 SV
R-W Oberhausen	0 - 3	Alemannia Aachen		Schalke 04	5 - 1	Vohwinkel 80 TSG
R-W Oberhausen	4 - 0	Erkenschwick SpVgg		Schalke 04	0 - 0	Alemannia Aachen
R-W Oberhausen	1 - 0	Rhenania Wurselen		Schalke 04	0 - 2	Erkenschwick SpVgg
R-W Oberhausen	2 - 2	Fortuna Dusseldorf		Schalke 04	2 - 3	Rhenania Wurselen
R-W Oberhausen	0 - 1	Schalke 04		Schalke 04	2 - 0	Fortuna Dusseldorf
R-W Oberhausen	6 - 1	Sp Katernburg		Schalke 04	1 - 2	Sp Katernburg
Hamborn 07 SV	0 - 0	Borussia Dortmund		Sp Katernburg	1 - 1	Borussia Dortmund
Hamborn 07 SV	1 - 2	Rot Weiss Essen		Sp Katernburg	1 - 1	Rot Weiss Essen
Hamborn 07 SV	1 - 2	Horst-Emscher STV		Sp Katernburg	1 - 2	Horst-Emscher STV
Hamborn 07 SV	0 - 0	Preussen Munster		Sp Katernburg	1 - 2	Preussen Munster
Hamborn 07 SV	1 - 1	R-W Oberhausen		Sp Katernburg	1 - 2	R-W Oberhausen
Hamborn 07 SV	4 - 2	Vohwinkel 80 TSG		Sp Katernburg	1 - 3	Hamborn 07 SV
Hamborn 07 SV	2 - 1	Alemannia Aachen		Sp Katernburg	1 - 0	Vohwinkel 80 TSG
Hamborn 07 SV	5 - 1	Erkenschwick SpVgg		Sp Katernburg	4 - 1	Alemannia Aachen
Hamborn 07 SV	1 - 1	Rhenania Wurselen		Sp Katernburg	3 - 2	Erkenschwick SpVgg
Hamborn 07 SV	3 - 0	Fortuna Dusseldorf		Sp Katernburg	1 - 1	Rhenania Wurselen
Hamborn 07 SV	4 - 1	Schalke 04		Sp Katernburg	1 - 0	Fortuna Dusseldorf
Hamborn 07 SV	2 - 1	Sp Katernburg		Sp Katernburg	2 - 3	Schalke 04
Vohwinkel 80 TSG	4 - 0	Borussia Dortmund				
Vohwinkel 80 TSG	2 - 1	Rot Weiss Essen				
Vohwinkel 80 TSG	1 - 4	Horst-Emscher STV				
Vohwinkel 80 TSG	2 - 1	Preussen Munster				
Vohwinkel 80 TSG	1 - 0	R-W Oberhausen				
Vohwinkel 80 TSG	4 - 1	Hamborn 07 SV				
Vohwinkel 80 TSG	2 - 3	Alemannia Aachen				
Vohwinkel 80 TSG	6 - 3	Erkenschwick SpVgg				

Vohwinkel 80 TSG	1 - 1	Rhenania Wurselen	
Vohwinkel 80 TSG	1 - 2	Fortuna Dusseldorf	
Vohwinkel 80 TSG	2 - 1	Schalke 04	
Vohwinkel 80 TSG	2 - 1	Sp Katernburg	

	SouthWest - North	Pld	W	D	L	F	A	GA	Pts
1	Kaiserslautern 1FC	24	21	1	2	142	22	6.45	42
2	Wormatia Worms	24	15	6	3	75	24	3.13	36
3	Neuendorf TuS	24	16	2	6	75	21	3.57	35
4	Pirmasens 03 FK	24	14	5	5	58	41	1.41	33
5	Neustadt/Wienstrasse	24	15	2	7	44	42	1.05	32
6	Phoenix Ludwigshafen	24	8	7	9	49	44	1.11	23
7	Eintracht 05 Trier	24	8	4	12	46	62	0.74	20
8	Mainz 05 FSV	24	7	6	11	39	67	0.58	20
9	Weisenau SG	24	7	4	13	44	86	0.51	18
10	Oppau ASV	24	4	8	12	39	60	0.65	16
11	Andernach 1910 SV	24	6	4	14	38	61	0.62	16
12	Kurenz FSV	24	6	3	15	23	55	0.42	15
13	Gonsenheim SG	24	2	2	20	19	106	0.18	6

Kaiserslautern were the class in the SouthWest, averaging nearly six goals a game and very easily won the divisional play-off against Fortuna Freiburg, who needed a play-off to progress to the title match.

SouthWest Championship play-off

May 15, 1949 Kaiserslautern 1FC	4 - 0	Fortuna Frieburg
May 22, 1949 Fortuna Frieburg	3 - 6	Kaiserslautern 1FC

Matches marked * Kurenz - Andernach finished 1-1 but points were awarded to Andernach. Also Neuendorf - Kaiserslautern 0-0, points awarded to Kaiserslautern. Neither decision in the end affected final positions.

Kaiserslautern 1FC	1 - 0	Wormatia Worms	Mainz 05 FSV	1 - 5	Kaiserslautern 1FC
Kaiserslautern 1FC	5 - 2	Neuendorf TuS	Mainz 05 FSV	1 - 4	Wormatia Worms
Kaiserslautern 1FC	4 - 0	Pirmasens 03 FK	Mainz 05 FSV	3 - 1	Neuendorf TuS
Kaiserslautern 1FC	7 - 1	Neustadt/Wienstrasse	Mainz 05 FSV	1 - 1	Pirmasens 03 FK
Kaiserslautern 1FC	6 - 2	Ph Ludwigshafen	Mainz 05 FSV	2 - 4	Neustadt/Wienstrasse
Kaiserslautern 1FC	14 - 0	Eintracht 05 Trier	Mainz 05 FSV	1 - 1	Ph Ludwigshafen
Kaiserslautern 1FC	7 - 1	Mainz 05 FSV	Mainz 05 FSV	1 - 1	Eintracht 05 Trier
Kaiserslautern 1FC	16 - 1	Weisenau SG	Mainz 05 FSV	3 - 0	Weisenau SG
Kaiserslautern 1FC	12 - 0	Oppau ASV	Mainz 05 FSV	4 - 2	Oppau ASV
Kaiserslautern 1FC	5 - 3	Andernach 1910 SV	Mainz 05 FSV	2 - 1	Andernach 1910 SV

Kaiserslautern 1FC	9 - 1	Kurenz FSV	Mainz 05 FSV	2 - 0	Kurenz FSV
Kaiserslautern 1FC	13 - 0	Gonsenheim SG	Mainz 05 FSV	4 - 0	Gonsenheim SG
Wormatia Worms	2 - 2	Kaiserslautern 1FC	Weisenau SG	0 - 6	Kaiserslautern 1FC
Wormatia Worms	1 - 1	Neuendorf TuS	Weisenau SG	1 - 4	Wormatia Worms
Wormatia Worms	2 - 3	Pirmasens 03 FK	Weisenau SG	0 - 4	Neuendorf TuS
Wormatia Worms	3 - 1	Neustadt/Wienstrasse	Weisenau SG	3 - 3	Pirmasens 03 FK
Wormatia Worms	5 - 1	Ph Ludwigshafen	Weisenau SG	3 - 1	Neustadt/Wienstrasse
Wormatia Worms	2 - 1	Eintracht 05 Trier	Weisenau SG	1 - 0	Ph Ludwigshafen
Wormatia Worms	9 - 1	Mainz 05 FSV	Weisenau SG	4 - 3	Eintracht 05 Trier
Wormatia Worms	6 - 2	Weisenau SG	Weisenau SG	2 - 2	Mainz 05 FSV
Wormatia Worms	4 - 0	Oppau ASV	Weisenau SG	2 - 2	Oppau ASV
Wormatia Worms	1 - 1	Andernach 1910 SV	Weisenau SG	2 - 0	Andernach 1910 SV
Wormatia Worms	3 - 0	Kurenz FSV	Weisenau SG	1 - 3	Kurenz FSV
Wormatia Worms	9 - 1	Gonsenheim SG	Weisenau SG	7 - 1	Gonsenheim SG
Neuendorf TuS*	0 - 0	Kaiserslautern 1FC*	Oppau ASV	0 - 4	Kaiserslautern 1FC
Neuendorf TuS	0 - 1	Wormatia Worms	Oppau ASV	2 - 2	Wormatia Worms
Neuendorf TuS	8 - 0	Pirmasens 03 FK	Oppau ASV	0 - 2	Neuendorf TuS
Neuendorf TuS	0 - 1	Neustadt/Wienstrasse	Oppau ASV	1 - 1	Pirmasens 03 FK
Neuendorf TuS	2 - 0	Ph Ludwigshafen	Oppau ASV	1 - 3	Neustadt/Wienstrasse
Neuendorf TuS	4 - 1	Eintracht 05 Trier	Oppau ASV	1 - 1	Ph Ludwigshafen
Neuendorf TuS	5 - 1	Mainz 05 FSV	Oppau ASV	2 - 2	Eintracht 05 Trier
Neuendorf TuS	10 - 0	Weisenau SG	Oppau ASV	1 - 1	Mainz 05 FSV
Neuendorf TuS	1 - 0	Oppau ASV	Oppau ASV	3 - 2	Weisenau SG
Neuendorf TuS	5 - 0	Andernach 1910 SV	Oppau ASV	4 - 0	Andernach 1910 SV
Neuendorf TuS	3 - 0	Kurenz FSV	Oppau ASV	1 - 1	Kurenz FSV
Neuendorf TuS	10 - 0	Gonsenheim SG	Oppau ASV	7 - 0	Gonsenheim SG
Pirmasens 03 FK	2 - 0	Kaiserslautern 1FC	Andernach 1910 SV	1 - 7	Kaiserslautern 1FC
Pirmasens 03 FK	1 - 3	Wormatia Worms	Andernach 1910 SV	2 - 1	Wormatia Worms
Pirmasens 03 FK	2 - 2	Neuendorf TuS	Andernach 1910 SV	2 - 3	Neuendorf TuS
Pirmasens 03 FK	0 - 1	Neustadt/Wienstrasse	Andernach 1910 SV	2 - 5	Pirmasens 03 FK
Pirmasens 03 FK	1 - 0	Ph Ludwigshafen	Andernach 1910 SV	1 - 1	Neustadt/Wienstrasse
Pirmasens 03 FK	4 - 0	Eintracht 05 Trier	Andernach 1910 SV	3 - 3	Ph Ludwigshafen
Pirmasens 03 FK	5 - 0	Mainz 05 FSV	Andernach 1910 SV	0 - 2	Eintracht 05 Trier
Pirmasens 03 FK	6 - 1	Weisenau SG	Andernach 1910 SV	3 - 1	Mainz 05 FSV
Pirmasens 03 FK	6 - 3	Oppau ASV	Andernach 1910 SV	3 - 2	Weisenau SG
Pirmasens 03 FK	3 - 2	Andernach 1910 SV	Andernach 1910 SV	0 - 4	Oppau ASV
Pirmasens 03 FK	2 - 1	Kurenz FSV	Andernach 1910 SV	4 - 0	Kurenz FSV
Pirmasens 03 FK	4 - 1	Gonsenheim SG	Andernach 1910 SV	5 - 0	Gonsenheim SG
Neustadt/Wienstrasse	1 - 10	Kaiserslautern 1FC	Kurenz FSV	0 - 1	Kaiserslautern 1FC
Neustadt/Wienstrasse	0 - 3	Wormatia Worms	Kurenz FSV	1 - 1	Wormatia Worms
Neustadt/Wienstrasse	1 - 0	Neuendorf TuS	Kurenz FSV	0 - 3	Neuendorf TuS
Neustadt/Wienstrasse	1 - 1	Pirmasens 03 FK	Kurenz FSV	3 - 2	Pirmasens 03 FK
Neustadt/Wienstrasse	2 - 1	Ph Ludwigshafen	Kurenz FSV	0 - 1	Neustadt/Wienstrasse
Neustadt/Wienstrasse	2 - 1	Eintracht 05 Trier	Kurenz FSV	0 - 2	Ph Ludwigshafen
Neustadt/Wienstrasse	2 - 0	Mainz 05 FSV	Kurenz FSV	1 - 0	Eintracht 05 Trier
Neustadt/Wienstrasse	3 - 1	Weisenau SG	Kurenz FSV	2 - 0	Mainz 05 FSV
Neustadt/Wienstrasse	2 - 1	Oppau ASV	Kurenz FSV	1 - 4	Weisenau SG
Neustadt/Wienstrasse	3 - 1	Andernach 1910 SV	Kurenz FSV	2 - 1	Oppau ASV
Neustadt/Wienstrasse	7 - 1	Kurenz FSV	Kurenz FSV*	1 - 1	Andernach 1910 SV*
Neustadt/Wienstrasse	2 - 0	Gonsenheim SG	Kurenz FSV	2 - 1	Gonsenheim SG
Ph Ludwigshafen	1 - 0	Kaiserslautern 1FC	Gonsenheim SG	2 - 3	Kaiserslautern 1FC
Ph Ludwigshafen	1 - 1	Wormatia Worms	Gonsenheim SG	0 - 3	Wormatia Worms

Ph Ludwigshafen	2	-	3	Neuendorf TuS	Gonsenheim SG	1	- 4	Neuendorf TuS
Ph Ludwigshafen	0	-	2	Pirmasens 03 FK	Gonsenheim SG	1	- 2	Pirmasens 03 FK
Ph Ludwigshafen	1	-	0	Neustadt/Wienstrasse	Gonsenheim SG	2	- 3	Neustadt/Wienstrasse
Ph Ludwigshafen	5	-	2	Eintracht 05 Trier	Gonsenheim SG	1	- 1	Ph Ludwigshafen
Ph Ludwigshafen	8	-	2	Mainz 05 FSV	Gonsenheim SG	0	- 4	Eintracht 05 Trier
Ph Ludwigshafen	4	-	0	Weisenau SG	Gonsenheim SG	0	- 2	Mainz 05 FSV
Ph Ludwigshafen	2	-	2	Oppau ASV	Gonsenheim SG	1	- 4	Weisenau SG
Ph Ludwigshafen	2	-	2	Andernach 1910 SV	Gonsenheim SG	2	- 1	Oppau ASV
Ph Ludwigshafen	3	-	1	Kurenz FSV	Gonsenheim SG	2	- 0	Andernach 1910 SV
Ph Ludwigshafen	6	-	2	Gonsenheim SG	Gonsenheim SG	1	- 1	Kurenz FSV
Eintracht 05 Trier	1	-	5	Kaiserslautern 1FC				
Eintracht 05 Trier	0	-	5	Wormatia Worms				
Eintracht 05 Trier	0	-	2	Neuendorf TuS				
Eintracht 05 Trier	1	-	2	Pirmasens 03 FK				
Eintracht 05 Trier	2	-	1	Neustadt/Wienstrasse				
Eintracht 05 Trier	4	-	2	Ph Ludwigshafen				
Eintracht 05 Trier	3	-	3	Mainz 05 FSV				
Eintracht 05 Trier	1	-	1	Weisenau SG				
Eintracht 05 Trier	4	-	0	Oppau ASV				
Eintracht 05 Trier	2	-	1	Andernach 1910 SV				
Eintracht 05 Trier	2	-	1	Kurenz FSV				
Eintracht 05 Trier	9	-	0	Gonsenheim SG				

	SouthWest South	Pld	W	D	L	F	A	GA	Pts
1	Fortuna Frieburg	22	13	5	4	49	28	1.75	31
2	Tubinger SV 03	22	12	7	3	48	25	1.92	31
3	Villingen ASV	22	10	6	6	37	28	1.32	26
4	Eintracht Singen	22	10	4	8	34	22	1.55	24
5	Fortuna Rastatt	22	10	3	9	53	54	0.98	23
6	Reulingen 1946 SSV	22	7	8	7	34	26	1.31	22
7	Schwenningen Vfl	22	7	7	8	31	40	0.78	21
8	Konstanz Vfl	22	7	6	9	40	37	1.08	20
9	Freiburg Vfl	22	8	4	10	31	39	0.79	20
10	Friedrichshafen SG	22	8	4	10	40	51	0.78	20
11	Biberach/Riss SV	22	5	6	11	32	52	0.62	16
12	Offenburger SV	22	2	6	14	26	53	0.49	10

Championship play-off Tubinger SV 03   0 - 6 Fortuna Frieburg

Fortuna Frieburg	2	-	2	Tubinger SV 03	Schwenningen Vfl	2	- 0	Fortuna Frieburg
Fortuna Frieburg	1	-	1	Villingen ASV	Schwenningen Vfl	2	- 0	Tubinger SV 03
Fortuna Frieburg	1	-	0	Eintracht Singen	Schwenningen Vfl	4	- 0	Villingen ASV
Fortuna Frieburg	9	-	1	Fortuna Rastatt	Schwenningen Vfl	1	- 1	Eintracht Singen

Fortuna Frieburg	1	-	2	Reulingen 1946 SSV	Schwenningen Vfl	6	-	0	Fortuna Rastatt
Fortuna Frieburg	5	-	0	Schwenningen Vfl	Schwenningen Vfl	1	-	1	Reulingen 1946 SSV
Fortuna Frieburg	1	-	0	Konstanz Vfl	Schwenningen Vfl	1	-	1	Konstanz Vfl
Fortuna Frieburg	2	-	2	Freiburg Vfl	Schwenningen Vfl	2	-	2	Freiburg Vfl
Fortuna Frieburg	4	-	2	Friedrichshafen SG	Schwenningen Vfl	5	-	3	Friedrichshafen SG
Fortuna Frieburg	3	-	0	Biberach/Riss SV	Schwenningen Vfl	3	-	2	Biberach/Riss SV
Fortuna Frieburg	2	-	0	Offenburger SV	Schwenningen Vfl	1	-	0	Offenburger SV
Tubinger SV 03	2	-	0	Fortuna Frieburg	Konstanz Vfl	4	-	1	Fortuna Frieburg
Tubinger SV 03	1	-	1	Villingen ASV	Konstanz Vfl	3	-	3	Tubinger SV 03
Tubinger SV 03	2	-	1	Eintracht Singen	Konstanz Vfl	0	-	2	Villingen ASV
Tubinger SV 03	0	-	0	Fortuna Rastatt	Konstanz Vfl	1	-	0	Eintracht Singen
Tubinger SV 03	0	-	0	Reulingen 1946 SSV	Konstanz Vfl	4	-	0	Fortuna Rastatt
Tubinger SV 03	6	-	0	Schwenningen Vfl	Konstanz Vfl	1	-	4	Reulingen 1946 SSV
Tubinger SV 03	2	-	1	Konstanz Vfl	Konstanz Vfl	1	-	1	Schwenningen Vfl
Tubinger SV 03	3	-	0	Freiburg Vfl	Konstanz Vfl	3	-	1	Freiburg Vfl
Tubinger SV 03	2	-	0	Friedrichshafen SG	Konstanz Vfl	2	-	3	Friedrichshafen SG
Tubinger SV 03	4	-	1	Biberach/Riss SV	Konstanz Vfl	3	-	2	Biberach/Riss SV
Tubinger SV 03	5	-	0	Offenburger SV	Konstanz Vfl	8	-	3	Offenburger SV
Villingen ASV	0	-	2	Fortuna Frieburg	Freiburg Vfl	0	-	1	Fortuna Frieburg
Villingen ASV	0	-	2	Tubinger SV 03	Freiburg Vfl	3	-	0	Tubinger SV 03
Villingen ASV	3	-	2	Eintracht Singen	Freiburg Vfl	4	-	1	Villingen ASV
Villingen ASV	4	-	2	Fortuna Rastatt	Freiburg Vfl	0	-	3	Eintracht Singen
Villingen ASV	2	-	0	Reulingen 1946 SSV	Freiburg Vfl	3	-	1	Fortuna Rastatt
Villingen ASV	0	-	0	Schwenningen Vfl	Freiburg Vfl	1	-	0	Reulingen 1946 SSV
Villingen ASV	4	-	1	Konstanz Vfl	Freiburg Vfl	1	-	0	Schwenningen Vfl
Villingen ASV	3	-	0	Freiburg Vfl	Freiburg Vfl	2	-	2	Konstanz Vfl
Villingen ASV	3	-	2	Friedrichshafen SG	Freiburg Vfl	1	-	2	Friedrichshafen SG
Villingen ASV	6	-	0	Biberach/Riss SV	Freiburg Vfl	0	-	1	Biberach/Riss SV
Villingen ASV	0	-	0	Offenburger SV	Freiburg Vfl	4	-	3	Offenburger SV
Eintracht Singen	2	-	2	Fortuna Frieburg	Friedrichshafen SG	1	-	2	Fortuna Frieburg
Eintracht Singen	0	-	1	Tubinger SV 03	Friedrichshafen SG	1	-	4	Tubinger SV 03
Eintracht Singen	2	-	1	Villingen ASV	Friedrichshafen SG	1	-	1	Villingen ASV
Eintracht Singen	6	-	0	Fortuna Rastatt	Friedrichshafen SG	0	-	1	Eintracht Singen
Eintracht Singen	1	-	2	Reulingen 1946 SSV	Friedrichshafen SG	3	-	2	Fortuna Rastatt
Eintracht Singen	3	-	0	Schwenningen Vfl	Friedrichshafen SG	2	-	1	Reulingen 1946 SSV
Eintracht Singen	1	-	0	Konstanz Vfl	Friedrichshafen SG	4	-	1	Schwenningen Vfl
Eintracht Singen	2	-	3	Freiburg Vfl	Friedrichshafen SG	1	-	0	Konstanz Vfl
Eintracht Singen	2	-	0	Friedrichshafen SG	Friedrichshafen SG	1	-	1	Freiburg Vfl
Eintracht Singen	2	-	1	Biberach/Riss SV	Friedrichshafen SG	2	-	3	Biberach/Riss SV
Eintracht Singen	2	-	1	Offenburger SV	Friedrichshafen SG	3	-	2	Offenburger SV
Fortuna Rastatt	3	-	4	Fortuna Frieburg	Biberach/Riss SV	2	-	3	Fortuna Frieburg
Fortuna Rastatt	4	-	1	Tubinger SV 03	Biberach/Riss SV	1	-	3	Tubinger SV 03
Fortuna Rastatt	4	-	0	Villingen ASV	Biberach/Riss SV	0	-	4	Villingen ASV
Fortuna Rastatt	0	-	0	Eintracht Singen	Biberach/Riss SV	2	-	1	Eintracht Singen
Fortuna Rastatt	5	-	1	Reulingen 1946 SSV	Biberach/Riss SV	3	-	3	Fortuna Rastatt
Fortuna Rastatt	5	-	0	Schwenningen Vfl	Biberach/Riss SV	1	-	1	Reulingen 1946 SSV
Fortuna Rastatt	3	-	1	Konstanz Vfl	Biberach/Riss SV	0	-	0	Schwenningen Vfl
Fortuna Rastatt	3	-	1	Freiburg Vfl	Biberach/Riss SV	1	-	3	Konstanz Vfl
Fortuna Rastatt	8	-	2	Friedrichshafen SG	Biberach/Riss SV	3	-	1	Freiburg Vfl
Fortuna Rastatt	3	-	1	Biberach/Riss SV	Biberach/Riss SV	3	-	3	Friedrichshafen SG
Fortuna Rastatt	2	-	1	Offenburger SV	Biberach/Riss SV	2	-	2	Offenburger SV
Reulingen 1946 SSV	2	-	2	Fortuna Frieburg	Offenburger SV	0	-	1	Fortuna Frieburg

Reulingen 1946 SSV	3	-	3	Tubinger SV 03	Offenburger SV	2	-	2	Tubinger SV 03
Reulingen 1946 SSV	0	-	0	Villingen ASV	Offenburger SV	0	-	1	Villingen ASV
Reulingen 1946 SSV	1	-	2	Eintracht Singen	Offenburger SV	0	-	0	Eintracht Singen
Reulingen 1946 SSV	2	-	0	Fortuna Rastatt	Offenburger SV	2	-	4	Fortuna Rastatt
Reulingen 1946 SSV	2	-	0	Schwenningen Vfl	Offenburger SV	0	-	2	Reulingen 1946 SSV
Reulingen 1946 SSV	1	-	1	Konstanz Vfl	Offenburger SV	3	-	1	Schwenningen Vfl
Reulingen 1946 SSV	0	-	1	Freiburg Vfl	Offenburger SV	0	-	0	Konstanz Vfl
Reulingen 1946 SSV	0	-	0	Friedrichshafen SG	Offenburger SV	3	-	0	Freiburg Vfl
Reulingen 1946 SSV	1	-	2	Biberach/Riss SV	Offenburger SV	3	-	4	Friedrichshafen SG
Reulingen 1946 SSV	8	-	0	Offenburger SV	Offenburger SV	1	-	1	Biberach/Riss SV

	South	Pld	W	D	L	F	A	GA	Pts
1	Offenbach Kickers	30	21	7	2	79	29	2.72	49
2	Mannheim VfR	30	15	8	7	51	42	1.21	38
3	Bayern Munchen	30	14	7	9	61	42	1.45	35
4	Munchen 1860 TSV	30	13	8	9	61	41	1.49	34
5	Waldhof 07 SV	30	12	10	8	54	45	1.20	34
6	Stuttgart VfB	30	13	5	12	56	51	1.10	31
7	Schwaben Augsburg	30	12	6	12	49	50	0.98	30
8	Stuttgarter Kickers	30	11	8	11	53	65	0.82	30
9	Muhlburg VfB	30	10	9	11	51	45	1.13	29
10	Schweinfurt 05	30	12	5	13	46	56	0.82	29
11	Nurnberg 1FC	30	11	5	14	49	55	0.89	27
12	Frankfurt FSV	30	11	5	14	40	53	0.75	27
13	Eintracht Frankfurt	30	9	8	13	28	41	0.68	26
14	Ulm 1846 TSG	30	9	4	17	43	53	0.81	22
15	Augsburg BC	30	9	4	17	46	66	0.70	22
16	Rodelheimer FC	30	7	3	20	40	73	0.55	17

Offenbach Kickers easily won the division, though they only drew home and away with runners-up Mannheim, a portent of things to come in the National finals.

14th Place play-off   Augsburg BC   1 - 0   Ulm 1846 TSG

Offenbach Kickers	1	-	1	Mannheim VfR	Muhlburg VfB	2	-	2	Offenbach Kickers
Offenbach Kickers	3	-	1	Bayern Munchen	Muhlburg VfB	5	-	0	Mannheim VfR
Offenbach Kickers	2	-	1	Munchen 1860 TSV	Muhlburg VfB	3	-	3	Bayern Munchen
Offenbach Kickers	3	-	2	Waldhof 07 SV	Muhlburg VfB	1	-	1	Munchen 1860 TSV
Offenbach Kickers	4	-	1	Stuttgart VfB	Muhlburg VfB	1	-	1	Waldhof 07 SV
Offenbach Kickers	5	-	1	Schwaben Augsburg	Muhlburg VfB	0	-	0	Stuttgart VfB
Offenbach Kickers	3	-	0	Stuttgarter Kickers	Muhlburg VfB	0	-	1	Schwaben Augsburg

Offenbach Kickers	5	-	0	Muhlburg VfB	Muhlburg VfB	6	-	1	Stuttgarter Kickers
Offenbach Kickers	3	-	1	Schweinfurt 05	Muhlburg VfB	0	-	0	Schweinfurt 05
Offenbach Kickers	4	-	1	Nurnberg 1FC	Muhlburg VfB	4	-	0	Nurnberg 1FC
Offenbach Kickers	1	-	0	Frankfurt FSV	Muhlburg VfB	1	-	0	Frankfurt FSV
Offenbach Kickers	5	-	0	Eintracht Frankfurt	Muhlburg VfB	1	-	1	Eintracht Frankfurt
Offenbach Kickers	1	-	0	Ulm 1846 TSG	Muhlburg VfB	3	-	0	Ulm 1846 TSG
Offenbach Kickers	2	-	2	Augsburg BC	Muhlburg VfB	5	-	0	Augsburg BC
Offenbach Kickers	5	-	0	Rodelheimer FC	Muhlburg VfB	2	-	1	Rodelheimer FC
Mannheim VfR	1	-	1	Offenbach Kickers	Schweinfurt 05	0	-	2	Offenbach Kickers
Mannheim VfR	1	-	1	Bayern Munchen	Schweinfurt 05	3	-	0	Mannheim VfR
Mannheim VfR	1	-	0	Munchen 1860 TSV	Schweinfurt 05	1	-	0	Bayern Munchen
Mannheim VfR	1	-	1	Waldhof 07 SV	Schweinfurt 05	6	-	3	Munchen 1860 TSV
Mannheim VfR	4	-	1	Stuttgart VfB	Schweinfurt 05	4	-	0	Waldhof 07 SV
Mannheim VfR	4	-	0	Schwaben Augsburg	Schweinfurt 05	3	-	2	Stuttgart VfB
Mannheim VfR	1	-	1	Stuttgarter Kickers	Schweinfurt 05	0	-	1	Schwaben Augsburg
Mannheim VfR	1	-	2	Muhlburg VfB	Schweinfurt 05	2	-	2	Stuttgarter Kickers
Mannheim VfR	3	-	0	Schweinfurt 05	Schweinfurt 05	3	-	0	Muhlburg VfB
Mannheim VfR	3	-	3	Nurnberg 1FC	Schweinfurt 05	1	-	1	Nurnberg 1FC
Mannheim VfR	3	-	1	Frankfurt FSV	Schweinfurt 05	2	-	4	Frankfurt FSV
Mannheim VfR	1	-	0	Eintracht Frankfurt	Schweinfurt 05	3	-	0	Eintracht Frankfurt
Mannheim VfR	6	-	2	Ulm 1846 TSG	Schweinfurt 05	2	-	1	Ulm 1846 TSG
Mannheim VfR	1	-	0	Augsburg BC	Schweinfurt 05	3	-	2	Augsburg BC
Mannheim VfR	2	-	0	Rodelheimer FC	Schweinfurt 05	0	-	2	Rodelheimer FC
Bayern Munchen	0	-	1	Offenbach Kickers	Nurnberg 1FC	8	-	1	Offenbach Kickers
Bayern Munchen	7	-	0	Mannheim VfR	Nurnberg 1FC	1	-	3	Mannheim VfR
Bayern Munchen	1	-	0	Munchen 1860 TSV	Nurnberg 1FC	2	-	2	Bayern Munchen
Bayern Munchen	3	-	2	Waldhof 07 SV	Nurnberg 1FC	3	-	0	Munchen 1860 TSV
Bayern Munchen	0	-	1	Stuttgart VfB	Nurnberg 1FC	0	-	1	Waldhof 07 SV
Bayern Munchen	3	-	0	Schwaben Augsburg	Nurnberg 1FC	3	-	2	Stuttgart VfB
Bayern Munchen	4	-	2	Stuttgarter Kickers	Nurnberg 1FC	0	-	2	Schwaben Augsburg
Bayern Munchen	2	-	0	Muhlburg VfB	Nurnberg 1FC	3	-	2	Stuttgarter Kickers
Bayern Munchen	1	-	1	Schweinfurt 05	Nurnberg 1FC	1	-	0	Muhlburg VfB
Bayern Munchen	2	-	1	Nurnberg 1FC	Nurnberg 1FC	2	-	1	Schweinfurt 05
Bayern Munchen	1	-	1	Frankfurt FSV	Nurnberg 1FC	2	-	1	Frankfurt FSV
Bayern Munchen	4	-	0	Eintracht Frankfurt	Nurnberg 1FC	1	-	1	Eintracht Frankfurt
Bayern Munchen	1	-	3	Ulm 1846 TSG	Nurnberg 1FC	4	-	1	Ulm 1846 TSG
Bayern Munchen	4	-	1	Augsburg BC	Nurnberg 1FC	3	-	0	Augsburg BC
Bayern Munchen	5	-	3	Rodelheimer FC	Nurnberg 1FC	3	-	2	Rodelheimer FC
Munchen 1860 TSV	1	-	1	Offenbach Kickers	Frankfurt FSV	0	-	0	Offenbach Kickers
Munchen 1860 TSV	3	-	1	Mannheim VfR	Frankfurt FSV	1	-	2	Mannheim VfR
Munchen 1860 TSV	0	-	2	Bayern Munchen	Frankfurt FSV	0	-	2	Bayern Munchen
Munchen 1860 TSV	1	-	1	Waldhof 07 SV	Frankfurt FSV	0	-	2	Munchen 1860 TSV
Munchen 1860 TSV	4	-	1	Stuttgart VfB	Frankfurt FSV	4	-	2	Waldhof 07 SV
Munchen 1860 TSV	5	-	0	Schwaben Augsburg	Frankfurt FSV	2	-	0	Stuttgart VfB
Munchen 1860 TSV	5	-	1	Stuttgarter Kickers	Frankfurt FSV	2	-	0	Schwaben Augsburg
Munchen 1860 TSV	4	-	4	Muhlburg VfB	Frankfurt FSV	2	-	2	Stuttgarter Kickers
Munchen 1860 TSV	4	-	1	Schweinfurt 05	Frankfurt FSV	2	-	1	Muhlburg VfB
Munchen 1860 TSV	2	-	1	Nurnberg 1FC	Frankfurt FSV	0	-	3	Schweinfurt 05
Munchen 1860 TSV	6	-	0	Frankfurt FSV	Frankfurt FSV	1	-	0	Nurnberg 1FC
Munchen 1860 TSV	3	-	1	Eintracht Frankfurt	Frankfurt FSV	2	-	0	Eintracht Frankfurt
Munchen 1860 TSV	1	-	2	Ulm 1846 TSG	Frankfurt FSV	2	-	0	Ulm 1846 TSG
Munchen 1860 TSV	2	-	1	Augsburg BC	Frankfurt FSV	3	-	1	Augsburg BC

Munchen 1860 TSV	0	-	0	Rodelheimer FC	Frankfurt FSV	1	-	0	Rodelheimer FC
Waldhof 07 SV	2	-	2	Offenbach Kickers	Eintracht Frankfurt	1	-	3	Offenbach Kickers
Waldhof 07 SV	1	-	2	Mannheim VfR	Eintracht Frankfurt	1	-	0	Mannheim VfR
Waldhof 07 SV	3	-	1	Bayern Munchen	Eintracht Frankfurt	4	-	1	Bayern Munchen
Waldhof 07 SV	2	-	1	Munchen 1860 TSV	Eintracht Frankfurt	1	-	1	Munchen 1860 TSV
Waldhof 07 SV	2	-	3	Stuttgart VfB	Eintracht Frankfurt	1	-	0	Waldhof 07 SV
Waldhof 07 SV	1	-	1	Schwaben Augsburg	Eintracht Frankfurt	0	-	0	Stuttgart VfB
Waldhof 07 SV	4	-	1	Stuttgarter Kickers	Eintracht Frankfurt	2	-	2	Schwaben Augsburg
Waldhof 07 SV	2	-	2	Muhlburg VfB	Eintracht Frankfurt	0	-	0	Stuttgarter Kickers
Waldhof 07 SV	0	-	0	Schweinfurt 05	Eintracht Frankfurt	0	-	1	Muhlburg VfB
Waldhof 07 SV	2	-	0	Nurnberg 1FC	Eintracht Frankfurt	2	-	0	Schweinfurt 05
Waldhof 07 SV	2	-	2	Frankfurt FSV	Eintracht Frankfurt	0	-	0	Nurnberg 1FC
Waldhof 07 SV	2	-	0	Eintracht Frankfurt	Eintracht Frankfurt	3	-	2	Frankfurt FSV
Waldhof 07 SV	3	-	1	Ulm 1846 TSG	Eintracht Frankfurt	3	-	0	Ulm 1846 TSG
Waldhof 07 SV	6	-	3	Augsburg BC	Eintracht Frankfurt	0	-	2	Augsburg BC
Waldhof 07 SV	3	-	2	Rodelheimer FC	Eintracht Frankfurt	2	-	1	Rodelheimer FC
Stuttgart VfB	0	-	1	Offenbach Kickers	Ulm 1846 TSG	1	-	3	Offenbach Kickers
Stuttgart VfB	3	-	1	Mannheim VfR	Ulm 1846 TSG	0	-	0	Mannheim VfR
Stuttgart VfB	2	-	1	Bayern Munchen	Ulm 1846 TSG	4	-	1	Bayern Munchen
Stuttgart VfB	2	-	0	Munchen 1860 TSV	Ulm 1846 TSG	0	-	1	Munchen 1860 TSV
Stuttgart VfB	1	-	0	Waldhof 07 SV	Ulm 1846 TSG	1	-	1	Waldhof 07 SV
Stuttgart VfB	1	-	1	Schwaben Augsburg	Ulm 1846 TSG	1	-	1	Stuttgart VfB
Stuttgart VfB	2	-	3	Stuttgarter Kickers	Ulm 1846 TSG	0	-	0	Schwaben Augsburg
Stuttgart VfB	1	-	0	Muhlburg VfB	Ulm 1846 TSG	0	-	2	Stuttgarter Kickers
Stuttgart VfB	9	-	0	Schweinfurt 05	Ulm 1846 TSG	2	-	0	Muhlburg VfB
Stuttgart VfB	3	-	2	Nurnberg 1FC	Ulm 1846 TSG	6	-	1	Schweinfurt 05
Stuttgart VfB	4	-	2	Frankfurt FSV	Ulm 1846 TSG	4	-	0	Nurnberg 1FC
Stuttgart VfB	1	-	1	Eintracht Frankfurt	Ulm 1846 TSG	6	-	0	Frankfurt FSV
Stuttgart VfB	3	-	1	Ulm 1846 TSG	Ulm 1846 TSG	1	-	0	Eintracht Frankfurt
Stuttgart VfB	4	-	3	Augsburg BC	Ulm 1846 TSG	3	-	0	Augsburg BC
Stuttgart VfB	3	-	1	Rodelheimer FC	Ulm 1846 TSG	1	-	2	Rodelheimer FC
Schwaben Augsburg	0	-	3	Offenbach Kickers	Augsburg BC	1	-	2	Offenbach Kickers
Schwaben Augsburg	0	-	3	Mannheim VfR	Augsburg BC	1	-	2	Mannheim VfR
Schwaben Augsburg	1	-	1	Bayern Munchen	Augsburg BC	0	-	0	Bayern Munchen
Schwaben Augsburg	1	-	3	Munchen 1860 TSV	Augsburg BC	1	-	4	Munchen 1860 TSV
Schwaben Augsburg	0	-	2	Waldhof 07 SV	Augsburg BC	1	-	2	Waldhof 07 SV
Schwaben Augsburg	3	-	2	Stuttgart VfB	Augsburg BC	4	-	2	Stuttgart VfB
Schwaben Augsburg	7	-	0	Stuttgarter Kickers	Augsburg BC	0	-	4	Schwaben Augsburg
Schwaben Augsburg	5	-	2	Muhlburg VfB	Augsburg BC	5	-	2	Stuttgarter Kickers
Schwaben Augsburg	1	-	2	Schweinfurt 05	Augsburg BC	1	-	0	Muhlburg VfB
Schwaben Augsburg	3	-	0	Nurnberg 1FC	Augsburg BC	2	-	1	Schweinfurt 05
Schwaben Augsburg	3	-	0	Frankfurt FSV	Augsburg BC	0	-	2	Nurnberg 1FC
Schwaben Augsburg	1	-	0	Eintracht Frankfurt	Augsburg BC	1	-	1	Frankfurt FSV
Schwaben Augsburg	3	-	0	Ulm 1846 TSG	Augsburg BC	2	-	0	Eintracht Frankfurt
Schwaben Augsburg	2	-	3	Augsburg BC	Augsburg BC	2	-	1	Ulm 1846 TSG
Schwaben Augsburg	1	-	1	Rodelheimer FC	Augsburg BC	4	-	1	Rodelheimer FC
Stuttgarter Kickers	1	-	0	Offenbach Kickers	Rodelheimer FC	0	-	10	Offenbach Kickers
Stuttgarter Kickers	1	-	1	Mannheim VfR	Rodelheimer FC	1	-	2	Mannheim VfR
Stuttgarter Kickers	0	-	4	Bayern Munchen	Rodelheimer FC	2	-	3	Bayern Munchen
Stuttgarter Kickers	2	-	2	Munchen 1860 TSV	Rodelheimer FC	1	-	1	Munchen 1860 TSV
Stuttgarter Kickers	2	-	2	Waldhof 07 SV	Rodelheimer FC	1	-	2	Waldhof 07 SV
Stuttgarter Kickers	2	-	1	Stuttgart VfB	Rodelheimer FC	2	-	0	Stuttgart VfB

Stuttgarter Kickers	1 - 3	Schwaben Augsburg	Rodelheimer FC	4 - 2	Schwaben Augsburg
Stuttgarter Kickers	4 - 0	Muhlburg VfB	Rodelheimer FC	1 - 2	Stuttgarter Kickers
Stuttgarter Kickers	3 - 0	Schweinfurt 05	Rodelheimer FC	1 - 5	Muhlburg VfB
Stuttgarter Kickers	3 - 1	Nurnberg 1FC	Rodelheimer FC	0 - 2	Schweinfurt 05
Stuttgarter Kickers	3 - 1	Frankfurt FSV	Rodelheimer FC	4 - 1	Nurnberg 1FC
Stuttgarter Kickers	1 - 2	Eintracht Frankfurt	Rodelheimer FC	0 - 3	Frankfurt FSV
Stuttgarter Kickers	6 - 1	Ulm 1846 TSG	Rodelheimer FC	0 - 2	Eintracht Frankfurt
Stuttgarter Kickers	0 - 0	Augsburg BC	Rodelheimer FC	1 - 0	Ulm 1846 TSG
Stuttgarter Kickers	3 - 2	Rodelheimer FC	Rodelheimer FC	4 - 3	Augsburg BC

	Berlin	Pld	W	D	L	F	A	GA	Pts
1	Berliner SV 92	22	17	3	2	54	23	2.35	37
2	Tennis Borussia Berlin	22	14	5	3	52	16	3.25	33
3	Union Oberschoneweide	22	14	4	4	54	28	1.93	32
4	Alemannia 90 Berlin	22	12	5	5	58	48	1.21	29
5	Viktoria 89 Berlin	22	11	5	6	51	47	1.09	27
6	Wacker 04 Reinickendorf	22	9	2	11	49	40	1.23	20
7	Pankow Vfb	22	5	8	9	34	47	0.72	18
8	Sudring Berlin	22	6	6	10	32	50	0.64	18
9	Tiergarten/Minerva	22	7	3	12	25	43	0.58	17
10	Kopenick SG	22	5	5	12	32	43	0.74	15
11	Spandau-Altstadt	22	4	1	17	29	47	0.62	9
12	Lichtenberg 47 SG	22	4	1	17	17	55	0.31	9

Matches marked * were awarded as losses against Spandau.

Berliner SV 92	1 - 0	Tennis Borussia Berlin	Pankow Vfb	0 - 4	Berliner SV 92
Berliner SV 92	2 - 1	U Oberschoneweide	Pankow Vfb	1 - 2	Tennis Borussia Berlin
Berliner SV 92	0 - 0	Alemannia 90 Berlin	Pankow Vfb	0 - 3	U Oberschoneweide
Berliner SV 92	5 - 0	Viktoria 89 Berlin	Pankow Vfb	2 - 6	Alemannia 90 Berlin
Berliner SV 92	3 - 0	Wacker 04	Pankow Vfb	1 - 4	Viktoria 89 Berlin
Berliner SV 92	3 - 2	Pankow Vfb	Pankow Vfb	1 - 1	Wacker 04
Berliner SV 92	1 - 0	Sudring Berlin	Pankow Vfb	1 - 1	Sudring Berlin
Berliner SV 92	3 - 0	Tiergarten/Minerva	Pankow Vfb	1 - 1	Tiergarten/Minerva
Berliner SV 92	4 - 1	Kopenick SG	Pankow Vfb	3 - 3	Kopenick SG
Berliner SV 92	1 - 0	Spandau-Altstadt	Pankow Vfb	2 - 1	Spandau-Altstadt
Berliner SV 92	0 - 3	Lichtenberg 47 SG	Pankow Vfb	1 - 0	Lichtenberg 47 SG
Tennis Borussia Berlin	3 - 0	Berliner SV 92	Sudring Berlin	1 - 5	Berliner SV 92
Tennis Borussia Berlin	3 - 0	U Oberschoneweide	Sudring Berlin	1 - 6	Tennis Borussia Berlin
Tennis Borussia Berlin	0 - 1	Alemannia 90 Berlin	Sudring Berlin	1 - 5	U Oberschoneweide
Tennis Borussia Berlin	5 - 0	Viktoria 89 Berlin	Sudring Berlin	3 - 3	Alemannia 90 Berlin
Tennis Borussia Berlin	1 - 0	Wacker 04	Sudring Berlin	1 - 1	Viktoria 89 Berlin
Tennis Borussia Berlin	1 - 1	Pankow Vfb	Sudring Berlin	1 - 0	Wacker 04
Tennis Borussia Berlin	3 - 3	Sudring Berlin	Sudring Berlin	2 - 2	Pankow Vfb
Tennis Borussia Berlin	2 - 0	Tiergarten/Minerva	Sudring Berlin	2 - 1	Tiergarten/Minerva

Tennis Borussia Berlin	4	-	0	Kopenick SG	Sudring Berlin	1	-	2	Kopenick SG
Tennis Borussia Berlin	3	-	1	Spandau-Altstadt	Sudring Berlin	w	-	1	Spandau-Altstadt
Tennis Borussia Berlin	1	-	0	Lichtenberg 47 SG	Sudring Berlin	1	-	0	Lichtenberg 47 SG
U Oberschoneweide	1	-	1	Berliner SV 92	Tiergarten/Minerva	2	-	3	Berliner SV 92
U Oberschoneweide	1	-	2	Tennis Borussia Berlin	Tiergarten/Minerva	0	-	3	Tennis Borussia Berlin
U Oberschoneweide	4	-	1	Alemannia 90 Berlin	Tiergarten/Minerva	2	-	5	U Oberschoneweide
U Oberschoneweide	4	-	0	Viktoria 89 Berlin	Tiergarten/Minerva	2	-	2	Alemannia 90 Berlin
U Oberschoneweide	1	-	2	Wacker 04	Tiergarten/Minerva	2	-	0	Viktoria 89 Berlin
U Oberschoneweide	2	-	1	Pankow Vfb	Tiergarten/Minerva	1	-	0	Wacker 04
U Oberschoneweide	3	-	1	Sudring Berlin	Tiergarten/Minerva	0	-	2	Pankow Vfb
U Oberschoneweide	5	-	2	Tiergarten/Minerva	Tiergarten/Minerva	4	-	2	Sudring Berlin
U Oberschoneweide	3	-	1	Kopenick SG	Tiergarten/Minerva	2	-	0	Kopenick SG
U Oberschoneweide	1	-	0	Spandau-Altstadt	Tiergarten/Minerva	w	-	1	Spandau-Altstadt
U Oberschoneweide	0	-	0	Lichtenberg 47 SG	Tiergarten/Minerva	4	-	1	Lichtenberg 47 SG
Alemannia 90 Berlin	2	-	4	Berliner SV 92	Kopenick SG	2	-	3	Berliner SV 92
Alemannia 90 Berlin	2	-	1	Tennis Borussia Berlin	Kopenick SG	0	-	0	Tennis Borussia Berlin
Alemannia 90 Berlin	2	-	2	U Oberschoneweide	Kopenick SG	2	-	3	U Oberschoneweide
Alemannia 90 Berlin	3	-	2	Viktoria 89 Berlin	Kopenick SG	1	-	4	Alemannia 90 Berlin
Alemannia 90 Berlin	3	-	2	Wacker 04	Kopenick SG	1	-	2	Viktoria 89 Berlin
Alemannia 90 Berlin	2	-	5	Pankow Vfb	Kopenick SG	3	-	1	Wacker 04
Alemannia 90 Berlin	2	-	2	Sudring Berlin	Kopenick SG	1	-	1	Pankow Vfb
Alemannia 90 Berlin	2	-	0	Tiergarten/Minerva	Kopenick SG	1	-	3	Sudring Berlin
Alemannia 90 Berlin	4	-	3	Kopenick SG	Kopenick SG	0	-	0	Tiergarten/Minerva
Alemannia 90 Berlin	4	-	3	Spandau-Altstadt	Kopenick SG	4	-	0	Spandau-Altstadt
Alemannia 90 Berlin	3	-	1	Lichtenberg 47 SG	Kopenick SG	3	-	0	Lichtenberg 47 SG
Viktoria 89 Berlin	3	-	3	Berliner SV 92	Spandau-Altstadt	1	-	5	Berliner SV 92
Viktoria 89 Berlin	1	-	1	Tennis Borussia Berlin	Spandau-Altstadt	1	-	1	Tennis Borussia Berlin
Viktoria 89 Berlin	2	-	2	U Oberschoneweide	Spandau-Altstadt	1	-	2	U Oberschoneweide
Viktoria 89 Berlin	4	-	0	Alemannia 90 Berlin	Spandau-Altstadt	1	-	4	Alemannia 90 Berlin
Viktoria 89 Berlin	5	-	0	Wacker 04	Spandau-Altstadt	1	-	2	Viktoria 89 Berlin
Viktoria 89 Berlin	5	-	3	Pankow Vfb	Spandau-Altstadt	3	-	0	Wacker 04
Viktoria 89 Berlin	3	-	1	Sudring Berlin	Spandau-Altstadt	1	-	2	Pankow Vfb
Viktoria 89 Berlin	4	-	1	Tiergarten/Minerva	Spandau-Altstadt	2	-	4	Sudring Berlin
Viktoria 89 Berlin	0	-	0	Kopenick SG	Spandau-Altstadt	1	-	w	Tiergarten/Minerva
Viktoria 89 Berlin	4	-	1	Spandau-Altstadt	Spandau-Altstadt	2	-	1	Kopenick SG
Viktoria 89 Berlin	3	-	0	Lichtenberg 47 SG	Spandau-Altstadt	6	-	1	Lichtenberg 47 SG
Wacker 04	0	-	1	Berliner SV 92	Lichtenberg 47 SG	1	-	2	Berliner SV 92
Wacker 04	1	-	3	Tennis Borussia Berlin	Lichtenberg 47 SG	1	-	7	Tennis Borussia Berlin
Wacker 04	2	-	3	U Oberschoneweide	Lichtenberg 47 SG	0	-	3	U Oberschoneweide
Wacker 04	5	-	2	Alemannia 90 Berlin	Lichtenberg 47 SG	1	-	6	Alemannia 90 Berlin
Wacker 04	11	-	2	Viktoria 89 Berlin	Lichtenberg 47 SG	1	-	4	Viktoria 89 Berlin
Wacker 04	2	-	2	Pankow Vfb	Lichtenberg 47 SG	1	-	3	Wacker 04
Wacker 04	3	-	1	Sudring Berlin	Lichtenberg 47 SG	2	-	0	Pankow Vfb
Wacker 04	5	-	1	Tiergarten/Minerva	Lichtenberg 47 SG	2	-	0	Sudring Berlin
Wacker 04	2	-	1	Kopenick SG	Lichtenberg 47 SG	1	-	0	Tiergarten/Minerva
Wacker 04	6	-	1	Spandau-Altstadt	Lichtenberg 47 SG	1	-	2	Kopenick SG
Wacker 04	3	-	0	Lichtenberg 47 SG	Lichtenberg 47 SG	0	-	3	Spandau-Altstadt

Greece

Once more only the three regional winners played off for the championship. Two of the six matches were awarded 2-0. Panathinaikos won the title on GA, despite having been deducted one point. Three for a win, 2 draw, 1 loss and zero for no show.

		Pld	W	D	L	F	A	GA	Pts
1	Panathinaikos AO	4	3	0	1	7	4	1.75	9
2	Olympiakos Piraeus	4	2	1	1	12	8	1.50	9
3	Aris Thessaloniki	4	0	1	3	5	12	0.42	4

Panathinaikos	3 - 2	Olympiakos Piraeus
Panathinaikos*	2 - 0	Aris Thessaloniki*
Olympiakos Piraeus*	2 - 0	Panathinaikos*
Olympiakos Piraeus	4 - 1	Aris Thessaloniki
Aris Thessaloniki	0 - 2	Panathinaikos
Aris Thessaloniki	4 - 4	Olympiakos Piraeus

Athens Region

		Pld	F	A	GD	Pts
1	Panathinaikos AO	16	40	16	24	41
2	Panionios GSS	16	33	18	15	39
3	Fostiras Tavros	16	27	17	10	36
4	Apollonas Athinas	16	25	16	9	36
5	AEK Athens	16	28	16	12	35
6	Asteras Athinas	16	16	28	-12	30
7	Esperos Kallitheas	16	13	27	-14	27
8	AO Dafnis	16	19	27	-8	26
9	Athinaikos Vironas	16	6	41	-35	16

Piraeus Region

		Pld	F	A	GD	Pts
1	Olympiakos Piraeus	14	49	13	36	41
2	Ethnikos AO	14	33	20	13	34
3	Panelefsiniakos AO	14	31	20	11	32
4	Atromitos Piraeus	14	28	27	1	27
5	Argonaftis Piraeus	14	19	20	-1	26
6	Proodeftiki Piraeus	14	24	24	0	22
7	AE Nikeas	14	19	36	-17	22
8	Aris Nikeas	14	18	61	-43	17

Thessalonika Region	Pld	F	A	GD	Pts
1 Aris Thessaloniki	10	31	11	20	25
2 PAOK Thessaloniki	10	21	9	12	25
3 Iraklis Thessaloniki	10	16	14	2	21
4 Makedonikos Neas Efkarpias	10	13	15	-2	20
5 Apollonas Kalamarias	10	14	25	-11	16
6 Megas Alexandros	10	8	29	-21	13

Hungary

Easy win for Ferencvaros with a hatful of goals too. Bottom two relegated. Next season a host of name changes.

		Pld	W	D	L	F	A	GA	Pts
1	Ferencvaros	30	26	1	3	140	36	3.89	53
2	MTK Budapest	30	18	6	6	91	38	2.39	42
3	Honved Kispest Budapest	30	19	3	8	94	46	2.04	41
4	Ujpest Dozsa	30	18	5	7	89	47	1.89	41
5	Csepel Weisz Manfred FC	30	15	5	10	67	66	1.02	35
6	Szentorinc	30	13	8	9	39	44	0.89	34
7	Vasas Budapest	30	15	2	13	68	51	1.33	32
8	MATEOSZ	30	12	5	13	67	53	1.26	29
9	Gyori ETO	30	12	5	13	56	88	0.64	29
10	Szombathely Haladas	30	11	6	13	56	60	0.93	28
11	Salgotarjan BTC	30	10	6	14	58	69	0.84	26
12	Soroksar	30	11	4	15	40	63	0.63	26
13	Tatabanya	30	9	3	18	53	87	0.61	21
14	Szeged MTE	30	7	5	18	38	80	0.48	19
15	Kistext	30	4	4	22	40	104	0.38	12
16	Goldberger	30	4	4	22	24	88	0.27	12

Ferencvaros	1 - 1	MTK Budapest	Gyori ETO	0 - 4	Ferencvaros
Ferencvaros	4 - 1	Honved Kispest	Gyori ETO	0 - 0	MTK Budapest
Ferencvaros	5 - 3	Ujpest Dozsa	Gyori ETO	4 - 0	Honved Kispest
Ferencvaros	6 - 2	Csepel Weisz	Gyori ETO	3 - 3	Ujpest Dozsa
Ferencvaros	2 - 1	Szentorinc	Gyori ETO	3 - 5	Csepel Weisz
Ferencvaros	4 - 2	Vasas Budapest	Gyori ETO	5 - 0	Szentorinc
Ferencvaros	2 - 1	MATEOSZ	Gyori ETO	2 - 1	Vasas Budapest
Ferencvaros	13 - 0	Gyori ETO	Gyori ETO	4 - 2	MATEOSZ
Ferencvaros	5 - 1	Szombathely	Gyori ETO	3 - 2	Szombathely
Ferencvaros	3 - 1	Salgotarjan BTC	Gyori ETO	1 - 0	Salgotarjan BTC
Ferencvaros	6 - 0	Soroksar	Gyori ETO	1 - 4	Soroksar
Ferencvaros	5 - 0	Tatabanya	Gyori ETO	1 - 3	Tatabanya
Ferencvaros	7 - 0	Szeged MTE	Gyori ETO	2 - 1	Szeged MTE
Ferencvaros	8 - 0	Kistext	Gyori ETO	1 - 1	Kistext
Ferencvaros	2 - 0	Goldberger	Gyori ETO	0 - 1	Goldberger
MTK Budapest	4 - 2	Ferencvaros	Szombathely	0 - 4	Ferencvaros
MTK Budapest	0 - 0	Honved Kispest	Szombathely	1 - 0	MTK Budapest
MTK Budapest	2 - 3	Ujpest Dozsa	Szombathely	3 - 3	Honved Kispest
MTK Budapest	4 - 1	Csepel Weisz	Szombathely	2 - 1	Ujpest Dozsa

MTK Budapest	3	-	3	Szentorinc	Szombathely	1	-	3	Csepel Weisz
MTK Budapest	1	-	2	Vasas Budapest	Szombathely	2	-	3	Szentorinc
MTK Budapest	3	-	0	MATEOSZ	Szombathely	2	-	1	Vasas Budapest
MTK Budapest	8	-	1	Gyori ETO	Szombathely	2	-	2	MATEOSZ
MTK Budapest	3	-	0	Szombathely	Szombathely	1	-	1	Gyori ETO
MTK Budapest	4	-	2	Salgotarjan BTC	Szombathely	0	-	3	Salgotarjan BTC
MTK Budapest	3	-	1	Soroksar	Szombathely	2	-	3	Soroksar
MTK Budapest	4	-	0	Tatabanya	Szombathely	4	-	3	Tatabanya
MTK Budapest	6	-	1	Szeged MTE	Szombathely	3	-	3	Szeged MTE
MTK Budapest	4	-	2	Kistext	Szombathely	1	-	2	Kistext
MTK Budapest	7	-	0	Goldberger	Szombathely	1	-	1	Goldberger
Honved Kispest	1	-	2	Ferencvaros	Salgotarjan BTC	1	-	7	Ferencvaros
Honved Kispest	1	-	2	MTK Budapest	Salgotarjan BTC	3	-	5	MTK Budapest
Honved Kispest	3	-	1	Ujpest Dozsa	Salgotarjan BTC	3	-	3	Honved Kispest
Honved Kispest	6	-	1	Csepel Weisz	Salgotarjan BTC	1	-	2	Ujpest Dozsa
Honved Kispest	4	-	0	Szentorinc	Salgotarjan BTC	2	-	0	Csepel Weisz
Honved Kispest	2	-	0	Vasas Budapest	Salgotarjan BTC	0	-	0	Szentorinc
Honved Kispest	5	-	1	MATEOSZ	Salgotarjan BTC	3	-	2	Vasas Budapest
Honved Kispest	11	-	3	Gyori ETO	Salgotarjan BTC	0	-	3	MATEOSZ
Honved Kispest	1	-	0	Szombathely	Salgotarjan BTC	3	-	5	Gyori ETO
Honved Kispest	5	-	1	Salgotarjan BTC	Salgotarjan BTC	1	-	7	Szombathely
Honved Kispest	6	-	0	Soroksar	Salgotarjan BTC	2	-	0	Soroksar
Honved Kispest	3	-	1	Tatabanya	Salgotarjan BTC	6	-	1	Tatabanya
Honved Kispest	7	-	0	Szeged MTE	Salgotarjan BTC	3	-	1	Szeged MTE
Honved Kispest	3	-	1	Kistext	Salgotarjan BTC	1	-	1	Kistext
Honved Kispest	7	-	0	Goldberger	Salgotarjan BTC	3	-	2	Goldberger
Ujpest Dozsa	5	-	0	Ferencvaros	Soroksar	0	-	3	Ferencvaros
Ujpest Dozsa	2	-	3	MTK Budapest	Soroksar	3	-	1	MTK Budapest
Ujpest Dozsa	1	-	2	Honved Kispest	Soroksar	5	-	2	Honved Kispest
Ujpest Dozsa	6	-	1	Csepel Weisz	Soroksar	2	-	2	Ujpest Dozsa
Ujpest Dozsa	4	-	0	Szentorinc	Soroksar	2	-	2	Csepel Weisz
Ujpest Dozsa	1	-	3	Vasas Budapest	Soroksar	1	-	3	Szentorinc
Ujpest Dozsa	2	-	2	MATEOSZ	Soroksar	0	-	5	Vasas Budapest
Ujpest Dozsa	3	-	0	Gyori ETO	Soroksar	0	-	0	MATEOSZ
Ujpest Dozsa	2	-	1	Szombathely	Soroksar	1	-	0	Gyori ETO
Ujpest Dozsa	1	-	0	Salgotarjan BTC	Soroksar	0	-	3	Szombathely
Ujpest Dozsa	5	-	2	Soroksar	Soroksar	2	-	0	Salgotarjan BTC
Ujpest Dozsa	5	-	1	Tatabanya	Soroksar	1	-	0	Tatabanya
Ujpest Dozsa	2	-	1	Szeged MTE	Soroksar	0	-	2	Szeged MTE
Ujpest Dozsa	3	-	1	Kistext	Soroksar	3	-	3	Kistext
Ujpest Dozsa	4	-	0	Goldberger	Soroksar	1	-	0	Goldberger
Csepel Weisz	3	-	1	Ferencvaros	Tatabanya	2	-	6	Ferencvaros
Csepel Weisz	1	-	0	MTK Budapest	Tatabanya	2	-	5	MTK Budapest
Csepel Weisz	3	-	2	Honved Kispest	Tatabanya	2	-	1	Honved Kispest
Csepel Weisz	2	-	5	Ujpest Dozsa	Tatabanya	1	-	2	Ujpest Dozsa
Csepel Weisz	1	-	1	Szentorinc	Tatabanya	2	-	2	Csepel Weisz
Csepel Weisz	2	-	4	Vasas Budapest	Tatabanya	0	-	3	Szentorinc
Csepel Weisz	2	-	1	MATEOSZ	Tatabanya	2	-	1	Vasas Budapest
Csepel Weisz	7	-	2	Gyori ETO	Tatabanya	3	-	1	MATEOSZ
Csepel Weisz	1	-	1	Szombathely	Tatabanya	3	-	4	Gyori ETO
Csepel Weisz	4	-	1	Salgotarjan BTC	Tatabanya	1	-	2	Szombathely
Csepel Weisz	2	-	0	Soroksar	Tatabanya	2	-	1	Salgotarjan BTC

Csepel Weisz	7	-	4	Tatabanya	Tatabanya	1 - 0	Soroksar
Csepel Weisz	2	-	0	Szeged MTE	Tatabanya	1 - 2	Szeged MTE
Csepel Weisz	3	-	1	Kistext	Tatabanya	3 - 2	Kistext
Csepel Weisz	3	-	2	Goldberger	Tatabanya	0 - 0	Goldberger
Szentorinc	0	-	5	Ferencvaros	Szeged MTE	2 - 9	Ferencvaros
Szentorinc	0	-	0	MTK Budapest	Szeged MTE	1 - 1	MTK Budapest
Szentorinc	0	-	1	Honved Kispest	Szeged MTE	1 - 2	Honved Kispest
Szentorinc	2	-	2	Ujpest Dozsa	Szeged MTE	1 - 5	Ujpest Dozsa
Szentorinc	1	-	0	Csepel Weisz	Szeged MTE	1 - 3	Csepel Weisz
Szentorinc	1	-	1	Vasas Budapest	Szeged MTE	1 - 0	Szentorinc
Szentorinc	2	-	1	MATEOSZ	Szeged MTE	2 - 2	Vasas Budapest
Szentorinc	2	-	3	Gyori ETO	Szeged MTE	1 - 2	MATEOSZ
Szentorinc	2	-	0	Szombathely	Szeged MTE	0 - 3	Gyori ETO
Szentorinc	1	-	1	Salgotarjan BTC	Szeged MTE	1 - 3	Szombathely
Szentorinc	0	-	2	Soroksar	Szeged MTE	3 - 3	Salgotarjan BTC
Szentorinc	5	-	3	Tatabanya	Szeged MTE	2 - 1	Soroksar
Szentorinc	2	-	1	Szeged MTE	Szeged MTE	1 - 1	Tatabanya
Szentorinc	2	-	0	Kistext	Szeged MTE	1 - 0	Kistext
Szentorinc	1	-	0	Goldberger	Szeged MTE	1 - 2	Goldberger
Vasas Budapest	2	-	7	Ferencvaros	Kistext	1 - 5	Ferencvaros
Vasas Budapest	2	-	1	MTK Budapest	Kistext	2 - 10	MTK Budapest
Vasas Budapest	1	-	2	Honved Kispest	Kistext	2 - 6	Honved Kispest
Vasas Budapest	2	-	1	Ujpest Dozsa	Kistext	1 - 9	Ujpest Dozsa
Vasas Budapest	3	-	1	Csepel Weisz	Kistext	1 - 1	Csepel Weisz
Vasas Budapest	0	-	1	Szentorinc	Kistext	1 - 2	Szentorinc
Vasas Budapest	4	-	3	MATEOSZ	Kistext	0 - 2	Vasas Budapest
Vasas Budapest	5	-	0	Gyori ETO	Kistext	0 - 6	MATEOSZ
Vasas Budapest	0	-	2	Szombathely	Kistext	0 - 3	Gyori ETO
Vasas Budapest	1	-	2	Salgotarjan BTC	Kistext	1 - 3	Szombathely
Vasas Budapest	1	-	2	Soroksar	Kistext	2 - 8	Salgotarjan BTC
Vasas Budapest	5	-	2	Tatabanya	Kistext	0 - 1	Soroksar
Vasas Budapest	3	-	2	Szeged MTE	Kistext	2 - 4	Tatabanya
Vasas Budapest	4	-	0	Kistext	Kistext	1 - 2	Szeged MTE
Vasas Budapest	2	-	1	Goldberger	Kistext	3 - 2	Goldberger
MATEOSZ	1	-	5	Ferencvaros	Goldberger	1 - 7	Ferencvaros
MATEOSZ	1	-	3	MTK Budapest	Goldberger	0 - 3	MTK Budapest
MATEOSZ	2	-	3	Honved Kispest	Goldberger	2 - 1	Honved Kispest
MATEOSZ	2	-	2	Ujpest Dozsa	Goldberger	1 - 2	Ujpest Dozsa
MATEOSZ	2	-	0	Csepel Weisz	Goldberger	1 - 2	Csepel Weisz
MATEOSZ	0	-	1	Szentorinc	Goldberger	0 - 0	Szentorinc
MATEOSZ	2	-	0	Vasas Budapest	Goldberger	0 - 7	Vasas Budapest
MATEOSZ	3	-	0	Gyori ETO	Goldberger	0 - 7	MATEOSZ
MATEOSZ	6	-	1	Szombathely	Goldberger	1 - 1	Gyori ETO
MATEOSZ	1	-	1	Salgotarjan BTC	Goldberger	0 - 5	Szombathely
MATEOSZ	3	-	1	Soroksar	Goldberger	0 - 2	Salgotarjan BTC
MATEOSZ	4	-	2	Tatabanya	Goldberger	3 - 2	Soroksar
MATEOSZ	3	-	1	Szeged MTE	Goldberger	2 - 3	Tatabanya
MATEOSZ	2	-	3	Kistext	Goldberger	1 - 2	Szeged MTE
MATEOSZ	3	-	0	Goldberger	Goldberger	1 - 6	Kistext

Iceland

Only four teams played the full season, two of them unbeaten! KR champions by virtue of beating Valur and Fram, while Vikingur dropped a point against Fram. However Akranes played two matches, won them both and then went home! Three out of five teams unbeaten, surely unique in league football. They were unranked officially, but for completeness they are listed fifth.

		Pld	W	D	L	F	A	GA	Pts
1	KR Reykjavik	3	2	1	0	7	1	7.00	5
2	Vikingur Reykjavik	3	1	2	0	5	4	1.25	4
3	Valur Reykjavik	4	1	0	3	5	12	0.42	2
4	Fram Reykjavik	4	0	1	3	4	9	0.44	1
5	IA Akranes	2	2	0	0	6	1	6.00	4

KR Reykjavik	1 - 1	Vikingur Reykjavik
KR Reykjavik	4 - 0	Valur Reykjavik
KR Reykjavik	2 - 0	Fram Reykjavik
Vikingur Reykjavik	3 - 2	Valur Reykjavik
Vikingur Reykjavik	1 - 1	Fram Reykjavik
Valur Reykjavik	3 - 2	Fram Reykjavik
Fram Reykjavik	1 - 3	IA Akranes
Valur Reykjavik	0 - 3	IA Akranes

Israel

League begins in 1949-1950 season

Republic of Ireland

Dundalk were early season favourites, winning the Dublin City Cup unbeaten. High-scoring Shelbourne won the Shield, but it was Drumcondra that played the second half of the season better than them all and took the title by six points, losing only one game in the League schedule. Cork United's demise in October was offset by Cork Athletic taking their place in the league.
Dundalk beat Drumcondra 2-1 in the final of the FAI Cup (see Cup section at back of this volume).

	League	Pld	W	D	L	F	A	GA	Pts
1	Drumcondra	18	12	5	1	34	23	1.48	29
2	Shelbourne	18	9	5	4	39	23	1.70	23
3	Dundalk	18	9	5	4	33	24	1.38	23
4	Shamrock Rovers	18	6	8	4	33	25	1.32	20
5	Transport Bray	18	5	8	5	35	41	0.85	18
6	Limerick	18	6	5	7	27	35	0.77	17
7	Waterford	18	7	1	10	39	34	1.15	15
8	Sligo Rovers	18	4	5	9	31	37	0.84	13
9	Cork Athletic	18	6	1	11	33	41	0.80	13
10	Bohemians Dublin	18	2	5	11	28	49	0.57	9

December 12, 1948
Limerick	3 - 2	Dundalk
Shamrock Rovers	3 - 1	Cork Athletic
Transport Bray	4 - 3	Bohemians Dublin
Waterford	1 - 2	Sligo Rovers

December 18, 1948
Shelbourne	3 - 1	Transport Bray

December 19, 1948
Bohemians Dublin	3 - 2	Waterford
Cork Athletic	2 - 0	Limerick
Dundalk	0 - 0	Drumcondra
Sligo Rovers	1 - 1	Shamrock Rovers

December 26, 1948
Sligo Rovers	3 - 1	Bohemians Dublin

December 27, 1948
Drumcondra	1 - 0	Cork Athletic
Shamrock Rovers	0 - 0	Limerick
Transport Bray	3 - 3	Dundalk
Waterford	2 - 3	Shelbourne

January 1, 1949
Bohemians Dublin	2 - 1	Shamrock Rovers

January 2, 1949
Cork Athletic	3 - 0	Transport Bray

February 26, 1949
Drumcondra	1 - 0	Dundalk

February 27, 1949
Limerick	5 - 2	Cork Athletic
Shamrock Rovers	2 - 2	Sligo Rovers
Transport Bray	2 - 2	Shelbourne
Waterford	5 - 2	Bohemians Dublin

March 6, 1949
Bohemians Dublin	1 - 2	Sligo Rovers
Cork Athletic	2 - 4	Drumcondra
Limerick	1 - 1	Shamrock Rovers

March 12, 1949
Shamrock Rovers	2 - 2	Bohemians Dublin

March 13, 1949
Drumcondra	1 - 1	Limerick
Sligo Rovers	1 - 4	Shelbourne
Transport Bray	2 - 6	Cork Athletic
Waterford	1 - 2	Dundalk

March 19, 1949
Shelbourne	0 - 0	Bohemians Dublin

March 20, 1949
Cork Athletic	0 - 2	Waterford
Drumcondra	1 - 1	Shamrock Rovers

Dundalk	4	-	0	Waterford	Dundalk	1	-	1	Sligo Rovers
Limerick	0	-	1	Drumcondra	Limerick	1	-	1	Transport Bray

Dundalk 4 - 0 Waterford
Limerick 0 - 1 Drumcondra
Shelbourne 2 - 1 Sligo Rovers
   January 8, 1949
Bohemians Dublin 0 - 6 Shelbourne
   January 9, 1949
Shamrock Rovers 2 - 3 Drumcondra
Sligo Rovers 3 - 4 Dundalk
Transport Bray 6 - 2 Limerick
Waterford 1 - 0 Cork Athletic
   January 15, 1949
Shamrock Rovers 2 - 2 Transport Bray
   January 16, 1949
Cork Athletic 3 - 1 Bohemians Dublin
Drumcondra 1 - 4 Waterford
Dundalk 1 - 1 Shelbourne
Limerick 3 - 2 Sligo Rovers
   January 22, 1949
Bohemians Dublin 2 - 3 Limerick
   January 23, 1949
Dundalk 2 - 1 Shamrock Rovers
Shelbourne 0 - 1 Cork Athletic
Sligo Rovers 0 - 1 Drumcondra
Waterford 5 - 0 Transport Bray
   January 29, 1949
Shamrock Rovers 4 - 1 Waterford
   January 30, 1949
Cork Athletic 0 - 2 Dundalk
Drumcondra 3 - 2 Bohemians Dublin
Limerick 0 - 2 Shelbourne
Transport Bray 4 - 3 Sligo Rovers
   February 5, 1949
Shelbourne 1 - 0 Shamrock Rovers
   February 6, 1949
Bohemians Dublin 1 - 4 Dundalk
Sligo Rovers 5 - 2 Cork Athletic
Transport Bray 1 - 1 Drumcondra
Waterford 1 - 2 Limerick
   February 12, 1949
Shelbourne 3 - 4 Drumcondra
   February 13, 1949
Bohemians Dublin 2 - 2 Transport Bray
Cork Athletic 3 - 4 Shamrock Rovers
Dundalk 2 - 1 Limerick
Sligo Rovers 0 - 3 Waterford

Dundalk 1 - 1 Sligo Rovers
Limerick 1 - 1 Transport Bray
   March 26, 1949
Bohemians Dublin 2 - 2 Cork Athletic
   March 27, 1949
Sligo Rovers 1 - 1 Limerick
Transport Bray 1 - 1 Shamrock Rovers
   April 2, 1949
Drumcondra 2 - 1 Sligo Rovers
   April 3, 1949
Cork Athletic 2 - 5 Shelbourne
Limerick 2 - 1 Bohemians Dublin
Shamrock Rovers 3 - 0 Dundalk
Transport Bray 2 - 0 Waterford
   April 10, 1949
Waterford 2 - 3 Drumcondra
   April 13, 1949
Drumcondra 2 - 2 Shelbourne
   April 16, 1949
Bohemians Dublin 1 - 3 Drumcondra
   April 17, 1949
Dundalk 2 - 1 Cork Athletic
Sligo Rovers 1 - 1 Transport Bray
Waterford 2 - 3 Shamrock Rovers
   April 18, 1949
Shelbourne 3 - 1 Limerick
   April 19, 1949
Dundalk 1 - 2 Transport Bray
   April 21, 1949
Shelbourne 0 - 1 Dundalk
   April 23, 1949
Drumcondra 2 - 1 Transport Bray
Dundalk 2 - 2 Bohemians Dublin
Shamrock Rovers 2 - 0 Shelbourne
   April 24, 1949
Cork Athletic 3 - 2 Sligo Rovers
Limerick 1 - 5 Waterford
   April 28, 1949
Shelbourne 2 - 2 Waterford

	Dublin City Cup	Pld	W	D	L	F	A	GA	Pts
1	Dundalk	9	6	3	0	27	7	3.86	15
2	Shamrock Rovers	9	7	0	2	22	14	1.57	14
3	Drumcondra	9	5	2	2	20	10	2.00	12
4	Transport Bray	9	3	4	2	18	14	1.29	10
5	Sligo Rovers	9	4	1	4	20	17	1.18	9
6	Waterford	9	4	1	4	16	24	0.67	9
7	Shelbourne	9	3	2	4	20	17	1.18	8
8	Cork United	9	3	1	5	19	26	0.73	7
9	Limerick	9	1	2	6	13	23	0.57	4
10	Bohemians Dublin	9	1	0	8	8	31	0.26	2

August 21, 1948
Shelbourne 1 - 2 Drumcondra
August 22, 1948
Transport Bray 3 - 0 Bohemians Dublin
Shamrock Rovers 4 - 1 Cork United
Limerick 2 - 2 Dundalk
Waterford 2 - 1 Sligo Rovers
August 25, 1948
Dundalk 0 - 0 Drumcondra
Cork United 2 - 1 Limerick
Sligo Rovers 1 - 2 Shamrock Rovers
Bohemians Dublin 0 - 2 Waterford
August 26, 1948
Shelbourne 0 - 1 Transport Bray
August 28, 1948
Shamrock Rovers 2 - 1 Limerick
August 29, 1948
Sligo Rovers 5 - 2 Bohemians Dublin
Drumcondra 6 - 1 Cork United
Transport Bray 1 - 2 Dundalk
Waterford 2 - 0 Shelbourne
September 2, 1948
Waterford 2 - 2 Transport Bray
September 4, 1948
Bohemians Dublin 0 - 3 Shamrock Rovers
September 5, 1948
Limerick 2 - 1 Drumcondra
Shelbourne 4 - 1 Sligo Rovers
Cork United 3 - 3 Transport Bray
Dundalk 7 - 0 Waterford
September 7, 1948
Bohemians Dublin 2 - 5 Shelbourne
September 8, 1948
Shamrock Rovers 1 - 2 Drumcondra

September 9, 1948
Waterford 2 - 5 Cork United
September 11, 1948
Shamrock Rovers 2 - 1 Transport Bray
September 12, 1948
Cork United 5 - 0 Bohemians Dublin
Dundalk 2 - 2 Shelbourne
Limerick 2 - 4 Sligo Rovers
Drumcondra 5 - 2 Waterford
September 14, 1948
Shelbourne 5 - 0 Cork United
September 15, 1948
Sligo Rovers 2 - 0 Drumcondra
Bohemians Dublin 4 - 0 Limerick
Dundalk 5 - 0 Shamrock Rovers
September 18, 1948
Drumcondra 3 - 0 Bohemians Dublin
September 19, 1948
Cork United 1 - 2 Dundalk
Limerick 1 - 1 Shelbourne
Transport Bray 2 - 2 Sligo Rovers
Shamrock Rovers 2 - 1 Waterford
September 25, 1948
Shelbourne 2 - 6 Shamrock Rovers
September 26, 1948
Sligo Rovers 3 - 1 Cork United
Transport Bray 1 - 1 Drumcondra
Bohemians Dublin 0 - 5 Dundalk
Waterford 3 - 2 Limerick

Sligo Rovers 1 - 2 Dundalk
Transport Bray 4 - 2 Limerick

	Shield	Pld	W	D	L	F	A	GA	Pts
1	Shelbourne	8	6	1	1	22	7	3.14	13
2	Drumcondra	8	5	2	1	16	8	2.00	12
3	Transport Bray	8	5	2	1	22	18	1.22	12
4	Dundalk	8	4	1	3	19	18	1.06	9
5	Shamrock Rovers	8	2	4	2	15	12	1.25	8
6	Sligo Rovers	8	2	3	3	14	16	0.88	7
7	Bohemians Dublin	8	2	1	5	10	21	0.48	5
8	Waterford	8	1	1	6	14	19	0.74	3
9	Limerick	8	0	3	5	6	19	0.32	3
10	Cork United							withdrew	

*Cork United played two games only in the Shield before disbanding. These results are not counted in the table.

October 2, 1948
Drumcondra 4 - 0 Shelbourne
October 3, 1948
Dundalk 3 - 1 Limerick
Cork United* 1 - 0 Shamrock Rovers*
Bohemians Dublin 1 - 4 Transport Bray
Sligo Rovers 2 - 1 Waterford
October 9, 1948
Drumcondra 1 - 3 Dundalk
October 10, 1948
Waterford 4 - 0 Bohemians Dublin
Limerick* 1 - 1 Cork United*
Transport Bray 0 - 3 Shelbourne
Shamrock Rovers 2 - 2 Sligo Rovers
October 16, 1948
Shelbourne 4 - 1 Waterford
October 17, 1948
Limerick 1 - 4 Shamrock Rovers
Dundalk 4 - 5 Transport Bray
October 20, 1948
Bohemians Dublin 1 - 3 Sligo Rovers
October 23, 1948
Shamrock Rovers 2 - 2 Bohemians Dublin
October 24, 1948
Waterford 3 - 4 Dundalk
Drumcondra 0 - 0 Limerick
Sligo Rovers 0 - 1 Shelbourne
October 30, 1948
Shelbourne 4 - 1 Bohemians Dublin

October 31, 1948
Drumcondra 1 - 0 Shamrock Rovers
Dundalk 3 - 1 Sligo Rovers
Limerick 1 - 2 Transport Bray
November 7, 1948
Waterford 1 - 3 Drumcondra
Shelbourne 3 - 0 Dundalk
Sligo Rovers 2 - 2 Limerick
Transport Bray 2 - 1 Shamrock Rovers
November 13, 1948
Drumcondra 3 - 1 Sligo Rovers
November 14, 1948
Limerick 1 - 2 Bohemians Dublin
Shamrock Rovers 1 - 1 Dundalk
Transport Bray 3 - 2 Waterford
November 21, 1948
Dundalk 1 - 3 Bohemians Dublin
November 27, 1948
Bohemians Dublin 0 - 2 Drumcondra
November 28, 1948
Shelbourne 6 - 0 Limerick
Waterford 2 - 4 Shamrock Rovers
Sligo Rovers 3 - 3 Transport Bray
December 4, 1948
Shamrock Rovers 1 - 1 Shelbourne
Drumcondra 3 - 3 Transport Bray
April 20, 1949
Limerick 0 - 0 Waterford

Italy

With four games remaining, Torino's team were all on board the plane that crashed at Superga. Torino decided to play out those 4 games with their youth team. All four opponents fielded their own youth team. Torino won all four for their fourth successive title. Como and Venezia replace Modena and Livorno.

	Serie A	Pld	W	D	L	F	A	GD	Pts
1	Torino	38	25	10	3	78	34	44	60
2	Internazionale Milan	38	22	11	5	85	39	46	55
3	AC Milan	38	21	8	9	83	52	31	50
4	Juventus Turin	38	18	8	12	64	47	17	44
5	Sampdoria Genoa	38	16	9	13	74	63	11	41
6	Bologna	38	12	17	9	53	46	7	41
7	Genoa	38	14	12	12	51	51	0	40
8	Triestina	38	13	12	13	59	59	0	38
9	Lucchese	38	14	10	14	55	55	0	38
10	Fiorentina	38	15	8	15	51	60	-9	38
11	Palermo	38	14	8	16	57	58	-1	36
12	Padova	38	12	12	14	45	64	-19	36
13	Lazio Roma	38	11	12	15	60	62	-2	34
14	AS Roma	38	12	8	18	47	57	-10	32
15	Atalanta Bergamo	38	11	9	18	40	58	-18	31
16	Novara	38	12	7	19	52	74	-22	31
17	Pro Patria	38	11	8	19	51	61	-10	30
18	Bari	38	10	10	18	30	50	-20	30
19	Modena	38	9	11	18	36	49	-13	29
20	Livorno	38	9	8	21	39	71	-32	26

*April 24th – Juventus - Bologna was originally 1-2, but was awarded 2-0.
*April 30th – Inter - Torino was the last game played by Il Grande Torino.

September 19, 1948				
Bari	0	-	2	AC Milan
Bologna	1	-	2	AS Roma
Fiorentina	0	-	3	Palermo
Genoa	7	-	1	Padova
Internazionale Milan	4	-	2	Sampdoria Genoa
Lazio, Roma	0	-	4	Juventus Turin
Lucchese	3	-	1	Triestina
Modena	0	-	0	Livorno
Novara	2	-	0	Atalanta Bergamo
Torino	4	-	1	Pro Patria

January 13, 1949				
Internazionale Milan	1	-	1	Padova
January 16, 1949				
AC Milan	2	-	1	Palermo
Bari	1	-	2	Sampdoria Genoa
Fiorentina	0	-	0	Juventus Turin
Genoa	3	-	2	Livorno
Lazio, Roma	1	-	1	Padova
Modena	4	-	0	Lucchese
Novara	1	-	1	Internazionale Milan
Pro Patria	0	-	3	Bologna

September 26, 1948								
				Torino	2	-	0	Atalanta Bergamo
AS Roma	4	-	2 Triestina	Triestina	2	-	0	AS Roma
Atalanta Bergamo	3	-	2 Torino	January 23, 1949				
Bologna	2	-	0 Pro Patria	AS Roma	1	-	2	Torino
Internazionale Milan	5	-	0 Novara	Atalanta Bergamo	1	-	1	AC Milan
Juventus Turin	3	-	2 Fiorentina	Bari	1	-	1	Triestina
Livorno	2	-	2 Genoa	Bologna	0	-	0	Padova
Lucchese	1	-	0 Modena	Internazionale Milan	1	-	0	Lazio Roma
Padova	2	-	0 Lazio Roma	Juventus Turin	2	-	1	Genoa
Palermo	2	-	1 AC Milan	Livorno	0	-	2	Palermo
Sampdoria Genoa	2	-	1 Bari	Lucchese	1	-	0	Pro Patria
October 3, 1948				Novara	2	-	1	Modena
AC Milan	3	-	0 Atalanta Bergamo	Sampdoria Genoa	2	-	1	Fiorentina
Fiorentina	1	-	0 Sampdoria Genoa	January 27, 1949				
Genoa	2	-	1 Juventus Turin	AC Milan	3	-	2	Pro Patria
Lazio, Roma	2	-	2 Internazionale Milan	Torino	2	-	1	Sampdoria Genoa
Modena	1	-	1 Novara	January 30, 1949				
Padova	2	-	0 Bologna	AC Milan	3	-	0	AS Roma
Palermo	4	-	2 Livorno	Fiorentina	0	-	2	Bari
Pro Patria	0	-	2 Lucchese	Genoa	0	-	0	Bologna
Torino	4	-	0 AS Roma	Lazio, Roma	2	-	1	Lucchese
Triestina	2	-	0 Bari	Modena	2	-	0	Atalanta Bergamo
October 10, 1948				Padova	3	-	2	Novara
AS Roma	1	-	2 AC Milan	Palermo	2	-	1	Internazionale Milan
Atalanta Bergamo	2	-	0 Modena	Pro Patria	1	-	4	Sampdoria Genoa
Bari	0	-	0 Fiorentina	Torino	1	-	0	Livorno
Bologna	2	-	2 Genoa	Triestina	1	-	0	Juventus Turin
Internazionale Milan	0	-	0 Palermo	February 3, 1949				
Juventus Turin	2	-	0 Triestina	Novara	0	-	0	Juventus Turin
Livorno	0	-	2 Torino	February 6, 1949				
Lucchese	2	-	1 Lazio Roma	Bari	1	-	0	Pro Patria
Novara	2	-	1 Padova	Bologna	6	-	2	Livorno
Sampdoria Genoa	4	-	4 Pro Patria	Genoa	0	-	0	Sampdoria Genoa
October 17, 1948				Internazionale Milan	4	-	4	AC Milan
AC Milan	0	-	2 Internazionale Milan	Juventus Turin	1	-	0	Atalanta Bergamo
AS Roma	1	-	1 Lazio Roma	Lazio, Roma	0	-	0	AS Roma
Atalanta Bergamo	2	-	4 Juventus Turin	Lucchese	1	-	1	Torino
Fiorentina	2	-	0 Novara	Novara	2	-	0	Fiorentina
Livorno	1	-	1 Bologna	Padova	0	-	0	Modena
Modena	0	-	2 Padova	Palermo	4	-	0	Triestina
Pro Patria	0	-	1 Bari	February 13, 1949				
Sampdoria Genoa	5	-	1 Genoa	AS Roma	0	-	0	Bari
Torino	2	-	1 Lucchese	Atalanta Bergamo	1	-	1	Lazio Roma
Triestina	3	-	1 Palermo	Bologna	3	-	1	Novara
October 24, 1948				Fiorentina	0	-	0	Padova
AC Milan	3	-	1 Triestina	Internazionale Milan	2	-	1	Genoa
Bari	0	-	4 AS Roma	Livorno	2	-	0	Pro Patria
Genoa	4	-	1 Internazionale Milan	Lucchese	6	-	2	Palermo
Juventus Turin	1	-	2 Torino	Sampdoria Genoa	1	-	1	Modena
Lazio, Roma	1	-	1 Atalanta Bergamo	Torino	3	-	1	Juventus Turin
Modena	2	-	1 Sampdoria Genoa	Triestina	1	-	3	AC Milan
Novara	1	-	1 Bologna	February 20, 1949				

Padova	2	-	0	Fiorentina	AC Milan	4	-	0	Lucchese
Palermo	1	-	3	Lucchese	Bari	1	-	2	Internazionale Milan
Pro Patria	1	-	0	Livorno	Genoa	1	-	0	AS Roma

October 31, 1948

					Juventus Turin	5	-	1	Sampdoria Genoa
AS Roma	1	-	0	Genoa	Lazio, Roma	5	-	1	Palermo
Atalanta Bergamo	0	-	1	Pro Patria	Livorno	1	-	1	Fiorentina
Bologna	2	-	0	Modena	Modena	0	-	1	Bologna
Fiorentina	3	-	2	Livorno	Novara	3	-	0	Triestina
Internazionale Milan	9	-	1	Bari	Padova	4	-	4	Torino
Lucchese	2	-	2	AC Milan	Pro Patria	0	-	0	Atalanta Bergamo
Palermo	1	-	0	Lazio Roma					
Sampdoria Genoa	2	-	0	Juventus Turin					

March 6, 1949

Torino	3	-	1	Padova	AS Roma	2	-	1	Modena
Triestina	1	-	1	Novara	Atalanta Bergamo	0	-	1	Padova

November 4, 1948

					Bologna	1	-	1	Triestina
					Fiorentina	3	-	1	Pro Patria
AC Milan	1	-	0	Torino	Internazionale Milan	1	-	1	Juventus Turin
Genoa	1	-	1	Palermo	Lucchese	0	-	1	Livorno
Juventus Turin	0	-	1	Internazionale Milan	Palermo	3	-	0	Genoa
Lazio, Roma	1	-	1	Bari	Sampdoria Genoa	1	-	3	Novara
Livorno	0	-	0	Lucchese	Torino	4	-	1	AC Milan

March 13, 1949

Modena	2	-	2	AS Roma	AC Milan	3	-	1	Fiorentina
Novara	2	-	3	Sampdoria Genoa	Atalanta Bergamo	1	-	1	Bologna
Padova	3	-	0	Atalanta Bergamo	Genoa	2	-	1	Bari
Pro Patria	2	-	4	Fiorentina	Juventus Turin	2	-	1	Lucchese
Triestina	1	-	1	Bologna	Lazio, Roma	2	-	2	Torino

November 7, 1948

					Livorno	2	-	1	AS Roma
AS Roma	4	-	0	Livorno	Modena	2	-	3	Internazionale Milan
Bari	0	-	0	Genoa	Palermo	3	-	0	Novara
Bologna	1	-	1	Atalanta Bergamo	Pro Patria	3	-	0	Padova
Fiorentina	4	-	2	AC Milan	Triestina	3	-	1	Sampdoria Genoa

March 19, 1949

Internazionale Milan	2	-	0	Modena	Novara	1	-	2	AC Milan
Lucchese	2	-	1	Juventus Turin					

March 20, 1949

Novara	1	-	0	Palermo					
Padova	1	-	1	Pro Patria	Bari	2	-	1	Palermo
Sampdoria Genoa	1	-	1	Triestina	Fiorentina	1	-	0	Lucchese
Torino	1	-	0	Lazio Roma	Internazionale Milan	2	-	1	Pro Patria

November 14, 1948

					Lazio, Roma	5	-	1	Genoa
AC Milan	4	-	1	Novara	Modena	2	-	2	Juventus Turin
AS Roma	2	-	4	Sampdoria Genoa	Padova	2	-	1	Livorno
Atalanta Bergamo	0	-	1	Triestina	Sampdoria Genoa	2	-	0	AS Roma
Bologna	2	-	2	Torino	Torino	1	-	0	Bologna
Genoa	1	-	0	Lazio Roma	Triestina	1	-	1	Atalanta Bergamo
Juventus Turin	0	-	1	Modena					

March 27, 1949

Livorno	2	-	2	Padova					
Lucchese	4	-	0	Fiorentina	Bari	0	-	0	Lazio Roma
Palermo	3	-	0	Bari					

April 3, 1949

Pro Patria	1	-	1	Internazionale Milan	AC Milan	5	-	1	Modena

November 21, 1948

					AS Roma	1	-	1	Fiorentina
Fiorentina	3	-	1	AS Roma	Atalanta Bergamo	0	-	0	Genoa
Genoa	2	-	0	Atalanta Bergamo	Bari	2	-	1	Juventus Turin
Internazionale Milan	3	-	1	Livorno	Bologna	2	-	0	Lazio Roma
Juventus Turin	1	-	0	Bari	Livorno	0	-	2	Internazionale Milan

Lazio, Roma	8	-	2	Bologna	Lucchese	4	-	0	Padova
Modena	0	-	0	AC Milan	Pro Patria	3	-	1	Triestina
Novara	0	-	2	Torino	Sampdoria Genoa	2	-	2	Palermo
Padova	0	-	1	Lucchese	Torino	4	-	0	Novara
Palermo	1	-	1	Sampdoria Genoa					
Triestina	0	-	0	Pro Patria					

April 10, 1949

November 28, 1948

					Fiorentina	1	-	0	Bologna
					Genoa	0	-	0	Lucchese
AC Milan	1	-	1	Juventus Turin	Internazionale Milan	1	-	0	AS Roma
AS Roma	1	-	0	Internazionale Milan	Juventus Turin	1	-	1	AC Milan
Atalanta Bergamo	2	-	1	Palermo	Lazio, Roma	2	-	0	Livorno
Bari	0	-	1	Modena	Modena	0	-	0	Bari
Bologna	0	-	0	Fiorentina	Novara	1	-	1	Pro Patria
Livorno	1	-	1	Lazio Roma	Padova	1	-	3	Sampdoria Genoa
Lucchese	0	-	0	Genoa	Palermo	1	-	2	Atalanta Bergamo
Pro Patria	5	-	0	Novara	Triestina	1	-	1	Torino
Sampdoria Genoa	0	-	0	Padova					
Torino	1	-	1	Triestina					

April 17, 1949

December 5, 1948

					AC Milan	2	-	0	Padova
					AS Roma	3	-	2	Palermo
Fiorentina	2	-	0	Atalanta Bergamo	Atalanta Bergamo	2	-	1	Fiorentina
Internazionale Milan	2	-	2	Bologna	Bari	2	-	0	Novara
Juventus Turin	2	-	2	Livorno	Bologna	1	-	3	Internazionale Milan
Lazio, Roma	2	-	5	Pro Patria	Genoa	5	-	1	Triestina
Modena	0	-	1	Torino	Lucchese	3	-	1	Sampdoria Genoa
Novara	3	-	1	Bari	Pro Patria	1	-	2	Lazio Roma
Padova	1	-	4	AC Milan	Torino	3	-	1	Modena
Palermo	2	-	1	AS Roma					
Sampdoria Genoa	5	-	0	Lucchese					
Triestina	0	-	0	Genoa					

April 18, 1949

Livorno	1	-	3	Juventus Turin

December 8, 1948

April 24, 1949

AS Roma	0	-	2	Padova	AC Milan	2	-	2	Genoa
Fiorentina	1	-	1	Modena	Bari	1	-	1	Torino
Genoa	1	-	0	AC Milan	Juventus Turin	2	-	0	Bologna
Internazionale Milan	4	-	0	Lucchese	Lazio, Roma	4	-	0	Triestina
Livorno	1	-	0	Novara	Lucchese	0	-	0	Internazionale Milan
Palermo	3	-	1	Pro Patria	Novara	3	-	1	Livorno
Triestina	4	-	1	Lazio Roma	Pro Patria	1	-	0	Palermo
					Sampdoria Genoa	4	-	2	Atalanta Bergamo

December 12, 1948

April 25, 1949

AC Milan	3	-	0	Lazio Roma	Modena	1	-	2	Fiorentina
AS Roma	4	-	1	Novara	Padova	2	-	0	AS Roma

April 30, 1949

Bari	1	-	0	Padova					
Bologna	1	-	2	Sampdoria Genoa	Atalanta Bergamo	2	-	2	Lucchese
Genoa	4	-	2	Fiorentina	Fiorentina	2	-	1	Genoa
Livorno	1	-	0	Triestina	Internazionale Milan	0	-	0	Torino
Lucchese	0	-	1	Atalanta Bergamo	Juventus Turin	4	-	3	Pro Patria
Modena	4	-	0	Palermo	Lazio, Roma	2	-	3	AC Milan
Pro Patria	0	-	1	Juventus Turin	Novara	2	-	1	AS Roma
Torino	4	-	2	Internazionale Milan	Padova	1	-	0	Bari
					Palermo	0	-	0	Modena

December 19, 1948

AC Milan	2	-	2	Bologna	Sampdoria Genoa	1	-	1	Bologna
Atalanta Bergamo	1	-	2	Internazionale Milan	Triestina	5	-	4	Livorno
Bari	0	-	0	Lucchese					

May 8, 1949

Fiorentina	0	-	0	Torino
AS Roma	3	-	1	Pro Patria

Juventus Turin	3	-	2	Palermo	Bologna	3	-	1	AC Milan
Lazio, Roma	5	-	1	Modena	Genoa	0	-	4	Novara
Novara	1	-	2	Genoa	Internazionale Milan	4	-	0	Atalanta Bergamo
Padova	0	-	0	Triestina	Livorno	1	-	0	Sampdoria Genoa
Pro Patria	1	-	1	AS Roma	Lucchese	1	-	1	Bari
Sampdoria Genoa	3	-	0	Livorno	Modena	2	-	0	Lazio Roma

December 23, 1948

					Palermo	2	-	0	Juventus Turin
Atalanta Bergamo	1	-	5	Sampdoria Genoa	Triestina	9	-	1	Padova

December 26, 1948 / **May 15, 1949**

Atalanta Bergamo	0	-	2	Bari	AC Milan	2	-	0	Livorno
Bologna	1	-	0	Palermo	AS Roma	0	-	1	Juventus Turin
Genoa	3	-	0	Torino	Bari	0	-	2	Atalanta Bergamo
Juventus Turin	0	-	0	AS Roma	Fiorentina	5	-	3	Triestina
Lazio, Roma	2	-	0	Sampdoria Genoa	Novara	5	-	2	Lucchese
Livorno	2	-	1	AC Milan	Padova	1	-	3	Internazionale Milan
Lucchese	5	-	1	Novara	Palermo	0	-	0	Bologna
Modena	1	-	1	Pro Patria	Pro Patria	2	-	0	Modena
Triestina	4	-	0	Fiorentina	Sampdoria Genoa	2	-	2	Lazio Roma
					Torino	4	-	0	Genoa

December 29, 1948 / **May 29, 1949**

Bologna	3	-	0	Juventus Turin	Atalanta Bergamo	3	-	0	AS Roma

December 30, 1948

					Bologna	4	-	1	Lucchese
Torino	2	-	0	Bari	Internazionale Milan	1	-	1	Triestina

January 2, 1949

					Juventus Turin	4	-	1	Novara
AS Roma	1	-	0	Atalanta Bergamo	Lazio, Roma	2	-	1	Fiorentina
Bari	3	-	0	Livorno	Livorno	1	-	0	Bari
Fiorentina	4	-	0	Lazio Roma	Modena	2	-	0	Genoa
Genoa	1	-	0	Modena	Padova	3	-	3	Palermo
Lucchese	1	-	1	Bologna	Pro Patria	3	-	2	AC Milan
Palermo	1	-	0	Padova	Sampdoria Genoa	2	-	3	Torino
Triestina	2	-	0	Internazionale Milan					

January 6, 1949 / **June 5, 1949**

Atalanta Bergamo	4	-	2	Livorno	AC Milan	3	-	2	Sampdoria Genoa
Bari	3	-	0	Bologna	AS Roma	3	-	0	Lucchese
Internazionale Milan	7	-	1	Fiorentina	Bologna	1	-	0	Bari
Juventus Turin	6	-	1	Padova	Fiorentina	0	-	2	Internazionale Milan
Lazio, Roma	2	-	1	Novara	Genoa	0	-	2	Pro Patria
Lucchese	5	-	1	AS Roma	Livorno	0	-	2	Atalanta Bergamo
Modena	0	-	2	Triestina	Novara	2	-	2	Lazio Roma
Palermo	2	-	2	Torino	Padova	3	-	0	Juventus Turin
Pro Patria	2	-	1	Genoa	Torino	3	-	0	Palermo
Sampdoria Genoa	2	-	1	AC Milan	Triestina	1	-	2	Modena

January 9, 1949 / **June 12, 1949**

AC Milan	4	-	1	Bari	Torino	2	-	0	Fiorentina
AS Roma	1	-	1	Bologna					
Atalanta Bergamo	3	-	1	Novara					
Juventus Turin	4	-	1	Lazio Roma					
Livorno	1	-	0	Modena					
Padova	0	-	0	Genoa					
Palermo	0	-	2	Fiorentina					
Pro Patria	0	-	1	Torino					
Sampdoria Genoa	0	-	4	Internazionale Milan					
Triestina	1	-	0	Lucchese					

	Serie B	Pld	W	D	L	F	A	GD	Pts
1	Como	42	25	10	7	83	39	46	60
2	Venezia	42	21	10	11	69	44	25	52
3	Vicenza	42	21	9	12	69	48	21	51
4	Salernitana 1919	42	21	5	16	75	64	11	47
5	Brescia	42	17	11	14	61	50	11	45
6	Napoli	42	17	11	14	43	40	3	45
7	Pro Sesto San Giovanni	42	18	8	16	61	51	10	44
8	Legnano	42	17	8	17	73	66	5	42
9	Pisa	42	17	8	17	63	58	7	42
10	SPAL Ferrara	42	16	9	17	72	57	15	41
11	US Alessandria 1912	42	17	6	19	70	54	16	40
12	Hellas Verona	42	16	8	18	62	73	-11	40
13	Siracusa	42	17	6	19	55	70	-15	40
14	Arsenaltaranto	42	18	4	20	56	72	-16	40
15	Cremonese	42	16	8	18	60	78	-18	40
16	Reggiana 1919	42	18	3	21	56	56	0	39
17	Empoli	42	15	8	19	53	76	-23	38
18	Spezia	42	12	13	17	49	63	-14	37
19	Parma	42	12	13	17	42	59	-17	37
20	Lecce US	42	14	8	20	57	68	-11	36
21	Seregno	42	11	12	19	51	72	-21	34
22	Pescara	42	11	12	19	49	71	-22	34

July 10th 1949 – Play-off for relegation place Parma - Spezia 1-4, played in Milan.

September 19, 1948
Arsenaltaranto 2 - 1 US Alessandria 1912
Como 2 - 1 Pescara
Napoli 2 - 2 Cremonese
Parma 0 - 2 Legnano
Pisa 2 - 0 Brescia
Pro Sesto 1 - 0 Salernitana 1919
Seregno 2 - 0 Hellas Verona
Siracusa 6 - 2 Lecce US
SPAL Ferrara 3 - 0 Empoli
Venezia 3 - 0 Reggiana 1919
Vicenza 2 - 1 Spezia

September 26, 1948
Arsenaltaranto 2 - 3 Como
Empoli 0 - 0 Vicenza

January 23, 1949
Brescia 1 - 0 Pisa
Cremonese 0 - 0 Napoli
Empoli 1 - 0 SPAL Ferrara
Hellas Verona 1 - 0 Seregno
Lecce US 1 - 2 Siracusa
Legnano 1 - 1 Parma
Pescara 2 - 2 Como
Reggiana 1919 0 - 1 Venezia
Salernitana 1919 3 - 2 Pro Sesto
Spezia 1 - 1 Vicenza
US Alessandria 1912 9 - 0 Arsenaltaranto

January 30, 1949
Brescia 1 - 0 Spezia
Como 2 - 0 Arsenaltaranto

Hellas Verona	1	-	0	Pisa	Cremonese	3 - 0	Pescara
Lecce US	0	-	2	US Alessandria 1912	Pisa	2 - 2	Hellas Verona
Legnano	0	-	1	Salernitana 1919	Salernitana 1919	1 - 0	Legnano
Napoli	1	-	0	Venezia	Seregno	0 - 0	Reggiana 1919
Parma	4	-	3	SPAL Ferrara	Siracusa	1 - 0	Pro Sesto
Pescara	1	-	1	Cremonese	SPAL Ferrara	5 - 0	Parma
Pro Sesto	1	-	1	Siracusa	US Alessandria 1912	4 - 0	Lecce US
Reggiana 1919	4	-	0	Seregno	Venezia	3 - 2	Napoli
Spezia	2	-	0	Brescia	Vicenza	4 - 1	Empoli

October 3, 1948 | | | | | February 6, 1949 | | |

Brescia	3 - 0	Arsenaltaranto	Arsenaltaranto	3 - 1	Brescia
Cremonese	2 - 0	Hellas Verona	Como	4 - 0	Lecce US
Lecce US	1 - 0	Como	Empoli	2 - 2	Seregno
Legnano	5 - 2	Siracusa	Hellas Verona	2 - 1	Cremonese
Pescara	1 - 1	Pro Sesto	Napoli	0 - 0	SPAL Ferrara
Pisa	1 - 2	Vicenza	Parma	1 - 0	US Alessandria 1912
Salernitana 1919	2 - 0	Venezia	Pro Sesto	1 - 0	Pescara
Seregno	1 - 1	Empoli	Reggiana 1919	4 - 1	Spezia
SPAL Ferrara	1 - 0	Napoli	Siracusa	4 - 1	Legnano
Spezia	0 - 2	Reggiana 1919	Venezia	3 - 1	Salernitana 1919
US Alessandria 1912	2 - 2	Parma	Vicenza	2 - 2	Pisa

October 10, 1948 | | | February 13, 1949 | | |

Brescia	2 - 0	Pescara	Arsenaltaranto	2 - 1	Hellas Verona
Como	2 - 0	Parma	Cremonese	1 - 2	Venezia
Empoli	3 - 2	Legnano	Lecce US	4 - 1	Vicenza
Hellas Verona	3 - 1	Arsenaltaranto	Legnano	1 - 0	Empoli
Napoli	0 - 0	Spezia	Parma	0 - 0	Como
Pro Sesto	0 - 0	SPAL Ferrara	Pescara	0 - 0	Brescia
Reggiana 1919	0 - 2	US Alessandria 1912	Pisa	6 - 2	Siracusa
Salernitana 1919	1 - 0	Seregno	Seregno	2 - 1	Salernitana 1919
Siracusa	1 - 0	Pisa	SPAL Ferrara	0 - 0	Pro Sesto
Venezia	2 - 2	Cremonese	Spezia	2 - 0	Napoli
Vicenza	1 - 2	Lecce US	US Alessandria 1912	4 - 0	Reggiana 1919

October 17, 1948 | | | February 20, 1949 | | |

Arsenaltaranto	1 - 1	Pisa	Brescia	1 - 0	US Alessandria 1912
Como	1 - 2	Empoli	Empoli	0 - 0	Como
Cremonese	0 - 1	Reggiana 1919	Lecce US	3 - 1	Hellas Verona
Hellas Verona	1 - 1	Lecce US	Napoli	1 - 1	Pescara
Legnano	2 - 0	Venezia	Pisa	1 - 0	Arsenaltaranto
Parma	1 - 0	Pro Sesto	Pro Sesto	3 - 0	Parma
Pescara	1 - 1	Napoli	Reggiana 1919	2 - 0	Cremonese
Siracusa	2 - 3	Seregno	Salernitana 1919	4 - 0	Vicenza
Spezia	1 - 1	SPAL Ferrara	Seregno	4 - 0	Siracusa
US Alessandria 1912	1 - 4	Brescia	SPAL Ferrara	1 - 1	Spezia
Vicenza	3 - 0	Salernitana 1919	Venezia	1 - 1	Legnano

October 24, 1948 | | | March 6, 1949 | | |

Arsenaltaranto	1 - 0	Pescara	Como	1 - 0	Brescia
Brescia	2 - 3	Como	Hellas Verona	3 - 1	SPAL Ferrara
Cremonese	3 - 1	US Alessandria 1912	Legnano	4 - 0	Pisa
Empoli	2 - 0	Salernitana 1919	Pescara	2 - 1	Arsenaltaranto
Lecce US	1 - 1	Spezia	Pro Sesto	1 - 0	Venezia
Napoli	3 - 0	Siracusa	Reggiana 1919	1 - 1	Parma

Parma	0	-	2 Reggiana 1919	Salernitana 1919	5	-	2 Empoli
Pisa	4	-	1 Legnano	Siracusa	1	-	0 Napoli
Seregno	0	-	1 Vicenza	Spezia	1	-	1 Lecce US
SPAL Ferrara	4	-	0 Hellas Verona	US Alessandria 1912	5	-	0 Cremonese
Venezia	2	-	1 Pro Sesto	Vicenza	1	-	1 Seregno

October 31, 1948 / March 13, 1949

Como	1	-	1 Cremonese	Arsenaltaranto	1	-	0 Venezia
Empoli	1	-	0 Siracusa	Brescia	3	-	1 Reggiana 1919
Hellas Verona	1	-	1 Parma	Cremonese	1	-	3 Como
Lecce US	1	-	0 Pescara	Napoli	2	-	0 Legnano
Legnano	1	-	2 Napoli	Parma	1	-	0 Hellas Verona
Pro Sesto	3	-	1 Seregno	Pescara	2	-	1 Lecce US
Reggiana 1919	0	-	0 Brescia	Pisa	1	-	2 US Alessandria 1912
Salernitana 1919	4	-	1 Spezia	Seregno	1	-	0 Pro Sesto
US Alessandria 1912	0	-	2 Pisa	Siracusa	4	-	3 Empoli
Venezia	6	-	1 Arsenaltaranto	SPAL Ferrara	5	-	0 Vicenza
Vicenza	1	-	0 SPAL Ferrara	Spezia	2	-	3 Salernitana 1919

November 4, 1948 / March 20, 1949

Brescia	1	-	1 Legnano	Arsenaltaranto	2	-	0 Spezia
Cremonese	3	-	1 Empoli	Como	1	-	1 Seregno
Napoli	1	-	0 Lecce US	Empoli	2	-	0 Cremonese
Parma	0	-	1 Vicenza	Hellas Verona	4	-	1 US Alessandria 1912
Pescara	4	-	2 Reggiana 1919	Lecce US	2	-	3 Napoli
Pisa	3	-	2 Pro Sesto	Legnano	1	-	1 Brescia
Seregno	0	-	3 Como	Pro Sesto	1	-	0 Pisa
Siracusa	3	-	0 Salernitana 1919	Reggiana 1919	1	-	0 Pescara
SPAL Ferrara	1	-	3 Venezia	Salernitana 1919	2	-	0 Siracusa
Spezia	3	-	1 Arsenaltaranto	Venezia	1	-	0 SPAL Ferrara
US Alessandria 1912	1	-	0 Hellas Verona	Vicenza	1	-	1 Parma

November 7, 1948 / April 3, 1949

Arsenaltaranto	6	-	0 Siracusa	Empoli	4	-	1 Hellas Verona
Brescia	2	-	2 Venezia	Lecce US	3	-	1 Pro Sesto
Como	3	-	0 US Alessandria 1912	Napoli	1	-	0 Salernitana 1919
Cremonese	3	-	2 Parma	Parma	0	-	1 Cremonese
Hellas Verona	1	-	0 Empoli	Pescara	1	-	0 Spezia
Legnano	2	-	0 Vicenza	Seregno	1	-	1 Pisa
Pisa	0	-	1 Seregno	Siracusa	3	-	1 Arsenaltaranto
Pro Sesto	3	-	1 Lecce US	SPAL Ferrara	3	-	1 Reggiana 1919
Reggiana 1919	0	-	1 SPAL Ferrara	US Alessandria 1912	0	-	3 Como
Salernitana 1919	1	-	1 Napoli	Venezia	1	-	0 Brescia
Spezia	3	-	0 Pescara	Vicenza	5	-	1 Legnano

November 14, 1948 / April 10, 1949

Arsenaltaranto	0	-	0 Salernitana 1919	Brescia	2	-	1 Seregno
Empoli	1	-	0 Spezia	Como	1	-	1 Venezia
Lecce US	2	-	1 Legnano	Cremonese	1	-	0 Vicenza
Napoli	1	-	0 Reggiana 1919	Hellas Verona	2	-	1 Pescara
Parma	1	-	0 Pisa	Legnano	4	-	0 Lecce US
Pescara	4	-	1 Hellas Verona	Pisa	4	-	1 Parma
Seregno	0	-	1 Brescia	Pro Sesto	1	-	0 US Alessandria 1912
SPAL Ferrara	2	-	0 Siracusa	Reggiana 1919	1	-	0 Napoli
US Alessandria 1912	0	-	2 Pro Sesto	Salernitana 1919	2	-	1 Arsenaltaranto
Venezia	1	-	1 Como	Siracusa	2	-	1 SPAL Ferrara

Vicenza	3	-	0	Cremonese	Spezia	2 - 1	Empoli

November 21, 1948

Brescia	4	-	0	Cremonese	Arsenaltaranto	2 - 0	SPAL Ferrara
Hellas Verona	2	-	2	Como	Como	1 - 0	Hellas Verona
Lecce US	1	-	1	Venezia	Cremonese	0 - 2	Brescia
Pescara	1	-	3	Legnano	Empoli	4 - 3	Reggiana 1919
Pisa	0	-	0	Napoli	Legnano	2 - 0	Pescara
Pro Sesto	0	-	0	Vicenza	Napoli	3 - 0	Pisa
Reggiana 1919	0	-	1	Empoli	Parma	1 - 0	Siracusa
Salernitana 1919	3	-	1	US Alessandria 1912	Seregno	2 - 2	Spezia
Siracusa	3	-	1	Parma	US Alessandria 1912	2 - 0	Salernitana 1919
SPAL Ferrara	4	-	0	Arsenaltaranto	Venezia	1 - 1	Lecce US
Spezia	2	-	0	Seregno	Vicenza	0 - 0	Pro Sesto

November 28, 1948

April 24, 1949

Como	5	-	1	Pisa	Arsenaltaranto	4 - 0	Legnano
Cremonese	1	-	1	SPAL Ferrara	Brescia	3 - 1	Salernitana 1919
Empoli	4	-	0	Lecce US	Hellas Verona	4 - 3	Vicenza
Legnano	0	-	0	Arsenaltaranto	Lecce US	1 - 0	Empoli
Napoli	2	-	1	Seregno	Pescara	1 - 1	Parma
Parma	0	-	2	Pescara	Pisa	3 - 3	Como
Reggiana 1919	2	-	1	Pro Sesto	Pro Sesto	3 - 1	Reggiana 1919
Salernitana 1919	2	-	1	Brescia	Seregno	2 - 1	Napoli
Siracusa	1	-	0	US Alessandria 1912	SPAL Ferrara	4 - 1	Cremonese
Venezia	3	-	2	Spezia	Spezia	0 - 0	Venezia
Vicenza	4	-	1	Hellas Verona	US Alessandria 1912	0 - 0	Siracusa

December 5, 1948

May 1, 1949

Arsenaltaranto	1	-	0	Reggiana 1919	Cremonese	1 - 0	Pisa
Brescia	0	-	2	Vicenza	Empoli	2 - 2	Pescara
Como	3	-	0	Siracusa	Lecce US	1 - 1	SPAL Ferrara
Hellas Verona	3	-	2	Venezia	Legnano	2 - 2	Seregno
Parma	1	-	1	Salernitana 1919	Napoli	2 - 0	Pro Sesto
Pescara	7	-	0	Empoli	Reggiana 1919	4 - 0	Arsenaltaranto
Pisa	1	-	2	Cremonese	Salernitana 1919	2 - 0	Parma
Pro Sesto	0	-	0	Napoli	Siracusa	2 - 1	Como
Seregno	1	-	1	Legnano	Spezia	2 - 0	US Alessandria 1912
SPAL Ferrara	0	-	0	Lecce US	Venezia	3 - 1	Hellas Verona
US Alessandria 1912	1	-	0	Spezia	Vicenza	3 - 0	Brescia

December 12, 1948

May 8, 1949

Brescia	2	-	2	SPAL Ferrara	Brescia	3 - 0	Pro Sesto
Como	3	-	1	Vicenza	Como	4 - 0	Spezia
Cremonese	3	-	2	Salernitana 1919	Empoli	2 - 1	Arsenaltaranto
Empoli	1	-	1	Venezia	Hellas Verona	2 - 3	Legnano
Hellas Verona	3	-	2	Pro Sesto	Lecce US	6 - 0	Pisa
Lecce US	1	-	0	Arsenaltaranto	Napoli	1 - 0	Vicenza
Napoli	1	-	1	Parma	Parma	4 - 2	Seregno
Pescara	0	-	1	Pisa	Pescara	2 - 1	SPAL Ferrara
Reggiana 1919	3	-	1	Legnano	Reggiana 1919	2 - 0	Salernitana 1919
Spezia	2	-	2	Siracusa	Siracusa	2 - 1	Cremonese
US Alessandria 1912	4	-	1	Seregno	US Alessandria 1912	5 - 0	Venezia

December 19, 1948

May 15, 1949

Arsenaltaranto	0	-	2	Cremonese	Arsenaltaranto	2 - 1	Lecce US
Empoli	2	-	1	Napoli	Legnano	4 - 0	Reggiana 1919

Lecce US	1	-	0 Reggiana 1919	Parma	1	-	0 Napoli
Legnano	2	-	3 Como	Pisa	3	-	1 Pescara
Parma	2	-	2 Brescia	Pro Sesto	1	-	0 Hellas Verona
Pisa	3	-	1 Salernitana 1919	Salernitana 1919	6	-	2 Cremonese
Pro Sesto	6	-	0 Spezia	Seregno	1	-	0 US Alessandria 1912
Seregno	4	-	0 SPAL Ferrara	Siracusa	0	-	1 Spezia
Siracusa	2	-	2 Hellas Verona	SPAL Ferrara	1	-	0 Brescia
Venezia	1	-	2 Pescara	Venezia	5	-	0 Empoli
Vicenza	4	-	1 US Alessandria 1912	Vicenza	2	-	1 Como

December 25, 1948 / May 29, 1949

Arsenaltaranto	1	-	0 Parma	Brescia	2	-	2 Parma
Brescia	1	-	0 Empoli	Como	2	-	0 Legnano
Como	2	-	0 Pro Sesto	Cremonese	1	-	1 Arsenaltaranto
Napoli	0	-	1 Hellas Verona	Hellas Verona	0	-	0 Siracusa
Pescara	2	-	0 Seregno	Napoli	2	-	0 Empoli
Salernitana 1919	2	-	0 Lecce US	Pescara	0	-	1 Venezia
Siracusa	1	-	0 Reggiana 1919	Reggiana 1919	3	-	0 Lecce US
SPAL Ferrara	0	-	1 Pisa	Salernitana 1919	1	-	1 Pisa
Spezia	3	-	1 Cremonese	SPAL Ferrara	2	-	1 Seregno
US Alessandria 1912	3	-	2 Legnano	Spezia	1	-	1 Pro Sesto
Vicenza	2	-	1 Venezia	US Alessandria 1912	0	-	0 Vicenza

December 30, 1948 / June 5, 1949

Arsenaltaranto	1	-	0 Empoli	Cremonese	2	-	1 Spezia
Cremonese	4	-	2 Siracusa	Empoli	3	-	3 Brescia
Legnano	2	-	1 Hellas Verona	Hellas Verona	3	-	1 Napoli
Pisa	1	-	0 Lecce US	Lecce US	4	-	0 Salernitana 1919
Pro Sesto	2	-	0 Brescia	Legnano	1	-	1 US Alessandria 1912
Salernitana 1919	3	-	0 Reggiana 1919	Parma	1	-	2 Arsenaltaranto
Seregno	2	-	1 Parma	Pisa	6	-	0 SPAL Ferrara
SPAL Ferrara	7	-	0 Pescara	Pro Sesto	2	-	5 Como
Spezia	0	-	0 Como	Reggiana 1919	2	-	1 Siracusa
Venezia	2	-	1 US Alessandria 1912	Seregno	2	-	2 Pescara
Vicenza	2	-	0 Napoli	Venezia	2	-	0 Vicenza

January 2, 1949 / June 12, 1949

Cremonese	6	-	3 Pro Sesto	Arsenaltaranto	3	-	2 Seregno
Empoli	1	-	0 US Alessandria 1912	Brescia	2	-	2 Hellas Verona
Hellas Verona	2	-	2 Brescia	Como	1	-	0 Napoli
Lecce US	1	-	2 Parma	Parma	2	-	0 Lecce US
Legnano	3	-	0 SPAL Ferrara	Pro Sesto	3	-	1 Cremonese
Napoli	1	-	0 Como	Salernitana 1919	8	-	2 Pescara
Pescara	0	-	0 Salernitana 1919	Siracusa	0	-	0 Venezia
Pisa	5	-	0 Spezia	SPAL Ferrara	6	-	2 Legnano
Reggiana 1919	2	-	0 Vicenza	Spezia	2	-	0 Pisa
Seregno	3	-	1 Arsenaltaranto	US Alessandria 1912	5	-	3 Empoli
Venezia	2	-	0 Siracusa	Vicenza	2	-	0 Reggiana 1919

January 6, 1949 / June 19, 1949

Como	4	-	1 Reggiana 1919	Arsenaltaranto	2	-	0 Vicenza
Cremonese	3	-	1 Seregno	Brescia	3	-	1 Lecce US
Empoli	1	-	1 Pisa	Hellas Verona	2	-	1 Spezia
Lecce US	0	-	2 Brescia	Legnano	4	-	0 Pro Sesto
Parma	1	-	0 Venezia	Napoli	0	-	0 US Alessandria 1912
Pro Sesto	2	-	0 Legnano	Pescara	1	-	0 Siracusa

Salernitana 1919	3	-	0	SPAL Ferrara	Pisa	2	-	0	Empoli
Siracusa	3	-	0	Pescara	Reggiana 1919	3	-	1	Como
Spezia	2	-	1	Hellas Verona	Seregno	0	-	0	Cremonese
US Alessandria 1912	3	-	0	Napoli	SPAL Ferrara	8	-	1	Salernitana 1919
Vicenza	4	-	1	Arsenaltaranto	Venezia	1	-	0	Parma

January 9, 1949

June 26, 1949

Como	1	-	0	Salernitana 1919	Arsenaltaranto	3	-	0	Napoli
Legnano	4	-	0	Cremonese	Brescia	2	-	0	Siracusa
Napoli	3	-	2	Arsenaltaranto	Cremonese	1	-	2	Legnano
Parma	1	-	1	Spezia	Empoli	0	-	2	Pro Sesto
Pescara	0	-	0	Vicenza	Hellas Verona	0	-	3	Reggiana 1919
Pro Sesto	6	-	0	Empoli	Lecce US	5	-	1	Seregno
Reggiana 1919	1	-	2	Hellas Verona	Pisa	1	-	0	Venezia
Seregno	1	-	1	Lecce US	Salernitana 1919	4	-	1	Como
Siracusa	2	-	0	Brescia	Spezia	1	-	1	Parma
SPAL Ferrara	3	-	1	US Alessandria 1912	US Alessandria 1912	4	-	0	SPAL Ferrara
Venezia	2	-	1	Pisa	Vicenza	6	-	2	Pescara

January 16, 1949

July 3, 1949

Arsenaltaranto	3	-	0	Pro Sesto	Como	2	-	0	SPAL Ferrara
Brescia	1	-	2	Napoli	Lecce US	4	-	0	Cremonese
Cremonese	3	-	2	Lecce US	Legnano	3	-	2	Spezia
Empoli	2	-	1	Parma	Napoli	2	-	1	Brescia
Hellas Verona	5	-	1	Salernitana 1919	Parma	1	-	0	Empoli
Pisa	2	-	1	Reggiana 1919	Pescara	0	-	0	US Alessandria 1912
SPAL Ferrara	0	-	2	Como	Pro Sesto	3	-	0	Arsenaltaranto
Spezia	2	-	1	Legnano	Reggiana 1919	3	-	0	Pisa
US Alessandria 1912	3	-	1	Pescara	Salernitana 1919	3	-	0	Hellas Verona
Venezia	7	-	0	Seregno	Seregno	1	-	2	Venezia
Vicenza	4	-	0	Siracusa	Siracusa	0	-	1	Vicenza

Luxembourg

Spora held off Fola to the Luxembourg title, champions Dudelange fished a distant third. At the bottom there was a tie for 9th place, Tetange defeated Obercorn to send them down to the B Liga with Rodange and Petange. Three clubs promoted were Jeunesse Esch-sur-Alzette, Rumelange US and Grevenmacher CD.

		Pld	W	D	L	F	A	GA	Pts
1	Spora Luxembourg	22	18	2	2	65	26	2.50	38
2	Fola Esch sur Alzette	22	16	2	4	57	24	2.38	34
3	Stade Dudelange	22	12	5	5	45	25	1.80	29
4	The National Schifflange	22	11	2	9	46	35	1.31	24
5	Progres Niedercorn	22	7	8	7	35	34	1.03	22
6	Red Boys Differdange	22	8	5	9	50	38	1.32	21
7	Union Luxembourg	22	6	9	7	44	39	1.13	21
8	US Dudelange	22	8	5	9	40	46	0.87	21
9	Tetange	22	7	3	12	34	50	0.68	17
10	Obercorn CS	22	7	3	12	32	63	0.51	17
11	Racing Rodange	22	7	2	13	36	46	0.78	16
12	Petange	22	1	2	19	23	81	0.28	4

US Dudelange	3 - 2	Red Boys Differdange	Red Boys Differdange	2 - 1	Obercorn CS
US Dudelange	3 - 4	Obercorn CS	Red Boys Differdange	1 - 1	US Dudelange
US Dudelange	3 - 1	The National	Red Boys Differdange	0 - 2	The National
US Dudelange	1 - 2	Spora Luxembourg	Red Boys Differdange	1 - 1	Spora Luxembourg
US Dudelange	0 - 1	Fola Esch	Red Boys Differdange	0 - 1	Fola Esch
US Dudelange	1 - 0	Tetange	Red Boys Differdange	3 - 1	Tetange
US Dudelange	1 - 1	Petange	Red Boys Differdange	10 - 0	Petange
US Dudelange	1 - 3	Stade Dudelange	Red Boys Differdange	2 - 3	Stade Dudelange
US Dudelange	2 - 0	Progres Niedercorn	Red Boys Differdange	1 - 1	Progres Niedercorn
US Dudelange	0 - 0	Union Luxembourg	Red Boys Differdange	3 - 3	Union Luxembourg
US Dudelange	7 - 4	Racing Rodange	Red Boys Differdange	0 - 2	Racing Rodange
Union Luxembourg	3 - 1	Red Boys Differdange	Racing Rodange	3 - 4	Red Boys Differdange
Union Luxembourg	0 - 1	Obercorn CS	Racing Rodange	0 - 1	Obercorn CS
Union Luxembourg	3 - 3	US Dudelange	Racing Rodange	3 - 1	US Dudelange
Union Luxembourg	3 - 2	The National	Racing Rodange	1 - 2	The National
Union Luxembourg	2 - 3	Spora Luxembourg	Racing Rodange	2 - 3	Spora Luxembourg
Union Luxembourg	3 - 1	Fola Esch	Racing Rodange	2 - 3	Fola Esch
Union Luxembourg	2 - 4	Tetange	Racing Rodange	2 - 0	Tetange
Union Luxembourg	10 - 2	Petange	Racing Rodange	1 - 0	Petange
Union Luxembourg	0 - 3	Stade Dudelange	Racing Rodange	0 - 1	Stade Dudelange
Union Luxembourg	1 - 1	Progres Niedercorn	Racing Rodange	0 - 1	Progres Niedercorn
Union Luxembourg	0 - 1	Racing Rodange	Racing Rodange	3 - 4	Union Luxembourg
The National	1 - 4	Red Boys Differdange	Progres Niedercorn	2 - 1	Red Boys Differdange
The National	10 - 1	Obercorn CS	Progres Niedercorn	2 - 3	Obercorn CS

The National	4	-	2	US Dudelange	Progres Niedercorn	1	-	2	US Dudelange
The National	0	-	2	Spora Luxembourg	Progres Niedercorn	0	-	5	The National
The National	1	-	5	Fola Esch	Progres Niedercorn	1	-	5	Spora Luxembourg
The National	0	-	1	Tetange	Progres Niedercorn	0	-	0	Fola Esch
The National	4	-	2	Petange	Progres Niedercorn	3	-	0	Tetange
The National	1	-	0	Stade Dudelange	Progres Niedercorn	4	-	0	Petange
The National	0	-	0	Progres Niedercorn	Progres Niedercorn	0	-	0	Stade Dudelange
The National	0	-	2	Union Luxembourg	Progres Niedercorn	2	-	1	Union Luxembourg
The National	5	-	1	Racing Rodange	Progres Niedercorn	2	-	2	Racing Rodange
Tetange	1	-	1	Red Boys Differdange	Petange	1	-	4	Red Boys Differdange
Tetange	4	-	0	Obercorn CS	Petange	1	-	3	Obercorn CS
Tetange	2	-	0	US Dudelange	Petange	2	-	6	US Dudelange
Tetange	2	-	3	The National	Petange	1	-	2	The National
Tetange	0	-	6	Spora Luxembourg	Petange	1	-	4	Spora Luxembourg
Tetange	3	-	0	Fola Esch	Petange	0	-	1	Fola Esch
Tetange	2	-	1	Petange	Petange	2	-	1	Tetange
Tetange	3	-	2	Stade Dudelange	Petange	2	-	5	Stade Dudelange
Tetange	3	-	3	Progres Niedercorn	Petange	2	-	6	Progres Niedercorn
Tetange	3	-	3	Union Luxembourg	Petange	1	-	1	Union Luxembourg
Tetange	0	-	2	Racing Rodange	Petange	1	-	2	Racing Rodange
Stade Dudelange	0	-	3	Red Boys Differdange	Obercorn CS	0	-	4	Red Boys Differdange
Stade Dudelange	7	-	1	Obercorn CS	Obercorn CS	0	-	2	US Dudelange
Stade Dudelange	1	-	1	US Dudelange	Obercorn CS	1	-	1	The National
Stade Dudelange	2	-	0	The National	Obercorn CS	1	-	6	Spora Luxembourg
Stade Dudelange	2	-	1	Spora Luxembourg	Obercorn CS	3	-	4	Fola Esch
Stade Dudelange	0	-	1	Fola Esch	Obercorn CS	4	-	1	Tetange
Stade Dudelange	3	-	1	Tetange	Obercorn CS	2	-	1	Petange
Stade Dudelange	3	-	0	Petange	Obercorn CS	1	-	2	Stade Dudelange
Stade Dudelange	1	-	1	Progres Niedercorn	Obercorn CS	1	-	3	Progres Niedercorn
Stade Dudelange	2	-	2	Union Luxembourg	Obercorn CS	1	-	1	Union Luxembourg
Stade Dudelange	3	-	1	Racing Rodange	Obercorn CS	1	-	1	Racing Rodange
Spora Luxembourg	5	-	3	Red Boys Differdange	Fola Esch	3	-	0	Red Boys Differdange
Spora Luxembourg	4	-	2	Obercorn CS	Fola Esch	4	-	0	Obercorn CS
Spora Luxembourg	6	-	0	US Dudelange	Fola Esch	5	-	0	US Dudelange
Spora Luxembourg	1	-	0	The National	Fola Esch	1	-	2	The National
Spora Luxembourg	1	-	3	Fola Esch	Fola Esch	2	-	3	Spora Luxembourg
Spora Luxembourg	3	-	1	Tetange	Fola Esch	6	-	1	Tetange
Spora Luxembourg	3	-	1	Petange	Fola Esch	6	-	1	Petange
Spora Luxembourg	1	-	0	Stade Dudelange	Fola Esch	2	-	2	Stade Dudelange
Spora Luxembourg	2	-	1	Progres Niedercorn	Fola Esch	2	-	1	Progres Niedercorn
Spora Luxembourg	0	-	0	Union Luxembourg	Fola Esch	2	-	0	Union Luxembourg
Spora Luxembourg	3	-	2	Racing Rodange	Fola Esch	4	-	1	Racing Rodange

Malta

Inconsistency cost champions Valletta dear, they beat Sliema 3-0 in the second round, but managed only 1 point against the two Saints teams. Naxxar and St George's tie for relegation was decided by a play-off match – the Lions lost 4-1.

		Pld	W	D	L	F	A	GA	Pts
1	Sliema Wanderers	14	11	0	3	33	15	2.20	22
2	Hamrun Spartans	14	9	2	3	38	22	1.73	20
3	Valletta FC	14	9	1	4	40	20	2.00	19
4	Floriana Valletta	14	6	5	3	24	19	1.26	17
5	Hibernians Valletta	14	5	5	4	24	20	1.20	15
6	St Andrew's Luqa	14	3	1	10	13	33	0.39	7
7	St George's	14	1	4	9	19	42	0.45	6
8	Naxxar Lions	14	2	2	10	13	33	0.39	6

1st Round

Sliema Wanderers	1 - 3	Hamrun Spartans
Sliema Wanderers	0 - 1	Valletta FC
Sliema Wanderers	3 - 2	Floriana Valletta
Sliema Wanderers	6 - 2	Hibernians Valletta
Sliema Wanderers	3 - 1	St Andrew's Luqa
Sliema Wanderers	3 - 0	Naxxar Lions
Sliema Wanderers	4 - 0	St George's
Hamrun Spartans	1 - 4	Valletta FC
Hamrun Spartans	2 - 3	Floriana Valletta
Hamrun Spartans	3 - 1	Hibernians Valletta
Hamrun Spartans	3 - 0	St Andrew's Luqa
Hamrun Spartans	3 - 2	Naxxar Lions
Hamrun Spartans	4 - 2	St George's
Valletta FC	3 - 2	Floriana Valletta
Valletta FC	0 - 2	Hibernians Valletta
Valletta FC	4 - 0	St Andrew's Luqa
Valletta FC	5 - 3	Naxxar Lions
Valletta FC	7 - 1	St George's
Floriana Valletta	1 - 1	Hibernians Valletta
Floriana Valletta	1 - 0	St Andrew's Luqa
Floriana Valletta	1 - 0	Naxxar Lions
Floriana Valletta	2 - 1	St George's
Hibernians Valletta	5 - 1	St Andrew's Luqa
Hibernians Valletta	3 - 0	Naxxar Lions
Hibernians Valletta	1 - 1	St George's
St Andrew's Luqa	0 - 1	Naxxar Lions
St Andrew's Luqa	2 - 2	St George's
Naxxar Lions	2 - 1	St George's

2nd Round

Sliema Wanderers	3 - 2	Hamrun Spartans
Sliema Wanderers	0 - 3	Valletta FC
Sliema Wanderers	1 - 0	Floriana Valletta
Sliema Wanderers	2 - 1	Hibernians Valletta
Sliema Wanderers	2 - 0	St Andrew's Luqa
Sliema Wanderers	2 - 0	Naxxar Lions
Sliema Wanderers	3 - 0	St George's
Hamrun Spartans	1 - 0	Valletta FC
Hamrun Spartans	3 - 3	Floriana Valletta
Hamrun Spartans	0 - 0	Hibernians Valletta
Hamrun Spartans	5 - 2	St Andrew's Luqa
Hamrun Spartans	2 - 0	Naxxar Lions
Hamrun Spartans	6 - 1	St George's
Valletta FC	1 - 4	Floriana Valletta
Valletta FC	2 - 1	Hibernians Valletta
Valletta FC	1 - 2	St Andrew's Luqa
Valletta FC	6 - 0	Naxxar Lions
Valletta FC	3 - 3	St George's
Floriana Valletta	0 - 0	Hibernians Valletta
Floriana Valletta	1 - 0	St Andrew's Luqa
Floriana Valletta	1 - 1	Naxxar Lions
Floriana Valletta	3 - 3	St George's
Hibernians Valletta	2 - 0	St Andrew's Luqa
Hibernians Valletta	3 - 3	Naxxar Lions
Hibernians Valletta	2 - 1	St George's
St Andrew's Luqa	2 - 1	Naxxar Lions
St Andrew's Luqa	3 - 2	St George's
Naxxar Lions	0 - 1	St George's

Netherlands

Regional winners - Apeldoorn won the East, Heerenveen retained the North, Den Bosch South I, Tilburg South II, Velsen West II and champions Schiedam West I.

		Pld	W	D	L	F	A	GA	Pts
1	SVV Schiedam	10	6	3	1	20	13	1.54	15
2	BVV Den Bosch	10	6	1	3	37	29	1.28	13
3	AGOVV Apeldoorn	10	4	3	3	14	8	1.75	11
4	Heerenveen	10	5	1	4	28	21	1.33	11
5	VSV Velsen	10	4	0	6	16	18	0.89	8
6	NOAD Tilburg	10	0	2	8	5	28	0.18	2

SVV Schiedam	0 - 4	VSV Velsen	BVV Den Bosch	2 - 2	SVV Schiedam
SVV Schiedam	1 - 0	AGOVV Apeldoorn	BVV Den Bosch	3 - 0	VSV Velsen
SVV Schiedam	2 - 1	BVV Den Bosch	BVV Den Bosch	0 - 0	AGOVV Apeldoorn
SVV Schiedam	3 - 1	Heerenveen SC	BVV Den Bosch	2 - 3	Heerenveen SC
SVV Schiedam	4 - 0	NOAD Tilburg	BVV Den Bosch	0 - 0	NOAD Tilburg
VSV Velsen	1 - 3	SVV Schiedam	Heerenveen SC	4 - 4	SVV Schiedam
VSV Velsen	1 - 0	AGOVV Apeldoorn	Heerenveen SC	3 - 1	VSV Velsen
VSV Velsen	0 - 1	BVV Den Bosch	Heerenveen SC	1 - 3	AGOVV Apeldoorn
VSV Velsen	1 - 4	Heerenveen SC	Heerenveen SC	1 - 2	BVV Den Bosch
VSV Velsen	5 - 1	NOAD Tilburg	Heerenveen SC	7 - 2	NOAD Tilburg
AGOVV Apeldoorn	0 - 0	SVV Schiedam	NOAD Tilburg	0 - 1	SVV Schiedam
AGOVV Apeldoorn	3 - 1	VSV Velsen	NOAD Tilburg	0 - 2	VSV Velsen
AGOVV Apeldoorn	1 - 2	BVV Den Bosch	NOAD Tilburg	1 - 1	AGOVV Apeldoorn
AGOVV Apeldoorn	3 - 1	Heerenveen SC	NOAD Tilburg	1 - 2	BVV Den Bosch
AGOVV Apeldoorn	3 - 0	NOAD Tilburg	NOAD Tilburg	0 - 3	Heerenveen SC

	West 1	Pld	W	D	L	F	A	GA	Pts
1	SVV Schiedam	20	15	2	3	50	25	2.00	32
2	Xerxes Rotterdam	20	12	3	5	52	33	1.58	27
3	Blauw Wit Amsterdam	20	11	4	5	46	32	1.44	26
4	Ajax Amsterdam	20	9	5	6	51	42	1.21	23
5	DOS Utrecht	20	8	5	7	37	36	1.03	21
6	Haarlem HFC	20	8	2	10	42	41	1.02	18
7	ADO Den Haag	20	6	4	10	40	38	1.05	16
8	tGooi Hilversum	20	6	3	11	23	41	0.56	15
9	De Volewijckers Amsterdam	20	4	7	9	21	40	0.53	15
10	Stormvogels Ijmuiden	20	6	2	12	30	44	0.68	14
11	Sparta Rotterdam	20	5	3	12	22	42	0.52	13

ADO Den Haag	6	-	0	Ajax Amsterdam	Sparta Rotterdam	3	-	2	ADO Den Haag
ADO Den Haag	1	-	2	Blauw Wit	Sparta Rotterdam	1	-	6	Ajax Amsterdam
ADO Den Haag	5	-	2	DOS Utrecht	Sparta Rotterdam	1	-	3	Blauw Wit
ADO Den Haag	0	-	2	tGooi Hilversum	Sparta Rotterdam	1	-	0	DOS Utrecht
ADO Den Haag	1	-	1	Haarlem HFC	Sparta Rotterdam	0	-	1	tGooi Hilversum
ADO Den Haag	2	-	0	Sparta Rotterdam	Sparta Rotterdam	4	-	1	Haarlem HFC
ADO Den Haag	4	-	1	Stormvogels	Sparta Rotterdam	0	-	3	Stormvogels
ADO Den Haag	0	-	3	SVV Schiedam	Sparta Rotterdam	2	-	4	SVV Schiedam
ADO Den Haag	0	-	0	De Volewijckers	Sparta Rotterdam	0	-	1	De Volewijckers
ADO Den Haag	1	-	2	Xerxes Rotterdam	Sparta Rotterdam	0	-	3	Xerxes Rotterdam
Ajax Amsterdam	5	-	4	ADO Den Haag	Stormvogels	2	-	1	ADO Den Haag
Ajax Amsterdam	1	-	1	Blauw Wit	Stormvogels	4	-	0	Ajax Amsterdam
Ajax Amsterdam	2	-	1	DOS Utrecht	Stormvogels	3	-	6	Blauw Wit
Ajax Amsterdam	5	-	3	tGooi Hilversum	Stormvogels	1	-	1	DOS Utrecht
Ajax Amsterdam	2	-	5	Haarlem HFC	Stormvogels	3	-	1	tGooi Hilversum
Ajax Amsterdam	1	-	1	Sparta Rotterdam	Stormvogels	2	-	1	Haarlem HFC
Ajax Amsterdam	1	-	0	Stormvogels	Stormvogels	4	-	2	Sparta Rotterdam
Ajax Amsterdam	3	-	3	SVV Schiedam	Stormvogels	0	-	2	SVV Schiedam
Ajax Amsterdam	2	-	0	De Volewijckers	Stormvogels	2	-	4	De Volewijckers
Ajax Amsterdam	1	-	3	Xerxes Rotterdam	Stormvogels	1	-	6	Xerxes Rotterdam
Blauw Wit	3	-	2	ADO Den Haag	SVV Schiedam	5	-	3	ADO Den Haag
Blauw Wit	1	-	0	Ajax Amsterdam	SVV Schiedam	2	-	1	Ajax Amsterdam
Blauw Wit	1	-	1	DOS Utrecht	SVV Schiedam	1	-	2	Blauw Wit
Blauw Wit	7	-	1	tGooi Hilversum	SVV Schiedam	3	-	2	DOS Utrecht
Blauw Wit	2	-	1	Haarlem HFC	SVV Schiedam	0	-	0	tGooi Hilversum
Blauw Wit	3	-	0	Sparta Rotterdam	SVV Schiedam	2	-	0	Haarlem HFC
Blauw Wit	2	-	0	Stormvogels	SVV Schiedam	4	-	2	Sparta Rotterdam
Blauw Wit	1	-	2	SVV Schiedam	SVV Schiedam	2	-	0	Stormvogels
Blauw Wit	2	-	2	De Volewijckers	SVV Schiedam	2	-	0	De Volewijckers
Blauw Wit	1	-	3	Xerxes Rotterdam	SVV Schiedam	1	-	3	Xerxes Rotterdam
DOS Utrecht	0	-	0	ADO Den Haag	De Volewijckers	2	-	4	ADO Den Haag
DOS Utrecht	4	-	4	Ajax Amsterdam	De Volewijckers	0	-	7	Ajax Amsterdam
DOS Utrecht	3	-	3	Blauw Wit	De Volewijckers	1	-	0	Blauw Wit
DOS Utrecht	4	-	1	tGooi Hilversum	De Volewijckers	0	-	2	DOS Utrecht
DOS Utrecht	3	-	2	Haarlem HFC	De Volewijckers	0	-	0	tGooi Hilversum
DOS Utrecht	2	-	0	Sparta Rotterdam	De Volewijckers	2	-	3	Haarlem HFC
DOS Utrecht	3	-	1	Stormvogels	De Volewijckers	1	-	1	Sparta Rotterdam
DOS Utrecht	0	-	3	SVV Schiedam	De Volewijckers	1	-	1	Stormvogels
DOS Utrecht	3	-	1	De Volewijckers	De Volewijckers	0	-	2	SVV Schiedam
DOS Utrecht	3	-	1	Xerxes Rotterdam	De Volewijckers	1	-	5	Xerxes Rotterdam
tGooi Hilversum	1	-	3	ADO Den Haag	Xerxes Rotterdam	0	-	0	ADO Den Haag
tGooi Hilversum	2	-	2	Ajax Amsterdam	Xerxes Rotterdam	0	-	4	Ajax Amsterdam
tGooi Hilversum	1	-	0	Blauw Wit	Xerxes Rotterdam	6	-	3	Blauw Wit
tGooi Hilversum	0	-	2	DOS Utrecht	Xerxes Rotterdam	4	-	1	DOS Utrecht
tGooi Hilversum	2	-	1	Haarlem HFC	Xerxes Rotterdam	4	-	1	tGooi Hilversum
tGooi Hilversum	0	-	2	Sparta Rotterdam	Xerxes Rotterdam	3	-	1	Haarlem HFC
tGooi Hilversum	1	-	0	Stormvogels	Xerxes Rotterdam	1	-	1	Sparta Rotterdam
tGooi Hilversum	1	-	2	SVV Schiedam	Xerxes Rotterdam	1	-	0	Stormvogels
tGooi Hilversum	1	-	2	De Volewijckers	Xerxes Rotterdam	2	-	5	SVV Schiedam
tGooi Hilversum	2	-	1	Xerxes Rotterdam	Xerxes Rotterdam	2	-	2	De Volewijckers

Haarlem HFC	4	-	1	ADO Den Haag
Haarlem HFC	1	-	4	Ajax Amsterdam
Haarlem HFC	2	-	3	Blauw Wit
Haarlem HFC	3	-	0	DOS Utrecht
Haarlem HFC	3	-	2	tGooi Hilversum
Haarlem HFC	0	-	1	Sparta Rotterdam
Haarlem HFC	5	-	2	Stormvogels
Haarlem HFC	3	-	2	SVV Schiedam
Haarlem HFC	1	-	1	De Volewijckers
Haarlem HFC	4	-	2	Xerxes Rotterdam

	West 2	Pld	W	D	L	F	A	GA	Pts
1	VSV Velsen	20	17	0	3	56	26	2.15	34
2	Feyenoord Rotterdam	20	12	5	3	57	40	1.43	29
3	EDO Haarlem	20	9	7	4	40	24	1.67	25
4	Hermes DVS Schiedam	20	9	6	5	47	31	1.52	24
5	DWS Amsterdam	20	8	5	7	29	25	1.16	21
6	Neptunus Rotterdam	20	6	6	8	26	34	0.76	18
7	HBS Den Haag	20	7	3	10	42	52	0.81	17
8	Koog aan de Zaan	20	4	8	8	39	46	0.85	16
9	Zeeburgia Amsterdam	20	5	5	10	33	44	0.75	15
10	DFC Dordrecht	20	5	4	11	26	41	0.63	14
11	DHC Delft	20	3	1	16	22	54	0.41	7

DFC Dordrecht	2	-	1	DHC Delft	Hermes DVS	1	-	1	DFC Dordrecht
DFC Dordrecht	2	-	0	DWS Amsterdam	Hermes DVS	3	-	0	DHC Delft
DFC Dordrecht	1	-	1	EDO Haarlem	Hermes DVS	0	-	0	DWS Amsterdam
DFC Dordrecht	1	-	2	Feyenoord	Hermes DVS	0	-	1	EDO Haarlem
DFC Dordrecht	1	-	1	HBS Den Haag	Hermes DVS	3	-	3	Feyenoord
DFC Dordrecht	1	-	3	Hermes DVS	Hermes DVS	9	-	0	HBS Den Haag
DFC Dordrecht	3	-	5	Koog aan de Zaan	Hermes DVS	0	-	0	Koog aan de Zaan
DFC Dordrecht	2	-	0	Neptunus Rotterdam	Hermes DVS	1	-	1	Neptunus Rotterdam
DFC Dordrecht	0	-	1	VSV Velsen	Hermes DVS	2	-	3	VSV Velsen
DFC Dordrecht	0	-	1	Zeeburgia	Hermes DVS	5	-	3	Zeeburgia
DHC Delft	2	-	3	DFC Dordrecht	Koog aan de Zaan	1	-	1	DFC Dordrecht
DHC Delft	1	-	3	DWS Amsterdam	Koog aan de Zaan	5	-	1	DHC Delft
DHC Delft	0	-	4	EDO Haarlem	Koog aan de Zaan	1	-	1	DWS Amsterdam
DHC Delft	1	-	2	Feyenoord	Koog aan de Zaan	0	-	0	EDO Haarlem
DHC Delft	2	-	1	HBS Den Haag	Koog aan de Zaan	5	-	7	Feyenoord
DHC Delft	0	-	4	Hermes DVS	Koog aan de Zaan	2	-	2	HBS Den Haag
DHC Delft	5	-	2	Koog aan de Zaan	Koog aan de Zaan	2	-	3	Hermes DVS
DHC Delft	3	-	1	Neptunus Rotterdam	Koog aan de Zaan	4	-	0	Neptunus Rotterdam
DHC Delft	2	-	3	VSV Velsen	Koog aan de Zaan	1	-	4	VSV Velsen
DHC Delft	2	-	2	Zeeburgia	Koog aan de Zaan	4	-	3	Zeeburgia
DWS Amsterdam	1	-	0	DFC Dordrecht	Neptunus Rotterdam	0	-	3	DFC Dordrecht
DWS Amsterdam	4	-	0	DHC Delft	Neptunus Rotterdam	3	-	0	DHC Delft

DWS Amsterdam	0	-	1	EDO Haarlem	Neptunus Rotterdam	2	-	1	DWS Amsterdam
DWS Amsterdam	0	-	5	Feyenoord	Neptunus Rotterdam	2	-	2	EDO Haarlem
DWS Amsterdam	3	-	1	HBS Den Haag	Neptunus Rotterdam	3	-	1	Feyenoord
DWS Amsterdam	1	-	1	Hermes DVS	Neptunus Rotterdam	2	-	4	HBS Den Haag
DWS Amsterdam	1	-	1	Koog aan de Zaan	Neptunus Rotterdam	1	-	2	Hermes DVS
DWS Amsterdam	0	-	0	Neptunus Rotterdam	Neptunus Rotterdam	0	-	0	Koog aan de Zaan
DWS Amsterdam	1	-	2	VSV Velsen	Neptunus Rotterdam	3	-	1	VSV Velsen
DWS Amsterdam	4	-	0	Zeeburgia	Neptunus Rotterdam	1	-	2	Zeeburgia
EDO Haarlem	5	-	1	DFC Dordrecht	VSV Velsen	5	-	1	DFC Dordrecht
EDO Haarlem	3	-	0	DHC Delft	VSV Velsen	2	-	1	DHC Delft
EDO Haarlem	1	-	2	DWS Amsterdam	VSV Velsen	2	-	4	DWS Amsterdam
EDO Haarlem	2	-	2	Feyenoord	VSV Velsen	2	-	1	EDO Haarlem
EDO Haarlem	4	-	3	HBS Den Haag	VSV Velsen	2	-	1	Feyenoord
EDO Haarlem	3	-	0	Hermes DVS	VSV Velsen	3	-	2	HBS Den Haag
EDO Haarlem	3	-	1	Koog aan de Zaan	VSV Velsen	3	-	1	Hermes DVS
EDO Haarlem	0	-	0	Neptunus Rotterdam	VSV Velsen	5	-	1	Koog aan de Zaan
EDO Haarlem	2	-	1	VSV Velsen	VSV Velsen	5	-	1	Neptunus Rotterdam
EDO Haarlem	2	-	2	Zeeburgia	VSV Velsen	4	-	0	Zeeburgia
Feyenoord	4	-	1	DFC Dordrecht	Zeeburgia	2	-	0	DFC Dordrecht
Feyenoord	2	-	1	DHC Delft	Zeeburgia	4	-	0	DHC Delft
Feyenoord	3	-	1	DWS Amsterdam	Zeeburgia	2	-	1	DWS Amsterdam
Feyenoord	4	-	3	EDO Haarlem	Zeeburgia	1	-	1	EDO Haarlem
Feyenoord	4	-	1	HBS Den Haag	Zeeburgia	2	-	2	Feyenoord
Feyenoord	3	-	2	Hermes DVS	Zeeburgia	1	-	4	HBS Den Haag
Feyenoord	4	-	2	Koog aan de Zaan	Zeeburgia	2	-	3	Hermes DVS
Feyenoord	1	-	1	Neptunus Rotterdam	Zeeburgia	1	-	1	Koog aan de Zaan
Feyenoord	0	-	3	VSV Velsen	Zeeburgia	1	-	2	Neptunus Rotterdam
Feyenoord	2	-	1	Zeeburgia	Zeeburgia	1	-	3	VSV Velsen
HBS Den Haag	5	-	2	DFC Dordrecht					
HBS Den Haag	1	-	0	DHC Delft					
HBS Den Haag	0	-	1	DWS Amsterdam					
HBS Den Haag	2	-	1	EDO Haarlem					
HBS Den Haag	5	-	5	Feyenoord					
HBS Den Haag	3	-	4	Hermes DVS					
HBS Den Haag	2	-	1	Koog aan de Zaan					
HBS Den Haag	1	-	3	Neptunus Rotterdam					
HBS Den Haag	1	-	2	VSV Velsen					
HBS Den Haag	3	-	2	Zeeburgia					

	North	Pld	W	D	L	F	A	GA	Pts
1	Heerenveen SC	19	16	3	0	75	19	3.95	35
2	Be Quick 1887 Groningen	20	8	7	5	39	29	1.34	23
3	Frisia 1883 Leeuwarden	20	10	2	8	41	35	1.17	22
4	Friesland Leeuwarden	19	8	6	5	31	34	0.91	22
5	Sneek wit Swart	20	9	3	8	36	36	1.00	21
6	Leeuwarden VV	20	8	4	8	43	39	1.10	20
7	Velocitas Groningen	20	9	2	9	28	40	0.70	20
8	GVAV Groningen	20	5	5	10	34	39	0.87	15
9	Hoogezand HSC	20	4	6	10	23	37	0.62	14
10	Emmen BV	20	5	4	11	30	53	0.57	14
11	Achilles 1894 Assen	20	4	4	12	32	51	0.63	12

The match Heerenveen SC - Friesland Leeuwarden was never played.

Achilles 1894 Assen	1 - 1	Be Quick 1887	Heerenveen SC	3 - 2	Achilles 1894 Assen
Achilles 1894 Assen	1 - 1	Emmen BV	Heerenveen SC	2 - 1	Be Quick 1887
Achilles 1894 Assen	6 - 1	Friesland	Heerenveen SC	5 - 1	Emmen BV
Achilles 1894 Assen	3 - 1	Frisia 1883	Heerenveen SC	3 - 0	Frisia 1883
Achilles 1894 Assen	1 - 3	GVAV Groningen	Heerenveen SC	3 - 2	GVAV Groningen
Achilles 1894 Assen	0 - 5	Heerenveen SC	Heerenveen SC	5 - 1	Hoogezand HSC
Achilles 1894 Assen	2 - 2	Hoogezand HSC	Heerenveen SC	4 - 1	Leeuwarden VV
Achilles 1894 Assen	2 - 4	Leeuwarden VV	Heerenveen SC	4 - 1	Sneek wit Swart
Achilles 1894 Assen	3 - 1	Sneek wit Swart	Heerenveen SC	7 - 1	Velocitas Groningen
Achilles 1894 Assen	0 - 1	Velocitas Groningen	Hoogezand HSC	3 - 2	Achilles 1894 Assen
Be Quick 1887	0 - 1	Achilles 1894 Assen	Hoogezand HSC	0 - 0	Be Quick 1887
Be Quick 1887	2 - 0	Emmen BV	Hoogezand HSC	2 - 2	Emmen BV
Be Quick 1887	0 - 0	Friesland	Hoogezand HSC	1 - 3	Friesland
Be Quick 1887	6 - 2	Frisia 1883	Hoogezand HSC	1 - 2	Frisia 1883
Be Quick 1887	3 - 3	GVAV Groningen	Hoogezand HSC	1 - 0	GVAV Groningen
Be Quick 1887	0 - 7	Heerenveen SC	Hoogezand HSC	2 - 2	Heerenveen SC
Be Quick 1887	5 - 0	Hoogezand HSC	Hoogezand HSC	1 - 3	Leeuwarden VV
Be Quick 1887	2 - 2	Leeuwarden VV	Hoogezand HSC	0 - 1	Sneek wit Swart
Be Quick 1887	2 - 1	Sneek wit Swart	Hoogezand HSC	3 - 1	Velocitas Groningen
Be Quick 1887	1 - 1	Velocitas Groningen	Leeuwarden VV	4 - 2	Achilles 1894 Assen
Emmen BV	1 - 1	Achilles 1894 Assen	Leeuwarden VV	0 - 1	Be Quick 1887
Emmen BV	1 - 0	Be Quick 1887	Leeuwarden VV	8 - 2	Emmen BV
Emmen BV	3 - 1	Friesland	Leeuwarden VV	2 - 4	Friesland
Emmen BV	1 - 2	Frisia 1883	Leeuwarden VV	0 - 0	Frisia 1883
Emmen BV	0 - 4	GVAV Groningen	Leeuwarden VV	4 - 1	GVAV Groningen
Emmen BV	2 - 8	Heerenveen SC	Leeuwarden VV	0 - 3	Heerenveen SC
Emmen BV	3 - 2	Hoogezand HSC	Leeuwarden VV	1 - 0	Hoogezand HSC
Emmen BV	2 - 2	Leeuwarden VV	Leeuwarden VV	3 - 4	Sneek wit Swart
Emmen BV	1 - 2	Sneek wit Swart	Leeuwarden VV	1 - 3	Velocitas Groningen
Emmen BV	4 - 1	Velocitas Groningen	Sneek wit Swart	4 - 2	Achilles 1894 Assen
Friesland	4 - 2	Achilles 1894 Assen	Sneek wit Swart	3 - 2	Be Quick 1887
Friesland	2 - 2	Be Quick 1887	Sneek wit Swart	1 - 0	Emmen BV
Friesland	2 - 1	Emmen BV	Sneek wit Swart	0 - 0	Friesland

Friesland	1	-	3	Frisia 1883	Sneek wit Swart	1	-	3	Frisia 1883
Friesland	2	-	3	GVAV Groningen	Sneek wit Swart	3	-	2	GVAV Groningen
Friesland	2	-	2	Heerenveen SC	Sneek wit Swart	2	-	2	Heerenveen SC
Friesland	1	-	1	Hoogezand HSC	Sneek wit Swart	2	-	1	Hoogezand HSC
Friesland	1	-	0	Leeuwarden VV	Sneek wit Swart	2	-	3	Leeuwarden VV
Friesland	1	-	0	Sneek wit Swart	Sneek wit Swart	0	-	0	Velocitas Groningen
Friesland	3	-	0	Velocitas Groningen	Velocitas Groningen	4	-	0	Achilles 1894 Assen
Frisia 1883	4	-	0	Achilles 1894 Assen	Velocitas Groningen	1	-	5	Be Quick 1887
Frisia 1883	0	-	3	Be Quick 1887	Velocitas Groningen	3	-	0	Emmen BV
Frisia 1883	5	-	2	Emmen BV	Velocitas Groningen	0	-	3	Friesland
Frisia 1883	8	-	0	Friesland	Velocitas Groningen	2	-	1	Frisia 1883
Frisia 1883	3	-	1	GVAV Groningen	Velocitas Groningen	2	-	0	GVAV Groningen
Frisia 1883	1	-	6	Heerenveen SC	Velocitas Groningen	0	-	2	Heerenveen SC
Frisia 1883	0	-	1	Hoogezand HSC	Velocitas Groningen	1	-	0	Hoogezand HSC
Frisia 1883	1	-	2	Leeuwarden VV	Velocitas Groningen	3	-	2	Leeuwarden VV
Frisia 1883	2	-	0	Sneek wit Swart	Velocitas Groningen	1	-	5	Sneek wit Swart
Frisia 1883	2	-	1	Velocitas Groningen					
GVAV Groningen	4	-	1	Achilles 1894 Assen					
GVAV Groningen	2	-	3	Be Quick 1887					
GVAV Groningen	1	-	3	Emmen BV					
GVAV Groningen	0	-	0	Friesland					
GVAV Groningen	1	-	1	Frisia 1883					
GVAV Groningen	0	-	2	Heerenveen SC					
GVAV Groningen	1	-	1	Hoogezand HSC					
GVAV Groningen	1	-	1	Leeuwarden VV					
GVAV Groningen	4	-	3	Sneek wit Swart					
GVAV Groningen	1	-	2	Velocitas Groningen					

	East	Pld	W	D	L	F	A	GA	Pts
1	AGOVV Apeldoorn	20	11	4	5	40	30	1.33	26
2	Enschede	20	9	7	4	35	24	1.46	25
3	Heracles Almelo	20	9	5	6	29	23	1.26	23
4	Hengelo	20	6	8	6	34	31	1.10	20
5	Enschedese Boys	20	8	4	8	27	26	1.04	20
6	Quick Nijmegen	20	7	6	7	35	38	0.92	20
7	WVV Wageningen	20	6	7	7	34	35	0.97	19
8	Zwolsche Boys	20	6	6	8	26	26	1.00	18
9	Go Ahead Eagles Deventer	20	6	6	8	27	30	0.90	18
10	Be Quick Zutphen	20	7	3	10	27	39	0.69	17
11	NEC Nijmegen	20	5	4	11	26	38	0.68	14

AGOVV Apeldoorn	3	-	1	Be Quick Zutphen	Heracles Almelo	1	-	2	AGOVV Apeldoorn
AGOVV Apeldoorn	1	-	1	Enschede	Heracles Almelo	0	-	1	Be Quick Zutphen
AGOVV Apeldoorn	1	-	1	Enschedese Boys	Heracles Almelo	0	-	3	Enschede
AGOVV Apeldoorn	4	-	1	Go Ahead Eagles	Heracles Almelo	3	-	1	Enschedese Boys
AGOVV Apeldoorn	0	-	3	Hengelo	Heracles Almelo	0	-	1	Go Ahead Eagles
AGOVV Apeldoorn	2	-	1	Heracles Almelo	Heracles Almelo	1	-	1	Hengelo

AGOVV Apeldoorn	4	-	1	NEC Nijmegen	Heracles Almelo	6 - 2	NEC Nijmegen
AGOVV Apeldoorn	3	-	2	Quick Nijmegen	Heracles Almelo	3 - 2	Quick Nijmegen
AGOVV Apeldoorn	0	-	1	WVV Wageningen	Heracles Almelo	0 - 0	WVV Wageningen
AGOVV Apeldoorn	1	-	0	Zwolsche Boys	Heracles Almelo	0 - 0	Zwolsche Boys
Be Quick Zutphen	0	-	2	AGOVV Apeldoorn	NEC Nijmegen	3 - 2	AGOVV Apeldoorn
Be Quick Zutphen	2	-	2	Enschede	NEC Nijmegen	0 - 2	Be Quick Zutphen
Be Quick Zutphen	4	-	1	Enschedese Boys	NEC Nijmegen	1 - 0	Enschede
Be Quick Zutphen	1	-	0	Go Ahead Eagles	NEC Nijmegen	0 - 0	Enschedese Boys
Be Quick Zutphen	0	-	5	Hengelo	NEC Nijmegen	2 - 1	Go Ahead Eagles
Be Quick Zutphen	0	-	1	Heracles Almelo	NEC Nijmegen	2 - 2	Hengelo
Be Quick Zutphen	0	-	2	NEC Nijmegen	NEC Nijmegen	0 - 1	Heracles Almelo
Be Quick Zutphen	1	-	3	Quick Nijmegen	NEC Nijmegen	1 - 2	Quick Nijmegen
Be Quick Zutphen	2	-	1	WVV Wageningen	NEC Nijmegen	1 - 1	WVV Wageningen
Be Quick Zutphen	1	-	0	Zwolsche Boys	NEC Nijmegen	1 - 2	Zwolsche Boys
Enschede	5	-	3	AGOVV Apeldoorn	Quick Nijmegen	0 - 1	AGOVV Apeldoorn
Enschede	6	-	1	Be Quick Zutphen	Quick Nijmegen	1 - 1	Be Quick Zutphen
Enschede	2	-	1	Enschedese Boys	Quick Nijmegen	1 - 1	Enschede
Enschede	0	-	2	Go Ahead Eagles	Quick Nijmegen	2 - 1	Enschedese Boys
Enschede	1	-	1	Hengelo	Quick Nijmegen	1 - 1	Go Ahead Eagles
Enschede	0	-	2	Heracles Almelo	Quick Nijmegen	2 - 2	Hengelo
Enschede	3	-	2	NEC Nijmegen	Quick Nijmegen	3 - 3	Heracles Almelo
Enschede	3	-	1	Quick Nijmegen	Quick Nijmegen	0 - 5	NEC Nijmegen
Enschede	3	-	3	WVV Wageningen	Quick Nijmegen	3 - 3	WVV Wageningen
Enschede	0	-	0	Zwolsche Boys	Quick Nijmegen	2 - 1	Zwolsche Boys
Enschedese Boys	2	-	3	AGOVV Apeldoorn	WVV Wageningen	3 - 1	AGOVV Apeldoorn
Enschedese Boys	3	-	1	Be Quick Zutphen	WVV Wageningen	1 - 0	Be Quick Zutphen
Enschedese Boys	0	-	0	Enschede	WVV Wageningen	3 - 2	Enschede
Enschedese Boys	0	-	1	Go Ahead Eagles	WVV Wageningen	0 - 1	Enschedese Boys
Enschedese Boys	1	-	1	Hengelo	WVV Wageningen	2 - 2	Go Ahead Eagles
Enschedese Boys	0	-	1	Heracles Almelo	WVV Wageningen	2 - 3	Hengelo
Enschedese Boys	1	-	0	NEC Nijmegen	WVV Wageningen	1 - 1	Heracles Almelo
Enschedese Boys	2	-	1	Quick Nijmegen	WVV Wageningen	4 - 0	NEC Nijmegen
Enschedese Boys	4	-	1	WVV Wageningen	WVV Wageningen	1 - 3	Quick Nijmegen
Enschedese Boys	2	-	0	Zwolsche Boys	WVV Wageningen	3 - 3	Zwolsche Boys
Go Ahead Eagles	1	-	4	AGOVV Apeldoorn	Zwolsche Boys	1 - 1	AGOVV Apeldoorn
Go Ahead Eagles	3	-	3	Be Quick Zutphen	Zwolsche Boys	1 - 3	Be Quick Zutphen
Go Ahead Eagles	0	-	1	Enschede	Zwolsche Boys	0 - 1	Enschede
Go Ahead Eagles	1	-	2	Enschedese Boys	Zwolsche Boys	4 - 2	Enschedese Boys
Go Ahead Eagles	1	-	1	Hengelo	Zwolsche Boys	2 - 0	Go Ahead Eagles
Go Ahead Eagles	4	-	1	Heracles Almelo	Zwolsche Boys	1 - 1	Hengelo
Go Ahead Eagles	1	-	1	NEC Nijmegen	Zwolsche Boys	0 - 1	Heracles Almelo
Go Ahead Eagles	1	-	2	Quick Nijmegen	Zwolsche Boys	2 - 1	NEC Nijmegen
Go Ahead Eagles	2	-	1	WVV Wageningen	Zwolsche Boys	2 - 3	Quick Nijmegen
Go Ahead Eagles	2	-	2	Zwolsche Boys	Zwolsche Boys	3 - 0	WVV Wageningen
Hengelo	2	-	2	AGOVV Apeldoorn			
Hengelo	4	-	3	Be Quick Zutphen			
Hengelo	0	-	1	Enschede			
Hengelo	0	-	2	Enschedese Boys			
Hengelo	0	-	2	Go Ahead Eagles			
Hengelo	0	-	3	Heracles Almelo			
Hengelo	4	-	1	NEC Nijmegen			
Hengelo	2	-	1	Quick Nijmegen			

Hengelo 1 - 3 WVV Wageningen
Hengelo 1 - 2 Zwolsche Boys

South 1	Pld	W	D	L	F	A	GA	Pts
1 BVV Den Bosch	20	15	1	4	44	13	3.38	31
2 Limburgia Brunssum	20	13	3	4	49	34	1.44	29
3 Willem II Tilburg	20	11	3	6	42	25	1.68	25
4 VVV Venlo	20	11	2	7	33	16	2.06	24
5 NAC Breda	20	10	3	7	39	32	1.22	23
6 MVV Maastricht	20	7	5	8	40	34	1.18	19
7 Ooserhout TSC	20	5	8	7	36	37	0.97	18
8 Brabantia Eindhoven	20	7	3	10	24	38	0.63	17
9 Juliana Kerkrade	20	6	4	10	43	62	0.69	16
10 Helmond	20	3	5	12	29	50	0.58	11
11 De Spechten Eindhoven	20	2	3	15	27	65	0.42	7

Brabantia 1 - 0 BVV Den Bosch
Brabantia 2 - 2 Helmond
Brabantia 5 - 0 Juliana Kerkrade
Brabantia 1 - 1 Limburgia Brunssum
Brabantia 0 - 2 MVV Maastricht
Brabantia 2 - 0 NAC Breda
Brabantia 2 - 1 De Spechten
Brabantia 3 - 1 Ooserhout TSC
Brabantia 1 - 4 VVV Venlo
Brabantia 0 - 1 Willem II Tilburg
BVV Den Bosch 7 - 0 Brabantia
BVV Den Bosch 2 - 1 Helmond
BVV Den Bosch 2 - 0 Juliana Kerkrade
BVV Den Bosch 3 - 0 Limburgia Brunssum
BVV Den Bosch 1 - 0 MVV Maastricht
BVV Den Bosch 4 - 0 NAC Breda
BVV Den Bosch 2 - 1 De Spechten
BVV Den Bosch 4 - 0 Ooserhout TSC
BVV Den Bosch 1 - 0 VVV Venlo
BVV Den Bosch 1 - 0 Willem II Tilburg
Helmond 1 - 0 Brabantia
Helmond 0 - 3 BVV Den Bosch
Helmond 5 - 3 Juliana Kerkrade
Helmond 2 - 1 Limburgia Brunssum
Helmond 0 - 5 MVV Maastricht
Helmond 1 - 3 NAC Breda
Helmond 2 - 4 De Spechten
Helmond 2 - 2 Ooserhout TSC

NAC Breda 3 - 2 Brabantia
NAC Breda 0 - 2 BVV Den Bosch
NAC Breda 3 - 2 Helmond
NAC Breda 2 - 1 Juliana Kerkrade
NAC Breda 1 - 2 Limburgia Brunssum
NAC Breda 2 - 0 MVV Maastricht
NAC Breda 7 - 0 De Spechten
NAC Breda 2 - 1 Ooserhout TSC
NAC Breda 1 - 2 VVV Venlo
NAC Breda 3 - 2 Willem II Tilburg
De Spechten 1 - 2 Brabantia
De Spechten 0 - 2 BVV Den Bosch
De Spechten 2 - 1 Helmond
De Spechten 2 - 3 Juliana Kerkrade
De Spechten 0 - 3 Limburgia Brunssum
De Spechten 2 - 2 MVV Maastricht
De Spechten 1 - 1 NAC Breda
De Spechten 1 - 4 Ooserhout TSC
De Spechten 1 - 4 VVV Venlo
De Spechten 1 - 5 Willem II Tilburg
Ooserhout TSC 0 - 1 Brabantia
Ooserhout TSC 2 - 2 BVV Den Bosch
Ooserhout TSC 1 - 1 Helmond
Ooserhout TSC 3 - 1 Juliana Kerkrade
Ooserhout TSC 3 - 3 Limburgia Brunssum
Ooserhout TSC 3 - 1 MVV Maastricht
Ooserhout TSC 1 - 1 NAC Breda
Ooserhout TSC 6 - 3 De Spechten

Helmond	1	-	3	VVV Venlo	Ooserhout TSC	1	-	1	VVV Venlo
Helmond	0	-	3	Willem II Tilburg	Ooserhout TSC	1	-	2	Willem II Tilburg
Juliana Kerkrade	4	-	2	Brabantia	VVV Venlo	5	-	0	Brabantia
Juliana Kerkrade	1	-	0	BVV Den Bosch	VVV Venlo	0	-	1	BVV Den Bosch
Juliana Kerkrade	3	-	3	Helmond	VVV Venlo	3	-	0	Helmond
Juliana Kerkrade	3	-	6	Limburgia Brunssum	VVV Venlo	2	-	0	Juliana Kerkrade
Juliana Kerkrade	3	-	3	MVV Maastricht	VVV Venlo	0	-	1	Limburgia Brunssum
Juliana Kerkrade	4	-	3	NAC Breda	VVV Venlo	0	-	1	MVV Maastricht
Juliana Kerkrade	3	-	3	De Spechten	VVV Venlo	1	-	3	NAC Breda
Juliana Kerkrade	4	-	2	Ooserhout TSC	VVV Venlo	3	-	0	De Spechten
Juliana Kerkrade	1	-	2	VVV Venlo	VVV Venlo	0	-	0	Ooserhout TSC
Juliana Kerkrade	2	-	1	Willem II Tilburg	VVV Venlo	1	-	0	Willem II Tilburg
Limburgia Brunssum	2	-	0	Brabantia	Willem II Tilburg	0	-	0	Brabantia
Limburgia Brunssum	3	-	2	BVV Den Bosch	Willem II Tilburg	1	-	0	BVV Den Bosch
Limburgia Brunssum	2	-	1	Helmond	Willem II Tilburg	3	-	2	Helmond
Limburgia Brunssum	5	-	5	Juliana Kerkrade	Willem II Tilburg	6	-	1	Juliana Kerkrade
Limburgia Brunssum	3	-	2	MVV Maastricht	Willem II Tilburg	4	-	2	Limburgia Brunssum
Limburgia Brunssum	2	-	0	NAC Breda	Willem II Tilburg	3	-	2	MVV Maastricht
Limburgia Brunssum	4	-	2	De Spechten	Willem II Tilburg	2	-	4	NAC Breda
Limburgia Brunssum	2	-	1	Ooserhout TSC	Willem II Tilburg	5	-	1	De Spechten
Limburgia Brunssum	1	-	2	VVV Venlo	Willem II Tilburg	1	-	1	Ooserhout TSC
Limburgia Brunssum	2	-	1	Willem II Tilburg	Willem II Tilburg	1	-	0	VVV Venlo
MVV Maastricht	3	-	0	Brabantia					
MVV Maastricht	3	-	5	BVV Den Bosch					
MVV Maastricht	2	-	2	Helmond					
MVV Maastricht	5	-	1	Juliana Kerkrade					
MVV Maastricht	1	-	4	Limburgia Brunssum					
MVV Maastricht	0	-	0	NAC Breda					
MVV Maastricht	4	-	1	De Spechten					
MVV Maastricht	2	-	3	Ooserhout TSC					
MVV Maastricht	1	-	0	VVV Venlo					
MVV Maastricht	1	-	1	Willem II Tilburg					

	South 2	Pld	W	D	L	F	A	GA	Pts
1	NOAD Tilburg	20	12	4	4	36	21	1.71	28
2	Bleijerheide Kerkrade	20	9	6	5	32	23	1.39	24
3	PSV Eindhoven	20	8	5	7	35	26	1.35	21
4	EVV Eindhoven	20	6	9	5	36	30	1.20	21
5	Helmondia	20	8	5	7	29	30	0.97	21
6	SC Emma Hoensbroek	20	7	5	8	22	28	0.79	19
7	Kerkrade	20	7	4	9	32	35	0.91	18
8	Maurits Geleen	20	6	6	8	21	25	0.84	18
9	Sittardse Boys	20	5	8	7	24	29	0.83	18
10	LONGA Tilburg	20	7	2	11	29	34	0.85	16
11	Baronie Breda	20	7	2	11	37	52	0.71	16

Baronie Breda	2	-	3	Bleijerheide	Maurits Geleen	2	-	1	Baronie Breda
Baronie Breda	1	-	3	EVV Eindhoven	Maurits Geleen	0	-	0	Bleijerheide
Baronie Breda	3	-	1	Helmondia	Maurits Geleen	0	-	0	EVV Eindhoven
Baronie Breda	0	-	0	Kerkrade	Maurits Geleen	1	-	1	Helmondia
Baronie Breda	2	-	0	LONGA Tilburg	Maurits Geleen	2	-	0	Kerkrade
Baronie Breda	5	-	1	Maurits Geleen	Maurits Geleen	2	-	1	LONGA Tilburg
Baronie Breda	0	-	2	NOAD Tilburg	Maurits Geleen	1	-	2	NOAD Tilburg
Baronie Breda	2	-	5	PSV Eindhoven	Maurits Geleen	0	-	1	PSV Eindhoven
Baronie Breda	5	-	2	Sittardse Boys	Maurits Geleen	2	-	0	Sittardse Boys
Baronie Breda	1	-	2	SC Emma	Maurits Geleen	4	-	0	SC Emma
Bleijerheide	5	-	2	Baronie Breda	NOAD Tilburg	5	-	0	Baronie Breda
Bleijerheide	1	-	1	EVV Eindhoven	NOAD Tilburg	3	-	0	Bleijerheide
Bleijerheide	3	-	1	Helmondia	NOAD Tilburg	2	-	1	EVV Eindhoven
Bleijerheide	2	-	1	Kerkrade	NOAD Tilburg	1	-	3	Helmondia
Bleijerheide	5	-	0	LONGA Tilburg	NOAD Tilburg	3	-	1	Kerkrade
Bleijerheide	2	-	1	Maurits Geleen	NOAD Tilburg	2	-	1	LONGA Tilburg
Bleijerheide	0	-	0	NOAD Tilburg	NOAD Tilburg	1	-	1	Maurits Geleen
Bleijerheide	2	-	0	PSV Eindhoven	NOAD Tilburg	0	-	1	PSV Eindhoven
Bleijerheide	1	-	3	Sittardse Boys	NOAD Tilburg	3	-	1	Sittardse Boys
Bleijerheide	1	-	1	SC Emma	NOAD Tilburg	2	-	1	SC Emma
EVV Eindhoven	3	-	4	Baronie Breda	PSV Eindhoven	4	-	0	Baronie Breda
EVV Eindhoven	2	-	1	Bleijerheide	PSV Eindhoven	1	-	2	Bleijerheide
EVV Eindhoven	4	-	3	Helmondia	PSV Eindhoven	0	-	0	EVV Eindhoven
EVV Eindhoven	1	-	1	Kerkrade	PSV Eindhoven	1	-	2	Helmondia
EVV Eindhoven	1	-	3	LONGA Tilburg	PSV Eindhoven	1	-	2	Kerkrade
EVV Eindhoven	4	-	0	Maurits Geleen	PSV Eindhoven	0	-	1	LONGA Tilburg
EVV Eindhoven	1	-	1	NOAD Tilburg	PSV Eindhoven	2	-	1	Maurits Geleen
EVV Eindhoven	2	-	0	PSV Eindhoven	PSV Eindhoven	1	-	1	NOAD Tilburg
EVV Eindhoven	3	-	1	Sittardse Boys	PSV Eindhoven	2	-	2	Sittardse Boys
EVV Eindhoven	1	-	1	SC Emma	PSV Eindhoven	1	-	1	SC Emma
Helmondia	1	-	1	Baronie Breda	Sittardse Boys	3	-	0	Baronie Breda
Helmondia	1	-	0	Bleijerheide	Sittardse Boys	1	-	1	Bleijerheide
Helmondia	2	-	2	EVV Eindhoven	Sittardse Boys	1	-	1	EVV Eindhoven
Helmondia	3	-	1	Kerkrade	Sittardse Boys	0	-	0	Helmondia
Helmondia	2	-	2	LONGA Tilburg	Sittardse Boys	3	-	1	Kerkrade
Helmondia	2	-	0	Maurits Geleen	Sittardse Boys	1	-	0	LONGA Tilburg
Helmondia	0	-	2	NOAD Tilburg	Sittardse Boys	0	-	0	Maurits Geleen
Helmondia	1	-	2	PSV Eindhoven	Sittardse Boys	0	-	1	NOAD Tilburg
Helmondia	3	-	0	Sittardse Boys	Sittardse Boys	3	-	3	PSV Eindhoven
Helmondia	1	-	0	SC Emma	Sittardse Boys	2	-	1	SC Emma
Kerkrade	4	-	5	Baronie Breda	SC Emma	1	-	2	Baronie Breda
Kerkrade	2	-	1	Bleijerheide	SC Emma	1	-	1	Bleijerheide
Kerkrade	4	-	4	EVV Eindhoven	SC Emma	1	-	0	EVV Eindhoven
Kerkrade	5	-	0	Helmondia	SC Emma	1	-	0	Helmondia
Kerkrade	1	-	3	LONGA Tilburg	SC Emma	1	-	2	Kerkrade
Kerkrade	2	-	1	Maurits Geleen	SC Emma	2	-	1	LONGA Tilburg
Kerkrade	1	-	2	NOAD Tilburg	SC Emma	1	-	1	Maurits Geleen
Kerkrade	2	-	0	PSV Eindhoven	SC Emma	3	-	2	NOAD Tilburg
Kerkrade	0	-	0	Sittardse Boys	SC Emma	1	-	5	PSV Eindhoven
Kerkrade	0	-	2	SC Emma	SC Emma	1	-	0	Sittardse Boys
LONGA Tilburg	5	-	1	Baronie Breda					
LONGA Tilburg	0	-	1	Bleijerheide					

LONGA Tilburg	3	-	2	EVV Eindhoven
LONGA Tilburg	1	-	2	Helmondia
LONGA Tilburg	1	-	2	Kerkrade
LONGA Tilburg	0	-	1	Maurits Geleen
LONGA Tilburg	4	-	1	NOAD Tilburg
LONGA Tilburg	1	-	5	PSV Eindhoven
LONGA Tilburg	1	-	1	Sittardse Boys
LONGA Tilburg	1	-	0	SC Emma

Northern Ireland

Linfield wrested the title away from Belfast Celtic in what turned out to be Celtic's final season. Crusaders will take their place next season.

		Pld	W	D	L	F	A	GA	Pts
1	Linfield Belfast	22	16	4	2	58	21	2.76	36
2	Belfast Celtic	22	14	3	5	69	32	2.16	31
3	Glentoran	22	13	3	6	45	28	1.61	29
4	Cliftonville Belfast	22	9	5	8	44	38	1.16	23
5	Bangor	22	8	5	9	43	45	0.96	21
6	Distillery Belfast	22	9	3	10	51	56	0.91	21
7	Portadown	22	8	4	10	41	48	0.85	20
8	Glenavon Lurgan	22	6	8	8	35	43	0.81	20
9	Derry City	22	8	3	11	40	52	0.77	19
10	Ballymena United	22	6	7	9	39	58	0.67	19
11	Ards	22	7	2	13	46	49	0.94	16
12	Coleraine	22	4	1	17	25	66	0.38	9

Ards	8 - 0 Ballymena United	Derry City	2 - 3 Ards
Ards	2 - 4 Bangor	Derry City	1 - 2 Ballymena United
Ards	4 - 4 Belfast Celtic	Derry City	3 - 1 Bangor
Ards	1 - 2 Cliftonville Belfast	Derry City	4 - 3 Belfast Celtic
Ards	7 - 0 Coleraine	Derry City	2 - 1 Cliftonville Belfast
Ards	3 - 1 Derry City	Derry City	7 - 1 Coleraine
Ards	0 - 1 Distillery Belfast	Derry City	2 - 2 Distillery Belfast
Ards	0 - 2 Glenavon Lurgan	Derry City	1 - 2 Glenavon Lurgan
Ards	2 - 1 Glentoran	Derry City	0 - 1 Glentoran
Ards	0 - 4 Linfield Belfast	Derry City	1 - 3 Linfield Belfast
Ards	2 - 2 Portadown	Derry City	3 - 2 Portadown
Ballymena United	1 - 0 Ards	Distillery Belfast	2 - 1 Ards
Ballymena United	1 - 1 Bangor	Distillery Belfast	6 - 2 Ballymena United
Ballymena United	0 - 5 Belfast Celtic	Distillery Belfast	5 - 0 Bangor
Ballymena United	3 - 4 Cliftonville Belfast	Distillery Belfast	1 - 2 Belfast Celtic
Ballymena United	5 - 2 Coleraine	Distillery Belfast	0 - 1 Cliftonville Belfast
Ballymena United	3 - 2 Derry City	Distillery Belfast	2 - 0 Coleraine
Ballymena United	7 - 5 Distillery Belfast	Distillery Belfast	2 - 3 Derry City
Ballymena United	0 - 0 Glenavon Lurgan	Distillery Belfast	2 - 0 Glenavon Lurgan
Ballymena United	1 - 1 Glentoran	Distillery Belfast	2 - 1 Glentoran
Ballymena United	0 - 3 Linfield Belfast	Distillery Belfast	3 - 2 Linfield Belfast
Ballymena United	1 - 1 Portadown	Distillery Belfast	2 - 2 Portadown
Bangor	2 - 3 Ards	Glenavon Lurgan	1 - 2 Ards
Bangor	2 - 2 Ballymena United	Glenavon Lurgan	2 - 2 Ballymena United
Bangor	0 - 1 Belfast Celtic	Glenavon Lurgan	4 - 2 Bangor

Bangor	2	-	1	Cliftonville Belfast	Glenavon Lurgan	1	-	0	Belfast Celtic
Bangor	1	-	0	Coleraine	Glenavon Lurgan	2	-	2	Cliftonville Belfast
Bangor	4	-	1	Derry City	Glenavon Lurgan	4	-	1	Coleraine
Bangor	5	-	2	Distillery Belfast	Glenavon Lurgan	4	-	1	Derry City
Bangor	1	-	1	Glenavon Lurgan	Glenavon Lurgan	2	-	2	Distillery Belfast
Bangor	3	-	0	Glentoran	Glenavon Lurgan	1	-	2	Glentoran
Bangor	3	-	3	Linfield Belfast	Glenavon Lurgan	0	-	3	Linfield Belfast
Bangor	2	-	3	Portadown	Glenavon Lurgan	2	-	2	Portadown
Belfast Celtic	4	-	3	Ards	Glentoran	2	-	0	Ards
Belfast Celtic	3	-	2	Ballymena United	Glentoran	4	-	2	Ballymena United
Belfast Celtic	3	-	0	Bangor	Glentoran	2	-	1	Bangor
Belfast Celtic	4	-	3	Cliftonville Belfast	Glentoran	0	-	0	Belfast Celtic
Belfast Celtic	4	-	0	Coleraine	Glentoran	2	-	0	Cliftonville Belfast
Belfast Celtic	8	-	0	Derry City	Glentoran	3	-	2	Coleraine
Belfast Celtic	10	-	2	Distillery Belfast	Glentoran	2	-	2	Derry City
Belfast Celtic	3	-	1	Glenavon Lurgan	Glentoran	4	-	1	Distillery Belfast
Belfast Celtic	0	-	3	Glentoran	Glentoran	7	-	1	Glenavon Lurgan
Belfast Celtic	0	-	1	Linfield Belfast	Glentoran	1	-	4	Linfield Belfast
Belfast Celtic	5	-	1	Portadown	Glentoran	2	-	1	Portadown
Cliftonville Belfast	3	-	2	Ards	Linfield Belfast	5	-	1	Ards
Cliftonville Belfast	1	-	1	Ballymena United	Linfield Belfast	4	-	2	Ballymena United
Cliftonville Belfast	2	-	2	Bangor	Linfield Belfast	1	-	2	Bangor
Cliftonville Belfast	2	-	5	Belfast Celtic	Linfield Belfast	1	-	1	Belfast Celtic
Cliftonville Belfast	6	-	0	Coleraine	Linfield Belfast	0	-	0	Cliftonville Belfast
Cliftonville Belfast	1	-	1	Derry City	Linfield Belfast	3	-	1	Coleraine
Cliftonville Belfast	2	-	1	Distillery Belfast	Linfield Belfast	3	-	0	Derry City
Cliftonville Belfast	5	-	2	Glenavon Lurgan	Linfield Belfast	5	-	2	Distillery Belfast
Cliftonville Belfast	1	-	0	Glentoran	Linfield Belfast	1	-	1	Glenavon Lurgan
Cliftonville Belfast	1	-	3	Linfield Belfast	Linfield Belfast	2	-	0	Glentoran
Cliftonville Belfast	5	-	0	Portadown	Linfield Belfast	3	-	1	Portadown
Coleraine	4	-	1	Ards	Portadown	2	-	1	Ards
Coleraine	1	-	2	Ballymena United	Portadown	2	-	0	Ballymena United
Coleraine	3	-	1	Bangor	Portadown	2	-	4	Bangor
Coleraine	1	-	0	Belfast Celtic	Portadown	2	-	4	Belfast Celtic
Coleraine	3	-	0	Cliftonville Belfast	Portadown	2	-	1	Cliftonville Belfast
Coleraine	1	-	2	Derry City	Portadown	2	-	1	Coleraine
Coleraine	0	-	6	Distillery Belfast	Portadown	0	-	1	Derry City
Coleraine	1	-	1	Glenavon Lurgan	Portadown	5	-	0	Distillery Belfast
Coleraine	1	-	3	Glentoran	Portadown	3	-	1	Glenavon Lurgan
Coleraine	0	-	2	Linfield Belfast	Portadown	1	-	4	Glentoran
Coleraine	2	-	4	Portadown	Portadown	1	-	2	Linfield Belfast

Norway

The new league system produces two group winners and a two-legged play-off final, which was easily won by Frederikstad. The bottom two in each group were relegated.

Championship play-off

June 6, 1949	Valerenga Oslo 1 - 3 Fredrikstad FK	
June 12, 1949	Fredrikstad FK 3 - 0 Valerenga Oslo	Agg 6-1

Group A	Pld	W	D	L	F	A	GA	Pts
1 Valerenga Oslo	14	9	2	3	23	13	1.77	20
2 Sparta Sarpsborg	14	9	1	4	30	18	1.67	19
3 Viking Stavanger	14	7	4	3	25	18	1.39	18
4 Algard FK	14	7	3	4	18	17	1.06	17
5 Skeid Oslo	14	7	0	7	34	25	1.36	14
6 Orn Horten	14	6	2	6	25	23	1.09	14
7 Pors Grenland Porsgrunn	14	1	4	9	11	34	0.32	6
8 Brann Bergen	14	1	2	11	25	43	0.58	4

Group B	Pld	W	D	L	F	A	GA	Pts
1 Fredrikstad FK	14	10	2	2	29	10	2.90	22
2 Sarpsborg FK	14	7	4	3	26	14	1.86	18
3 Lyn Oslo	14	5	6	3	19	17	1.12	16
4 Sandefjord BK	14	5	5	4	25	20	1.25	15
5 Mjondalen IF	14	6	0	8	18	26	0.69	12
6 Storms BK Skien	14	3	6	5	15	24	0.63	12
7 Freidig Trondheim	14	3	3	8	15	27	0.56	9
8 Sandaker Oslo	14	3	2	9	22	31	0.71	8

Group A

August 1, 1948

Pors Grenland	0 - 1	Skeid Oslo
Sparta Sarpsborg	4 - 1	Orn Horten
Valerenga Oslo	4 - 3	Brann Bergen
Viking Stavanger	1 - 3	Algard FK

August 8, 1948

Algard FK	0 - 2	Sparta Sarpsborg
Brann Bergen	2 - 2	Pors Grenland

Group B

August 1, 1948

Fredrikstad FK	5 - 0	Storms BK Skien
Freidig Trondheim	0 - 2	Mjondalen IF
Lyn Oslo	4 - 0	Sandaker Oslo
Sandefjord BK	1 - 1	Sarpsborg FK

August 8, 1948

Mjondalen IF	3 - 0	Sandefjord BK
Sandaker Oslo	2 - 1	Fredrikstad FK

Orn Horten	0	-	1 Viking Stavanger	Sarpsborg FK	1	-	0 Freidig Trondheim
Skeid Oslo	1	-	0 Valerenga Oslo	Storms BK Skien	0	-	0 Lyn Oslo

August 22, 1948   August 22, 1948

Pors Grenland	2	-	0 Orn Horten	Fredrikstad FK	1	-	2 Mjondalen IF
Sparta Sarpsborg	3	-	1 Skeid Oslo	Freidig Trondheim	1	-	1 Storms BK Skien
Valerenga Oslo	3	-	0 Algard FK	Lyn Oslo	1	-	1 Sarpsborg FK
Viking Stavanger	4	-	3 Brann Bergen	Sandefjord BK	4	-	1 Sandaker Oslo

September 12, 1948   September 12, 1948

Algard FK	1	-	0 Pors Grenland	Storms BK Skien	3	-	3 Sandefjord BK
Orn Horten	0	-	1 Valerenga Oslo				

September 26, 1948   September 26, 1948

Brann Bergen	1	-	3 Algard FK	Sandaker Oslo	0	-	3 Sarpsborg FK
Skeid Oslo	3	-	2 Orn Horten	Sandefjord BK	3	-	1 Lyn Oslo
Sparta Sarpsborg	5	-	1 Pors Grenland				

October 3, 1948   October 3, 1948

Algard FK	2	-	1 Skeid Oslo	Lyn Oslo	1	-	1 Fredrikstad FK
Orn Horten	4	-	2 Brann Bergen	Mjondalen IF	0	-	7 Sandaker Oslo
Valerenga Oslo	1	-	0 Sparta Sarpsborg	Sandefjord BK	4	-	5 Freidig Trondheim

October 10, 1948   October 10, 1948

Brann Bergen	2	-	3 Skeid Oslo	Freidig Trondheim	1	-	3 Fredrikstad FK
Orn Horten	2	-	0 Algard FK	Mjondalen IF	2	-	3 Sarpsborg FK
Pors Grenland	0	-	2 Valerenga Oslo	Sandaker Oslo	2	-	2 Storms BK Skien
Sparta Sarpsborg	3	-	1 Viking Stavanger				

October 17, 1948   October 16, 1948

Algard FK	0	-	0 Valerenga Oslo	Lyn Oslo	2	-	0 Mjondalen IF
Viking Stavanger	2	-	2 Orn Horten				

                            October 17, 1948

				Storms BK Skien	0	-	1 Freidig Trondheim

October 24, 1948   October 24, 1948

Algard FK	1	-	0 Viking Stavanger	Freidig Trondheim	2	-	1 Sandaker Oslo
Pors Grenland	1	-	1 Brann Bergen	Sandefjord BK	3	-	0 Mjondalen IF
Skeid Oslo	5	-	2 Sparta Sarpsborg	Sarpsborg FK	5	-	1 Lyn Oslo
Valerenga Oslo	2	-	1 Orn Horten	Storms BK Skien	0	-	2 Fredrikstad FK

October 26, 1948   October 31, 1948

Skeid Oslo	2	-	3 Viking Stavanger	Fredrikstad FK	4	-	2 Sandaker Oslo
				Freidig Trondheim	0	-	0 Lyn Oslo
				Sarpsborg FK	1	-	1 Sandefjord BK

November 5, 1948   November 5, 1948

Viking Stavanger	1	-	1 Valerenga Oslo	Fredrikstad FK	1	-	0 Sandefjord BK
				Mjondalen IF	0	-	2 Lyn Oslo

November 17, 1948

Skeid Oslo	8	-	1 Pors Grenland	Sandaker Oslo	3	-	2 Freidig Trondheim
Sparta Sarpsborg	3	-	1 Brann Bergen	Sarpsborg FK	4	-	1 Storms BK Skien

April 30, 1949   April 28, 1949

Algard FK	2	-	2 Orn Horten	Sandaker Oslo	1	-	3 Lyn Oslo

May 1, 1949   April 30, 1949

Skeid Oslo	7	-	1 Brann Bergen	Fredrikstad FK	3	-	1 Sarpsborg FK
Valerenga Oslo	2	-	0 Pors Grenland				
Viking Stavanger	1	-	1 Sparta Sarpsborg				

                            May 1, 1949

				Mjondalen IF	4	-	1 Freidig Trondheim
				Sandefjord BK	2	-	2 Storms BK Skien

May 8, 1949   May 8, 1949

Brann Bergen	2	-	4 Valerenga Oslo	Freidig Trondheim	0	-	2 Sarpsborg FK
Orn Horten	2	-	1 Sparta Sarpsborg	Lyn Oslo	0	-	0 Storms BK Skien
Pors Grenland	1	-	1 Algard FK	Mjondalen IF	0	-	1 Fredrikstad FK
Viking Stavanger	3	-	0 Skeid Oslo				

May 15, 1949   May 15, 1949

Brann Bergen	0	-	2 Viking Stavanger	Fredrikstad FK	2	-	0 Freidig Trondheim
Orn Horten	4	-	1 Pors Grenland	Lyn Oslo	1	-	0 Sandefjord BK

Sparta Sarpsborg	1 - 0	Algard FK	

May 22, 1949

Algard FK	3 - 2	Brann Bergen
Orn Horten	2 - 0	Skeid Oslo
Pors Grenland	0 - 3	Sparta Sarpsborg
Valerenga Oslo	0 - 2	Viking Stavanger

May 26, 1949

Brann Bergen	2 - 3	Orn Horten
Skeid Oslo	1 - 2	Algard FK
Sparta Sarpsborg	2 - 1	Valerenga Oslo
Viking Stavanger	1 - 1	Pors Grenland

May 29, 1949

Brann Bergen	3 - 0	Sparta Sarpsborg
Pors Grenland	1 - 3	Viking Stavanger

May 30, 1949

Valerenga Oslo	2 - 1	Skeid Oslo

Sarpsborg FK	2 - 0	Mjondalen IF
Storms BK Skien	1 - 0	Sandaker Oslo

May 22, 1949

Fredrikstad FK	4 - 1	Lyn Oslo
Freidig Trondheim	0 - 2	Sandefjord BK
Sandaker Oslo	1 - 2	Mjondalen IF
Storms BK Skien	2 - 1	Sarpsborg FK

May 26, 1949

Mjondalen IF	3 - 1	Storms BK Skien
Sandefjord BK	0 - 0	Fredrikstad FK
Sarpsborg FK	1 - 1	Sandaker Oslo

May 29, 1949

Lyn Oslo	2 - 2	Freidig Trondheim
Sandaker Oslo	1 - 2	Sandefjord BK
Sarpsborg FK	0 - 1	Fredrikstad FK
Storms BK Skien	2 - 0	Mjondalen IF

Poland

A tie on points is decided by a play-off, which Cracovia won. The second division was formed following the final round of group matches and begins next year. Poland for the moment is running a spring to autumn season.

Championship play-off
December 5th 1948   Cracovia   3 - 1   Wisla Krakow

	Division 1	Pld	W	D	L	F	A	GA	Pts
1	Cracovia	26	17	4	5	61	26	2.35	38
2	Wisla Krakow	26	17	4	5	86	34	2.53	38
3	Ruch Chorzow	26	12	6	8	71	40	1.78	30
4	Legia Warszawa	26	14	2	10	55	46	1.20	30
5	AKS Chorzow	26	13	3	10	50	49	1.02	29
6	ZZK Poznan	26	9	8	9	48	49	0.98	26
7	Polonia Warszawa	26	11	4	11	45	49	0.92	26
8	LKS Lodz	26	10	4	12	60	64	0.94	24
9	Warta Poznan	26	9	6	11	51	56	0.91	24
10	Polonia Bytom	26	9	5	12	48	55	0.87	23
11	Tarnovia	26	10	2	14	42	48	0.88	22
12	Garbarnia Krakow	26	9	4	13	38	52	0.73	22
13	Rymer Radlin	26	8	3	15	45	64	0.70	19
14	Widzew Lodz	26	5	3	18	31	99	0.31	13

Wisła Krakow	0 - 2	Cracovia	LKS Lodz	0 - 3	Wisła Krakow
Wisła Krakow	3 - 1	Ruch Chorzow	LKS Lodz	1 - 0	Cracovia
Wisła Krakow	8 - 0	Legia Warszawa	LKS Lodz	3 - 7	Ruch Chorzow
Wisła Krakow	4 - 0	AKS Chorzow	LKS Lodz	3 - 0	Legia Warszawa
Wisła Krakow	2 - 1	ZZK Poznan	LKS Lodz	1 - 4	AKS Chorzow
Wisła Krakow	6 - 0	Polonia Warszawa	LKS Lodz	3 - 2	ZZK Poznan
Wisła Krakow	5 - 1	LKS Lodz	LKS Lodz	2 - 4	Polonia Warszawa
Wisła Krakow	5 - 2	Warta Poznan	LKS Lodz	3 - 3	Warta Poznan
Wisła Krakow	5 - 0	Polonia Bytom	LKS Lodz	3 - 3	Polonia Bytom
Wisła Krakow	6 - 1	Tarnovia	LKS Lodz	2 - 1	Tarnovia
Wisła Krakow	4 - 0	Garbarnia Krakow	LKS Lodz	1 - 2	Garbarnia Krakow
Wisła Krakow	2 - 7	Rymer Radlin	LKS Lodz	6 - 1	Rymer Radlin
Wisła Krakow	8 - 0	Widzew Lodz	LKS Lodz	6 - 1	Widzew Lodz
Cracovia	1 - 1	Wisła Krakow	Warta Poznan	2 - 3	Wisła Krakow
Cracovia	0 - 4	Ruch Chorzow	Warta Poznan	0 - 2	Cracovia
Cracovia	2 - 0	Legia Warszawa	Warta Poznan	1 - 1	Ruch Chorzow
Cracovia	5 - 1	AKS Chorzow	Warta Poznan	4 - 1	Legia Warszawa

Cracovia	3	-	1	ZZK Poznan	Warta Poznan	1	- 3	AKS Chorzow
Cracovia	3	-	1	Polonia Warszawa	Warta Poznan	2	- 2	ZZK Poznan
Cracovia	6	-	1	LKS Lodz	Warta Poznan	3	- 0	Polonia Warszawa
Cracovia	2	-	2	Warta Poznan	Warta Poznan	2	- 2	LKS Lodz
Cracovia	2	-	1	Polonia Bytom	Warta Poznan	1	- 3	Polonia Bytom
Cracovia	3	-	0	Tarnovia	Warta Poznan	3	- 0	Tarnovia
Cracovia	2	-	0	Garbarnia Krakow	Warta Poznan	0	- 5	Garbarnia Krakow
Cracovia	4	-	0	Rymer Radlin	Warta Poznan	5	- 1	Rymer Radlin
Cracovia	7	-	0	Widzew Lodz	Warta Poznan	3	- 2	Widzew Lodz
Ruch Chorzow	1	-	1	Wisła Krakow	Polonia Bytom	2	- 4	Wisła Krakow
Ruch Chorzow	1	-	2	Cracovia	Polonia Bytom	2	- 3	Cracovia
Ruch Chorzow	3	-	3	Legia Warszawa	Polonia Bytom	1	- 1	Ruch Chorzow
Ruch Chorzow	1	-	1	AKS Chorzow	Polonia Bytom	1	- 2	Legia Warszawa
Ruch Chorzow	2	-	0	ZZK Poznan	Polonia Bytom	3	- 3	AKS Chorzow
Ruch Chorzow	1	-	2	Polonia Warszawa	Polonia Bytom	1	- 2	ZZK Poznan
Ruch Chorzow	3	-	0	LKS Lodz	Polonia Bytom	1	- 1	Polonia Warszawa
Ruch Chorzow	3	-	1	Warta Poznan	Polonia Bytom	4	- 3	LKS Lodz
Ruch Chorzow	1	-	2	Polonia Bytom	Polonia Bytom	3	- 0	Warta Poznan
Ruch Chorzow	4	-	2	Tarnovia	Polonia Bytom	1	- 0	Tarnovia
Ruch Chorzow	1	-	0	Garbarnia Krakow	Polonia Bytom	4	- 1	Garbarnia Krakow
Ruch Chorzow	5	-	1	Rymer Radlin	Polonia Bytom	3	- 1	Rymer Radlin
Ruch Chorzow	13	-	1	Widzew Lodz	Polonia Bytom	2	- 1	Widzew Lodz
Legia Warszawa	4	-	1	Wisła Krakow	Tarnovia	2	- 1	Wisła Krakow
Legia Warszawa	0	-	0	Cracovia	Tarnovia	1	- 1	Cracovia
Legia Warszawa	4	-	2	Ruch Chorzow	Tarnovia	3	- 0	Ruch Chorzow
Legia Warszawa	4	-	1	AKS Chorzow	Tarnovia	1	- 3	Legia Warszawa
Legia Warszawa	3	-	1	ZZK Poznan	Tarnovia	4	- 0	AKS Chorzow
Legia Warszawa	0	-	1	Polonia Warszawa	Tarnovia	2	- 2	ZZK Poznan
Legia Warszawa	1	-	3	LKS Lodz	Tarnovia	3	- 0	Polonia Warszawa
Legia Warszawa	2	-	1	Warta Poznan	Tarnovia	2	- 1	LKS Lodz
Legia Warszawa	3	-	1	Polonia Bytom	Tarnovia	4	- 1	Warta Poznan
Legia Warszawa	0	-	2	Tarnovia	Tarnovia	0	- 1	Polonia Bytom
Legia Warszawa	2	-	0	Garbarnia Krakow	Tarnovia	2	- 0	Garbarnia Krakow
Legia Warszawa	1	-	0	Rymer Radlin	Tarnovia	4	- 0	Rymer Radlin
Legia Warszawa	6	-	0	Widzew Lodz	Tarnovia	5	- 1	Widzew Lodz
AKS Chorzow	2	-	1	Wisła Krakow	Garbarnia Krakow	1	- 3	Wisła Krakow
AKS Chorzow	1	-	0	Cracovia	Garbarnia Krakow	3	- 2	Cracovia
AKS Chorzow	0	-	2	Ruch Chorzow	Garbarnia Krakow	2	- 6	Ruch Chorzow
AKS Chorzow	1	-	3	Legia Warszawa	Garbarnia Krakow	1	- 0	Legia Warszawa
AKS Chorzow	3	-	2	ZZK Poznan	Garbarnia Krakow	1	- 1	AKS Chorzow
AKS Chorzow	0	-	1	Polonia Warszawa	Garbarnia Krakow	1	- 1	ZZK Poznan
AKS Chorzow	2	-	5	LKS Lodz	Garbarnia Krakow	2	- 1	Polonia Warszawa
AKS Chorzow	2	-	4	Warta Poznan	Garbarnia Krakow	0	- 0	LKS Lodz
AKS Chorzow	3	-	2	Polonia Bytom	Garbarnia Krakow	3	- 4	Warta Poznan
AKS Chorzow	4	-	0	Tarnovia	Garbarnia Krakow	4	- 1	Polonia Bytom
AKS Chorzow	6	-	0	Garbarnia Krakow	Garbarnia Krakow	3	- 1	Tarnovia
AKS Chorzow	2	-	0	Rymer Radlin	Garbarnia Krakow	1	- 0	Rymer Radlin
AKS Chorzow	1	-	0	Widzew Lodz	Garbarnia Krakow	2	- 1	Widzew Lodz
ZZK Poznan	1	-	1	Wisła Krakow	Rymer Radlin	1	- 2	Wisła Krakow
ZZK Poznan	1	-	0	Cracovia	Rymer Radlin	1	- 2	Cracovia
ZZK Poznan	3	-	2	Ruch Chorzow	Rymer Radlin	1	- 1	Ruch Chorzow
ZZK Poznan	5	-	4	Legia Warszawa	Rymer Radlin	3	- 2	Legia Warszawa

ZZK Poznan	1	-	2	AKS Chorzow	Rymer Radlin	0 - 3	AKS Chorzow
ZZK Poznan	2	-	1	Polonia Warszawa	Rymer Radlin	1 - 2	ZZK Poznan
ZZK Poznan	1	-	3	LKS Lodz	Rymer Radlin	2 - 1	Polonia Warszawa
ZZK Poznan	2	-	0	Warta Poznan	Rymer Radlin	2 - 0	LKS Lodz
ZZK Poznan	4	-	2	Polonia Bytom	Rymer Radlin	2 - 3	Warta Poznan
ZZK Poznan	2	-	0	Tarnovia	Rymer Radlin	2 - 2	Polonia Bytom
ZZK Poznan	1	-	1	Garbarnia Krakow	Rymer Radlin	3 - 0	Tarnovia
ZZK Poznan	3	-	3	Rymer Radlin	Rymer Radlin	4 - 3	Garbarnia Krakow
ZZK Poznan	1	-	1	Widzew Lodz	Rymer Radlin	4 - 1	Widzew Lodz
Polonia Warszawa	0	-	5	Wisła Krakow	Widzew Lodz	2 - 2	Wisła Krakow
Polonia Warszawa	2	-	5	Cracovia	Widzew Lodz	1 - 2	Cracovia
Polonia Warszawa	0	-	3	Ruch Chorzow	Widzew Lodz	3 - 2	Ruch Chorzow
Polonia Warszawa	0	-	1	Legia Warszawa	Widzew Lodz	1 - 6	Legia Warszawa
Polonia Warszawa	4	-	1	AKS Chorzow	Widzew Lodz	0 - 3	AKS Chorzow
Polonia Warszawa	2	-	2	ZZK Poznan	Widzew Lodz	4 - 3	ZZK Poznan
Polonia Warszawa	3	-	1	LKS Lodz	Widzew Lodz	1 - 1	Polonia Warszawa
Polonia Warszawa	0	-	0	Warta Poznan	Widzew Lodz	2 - 6	LKS Lodz
Polonia Warszawa	3	-	1	Polonia Bytom	Widzew Lodz	0 - 3	Warta Poznan
Polonia Warszawa	3	-	0	Tarnovia	Widzew Lodz	2 - 1	Polonia Bytom
Polonia Warszawa	2	-	1	Garbarnia Krakow	Widzew Lodz	3 - 2	Tarnovia
Polonia Warszawa	6	-	2	Rymer Radlin	Widzew Lodz	2 - 1	Garbarnia Krakow
Polonia Warszawa	6	-	1	Widzew Lodz	Widzew Lodz	0 - 3	Rymer Radlin

Division 2 - Final Group	Pld	W	D	L	F	A	GA	Pts
1 Lechia Gdansk	8	7	1	0	32	10	3.20	15
2 Szombierki Bytom	8	4	1	3	21	13	1.62	9
3 Radomiak Radom	8	4	0	4	14	19	0.74	8
4 Skra Czestochowa	8	3	2	3	17	15	1.13	8
5 PTC Pabianice	8	0	0	8	9	36	0.25	0

* Match originally 2-2, awarded to Skra.

Lechia Gdansk	4 - 1	Szombierki Bytom
Lechia Gdansk	6 - 1	Radomiak Radom
Lechia Gdansk	3 - 0	Skra Czestochowa
Lechia Gdansk	7 - 2	PTC Pabianice
Szombierki Bytom	2 - 3	Lechia Gdansk
Szombierki Bytom	2 - 1	Radomiak Radom
Szombierki Bytom	2 - 2	Skra Czestochowa
Szombierki Bytom	9 - 0	PTC Pabianice
Radomiak Radom	1 - 3	Lechia Gdansk
Radomiak Radom	3 - 1	Szombierki Bytom
Radomiak Radom	3 - 2	Skra Czestochowa
Radomiak Radom	1 - 0	PTC Pabianice
Skra Czestochowa	1 - 1	Lechia Gdansk

Skra Czestochowa	0	- 3	Szombierki Bytom
Skra Czestochowa	3	- 0	Radomiak Radom
Skra Czestochowa	9	- 3	PTC Pabianice
PTC Pabianice	2	- 5	Lechia Gdansk
PTC Pabianice	0	- 1	Szombierki Bytom
PTC Pabianice	2	- 4	Radomiak Radom
PTC Pabianice*	o	- w	Skra Czestochowa*

Division 2 Group 1

	Pld	W	D	L	F	A	GA	Pts
1 Skra Czestochowa	6	5	0	1	19	8	2.38	10
2 KS Chelmek	6	4	1	1	17	8	2.13	9
3 Polonia Przemysl	6	2	0	4	11	19	0.58	4
4 Zaglebie Dabrowa Gornicza	6	0	1	5	6	18	0.33	1

Skra Czestochowa	3	- 1	KS Chelmek
Skra Czestochowa	3	- 2	Polonia Przemysl
Skra Czestochowa	8	- 1	Zaglebie Dabrowa Gornicza
KS Chelmek	1	- 0	Skra Czestochowa
KS Chelmek	6	- 3	Polonia Przemysl
KS Chelmek	3	- 1	Zaglebie Dabrowa Gornicza
Polonia Przemysl	2	- 3	Skra Czestochowa
Polonia Przemysl	0	- 5	KS Chelmek
Polonia Przemysl	2	- 1	Zaglebie Dabrowa Gornicza
Zaglebie Dabrowa Gornicza	1	- 2	Skra Czestochowa
Zaglebie Dabrowa Gornicza	1	- 1	KS Chelmek
Zaglebie Dabrowa Gornicza	1	- 2	Polonia Przemysl

Division 2 Group 2

	Pld	W	D	L	F	A	GA	Pts
1 Szombierki Bytom	6	4	1	1	17	5	3.40	9
2 Pomorzanin Torun	6	4	1	1	20	10	2.00	9
3 Baildon Katowice	6	1	1	4	12	19	0.63	3
4 Legia Krosno	6	1	1	4	9	24	0.38	3

Szombierki Bytom	1	- 2	Pomorzanin Torun
Szombierki Bytom	6	- 1	Baildon Katowice
Szombierki Bytom	5	- 0	Legia Krosno
Pomorzanin Torun	0	- 1	Szombierki Bytom
Pomorzanin Torun	4	- 3	Baildon Katowice
Pomorzanin Torun	8	- 0	Legia Krosno
Baildon Katowice	1	- 1	Szombierki Bytom
Baildon Katowice	2	- 3	Pomorzanin Torun
Baildon Katowice	3	- 2	Legia Krosno
Legia Krosno	1	- 3	Szombierki Bytom
Legia Krosno	3	- 3	Pomorzanin Torun
Legia Krosno	3	- 2	Baildon Katowice

Division 2 Group 3	Pld	W	D	L	F	A	GA	Pts
1 Radomiak Radom	6	3	1	2	16	8	2.00	7
2 Ostrovia Ostrow Wielkopolski	6	3	1	2	17	13	1.31	7
3 Polonia Swidnica	6	3	0	3	10	11	0.91	6
4 Gwardia Szczecin	6	2	0	4	8	19	0.42	4

Radomiak Radom	6	- 1	Ostrovia Ostrow Wielkopolski
Radomiak Radom	4	- 0	Polonia Swidnica
Radomiak Radom	1	- 2	Gwardia Szczecin
Ostrovia Ostrow Wielkopolski	2	- 2	Radomiak Radom
Ostrovia Ostrow Wielkopolski	3	- 2	Polonia Swidnica
Ostrovia Ostrow Wielkopolski	7	- 2	Gwardia Szczecin
Polonia Swidnica	2	- 1	Radomiak Radom
Polonia Swidnica	1	- 0	Ostrovia Ostrow Wielkopolski
Polonia Swidnica	3	- 0	Gwardia Szczecin
Gwardia Szczecin	1	- 2	Radomiak Radom
Gwardia Szczecin	0	- 4	Ostrovia Ostrow Wielkopolski
Gwardia Szczecin	3	- 2	Polonia Swidnica

Division 2 Group 4	Pld	W	D	L	F	A	GA	Pts
1 PTC Pabianice	6	4	1	1	17	3	5.67	9
2 Gwardia Kielce	6	4	1	1	24	6	4.00	9
3 Ognisko Siedlce	6	2	1	3	9	21	0.43	5
4 Wici Bialystok	6	0	1	5	6	26	0.23	1

PTC Pabianice	0	- 0	Gwardia Kielce
PTC Pabianice	5	- 0	Ognisko Siedlce
PTC Pabianice	6	- 1	Wici Bialystok
Gwardia Kielce	0	- 2	PTC Pabianice
Gwardia Kielce	8	- 1	Ognisko Siedlce
Gwardia Kielce	3	- 0	Wici Bialystok
Ognisko Siedlce	2	- 1	PTC Pabianice
Ognisko Siedlce	1	- 4	Gwardia Kielce
Ognisko Siedlce	4	- 2	Wici Bialystok
Wici Bialystok	0	- 3	PTC Pabianice
Wici Bialystok	2	- 9	Gwardia Kielce
Wici Bialystok	1	- 1	Ognisko Siedlce

Division 2 Group 5	Pld	W	D	L	F	A	GA	Pts
1 Lechia Gdansk	6	4	2	0	26	11	2.36	10
2 Lublinianka Lublin	6	2	3	1	13	12	1.08	7
3 Bzura Chodakow	6	1	4	1	15	12	1.25	6
4 Gwardia Olsztyn	6	0	1	5	8	27	0.30	1

Lechia Gdansk	3 - 0	Lublinianka Lublin
Lechia Gdansk	4 - 4	Bzura Chodakow
Lechia Gdansk	7 - 2	Gwardia Olsztyn
Lublinianka Lublin	3 - 3	Lechia Gdansk
Lublinianka Lublin	2 - 2	Bzura Chodakow
Lublinianka Lublin	4 - 1	Gwardia Olsztyn
Bzura Chodakow	0 - 2	Lechia Gdansk
Bzura Chodakow	2 - 2	Lublinianka Lublin
Bzura Chodakow	5 - 0	Gwardia Olsztyn
Gwardia Olsztyn	2 - 7	Lechia Gdansk
Gwardia Olsztyn	1 - 2	Lublinianka Lublin
Gwardia Olsztyn	2 - 2	Bzura Chodakow

Portugal

A hat-trick for Sporting, a little easier than the last and this time they scored their century of goals. Boavista were relegated to be replaced by Academica Coimbra.

		Pld	W	D	L	F	A	GA	Pts
1	Sporting Lisboa	26	20	2	4	100	35	2.86	42
2	Benfica Lisboa	26	17	3	6	72	34	2.12	37
3	Belenenses CF	26	16	3	7	68	36	1.89	35
4	Porto FC	26	16	1	9	55	37	1.49	33
5	Estoril Praia GD	26	12	5	9	76	54	1.41	29
6	Vitoria Guimaraes	26	11	4	11	47	50	0.94	26
7	Olhanense	26	10	4	12	51	55	0.93	24
8	Sporting Braga	26	11	2	13	39	54	0.72	24
9	CAD o Elvas	26	7	7	12	46	61	0.75	21
10	Atletico Lisboa	26	8	5	13	44	68	0.65	21
11	Covilha SC	26	9	2	15	50	59	0.85	20
12	Vitoria Setubal	26	8	4	14	39	61	0.64	20
13	Lusitano Vila Real de Santo Antonio	26	7	4	15	23	52	0.44	18
14	Boavista FC Porto	26	4	6	16	35	89	0.39	14

Atletico Lisboa	1 - 7	Belenenses CF	Lusitano Vila Real	0 - 1	Atletico Lisboa
Atletico Lisboa	1 - 2	Benfica Lisboa	Lusitano Vila Real	1 - 1	Belenenses CF
Atletico Lisboa	1 - 1	Boavista FC Porto	Lusitano Vila Real	1 - 2	Benfica Lisboa
Atletico Lisboa	3 - 1	CAD o Elvas	Lusitano Vila Real	1 - 0	Boavista FC Porto
Atletico Lisboa	5 - 1	Covilha SC	Lusitano Vila Real	2 - 1	CAD o Elvas
Atletico Lisboa	3 - 3	Estoril Praia GD	Lusitano Vila Real	2 - 1	Covilha SC
Atletico Lisboa	3 - 0	Lusitano Vila Real	Lusitano Vila Real	1 - 1	Estoril Praia GD
Atletico Lisboa	1 - 1	Olhanense	Lusitano Vila Real	2 - 1	Olhanense
Atletico Lisboa	3 - 2	Porto FC	Lusitano Vila Real	1 - 0	Porto FC
Atletico Lisboa	4 - 3	Sporting Braga	Lusitano Vila Real	2 - 0	Sporting Braga
Atletico Lisboa	0 - 3	Sporting Lisboa	Lusitano Vila Real	0 - 2	Sporting Lisboa
Atletico Lisboa	1 - 2	Vitoria Guimaraes	Lusitano Vila Real	1 - 0	Vitoria Guimaraes
Atletico Lisboa	5 - 1	Vitoria Setubal	Lusitano Vila Real	0 - 1	Vitoria Setubal
Belenenses CF	4 - 0	Atletico Lisboa	Olhanense	4 - 1	Atletico Lisboa
Belenenses CF	0 - 1	Benfica Lisboa	Olhanense	2 - 3	Belenenses CF
Belenenses CF	5 - 0	Boavista FC Porto	Olhanense	2 - 1	Benfica Lisboa
Belenenses CF	5 - 2	CAD o Elvas	Olhanense	10 - 3	Boavista FC Porto
Belenenses CF	6 - 1	Covilha SC	Olhanense	4 - 1	CAD o Elvas
Belenenses CF	6 - 2	Estoril Praia GD	Olhanense	4 - 0	Covilha SC
Belenenses CF	3 - 1	Lusitano Vila Real	Olhanense	2 - 7	Estoril Praia GD
Belenenses CF	2 - 1	Olhanense	Olhanense	1 - 0	Lusitano Vila Real

Belenenses CF	3	-	1	Porto FC	Olhanense	1	-	2	Porto FC
Belenenses CF	5	-	0	Sporting Braga	Olhanense	3	-	2	Sporting Braga
Belenenses CF	1	-	4	Sporting Lisboa	Olhanense	3	-	7	Sporting Lisboa
Belenenses CF	3	-	0	Vitoria Guimaraes	Olhanense	2	-	0	Vitoria Guimaraes
Belenenses CF	3	-	1	Vitoria Setubal	Olhanense	1	-	0	Vitoria Setubal
Benfica Lisboa	3	-	1	Atletico Lisboa	Porto FC	3	-	0	Atletico Lisboa
Benfica Lisboa	0	-	2	Belenenses CF	Porto FC	2	-	0	Belenenses CF
Benfica Lisboa	7	-	0	Boavista FC Porto	Porto FC	4	-	3	Benfica Lisboa
Benfica Lisboa	6	-	0	CAD o Elvas	Porto FC	3	-	1	Boavista FC Porto
Benfica Lisboa	6	-	1	Covilha SC	Porto FC	3	-	1	CAD o Elvas
Benfica Lisboa	1	-	2	Estoril Praia GD	Porto FC	4	-	1	Covilha SC
Benfica Lisboa	2	-	1	Lusitano Vila Real	Porto FC	2	-	1	Estoril Praia GD
Benfica Lisboa	1	-	0	Olhanense	Porto FC	3	-	0	Lusitano Vila Real
Benfica Lisboa	1	-	1	Porto FC	Porto FC	2	-	0	Olhanense
Benfica Lisboa	4	-	0	Sporting Braga	Porto FC	0	-	1	Sporting Braga
Benfica Lisboa	3	-	3	Sporting Lisboa	Porto FC	1	-	0	Sporting Lisboa
Benfica Lisboa	5	-	0	Vitoria Guimaraes	Porto FC	4	-	2	Vitoria Guimaraes
Benfica Lisboa	6	-	0	Vitoria Setubal	Porto FC	6	-	1	Vitoria Setubal
Boavista FC Porto	3	-	3	Atletico Lisboa	Sporting Braga	2	-	1	Atletico Lisboa
Boavista FC Porto	1	-	1	Belenenses CF	Sporting Braga	3	-	1	Belenenses CF
Boavista FC Porto	1	-	4	Benfica Lisboa	Sporting Braga	3	-	4	Benfica Lisboa
Boavista FC Porto	1	-	2	CAD o Elvas	Sporting Braga	4	-	2	Boavista FC Porto
Boavista FC Porto	2	-	1	Covilha SC	Sporting Braga	1	-	1	CAD o Elvas
Boavista FC Porto	1	-	2	Estoril Praia GD	Sporting Braga	2	-	1	Covilha SC
Boavista FC Porto	6	-	1	Lusitano Vila Real	Sporting Braga	2	-	1	Estoril Praia GD
Boavista FC Porto	5	-	1	Olhanense	Sporting Braga	3	-	1	Lusitano Vila Real
Boavista FC Porto	1	-	5	Porto FC	Sporting Braga	0	-	1	Olhanense
Boavista FC Porto	2	-	1	Sporting Braga	Sporting Braga	2	-	0	Porto FC
Boavista FC Porto	0	-	0	Sporting Lisboa	Sporting Braga	1	-	0	Sporting Lisboa
Boavista FC Porto	1	-	1	Vitoria Guimaraes	Sporting Braga	1	-	1	Vitoria Guimaraes
Boavista FC Porto	1	-	1	Vitoria Setubal	Sporting Braga	2	-	0	Vitoria Setubal
CAD o Elvas	7	-	0	Atletico Lisboa	Sporting Lisboa	5	-	1	Atletico Lisboa
CAD o Elvas	1	-	1	Belenenses CF	Sporting Lisboa	5	-	1	Belenenses CF
CAD o Elvas	0	-	1	Benfica Lisboa	Sporting Lisboa	5	-	1	Benfica Lisboa
CAD o Elvas	3	-	0	Boavista FC Porto	Sporting Lisboa	12	-	1	Boavista FC Porto
CAD o Elvas	0	-	1	Covilha SC	Sporting Lisboa	7	-	1	CAD o Elvas
CAD o Elvas	4	-	2	Estoril Praia GD	Sporting Lisboa	7	-	2	Covilha SC
CAD o Elvas	1	-	1	Lusitano Vila Real	Sporting Lisboa	5	-	3	Estoril Praia GD
CAD o Elvas	2	-	2	Olhanense	Sporting Lisboa	7	-	1	Lusitano Vila Real
CAD o Elvas	2	-	0	Porto FC	Sporting Lisboa	3	-	1	Olhanense
CAD o Elvas	4	-	1	Sporting Braga	Sporting Lisboa	1	-	2	Porto FC
CAD o Elvas	3	-	4	Sporting Lisboa	Sporting Lisboa	4	-	0	Sporting Braga
CAD o Elvas	3	-	2	Vitoria Guimaraes	Sporting Lisboa	3	-	0	Vitoria Guimaraes
CAD o Elvas	3	-	3	Vitoria Setubal	Sporting Lisboa	3	-	1	Vitoria Setubal
Covilha SC	1	-	2	Atletico Lisboa	Vitoria Guimaraes	1	-	1	Atletico Lisboa
Covilha SC	1	-	2	Belenenses CF	Vitoria Guimaraes	2	-	1	Belenenses CF
Covilha SC	1	-	0	Benfica Lisboa	Vitoria Guimaraes	3	-	3	Benfica Lisboa
Covilha SC	4	-	0	Boavista FC Porto	Vitoria Guimaraes	3	-	1	Boavista FC Porto
Covilha SC	5	-	0	CAD o Elvas	Vitoria Guimaraes	3	-	0	CAD o Elvas
Covilha SC	1	-	3	Estoril Praia GD	Vitoria Guimaraes	1	-	0	Covilha SC
Covilha SC	3	-	0	Lusitano Vila Real	Vitoria Guimaraes	4	-	1	Estoril Praia GD
Covilha SC	1	-	1	Olhanense	Vitoria Guimaraes	5	-	0	Lusitano Vila Real

Covilha SC	1	-	2	Porto FC	Vitoria Guimaraes	1	-	0 Olhanense
Covilha SC	2	-	0	Sporting Braga	Vitoria Guimaraes	2	-	1 Porto FC
Covilha SC	5	-	2	Sporting Lisboa	Vitoria Guimaraes	3	-	2 Sporting Braga
Covilha SC	6	-	2	Vitoria Guimaraes	Vitoria Guimaraes	1	-	3 Sporting Lisboa
Covilha SC	6	-	2	Vitoria Setubal	Vitoria Guimaraes	5	-	0 Vitoria Setubal
Estoril Praia GD	3	-	1	Atletico Lisboa	Vitoria Setubal	5	-	1 Atletico Lisboa
Estoril Praia GD	2	-	0	Belenenses CF	Vitoria Setubal	1	-	2 Belenenses CF
Estoril Praia GD	1	-	3	Benfica Lisboa	Vitoria Setubal	1	-	2 Benfica Lisboa
Estoril Praia GD	8	-	1	Boavista FC Porto	Vitoria Setubal	5	-	0 Boavista FC Porto
Estoril Praia GD	2	-	2	CAD o Elvas	Vitoria Setubal	1	-	1 CAD o Elvas
Estoril Praia GD	2	-	2	Covilha SC	Vitoria Setubal	2	-	1 Covilha SC
Estoril Praia GD	2	-	2	Lusitano Vila Real	Vitoria Setubal	2	-	0 Estoril Praia GD
Estoril Praia GD	6	-	1	Olhanense	Vitoria Setubal	2	-	1 Lusitano Vila Real
Estoril Praia GD	5	-	1	Porto FC	Vitoria Setubal	2	-	2 Olhanense
Estoril Praia GD	6	-	1	Sporting Braga	Vitoria Setubal	3	-	1 Porto FC
Estoril Praia GD	2	-	4	Sporting Lisboa	Vitoria Setubal	1	-	2 Sporting Braga
Estoril Praia GD	4	-	2	Vitoria Guimaraes	Vitoria Setubal	0	-	1 Sporting Lisboa
Estoril Praia GD	5	-	0	Vitoria Setubal	Vitoria Setubal	3	-	1 Vitoria Guimaraes

Romania

Oradea improved dramatically on last season's mid-table position by taking the title by five points from CFR Bucuresti, while two-time winners Arad fell to 9th place. There was another reduction in the size of the top division, so 4 teams were relegated, replaced by CFR Sibiu and Metalul Resita.

		Pld	W	D	L	F	A	GA	Pts
1	Oradea ICO	26	16	5	5	60	36	1.67	37
2	CFR Bucuresti	26	14	4	8	61	33	1.85	32
3	CFR Timisoara	26	12	6	8	47	30	1.57	30
4	RATA Tirgu Mures	26	13	4	9	51	37	1.38	30
5	Jiul Petrosani	26	11	8	7	44	41	1.07	30
6	Petrolul Bucuresti	26	11	7	8	47	36	1.31	29
7	CCA Bucuresti	26	10	9	7	58	53	1.09	29
8	Dinamo Bucuresti	26	11	6	9	55	50	1.10	28
9	Arad IT	26	9	9	8	45	34	1.32	27
10	Politehnica Timisoara	26	11	3	12	47	45	1.04	25
11	CFR Cluj	26	9	5	12	39	67	0.58	23
12	Universitatea Cluj	26	7	5	14	31	50	0.62	19
13	Metalochimic Bucuresti	26	5	4	17	50	80	0.63	14
14	Gaz Metan Medias	26	3	5	18	27	70	0.39	11

August 21, 1948
CFR Bucuresti 5 - 2 CCA Bucuresti
August 22, 1948
Dinamo Bucuresti 4 - 1 Jiul Petrosani
Gaz Metan Medias 4 - 5 CFR Cluj
Metal Bucuresti 1 - 6 CFR Timisoara
Oradea ICO 5 - 2 RATA Tirgu Mures
Poli Timisoara 3 - 1 Petrolul Bucuresti
Universitatea Cluj 2 - 1 Arad ITA
August 28, 1948
Dinamo Bucuresti 5 - 3 Metal Bucuresti
August 29, 1948
Arad ITA 2 - 0 Poli Timisoara
CCA Bucuresti 3 - 2 Universitatea Cluj
CFR Timisoara 4 - 0 Gaz Metan Medias
Jiul Petrosani 2 - 1 RATA Tirgu Mures
Petrolul Bucuresti 3 - 4 Oradea ICO
August 30, 1948
CFR Cluj 2 - 1 CFR Bucuresti
September 5, 1948

February 27, 1949
Arad ITA 4 - 1 Universitatea Cluj
CFR Cluj 2 - 2 Gaz Metan Medias
CFR Timisoara 2 - 0 Metal Bucuresti
Jiul Petrosani 3 - 2 Dinamo Bucuresti
Petrolul Bucuresti 1 - 2 Poli Timisoara
RATA Tirgu Mures 0 - 3 Oradea ICO
March 19, 1949
Metal Bucuresti 1 - 4 Dinamo Bucuresti
March 20, 1949
CFR Bucuresti 12 - 2 CFR Cluj
Gaz Metan Medias 1 - 1 CFR Timisoara
Oradea ICO 1 - 3 Petrolul Bucuresti
Poli Timisoara 0 - 0 Arad ITA
RATA Tirgu Mures 2 - 2 Jiul Petrosani
Universitatea Cluj 0 - 0 CCA Bucuresti
March 26, 1949
CCA Bucuresti 5 - 4 Poli Timisoara
March 27, 1949
Arad ITA 1 - 2 Oradea ICO

CFR Bucuresti	0	-	1	CFR Timisoara	CFR Cluj	1	-	0	Universitatea Cluj
Gaz Metan Medias	1	-	1	Dinamo Bucuresti	CFR Timisoara	1	-	2	CFR Bucuresti
Metal Bucuresti	4	-	3	Jiul Petrosani	Dinamo Bucuresti	1	-	2	Gaz Metan Medias
Oradea ICO	2	-	2	Arad ITA	Jiul Petrosani	3	-	2	Metal Bucuresti
Poli Timisoara	6	-	0	CCA Bucuresti	Petrolul Bucuresti	1	-	0	RATA Tirgu Mures
RATA Tirgu Mures	2	-	1	Petrolul Bucuresti			April 2, 1949		
Universitatea Cluj	0	-	1	CFR Cluj	CFR Bucuresti	5	-	2	Dinamo Bucuresti
	September 9, 1948						April 3, 1949		
Dinamo Bucuresti	0	-	1	CFR Bucuresti	Gaz Metan Medias	1	-	0	Metal Bucuresti
	September 12, 1948				Oradea ICO	2	-	1	CCA Bucuresti
Arad ITA	2	-	0	RATA Tirgu Mures	Petrolul Bucuresti	1	-	0	Jiul Petrosani
CFR Cluj	1	-	2	Poli Timisoara	Poli Timisoara	3	-	0	CFR Cluj
CFR Timisoara	5	-	1	Universitatea Cluj	RATA Tirgu Mures	1	-	0	Arad ITA
Jiul Petrosani	1	-	0	Petrolul Bucuresti	Universitatea Cluj	0	-	2	CFR Timisoara
	September 14, 1948						April 9, 1949		
Metal Bucuresti	5	-	3	Gaz Metan Medias	Metal Bucuresti	2	-	6	CFR Bucuresti
	September 16, 1948						April 10, 1949		
CCA Bucuresti	3	-	3	Oradea ICO	Arad ITA	2	-	2	Petrolul Bucuresti
	September 18, 1948				CCA Bucuresti	0	-	1	RATA Tirgu Mures
CFR Bucuresti	4	-	0	Metal Bucuresti	CFR Cluj	1	-	2	Oradea ICO
	September 19, 1948				CFR Timisoara	3	-	1	Poli Timisoara
Gaz Metan Medias	0	-	0	Jiul Petrosani	Dinamo Bucuresti	2	-	2	Universitatea Cluj
Oradea ICO	2	-	1	CFR Cluj	Jiul Petrosani	3	-	1	Gaz Metan Medias
Petrolul Bucuresti	1	-	1	Arad ITA			April 16, 1949		
Poli Timisoara	2	-	3	CFR Timisoara	Petrolul Bucuresti	2	-	3	CCA Bucuresti
RATA Tirgu Mures	3	-	2	CCA Bucuresti			April 17, 1949		
Universitatea Cluj	1	-	1	Dinamo Bucuresti	Arad ITA	0	-	1	Jiul Petrosani
	September 23, 1948				CFR Bucuresti	2	-	0	Gaz Metan Medias
Dinamo Bucuresti	3	-	2	Poli Timisoara	Oradea ICO	0	-	0	CFR Timisoara
Metal Bucuresti	1	-	3	Universitatea Cluj	Poli Timisoara	1	-	3	Dinamo Bucuresti
	September 26, 1948				RATA Tirgu Mures	1	-	2	CFR Cluj
CFR Cluj	0	-	0	RATA Tirgu Mures	Universitatea Cluj	2	-	1	Metal Bucuresti
CFR Timisoara	2	-	1	Oradea ICO			May 28, 1949		
Gaz Metan Medias	0	-	1	CFR Bucuresti	Dinamo Bucuresti	5	-	2	Oradea ICO
Jiul Petrosani	0	-	0	Arad ITA			May 29, 1949		
	September 28, 1948				CCA Bucuresti	4	-	3	Arad ITA
CCA Bucuresti	0	-	0	Petrolul Bucuresti	CFR Cluj	0	-	2	Petrolul Bucuresti
	October 3, 1948				CFR Timisoara	2	-	0	RATA Tirgu Mures
Arad ITA	3	-	3	CCA Bucuresti	Gaz Metan Medias	2	-	3	Universitatea Cluj
CFR Bucuresti	5	-	2	Jiul Petrosani	Jiul Petrosani	1	-	1	CFR Bucuresti
Oradea ICO	2	-	1	Dinamo Bucuresti	Metal Bucuresti	2	-	3	Poli Timisoara
Petrolul Bucuresti	3	-	4	CFR Cluj			June 4, 1949		
Poli Timisoara	2	-	2	Metal Bucuresti	Petrolul Bucuresti	1	-	1	CFR Timisoara
RATA Tirgu Mures	2	-	0	CFR Timisoara			June 5, 1949		
Universitatea Cluj	4	-	2	Gaz Metan Medias	CCA Bucuresti	3	-	1	Jiul Petrosani
	October 16, 1948						June 8, 1949		
Dinamo Bucuresti	2	-	2	RATA Tirgu Mures	Arad ITA	4	-	1	CFR Cluj
	October 17, 1948				Poli Timisoara	4	-	2	Gaz Metan Medias
CFR Bucuresti	1	-	2	Universitatea Cluj	Universitatea Cluj	0	-	1	CFR Bucuresti
CFR Cluj	1	-	0	Arad ITA			June 11, 1949		
CFR Timisoara	0	-	1	Petrolul Bucuresti	Dinamo Bucuresti	3	-	5	Petrolul Bucuresti
Gaz Metan Medias	2	-	0	Poli Timisoara	Metal Bucuresti	3	-	1	RATA Tirgu Mures

Jiul Petrosani	2 - 2	CCA Bucuresti	
Metal Bucuresti	1 - 6	Oradea ICO	

November 6, 1948

Petrolul Bucuresti	3 - 1	Dinamo Bucuresti	

November 7, 1948

Arad ITA	1 - 1	CFR Timisoara
CCA Bucuresti	1 - 4	CFR Cluj
Oradea ICO	4 - 1	Gaz Metan Medias
Poli Timisoara	1 - 0	CFR Bucuresti
RATA Tirgu Mures	3 - 0	Metal Bucuresti
Universitatea Cluj	1 - 1	Jiul Petrosani

November 14, 1948

CFR Bucuresti	2 - 1	Oradea ICO
CFR Timisoara	1 - 3	CCA Bucuresti
Dinamo Bucuresti	2 - 0	Arad ITA
Gaz Metan Medias	2 - 5	RATA Tirgu Mures
Jiul Petrosani	4 - 1	CFR Cluj
Metal Bucuresti	2 - 0	Petrolul Bucuresti
Universitatea Cluj	0 - 2	Poli Timisoara

November 21, 1948

Arad ITA	1 - 1	Metal Bucuresti
CCA Bucuresti	0 - 1	Dinamo Bucuresti
CFR Cluj	1 - 3	CFR Timisoara
Oradea ICO	1 - 0	Universitatea Cluj
Petrolul Bucuresti	2 - 0	Gaz Metan Medias
RATA Tirgu Mures	2 - 1	CFR Bucuresti

November 27, 1948

CFR Bucuresti	1 - 1	Petrolul Bucuresti

November 28, 1948

Dinamo Bucuresti	1 - 0	CFR Cluj
Gaz Metan Medias	1 - 1	Arad ITA
Jiul Petrosani	3 - 2	CFR Timisoara
Metal Bucuresti	2 - 7	CCA Bucuresti
Poli Timisoara	2 - 3	Oradea ICO
Universitatea Cluj	4 - 1	RATA Tirgu Mures

December 5, 1948

Arad ITA	3 - 2	CFR Bucuresti
CCA Bucuresti	3 - 0	Gaz Metan Medias
CFR Cluj	2 - 1	Metal Bucuresti
CFR Timisoara	2 - 0	Dinamo Bucuresti
Oradea ICO	3 - 0	Jiul Petrosani
Petrolul Bucuresti	3 - 1	Universitatea Cluj
RATA Tirgu Mures	4 - 1	Poli Timisoara

February 20, 1949

Poli Timisoara	3 - 0	Jiul Petrosani

February 26, 1949

CCA Bucuresti	1 - 1	CFR Bucuresti

June 12, 1949

CFR Bucuresti	2 - 0	Poli Timisoara
CFR Cluj	1 - 1	CCA Bucuresti
CFR Timisoara	1 - 2	Arad ITA
Gaz Metan Medias	0 - 2	Oradea ICO
Jiul Petrosani	3 - 0	Universitatea Cluj

June 15, 1949

RATA Tirgu Mures	2 - 2	Dinamo Bucuresti

June 18, 1949

Petrolul Bucuresti	3 - 3	Metal Bucuresti

June 19, 1949

Arad ITA	4 - 0	Dinamo Bucuresti
CCA Bucuresti	3 - 1	CFR Timisoara
CFR Cluj	2 - 2	Jiul Petrosani
Oradea ICO	1 - 1	CFR Bucuresti
Poli Timisoara	2 - 0	Universitatea Cluj
RATA Tirgu Mures	8 - 0	Gaz Metan Medias

June 26, 1949

Gaz Metan Medias	0 - 3	Petrolul Bucuresti
Jiul Petrosani	4 - 0	Poli Timisoara
Metal Bucuresti	2 - 4	Arad ITA

June 28, 1949

CFR Timisoara	2 - 2	CFR Cluj

June 29, 1949

CFR Bucuresti	0 - 1	RATA Tirgu Mures
Dinamo Bucuresti	3 - 3	CCA Bucuresti
Universitatea Cluj	2 - 3	Oradea ICO

July 2, 1949

Petrolul Bucuresti	4 - 1	CFR Bucuresti

July 3, 1949

Arad ITA	3 - 0	Gaz Metan Medias
CCA Bucuresti	2 - 2	Metal Bucuresti
CFR Cluj	2 - 5	Dinamo Bucuresti
CFR Timisoara	1 - 1	Jiul Petrosani
Oradea ICO	1 - 1	Poli Timisoara
RATA Tirgu Mures	6 - 0	Universitatea Cluj

July 9, 1949

Dinamo Bucuresti	1 - 0	CFR Timisoara
Metal Bucuresti	9 - 0	CFR Cluj

July 10, 1949

CFR Bucuresti	3 - 1	Arad ITA
Gaz Metan Medias	0 - 3	CCA Bucuresti
Jiul Petrosani	1 - 0	Oradea ICO
Poli Timisoara	0 - 1	RATA Tirgu Mures

July 13, 1949

Universitatea Cluj	0 - 0	Petrolul Bucuresti

July 17, 1949

Oradea ICO	4 - 0	Metal Bucuresti

Scotland

Rangers trailed Dundee by a point going into the last round of matches. Both were away from home, 'Gers at bottom club Albion, Dundee at Falkirk. The scorelines were both 4-1, unfortunately for Dundee they lost while Rangers won. Going down with Albion are Morton, while coming up will be Raith Rovers and Stirling Albion, Raith claimed the title thanks to a 4-0 win over Dunfermline.

Division 1	Pld	W	D	L	F	A	GA	Pts
1 Glasgow Rangers	30	20	6	4	63	32	1.97	46
2 Dundee	30	20	5	5	71	48	1.48	45
3 Hibernians Edinburgh	30	17	5	8	75	52	1.44	39
4 East Fife	30	16	3	11	64	46	1.39	35
5 Falkirk	30	12	8	10	70	54	1.30	32
6 Glasgow Celtic	30	12	7	11	48	40	1.20	31
7 Third Lanark	30	13	5	12	56	52	1.08	31
8 Heart of Midlothian	30	12	6	12	64	54	1.19	30
9 St Mirren Paisley	30	13	4	13	51	47	1.09	30
10 Queen of the South Dumfries	30	11	8	11	47	53	0.89	30
11 Partick Thistle	30	9	9	12	50	63	0.79	27
12 Motherwell	30	10	5	15	44	49	0.90	25
13 Aberdeen	30	7	11	12	39	48	0.81	25
14 Clyde	30	9	6	15	50	67	0.75	24
15 Greenock Morton	30	7	8	15	39	51	0.76	22
16 Albion Rovers	30	3	2	25	30	105	0.29	8

August 14, 1948
Dundee	2 - 1	Heart of Midlothian
Falkirk	3 - 2	Queen of the South
Glasgow Celtic	0 - 0	Greenock Morton
Hibernians, Edinburgh	5 - 2	East Fife
Motherwell	1 - 1	Glasgow Rangers
Partick Thistle	3 - 0	Albion Rovers
St Mirren Paisley	2 - 1	Clyde
Third Lanark	1 - 0	Aberdeen

August 18, 1948
Aberdeen	1 - 0	Glasgow Celtic
Albion Rovers	1 - 2	St Mirren Paisley
Clyde	3 - 3	Dundee
East Fife	0 - 1	Motherwell
Glasgow Rangers	4 - 3	Falkirk
Greenock Morton	2 - 1	Partick Thistle
Heart of Midlothian	3 - 2	Third Lanark
Queen of the South	1 - 1	Hibernians Edinburgh

January 3, 1949
Dundee	3 - 1	Glasgow Rangers
Falkirk	7 - 1	Albion Rovers
Glasgow Celtic	2 - 0	Heart of Midlothian
Hibernians, Edinburgh	3 - 0	Clyde
Partick Thistle	1 - 1	Queen of the South
St Mirren Paisley	2 - 0	East Fife
Third Lanark	1 - 0	Greenock Morton

January 8, 1949
Aberdeen	2 - 2	Third Lanark
Albion Rovers	2 - 3	Partick Thistle
Clyde	4 - 1	St Mirren Paisley
East Fife	2 - 3	Hibernians Edinburgh
Glasgow Rangers	2 - 0	Motherwell
Greenock Morton	0 - 0	Glasgow Celtic
Heart of Midlothian	0 - 1	Dundee
Queen of the South	0 - 0	Falkirk

January 15, 1949

August 21, 1948
Dundee	3 - 0	Aberdeen	
Falkirk	1 - 2	East Fife	
Gasgow Celtic	0 - 1	Glasgow Rangers	
Hibernians, Edinburgh	3 - 1	Heart of Midlothian	
Motherwell	5 - 1	Albion Rovers	
Partick Thistle	3 - 2	Clyde	
St Mirren Paisley	2 - 1	Greenock Morton	
Third Lanark	6 - 1	Queen of the South	

August 28, 1948
Aberdeen	2 - 0	Motherwell	
Albion Rovers	2 - 0	Falkirk	
Clyde	3 - 5	Hibernians Edinburgh	
East Fife	3 - 1	St Mirren Paisley	
Glasgow Rangers	1 - 1	Dundee	
Greenock Morton	3 - 3	Third Lanark	
Heart of Midlothian	1 - 2	Glasgow Celtic	
Queen of the South	8 - 2	Partick Thistle	

August 31, 1948
St Mirren Paisley	3 - 1	Aberdeen	

September 1, 1948
Dundee	2 - 5	East Fife	
Falkirk	5 - 1	Greenock Morton	
Gasgow Celtic	2 - 2	Queen of the South	
Hibernians, Edinburgh	4 - 4	Albion Rovers	
Motherwell	3 - 0	Heart of Midlothian	
Partick Thistle	1 - 1	Glasgow Rangers	
Third Lanark	0 - 1	Clyde	

September 4, 1948
Aberdeen	1 - 2	Hibernians Edinburgh	
Albion Rovers	3 - 3	Glasgow Celtic	
Clyde	3 - 3	Falkirk	
East Fife	2 - 0	Partick Thistle	
Glasgow Rangers	2 - 1	Third Lanark	
Heart of Midlothian	1 - 3	St Mirren Paisley	
Queen of the South	2 - 1	Motherwell	

October 23, 1948
Aberdeen	4 - 4	Clyde	
Albion Rovers	2 - 1	Greenock Morton	
Falkirk	5 - 1	Third Lanark	
Gasgow Celtic	0 - 1	Dundee	
Heart of Midlothian	2 - 0	Glasgow Rangers	
Partick Thistle	2 - 6	Hibernians Edinburgh	
Queen of the South	0 - 3	East Fife	
St Mirren Paisley	0 - 0	Motherwell	

October 30, 1948
Clyde	3 - 3	Heart of Midlothian	
Greenock Morton	2 - 1	Queen of the South	
Hibernians, Edinburgh	1 - 2	Glasgow Celtic	
Motherwell	0 - 3	Falkirk	
Partick Thistle	1 - 3	Third Lanark	

November 6, 1948
Dundee	3 - 1	Greenock Morton	
Falkirk	3 - 2	Clyde	
Gasgow Celtic	3 - 0	Albion Rovers	
Hibernians, Edinburgh	4 - 1	Aberdeen	
Motherwell	2 - 3	Queen of the South	
Partick Thistle	0 - 0	East Fife	
St Mirren Paisley	1 - 2	Heart of Midlothian	
Third Lanark	2 - 1	Glasgow Rangers	

January 29, 1949
Aberdeen	0 - 2	St Mirren Paisley	
Albion Rovers	0 - 3	Hibernians Edinburgh	
Clyde	2 - 0	Third Lanark	
East Fife	3 - 0	Dundee	
Glasgow Rangers	2 - 2	Partick Thistle	
Heart of Midlothian	5 - 1	Motherwell	
Queen of the South	1 - 0	Glasgow Celtic	

February 12, 1949
Aberdeen	0 - 2	Glasgow Rangers	
Albion Rovers	0 - 3	East Fife	
Falkirk	3 - 0	Motherwell	
Gasgow Celtic	1 - 2	Hibernians Edinburgh	
Heart of Midlothian	3 - 0	Clyde	
Partick Thistle	4 - 4	Dundee	
Queen of the South	2 - 1	Greenock Morton	
St Mirren Paisley	1 - 2	Third Lanark	

February 19, 1949
Dundee	5 - 0	Albion Rovers	
Falkirk	1 - 2	Aberdeen	
Hibernians, Edinburgh	0 - 1	Glasgow Rangers	
St Mirren Paisley	1 - 1	Queen of the South	
Third Lanark	2 - 2	East Fife	

February 26, 1949
Aberdeen	4 - 2	Partick Thistle	
Albion Rovers	1 - 5	Third Lanark	
Clyde	1 - 0	Motherwell	
East Fife	3 - 2	Glasgow Celtic	
Glasgow Rangers	2 - 1	St Mirren Paisley	
Greenock Morton	2 - 3	Hibernians Edinburgh	
Heart of Midlothian	3 - 1	Falkirk	
Queen of the South	0 - 1	Dundee	

March 5, 1949
Albion Rovers	2 - 1	Aberdeen	
Greenock Morton	0 - 1	Falkirk	

March 12, 1949
Aberdeen	4 - 0	Albion Rovers	
Clyde	4 - 0	Queen of the South	
Falkirk	1 - 1	Glasgow Celtic	
Heart of Midlothian	2 - 4	Greenock Morton	
Motherwell	3 - 1	Partick Thistle	
St Mirren Paisley	6 - 1	Dundee	

March 19, 1949
Dundee	4 - 3	Hibernians Edinburgh	

Aberdeen	1	-	4	Falkirk	Falkirk	2	-	1 St Mirren Paisley
Albion Rovers	0	-	6	Dundee	Gasgow Celtic	3	-	0 Partick Thistle
Clyde	0	-	4	Glasgow Celtic	Glasgow Rangers	4	-	1 Clyde
East Fife	4	-	0	Third Lanark	Greenock Morton	2	-	0 East Fife
Glasgow Rangers	2	-	4	Hibernians Edinburgh	Heart of Midlothian	1	-	1 Aberdeen
Greenock Morton	1	-	1	Motherwell	Motherwell	1	-	0 Third Lanark
Heart of Midlothian	1	-	3	Partick Thistle	Queen of the South	4	-	0 Albion Rovers
Queen of the South	3	-	2	St Mirren Paisley				March 26, 1949
				November 13, 1948	Gasgow Celtic	2	-	1 St Mirren Paisley
Dundee	2	-	1	Queen of the South	Queen of the South	0	-	0 Aberdeen
Falkirk	5	-	3	Heart of Midlothian				April 2, 1949
Gasgow Celtic	0	-	1	East Fife	Aberdeen	0	-	0 Greenock Morton
Hibernians, Edinburgh	3	-	4	Greenock Morton	Clyde	2	-	4 East Fife
Motherwell	2	-	3	Clyde	Falkirk	1	-	3 Partick Thistle
Partick Thistle	0	-	0	Aberdeen	Glasgow Rangers	3	-	0 Queen of the South
St Mirren Paisley	0	-	2	Glasgow Rangers	Heart of Midlothian	7	-	1 Albion Rovers
Third Lanark	4	-	1	Albion Rovers	Motherwell	0	-	1 Glasgow Celtic
				November 20, 1948	St Mirren Paisley	2	-	0 Hibernians Edinburgh
Aberdeen	3	-	1	East Fife	Third Lanark	2	-	3 Dundee
Clyde	0	-	3	Greenock Morton				April 5, 1949
Heart of Midlothian	1	-	1	Queen of the South	Glasgow Rangers	2	-	1 Heart of Midlothian
Motherwell	5	-	1	Hibernians Edinburgh				April 9, 1949
St Mirren Paisley	4	-	2	Partick Thistle	Clyde	0	-	0 Aberdeen
Third Lanark	3	-	2	Glasgow Celtic	Greenock Morton	3	-	0 Albion Rovers
				November 27, 1948	Hibernians, Edinburgh	2	-	1 Partick Thistle
Dundee	1	-	0	St Mirren Paisley	Motherwell	4	-	1 St Mirren Paisley
East Fife	1	-	2	Glasgow Rangers	Third Lanark	3	-	2 Falkirk
Gasgow Celtic	4	-	4	Falkirk				April 11, 1949
Greenock Morton	0	-	2	Heart of Midlothian	Dundee	3	-	2 Glasgow Celtic
Hibernians, Edinburgh	1	-	0	Third Lanark				April 13, 1949
Partick Thistle	1	-	1	Motherwell	Glasgow Rangers	3	-	1 East Fife
Queen of the South	4	-	1	Clyde	Greenock Morton	2	-	2 Clyde
				December 4, 1948	Partick Thistle	3	-	0 St Mirren Paisley
Aberdeen	2	-	2	Heart of Midlothian				April 15, 1949
Albion Rovers	1	-	3	Queen of the South	Albion Rovers	1	-	2 Clyde
Clyde	1	-	3	Glasgow Rangers				April 16, 1949
East Fife	3	-	1	Greenock Morton	East Fife	4	-	0 Queen of the South
Hibernians, Edinburgh	2	-	1	Dundee	Gasgow Celtic	1	-	2 Third Lanark
Partick Thistle	1	-	2	Glasgow Celtic	Glasgow Rangers	1	-	1 Aberdeen
St Mirren Paisley	2	-	0	Falkirk	Greenock Morton	2	-	2 Dundee
Third Lanark	1	-	3	Motherwell	Hibernians, Edinburgh	5	-	1 Motherwell
				December 11, 1948				April 18, 1949
Aberdeen	1	-	2	Queen of the South	Gasgow Celtic	2	-	1 Clyde
Clyde	1	-	0	Albion Rovers	Glasgow Rangers	3	-	1 Albion Rovers
Falkirk	1	-	1	Hibernians Edinburgh				April 19, 1949
Glasgow Rangers	4	-	1	Greenock Morton	Third Lanark	3	-	2 Hibernians Edinburgh
Heart of Midlothian	4	-	0	East Fife				April 20, 1949
Motherwell	0	-	2	Dundee	Dundee	3	-	1 Falkirk
St Mirren Paisley	1	-	1	Glasgow Celtic	East Fife	1	-	4 Aberdeen
Third Lanark	1	-	2	Partick Thistle	Partick Thistle	1	-	1 Heart of Midlothian
				December 18, 1948				April 22, 1949
Albion Rovers	1	-	5	Heart of Midlothian	Third Lanark	3	-	1 St Mirren Paisley

Dundee	1	-	1	Third Lanark				
East Fife	1	-	2	Clyde				
Gasgow Celtic	3	-	2	Motherwell				
Greenock Morton	1	-	1	Aberdeen				
Hibernians, Edinburgh	1	-	1	St Mirren Paisley				
Partick Thistle	3	-	3	Falkirk				
Queen of the South	0	-	2	Glasgow Rangers				

December 25, 1948

Dundee	3	-	1	Clyde
Falkirk	2	-	2	Glasgow Rangers
Gasgow Celtic	3	-	0	Aberdeen
Hibernians, Edinburgh	1	-	1	Queen of the South
Motherwell	1	-	2	East Fife
Partick Thistle	1	-	0	Greenock Morton
St Mirren Paisley	3	-	2	Albion Rovers
Third Lanark	1	-	1	Heart of Midlothian

January 1, 1949

Aberdeen	1	-	3	Dundee
Albion Rovers	1	-	3	Motherwell
Clyde	0	-	1	Partick Thistle
East Fife	1	-	1	Falkirk
Glasgow Rangers	4	-	0	Glasgow Celtic
Greenock Morton	1	-	4	St Mirren Paisley
Heart of Midlothian	3	-	2	Hibernians Edinburgh
Queen of the South	2	-	1	Third Lanark

April 23, 1949

Dundee	4	-	2	Partick Thistle
East Fife	5	-	1	Albion Rovers
Hibernians, Edinburgh	2	-	0	Falkirk
Motherwell	1	-	0	Greenock Morton
Queen of the South	1	-	4	Heart of Midlothian

April 25, 1949

Greenock Morton	0	-	1	Glasgow Rangers

April 27, 1949

Dundee	2	-	1	Motherwell

April 29, 1949

East Fife	5	-	1	Heart of Midlothian

April 30, 1949

Albion Rovers	1	-	4	Glasgow Rangers
Falkirk	4	-	1	Dundee
Motherwell	1	-	1	Aberdeen

	Division 2	Pld	W	D	L	F	A	GA	Pts
1	Raith Rovers	30	20	2	8	80	44	1.82	42
2	Stirling Albion	30	20	2	8	71	47	1.51	42
3	Airdrieonians	30	16	9	5	76	42	1.81	41
4	Dunfermline Athletic	30	16	9	5	80	58	1.38	41
5	Queens Park Glasgow	30	14	7	9	66	49	1.35	35
6	St Johnstone Perth	30	14	4	12	58	51	1.14	32
7	Arbroath	30	12	8	10	62	56	1.11	32
8	Dundee United	30	10	7	13	60	67	0.90	27
9	Ayr United	30	10	7	13	51	70	0.73	27
10	Hamilton Academicals	30	9	8	13	48	57	0.84	26
11	Kilmarnock	30	9	7	14	58	61	0.95	25
12	Stenhousemuir	30	8	8	14	50	54	0.93	24
13	Cowdenbeath	30	9	5	16	53	58	0.91	23
14	Alloa Athletic	30	10	3	17	42	85	0.49	23
15	Dumbarton	30	8	6	16	52	79	0.66	22
16	East Stirlingshire	30	6	6	18	38	67	0.57	18

August 14, 1948
Airdrieonians	3	-	1	Cowdenbeath
Alloa Athletic	1	-	1	Arbroath
Dumbarton	3	-	2	Dundee United
Dunfermline Ath	1	-	1	Stenhousemuir
Kilmarnock	3	-	2	East Stirlingshire
Raith Rovers	3	-	1	Queens Park Glasgow
St Johnstone Perth	2	-	4	Ayr United
Stirling Albion	3	-	0	Hamilton Acad

August 17, 1948
East Stirlingshire	1	-	1	Airdrieonians

August 18, 1948
Arbroath	3	-	2	St Johnstone Perth
Ayr United	3	-	2	Dumbarton
Cowdenbeath	2	-	1	Raith Rovers
Dundee United	0	-	1	Dunfermline Ath
Hamilton Acad	1	-	2	Alloa Athletic
Queens Park Glasgow	2	-	3	Kilmarnock
Stenhousemuir	2	-	5	Stirling Albion

August 21, 1948
Airdrieonians	2	-	1	Hamilton Acad
Alloa Athletic	1	-	0	Stenhousemuir
Dumbarton	5	-	2	Queens Park Glasgow
Dunfermline Ath	4	-	2	Cowdenbeath
Kilmarnock	1	-	2	Ayr United
Raith Rovers	5	-	1	East Stirlingshire
St Johnstone Perth	3	-	0	Dundee United
Stirling Albion	1	-	6	Arbroath

August 28, 1948
Arbroath	1	-	1	Kilmarnock
Ayr United	1	-	3	Dunfermline Ath
Cowdenbeath	0	-	3	St Johnstone Perth
Dundee United	1	-	3	Airdrieonians
East Stirlingshire	1	-	2	Alloa Athletic
Hamilton Acad	1	-	4	Raith Rovers
Queens Park Glasgow	2	-	3	Stirling Albion
Stenhousemuir	5	-	0	Dumbarton

August 31, 1948
Stirling Albion	2	-	1	Cowdenbeath

September 1, 1948
Airdrieonians	2	-	2	Ayr United
Alloa Athletic	3	-	3	Dundee United
Dumbarton	1	-	1	Arbroath
Dunfermline Ath	5	-	2	Queens Park Glasgow
Kilmarnock	3	-	1	Hamilton Acad
Raith Rovers	3	-	0	Stenhousemuir
St Johnstone Perth	2	-	0	East Stirlingshire

September 4, 1948
Arbroath	1	-	2	Raith Rovers

January 1, 1949
Arbroath	2	-	1	Stirling Albion
Ayr United	1	-	1	Kilmarnock
Cowdenbeath	4	-	0	Dunfermline Ath
Dundee United	4	-	3	St Johnstone Perth
East Stirlingshire	1	-	5	Raith Rovers
Hamilton Acad	2	-	0	Airdrieonians
Queens Park Glasgow	2	-	0	Dumbarton
Stenhousemuir	2	-	0	Alloa Athletic

January 3, 1949
Airdrieonians	1	-	1	Dundee United
Dumbarton	2	-	2	Stenhousemuir
Dunfermline Ath	5	-	0	Ayr United
Kilmarnock	8	-	0	Arbroath
Raith Rovers	3	-	0	Hamilton Acad
Stirling Albion	2	-	5	Queens Park Glasgow

January 8, 1949
Arbroath	2	-	1	Alloa Athletic
Ayr United	0	-	2	St Johnstone Perth
Cowdenbeath	5	-	1	Airdrieonians
Dundee United	4	-	0	Dumbarton
East Stirlingshire	3	-	0	Kilmarnock
Hamilton Acad	3	-	1	Stirling Albion
Queens Park Glasgow	1	-	1	Raith Rovers
Stenhousemuir	3	-	3	Dunfermline Ath

January 15, 1949
Airdrieonians	2	-	2	Queens Park Glasgow
Alloa Athletic	1	-	2	Ayr United
Dumbarton	1	-	3	Cowdenbeath
Dunfermline Ath	3	-	4	Hamilton Acad
Kilmarnock	3	-	3	Dundee United
Raith Rovers	3	-	1	Arbroath
St Johnstone Perth	1	-	1	Stenhousemuir
Stirling Albion	3	-	1	East Stirlingshire

January 29, 1949
Arbroath	3	-	0	Dumbarton
Ayr United	1	-	1	Airdrieonians
Cowdenbeath	0	-	2	Stirling Albion
Dundee United	5	-	1	Alloa Athletic
East Stirlingshire	3	-	1	St Johnstone Perth
Hamilton Acad	3	-	1	Kilmarnock
Queens Park Glasgow	4	-	4	Dunfermline Ath
Stenhousemuir	3	-	1	Raith Rovers

February 5, 1949
Kilmarnock	0	-	2	Stirling Albion
St Johnstone Perth	1	-	2	Dunfermline Ath

February 12, 1949
Alloa Athletic	2	-	4	Dumbarton
Ayr United	0	-	1	Arbroath

Ayr United	1 - 4	Alloa Athletic		Dundee United	2 - 1	Cowdenbeath
Cowdenbeath	1 - 2	Dumbarton		Dunfermline Ath	3 - 2	Kilmarnock
Dundee United	4 - 1	Kilmarnock		Hamilton Acad	2 - 1	East Stirlingshire
East Stirlingshire	1 - 2	Stirling Albion		Queens Park Glasgow	1 - 0	Stenhousemuir
Hamilton Acad	2 - 4	Dunfermline Ath		Raith Rovers	0 - 3	Airdrieonians
Queens Park Glasgow	1 - 0	Airdrieonians		Stirling Albion	2 - 1	St Johnstone Perth
Stenhousemuir	2 - 3	St Johnstone Perth			February 19, 1949	

October 23, 1948

Alloa Athletic	4 - 5	Airdrieonians		Airdrieonians	3 - 0	Stenhousemuir
Ayr United	2 - 1	Cowdenbeath		Alloa Athletic	2 - 6	Queens Park Glasgow
Dundee United	5 - 5	Arbroath		Dunfermline Ath	4 - 2	Arbroath
Dunfermline Ath	0 - 2	St Johnstone Perth		Kilmarnock	2 - 2	Cowdenbeath
Hamilton Acad	2 - 0	Stenhousemuir		Raith Rovers	1 - 3	Dundee United
Queens Park Glasgow	4 - 0	East Stirlingshire		St Johnstone Perth	1 - 1	Hamilton Acad
Raith Rovers	4 - 3	Dumbarton		Stirling Albion	4 - 1	Ayr United
Stirling Albion	3 - 1	Kilmarnock			February 26, 1949	

October 30, 1948

Arbroath	1 - 0	Ayr United		Arbroath	3 - 3	Airdrieonians
Cowdenbeath	2 - 3	Dundee United		Ayr United	2 - 3	Raith Rovers
Dumbarton	2 - 2	East Stirlingshire		Cowdenbeath	3 - 0	Alloa Athletic
Kilmarnock	1 - 2	Dunfermline Ath		Dundee United	0 - 1	Stirling Albion
St Johnstone Perth	2 - 1	Stirling Albion		East Stirlingshire	2 - 2	Dunfermline Ath
Stenhousemuir	1 - 3	Queens Park Glasgow		Hamilton Acad	4 - 0	Dumbarton
				Queens Park Glasgow	5 - 0	St Johnstone Perth
				Stenhousemuir	6 - 2	Kilmarnock

November 6, 1948

Arbroath	1 - 1	Dunfermline Ath			March 5, 1949	
Ayr United	1 - 2	Stirling Albion		Dunfermline Ath	3 - 2	Dumbarton
Cowdenbeath	1 - 0	Kilmarnock		East Stirlingshire	3 - 0	Dundee United
Dundee United	1 - 4	Raith Rovers		Hamilton Acad	4 - 0	Cowdenbeath
East Stirlingshire	2 - 3	Dumbarton		Kilmarnock	3 - 3	Airdrieonians
Hamilton Acad	0 - 3	St Johnstone Perth		Queens Park Glasgow	4 - 1	Ayr United
Queens Park Glasgow	3 - 0	Alloa Athletic		St Johnstone Perth	5 - 3	Raith Rovers
Stenhousemuir	1 - 3	Airdrieonians		Stirling Albion	5 - 1	Alloa Athletic

November 13, 1948

March 12, 1949

Airdrieonians	4 - 1	Arbroath		Airdrieonians	4 - 1	Stirling Albion
Alloa Athletic	4 - 2	Cowdenbeath		Alloa Athletic	2 - 1	St Johnstone Perth
Dumbarton	5 - 3	Hamilton Acad		Arbroath	1 - 2	Queens Park Glasgow
Dunfermline Ath	5 - 2	East Stirlingshire		Ayr United	3 - 1	Stenhousemuir
Kilmarnock	1 - 0	Stenhousemuir		Cowdenbeath	4 - 2	East Stirlingshire
Raith Rovers	6 - 0	Ayr United		Dumbarton	2 - 2	Kilmarnock
St Johnstone Perth	3 - 2	Queens Park Glasgow		Dundee United	2 - 2	Hamilton Acad
Stirling Albion	5 - 2	Dundee United			March 19, 1949	

November 20, 1948

Airdrieonians	5 - 0	Kilmarnock		Airdrieonians	3 - 1	Dumbarton
Alloa Athletic	1 - 0	Stirling Albion		Arbroath	2 - 2	Cowdenbeath
Arbroath	4 - 1	Stenhousemuir		Ayr United	8 - 0	Dundee United
Ayr United	3 - 2	Queens Park Glasgow		Dunfermline Ath	3 - 3	Stirling Albion
Dumbarton	3 - 3	Dunfermline Ath		Queens Park Glasgow	0 - 0	Hamilton Acad
Dundee United	1 - 1	East Stirlingshire		Raith Rovers	5 - 0	Alloa Athletic
St Johnstone Perth	3 - 0	Cowdenbeath		St Johnstone Perth	1 - 0	Kilmarnock
				Stenhousemuir	0 - 0	East Stirlingshire

November 27, 1948

March 26, 1949

Dunfermline Ath	2 - 0	Raith Rovers		Dunfermline Ath	2 - 2	Alloa Athletic
East Stirlingshire	2 - 0	Cowdenbeath		East Stirlingshire	0 - 4	Ayr United
				Hamilton Acad	3 - 2	Arbroath

133

Hamilton Acad	2 - 4	Dundee United
Kilmarnock	4 - 2	Dumbarton
Queens Park Glasgow	3 - 1	Arbroath
St Johnstone Perth	5 - 0	Alloa Athletic
Stenhousemuir	7 - 1	Ayr United
Stirling Albion	1 - 0	Airdrieonians

December 4, 1948

Alloa Athletic	1 - 5	Raith Rovers
Cowdenbeath	0 - 3	Arbroath
Dumbarton	0 - 4	Airdrieonians
Dundee United	1 - 2	Ayr United
East Stirlingshire	2 - 4	Stenhousemuir
Hamilton Acad	1 - 1	Queens Park Glasgow
Kilmarnock	3 - 1	St Johnstone Perth
Stirling Albion	2 - 3	Dunfermline Ath

December 11, 1948

Airdrieonians	7 - 1	St Johnstone Perth
Alloa Athletic	0 - 6	Dunfermline Ath
Arbroath	5 - 1	Hamilton Acad
Ayr United	1 - 1	East Stirlingshire
Cowdenbeath	1 - 1	Stenhousemuir
Dumbarton	1 - 5	Stirling Albion
Dundee United	5 - 2	Queens Park Glasgow
Raith Rovers	3 - 2	Kilmarnock

December 18, 1948

Dunfermline Ath	2 - 4	Airdrieonians
East Stirlingshire	2 - 1	Arbroath
Hamilton Acad	2 - 2	Ayr United
Kilmarnock	6 - 0	Alloa Athletic
Queens Park Glasgow	2 - 1	Cowdenbeath
St Johnstone Perth	3 - 1	Dumbarton
Stenhousemuir	3 - 2	Dundee United
Stirling Albion	5 - 2	Raith Rovers

December 25, 1948

Airdrieonians	3 - 0	East Stirlingshire
Alloa Athletic	2 - 1	Hamilton Acad
Dumbarton	0 - 0	Ayr United
Dunfermline Ath	2 - 0	Dundee United
Kilmarnock	1 - 1	Queens Park Glasgow
Raith Rovers	3 - 2	Cowdenbeath
St Johnstone Perth	2 - 2	Arbroath
Stirling Albion	1 - 0	Stenhousemuir

Kilmarnock	3 - 1	Raith Rovers
St Johnstone Perth	1 - 1	Airdrieonians
Stenhousemuir	2 - 2	Cowdenbeath
Stirling Albion	3 - 1	Dumbarton

April 2, 1949

Airdrieonians	2 - 2	Dunfermline Ath
Alloa Athletic	1 - 0	Kilmarnock
Arbroath	5 - 1	East Stirlingshire
Ayr United	1 - 1	Hamilton Acad
Cowdenbeath	1 - 0	Queens Park Glasgow
Dumbarton	1 - 0	St Johnstone Perth
Dundee United	2 - 0	Stenhousemuir
Raith Rovers	0 - 0	Stirling Albion

April 9, 1949

Arbroath	1 - 0	Dundee United
Cowdenbeath	9 - 2	Ayr United
Dumbarton	0 - 1	Raith Rovers
East Stirlingshire	0 - 1	Queens Park Glasgow
Stenhousemuir	1 - 1	Hamilton Acad

April 16, 1949

Airdrieonians	0 - 3	Raith Rovers
Cowdenbeath	0 - 0	Hamilton Acad
Dumbarton	5 - 3	Alloa Athletic
Stenhousemuir	1 - 0	Arbroath

April 20, 1949

Queens Park Glasgow	0 - 0	Dundee United

April 23, 1949

Airdrieonians	3 - 0	Alloa Athletic
East Stirlingshire	1 - 0	Hamilton Acad
Raith Rovers	1 - 0	St Johnstone Perth

April 30, 1949

Alloa Athletic	1 - 0	East Stirlingshire
Raith Rovers	4 - 0	Dunfermline Ath

Spain

Barcelona won the title once more in a very close race. In Segunda division 3 teams tied on points. Real Sociedad winning, Malaga were placed second and Granada unluckily missed out. Alcoyano and Sabadell were relegated.

	Primera Liga	Pld	W	D	L	F	A	GD	Pts
1	Barcelona CF	26	16	5	5	66	36	30	37
2	Valencia CF	26	16	3	7	78	47	31	35
3	Real Madrid CF	26	15	4	7	67	42	25	34
4	Atletico de Madrid	26	15	4	7	54	32	22	34
5	Real Oviedo	26	13	4	9	50	43	7	30
6	Athletic Bilbao	26	11	2	13	61	63	-2	24
7	Espanyol Barcleona	26	10	4	12	51	46	5	24
8	Sevilla FC	26	11	1	14	35	40	-5	23
9	Tarragona CG	26	10	3	13	59	72	-13	23
10	Deportivo La Coruna	26	9	4	13	56	60	-4	22
11	Celta de Vigo	26	9	4	13	51	64	-13	22
12	Real Valladolid	26	10	2	14	38	59	-21	22
13	Alcoyano CD Valencia	26	8	5	13	30	54	-24	21
14	Sabadell	26	5	3	18	43	81	-38	13

September 12, 1948
Alcoyano CF 1 - 0 Deportivo La Coruna
Athletic Bilbao 7 - 2 Real Valladolid
Atletico de Madrid 1 - 1 Sevilla FC
Barcelona CF 5 - 2 Real Oviedo
Celta de Vigo 6 - 4 Tarragona CG
Sabadell 1 - 2 Real Madrid CF
Valencia CF 4 - 1 Espanyol Barcleona

September 19, 1948
Deportivo La Coruna 5 - 2 Sabadell
Espanyol Barcleona 4 - 1 Atletico de Madrid
Real Madrid CF 1 - 2 Barcelona CF
Real Oviedo 2 - 1 Valencia CF
Real Valladolid 4 - 2 Celta de Vigo
Sevilla FC 6 - 0 Athletic Bilbao
Tarragona CG 3 - 1 Alcoyano CF

September 26, 1948
Athletic Bilbao 4 - 3 Espanyol Barcleona
Atletico de Madrid 6 - 0 Real Oviedo
Barcelona CF 5 - 1 Deportivo La Coruna
Celta de Vigo 5 - 1 Alcoyano CF
Real Valladolid 2 - 0 Sevilla FC
Sabadell 2 - 3 Tarragona CG
Valencia CF 4 - 4 Real Madrid CF

December 12, 1948
Deportivo La Coruna 6 - 1 Alcoyano CF
Espanyol Barcleona 3 - 0 Valencia CF
Real Madrid CF 5 - 1 Sabadell
Real Oviedo 2 - 0 Barcelona CF
Real Valladolid 1 - 0 Athletic Bilbao
Sevilla FC 0 - 1 Atletico de Madrid
Tarragona CG 3 - 2 Celta de Vigo

January 9, 1949
Alcoyano CF 2 - 2 Tarragona CG
Athletic Bilbao 4 - 0 Sevilla FC
Atletico de Madrid 2 - 1 Espanyol Barcleona
Barcelona CF 3 - 1 Real Madrid CF
Celta de Vigo 2 - 0 Real Valladolid
Sabadell 4 - 4 Deportivo La Coruna
Valencia CF 3 - 1 Real Ovledo

January 16, 1949
Alcoyano CF 1 - 0 Celta de Vigo
Deportivo La Coruna 2 - 2 Barcelona CF
Espanyol Barcleona 1 - 1 Athletic Bilbao
Real Madrid CF 4 - 3 Valencia CF
Real Oviedo 2 - 0 Atletico de Madrid
Sevilla FC 2 - 1 Real Valladolid
Tarragona CG 3 - 2 Sabadell

October 3, 1948
Alcoyano CF	2 - 1	Sabadell	
Deportivo La Coruna	1 - 2	Valencia CF	
Espanyol Barcelona	5 - 1	Real Valladolid	
Real Madrid CF	1 - 2	Atletico de Madrid	
Real Oviedo	6 - 3	Athletic Bilbao	
Sevilla FC	2 - 1	Celta de Vigo	
Tarragona CG	2 - 2	Barcelona CF	

October 10, 1948
Athletic Bilbao	2 - 3	Real Madrid CF	
Atletico de Madrid	4 - 0	Deportivo La Coruna	
Barcelona CF	4 - 0	Alcoyano CF	
Celta de Vigo	3 - 2	Sabadell	
Real Valladolid	2 - 1	Real Oviedo	
Sevilla FC	0 - 3	Espanyol Barcelona	
Valencia CF	7 - 0	Tarragona CG	

October 17, 1948
Alcoyano CF	0 - 1	Valencia CF	
Deportivo La Coruna	3 - 1	Athletic Bilbao	
Espanyol Barcelona	5 - 0	Celta de Vigo	
Real Madrid CF	4 - 1	Real Valladolid	
Real Oviedo	0 - 1	Sevilla FC	
Sabadell	1 - 0	Barcelona CF	
Tarragona CG	2 - 1	Atletico de Madrid	

October 24, 1948
Athletic Bilbao	4 - 1	Tarragona CG	
Atletico de Madrid	4 - 0	Alcoyano CF	
Celta de Vigo	2 - 2	Barcelona CF	
Espanyol Barcelona	0 - 0	Real Oviedo	
Real Valladolid	1 - 0	Deportivo La Coruna	
Sevilla FC	1 - 5	Real Madrid CF	
Valencia CF	3 - 0	Sabadell	

October 31, 1948
Alcoyano CF	1 - 0	Athletic Bilbao	
Barcelona CF	4 - 3	Valencia CF	
Deportivo La Coruna	2 - 0	Sevilla FC	
Real Madrid CF	3 - 1	Espanyol Barcelona	
Real Oviedo	5 - 2	Celta de Vigo	
Sabadell	1 - 3	Atletico de Madrid	
Tarragona CG	4 - 2	Real Valladolid	

November 7, 1948
Athletic Bilbao	7 - 2	Sabadell	
Atletico de Madrid	2 - 0	Barcelona CF	
Celta de Vigo	4 - 2	Valencia CF	
Espanyol Barcelona	4 - 1	Deportivo La Coruna	
Real Oviedo	1 - 1	Real Madrid CF	
Real Valladolid	4 - 2	Alcoyano CF	
Sevilla FC	3 - 1	Tarragona CG	

November 14, 1948
Alcoyano CF	2 - 0	Sevilla FC	
Barcelona CF	5 - 2	Athletic Bilbao	
Deportivo La Coruna	1 - 2	Real Oviedo	

January 23, 1949
Athletic Bilbao	0 - 1	Real Oviedo	
Atletico de Madrid	0 - 2	Real Madrid CF	
Barcelona CF	3 - 1	Tarragona CG	
Celta de Vigo	3 - 1	Sevilla FC	
Real Valladolid	1 - 0	Espanyol Barcelona	
Sabadell	3 - 1	Alcoyano CF	
Valencia CF	7 - 1	Deportivo La Coruna	

January 30, 1949
Alcoyano CF	1 - 2	Barcelona CF	
Deportivo La Coruna	3 - 1	Atletico de Madrid	
Espanyol Barcelona	1 - 0	Sevilla FC	
Real Madrid CF	4 - 2	Athletic Bilbao	
Real Oviedo	2 - 1	Real Valladolid	
Sabadell	3 - 0	Celta de Vigo	
Tarragona CG	6 - 1	Valencia CF	

February 6, 1949
Athletic Bilbao	3 - 1	Deportivo La Coruna	
Atletico de Madrid	1 - 0	Tarragona CG	
Barcelona CF	4 - 1	Sabadell	
Celta de Vigo	2 - 1	Espanyol Barcelona	
Real Valladolid	2 - 0	Real Madrid CF	
Sevilla FC	1 - 0	Real Oviedo	
Valencia CF	5 - 3	Alcoyano CF	

February 13, 1949
Alcoyano CF	0 - 0	Atletico de Madrid	
Barcelona CF	3 - 1	Celta de Vigo	
Deportivo La Coruna	5 - 0	Real Valladolid	
Real Madrid CF	1 - 0	Sevilla FC	
Real Oviedo	3 - 0	Espanyol Barcelona	
Sabadell	0 - 3	Valencia CF	
Tarragona CG	3 - 1	Athletic Bilbao	

February 20, 1949
Athletic Bilbao	3 - 0	Alcoyano CF	
Atletico de Madrid	6 - 0	Sabadell	
Celta de Vigo	2 - 1	Real Oviedo	
Espanyol Barcelona	3 - 2	Real Madrid CF	
Real Valladolid	3 - 1	Tarragona CG	
Sevilla FC	3 - 1	Deportivo La Coruna	
Valencia CF	4 - 2	Barcelona CF	

February 27, 1949
Alcoyano CF	2 - 1	Real Valladolid	
Barcelona CF	4 - 0	Atletico de Madrid	
Deportivo La Coruna	3 - 0	Espanyol Barcelona	
Real Madrid CF	0 - 2	Real Oviedo	
Sabadell	2 - 2	Athletic Bilbao	
Tarragona CG	1 - 3	Sevilla FC	
Valencia CF	1 - 0	Celta de Vigo	

March 6, 1949
Athletic Bilbao	2 - 0	Barcelona CF	
Atletico de Madrid	2 - 2	Valencia CF	
Celta de Vigo	3 - 1	Real Madrid CF	

Real Madrid CF	6 - 0	Celta de Vigo		Espanyol Barcleona	5 - 4	Tarragona CG
Sabadell	3 - 1	Real Valladolid		Real Oviedo	4 - 1	Deportivo La Coruna
Tarragona CG	4 - 1	Espanyol Barcleona		Real Valladolid	4 - 0	Sabadell
Valencia CF	4 - 3	Atletico de Madrid		Sevilla FC	2 - 0	Alcoyano CF

November 21, 1948   **April 3, 1949**

Athletic Bilbao	3 - 2	Valencia CF		Alcoyano CF	2 - 0	Espanyol Barcleona
Celta de Vigo	2 - 2	Atletico de Madrid		Atletico de Madrid	3 - 0	Celta de Vigo
Espanyol Barcleona	1 - 1	Alcoyano CF		Barcelona CF	6 - 0	Real Valladolid
Real Madrid CF	3 - 1	Deportivo La Coruna		Deportivo La Coruna	0 - 3	Real Madrid CF
Real Oviedo	0 - 2	Tarragona CG		Sabadell	1 - 3	Sevilla FC
Real Valladolid	1 - 1	Barcelona CF		Tarragona CG	2 - 4	Real Oviedo
Sevilla FC	4 - 1	Sabadell		Valencia CF	5 - 0	Athletic Bilbao

November 28, 1948   **April 10, 1949**

Alcoyano CF	2 - 1	Real Oviedo		Athletic Bilbao	1 - 3	Atletico de Madrid
Atletico de Madrid	3 - 2	Athletic Bilbao		Deportivo La Coruna	3 - 3	Celta de Vigo
Barcelona CF	2 - 1	Sevilla FC		Espanyol Barcleona	6 - 2	Sabadell
Celta de Vigo	1 - 1	Deportivo La Coruna		Real Madrid CF	3 - 1	Tarragona CG
Sabadell	2 - 0	Espanyol Barcleona		Real Oviedo	1 - 1	Alcoyano CF
Tarragona CG	3 - 3	Real Madrid CF		Real Valladolid	1 - 1	Valencia CF
Valencia CF	6 - 2	Real Valladolid		Sevilla FC	1 - 2	Barcelona CF

December 5, 1948   **April 17, 1949**

Athletic Bilbao	3 - 2	Celta de Vigo		Alcoyano CF	2 - 2	Real Madrid CF
Deportivo La Coruna	6 - 2	Tarragona CG		Atletico de Madrid	2 - 0	Real Valladolid
Espanyol Barcleona	1 - 1	Barcelona CF		Barcelona CF	2 - 1	Espanyol Barcleona
Real Madrid CF	3 - 1	Alcoyano CF		Celta de Vigo	3 - 4	Athletic Bilbao
Real Oviedo	5 - 4	Sabadell		Sabadell	2 - 2	Real Oviedo
Real Valladolid	0 - 1	Atletico de Madrid		Tarragona CG	1 - 4	Deportivo La Coruna
Sevilla FC	0 - 2	Valencia CF		Valencia CF	2 - 0	Sevilla FC

	Segunda Division	Pld	W	D	L	F	A	GD	Pts
1	Real Sociedad San Sebastian	26	17	1	8	80	41	39	35
2	Malaga CD	26	15	5	6	73	33	40	35
3	Granada CF	26	16	3	7	50	37	13	35
4	Hercules CF Alicante	26	14	4	8	64	53	11	32
5	Barakaldo CF	26	13	3	10	48	37	11	29
6	Sporting Gijon	26	12	5	9	56	44	12	29
7	Real Murcia CF	26	12	2	12	51	71	-20	26
8	Castellon CD	26	11	2	13	47	61	-14	24
9	Levante UD	26	9	4	13	48	53	-5	22
10	Girona CF	26	10	2	14	45	53	-8	22
11	Racing Santander	26	8	5	13	50	67	-17	21
12	Valencia CF Mestalla	26	9	2	15	43	50	-7	20
13	Badalona CF	26	8	3	15	40	63	-23	19
14	Racing Ferrol	26	6	3	17	39	71	-32	15

*Note Valencia CF Mestalla is Valencia's reserve team.

September 12, 1948
Racing Ferrol	1	-	0	Barakaldo CF
Granada CF	1	-	0	Castellon CD
Hercules CF Alicante	4	-	2	Real Sociedad
Malaga CD	8	-	0	Real Murcia CF
Racing Santander	7	-	1	Girona CF
Sporting Gijon	2	-	1	Levante UD
Valencia CF Mestalla	3	-	2	Badalona CF

September 19, 1948
Badalona CF	3	-	4	Hercules CF Alicante
Barakaldo CF	5	-	1	Granada CF
Castellon CD	3	-	2	Racing Santander
Girona CF	4	-	2	Sporting Gijon
Levante UD	1	-	0	Valencia CF Mestalla
Malaga CD	3	-	1	Real Sociedad
Real Murcia CF	6	-	2	Racing Ferrol

September 26, 1948
Racing Ferrol	1	-	1	Granada CF
Hercules CF Alicante	4	-	2	Levante UD
Malaga CD	6	-	1	Badalona CF
Racing Santander	2	-	0	Barakaldo CF
Real Murcia CF	3	-	0	Real Sociedad
Sporting Gijon	5	-	2	Castellon CD
Valencia CF Mestalla	3	-	1	Girona CF

October 3, 1948
Badalona CF	3	-	0	Real Murcia CF
Barakaldo CF	1	-	0	Sporting Gijon
Castellon CD	1	-	0	Valencia CF Mestalla
Girona CF	2	-	0	Hercules CF Alicante
Granada CF	3	-	0	Racing Santander
Levante UD	2	-	3	Malaga CD
Real Sociedad	3	-	1	Racing Ferrol

October 10, 1948
Racing Ferrol	2	-	2	Racing Santander
Hercules CF Alicante	5	-	3	Castellon CD
Malaga CD	4	-	2	Girona CF
Real Murcia CF	1	-	3	Levante UD
Real Sociedad	4	-	1	Badalona CF
Sporting Gijon	2	-	0	Granada CF
Valencia CF Mestalla	2	-	0	Barakaldo CF

October 17, 1948
Badalona CF	2	-	1	Racing Ferrol
Barakaldo CF	3	-	0	Hercules CF Alicante
Castellon CD	1	-	1	Malaga CD
Girona CF	2	-	1	Real Murcia CF
Granada CF	4	-	2	Valencia CF Mestalla
Levante UD	1	-	2	Real Sociedad
Racing Santander	3	-	2	Sporting Gijon

October 24, 1948
Badalona CF	3	-	2	Levante UD
Racing Ferrol	3	-	3	Sporting Gijon
Hercules CF Alicante	3	-	3	Granada CF

December 12, 1948
Badalona CF	2	-	1	Valencia CF Mestalla
Barakaldo CF	2	-	0	Racing Ferrol
Castellon CD	1	-	0	Granada CF
Girona CF	4	-	0	Racing Santander
Levante UD	1	-	1	Sporting Gijon
Real Murcia CF	1	-	0	Malaga CD
Real Sociedad	9	-	2	Hercules CF Alicante

January 9, 1949
Racing Ferrol	2	-	3	Real Murcia CF
Granada CF	3	-	1	Barakaldo CF
Hercules CF Alicante	2	-	1	Badalona CF
Racing Santander	4	-	4	Castellon CD
Real Sociedad	5	-	1	Malaga CD
Sporting Gijon	2	-	0	Girona CF
Valencia CF Mestalla	1	-	0	Levante UD

January 16, 1949
Badalona CF	2	-	2	Malaga CD
Barakaldo CF	2	-	3	Racing Santander
Castellon CD	4	-	1	Sporting Gijon
Girona CF	2	-	1	Valencia CF Mestalla
Granada CF	3	-	0	Racing Ferrol
Levante UD	1	-	1	Hercules CF Alicante
Real Sociedad	7	-	0	Real Murcia CF

January 23, 1949
Racing Ferrol	3	-	4	Real Sociedad
Hercules CF Alicante	2	-	0	Girona CF
Malaga CD	5	-	0	Levante UD
Racing Santander	1	-	2	Granada CF
Real Murcia CF	1	-	2	Badalona CF
Sporting Gijon	0	-	0	Barakaldo CF
Valencia CF Mestalla	3	-	1	Castellon CD

January 30, 1949
Badalona CF	2	-	1	Real Sociedad
Barakaldo CF	6	-	2	Valencia CF Mestalla
Castellon CD	1	-	2	Hercules CF Alicante
Girona CF	2	-	2	Malaga CD
Granada CF	1	-	0	Sporting Gijon
Levante UD	2	-	2	Real Murcia CF
Racing Santander	1	-	2	Racing Ferrol

February 6, 1949
Racing Ferrol	4	-	0	Badalona CF
Hercules CF Alicante	2	-	0	Barakaldo CF
Malaga CD	1	-	0	Castellon CD
Real Murcia CF	3	-	0	Girona CF
Real Sociedad	4	-	3	Levante UD
Sporting Gijon	3	-	0	Racing Santander
Valencia CF Mestalla	1	-	2	Granada CF

February 13, 1949
Barakaldo CF	3	-	2	Malaga CD
Castellon CD	4	-	0	Real Murcia CF
Girona CF	4	-	1	Real Sociedad

Malaga CD	3	-	0	Barakaldo CF	Granada CF	1 - 1	Hercules CF Alicante
Real Murcia CF	2	-	0	Castellon CD	Levante UD	4 - 0	Badalona CF
Real Sociedad	5	-	1	Girona CF	Racing Santander	0 - 1	Valencia CF Mestalla
Valencia CF Mestalla	4	-	2	Racing Santander	Sporting Gijon	6 - 1	Racing Ferrol

October 31, 1948 | **February 20, 1949**

Barakaldo CF	3	-	0	Real Murcia CF	Badalona CF	0 - 3	Girona CF
Castellon CD	3	-	1	Real Sociedad	Racing Ferrol	0 - 1	Levante UD
Girona CF	5	-	0	Badalona CF	Hercules CF Alicante	4 - 1	Racing Santander
Granada CF	1	-	0	Malaga CD	Malaga CD	5 - 0	Granada CF
Levante UD	5	-	2	Racing Ferrol	Real Murcia CF	5 - 1	Barakaldo CF
Racing Santander	6	-	5	Hercules CF Alicante	Real Sociedad	7 - 0	Castellon CD
Sporting Gijon	3	-	2	Valencia CF Mestalla	Valencia CF Mestalla	2 - 3	Sporting Gijon

November 7, 1948 | **February 27, 1949**

Badalona CF	4	-	1	Castellon CD	Barakaldo CF	1 - 2	Real Sociedad
Racing Ferrol	3	-	0	Valencia CF Mestalla	Castellon CD	2 - 1	Badalona CF
Hercules CF Alicante	3	-	1	Sporting Gijon	Girona CF	5 - 1	Levante UD
Levante UD	4	-	0	Girona CF	Granada CF	5 - 1	Real Murcia CF
Malaga CD	7	-	1	Racing Santander	Racing Santander	2 - 2	Malaga CD
Real Murcia CF	2	-	1	Granada CF	Sporting Gijon	3 - 2	Hercules CF Alicante
Real Sociedad	4	-	1	Barakaldo CF	Valencia CF Mestalla	6 - 1	Racing Ferrol

November 14, 1948 | **March 6, 1949**

Barakaldo CF	3	-	1	Badalona CF	Badalona CF	1 - 2	Barakaldo CF
Castellon CD	1	-	2	Levante UD	Racing Ferrol	1 - 0	Girona CF
Girona CF	4	-	1	Racing Ferrol	Hercules CF Alicante	4 - 1	Valencia CF Mestalla
Granada CF	3	-	0	Real Sociedad	Levante UD	4 - 1	Castellon CD
Racing Santander	2	-	2	Real Murcia CF	Malaga CD	3 - 0	Sporting Gijon
Sporting Gijon	2	-	1	Malaga CD	Real Murcia CF	4 - 1	Racing Santander
Valencia CF Mestalla	1	-	1	Hercules CF Alicante	Real Sociedad	5 - 1	Granada CF

November 21, 1948 | **April 3, 1949**

Badalona CF	2	-	0	Granada CF	Barakaldo CF	2 - 1	Levante UD
Racing Ferrol	0	-	1	Hercules CF Alicante	Castellon CD	3 - 1	Girona CF
Girona CF	2	-	3	Castellon CD	Granada CF	4 - 2	Badalona CF
Levante UD	1	-	1	Barakaldo CF	Hercules CF Alicante	0 - 1	Racing Ferrol
Malaga CD	1	-	1	Valencia CF Mestalla	Racing Santander	2 - 0	Real Sociedad
Real Murcia CF	3	-	2	Sporting Gijon	Sporting Gijon	7 - 0	Real Murcia CF
Real Sociedad	5	-	0	Racing Santander	Valencia CF Mestalla	0 - 1	Malaga CD

November 28, 1948 | **April 10, 1949**

Barakaldo CF	3	-	0	Girona CF	Badalona CF	1 - 1	Racing Santander
Racing Ferrol	2	-	4	Castellon CD	Castellon CD	3 - 2	Racing Ferrol
Granada CF	3	-	0	Levante UD	Girona CF	0 - 0	Barakaldo CF
Hercules CF Alicante	3	-	0	Malaga CD	Levante UD	2 - 3	Granada CF
Racing Santander	1	-	0	Badalona CF	Malaga CD	1 - 0	Hercules CF Alicante
Sporting Gijon	0	-	0	Real Sociedad	Real Murcia CF	4 - 3	Valencia CF Mestalla
Valencia CF Mestalla	2	-	0	Real Murcia CF	Real Sociedad	3 - 0	Sporting Gijon

December 5, 1948 | **April 17, 1949**

Badalona CF	1	-	1	Sporting Gijon	Barakaldo CF	6 - 1	Castellon CD
Castellon CD	0	-	2	Barakaldo CF	Racing Ferrol	1 - 5	Malaga CD
Girona CF	0	-	1	Granada CF	Granada CF	3 - 0	Girona CF
Levante UD	3	-	1	Racing Santander	Hercules CF Alicante	8 - 2	Real Murcia CF
Malaga CD	6	-	2	Racing Ferrol	Racing Santander	5 - 1	Levante UD
Real Murcia CF	5	-	1	Hercules CF Alicante	Sporting Gijon	5 - 3	Badalona CF
Real Sociedad	2	-	0	Valencia CF Mestalla	Valencia CF Mestalla	1 - 3	Real Sociedad

Sweden

It's Malmo over Helsingborgs on GA. Goteborgs in third needed a win and the top 2 to slip up on the last day, neither obliged and Halmia held them to a draw. Orebro and Landskrona go down, Djurgardens and Kalmar come up a level.

		Pld	W	D	L	F	A	GA	Pts
1	Malmo FF	22	12	5	5	72	29	2.48	29
2	Helsingborgs IF	22	11	7	4	48	30	1.60	29
3	Goteborgs AIS	22	12	3	7	41	29	1.41	27
4	Degerfors IF	22	10	5	7	45	33	1.36	25
5	Solna AIK	22	11	3	8	42	38	1.11	25
6	Goteborg IFK	22	9	5	8	36	33	1.09	23
7	Norrkoping IFK	22	8	6	8	38	33	1.15	22
8	Jonkoping Sodra IF	22	6	10	6	34	52	0.65	22
9	Halmia IS	22	6	7	9	33	39	0.85	19
10	Elfsborg IF	22	7	4	11	28	47	0.60	18
11	Orebro SK	22	5	4	13	30	50	0.60	14
12	Landskrona BoIS	22	3	5	14	26	60	0.43	11

August 8, 1948
Elfsborg IF   0 - 0 Landskrona BoIS
Goteborgs AIS   2 - 0 Jonkoping Sodra IF
Orebro SK   2 - 1 Halmia IS

August 15, 1948
Degerfors IF   3 - 1 Orebro SK

August 19, 1948
Goteborgs AIS   1 - 2 Elfsborg IF
Landskrona BoIS   1 - 4 Helsingborgs IF

August 22, 1948
Elfsborg IF   4 - 4 Jonkoping Sodra IF
Goteborg IFK   1 - 2 Goteborgs AIS
Helsingborgs IF   1 - 0 Degerfors IF
Malmo FF   5 - 0 Landskrona BoIS
Orebro SK   2 - 2 Norrkoping IFK
Solna AIK   3 - 1 Halmia IS

August 29, 1948
Degerfors IF   4 - 0 Landskrona BoIS
Goteborg IFK   4 - 4 Malmo FF
Halmia IS   0 - 2 Elfsborg IF
Norrkoping IFK   0 - 0 Jonkoping Sodra IF
Orebro SK   3 - 2 Goteborgs AIS
Solna AIK   3 - 2 Helsingborgs IF

September 5, 1948
Elfsborg IF   0 - 1 Goteborg IFK
Goteborgs AIS   1 - 0 Degerfors IF
Helsingborgs IF   5 - 3 Orebro SK
Jonkoping Sodra IF 3 - 2 Halmia IS

March 27, 1949
Goteborg IFK   3 - 2 Solna AIK
Helsingborgs IF   1 - 3 Norrkoping IFK
Malmo FF   2 - 0 Degerfors IF

April 3, 1949
Halmia IS   2 - 2 Goteborg IFK
Jonkoping Sodra IF 2 - 2 Malmo FF
Norrkoping IFK   1 - 4 Solna AIK

April 10, 1949
Elfsborg IF   3 - 2 Degerfors IF
Goteborgs AIS   1 - 1 Solna AIK
Helsingborgs IF   2 - 1 Halmia IS
Jonkoping Sodra IF 2 - 1 Landskrona BoIS
Malmo FF   4 - 0 Norrkoping IFK
Orebro SK   0 - 2 Goteborg IFK

April 18, 1949
Degerfors IF   1 - 1 Jonkoping Sodra IF
Goteborg IFK   0 - 0 Helsingborgs IF
Halmia IS   5 - 1 Malmo FF
Landskrona BoIS   2 - 4 Goteborgs AIS
Norrkoping IFK   2 - 1 Elfsborg IF
Solna AIK   2 - 0 Orebro SK

April 24, 1949
Elfsborg IF   0 - 0 Halmia IS
Goteborgs AIS   4 - 1 Orebro SK
Helsingborgs IF   1 - 1 Solna AIK
Jonkoping Sodra IF 1 - 1 Norrkoping IFK
Landskrona BoIS   5 - 1 Degerfors IF

Landskrona BoIS	3	-	1	Norrkoping IFK	Malmo FF	3 - 1	Goteborg IFK
Malmo FF	5	-	0	Solna AIK	*May 1, 1949*		
September 12, 1948					Degerfors IF	1 - 0	Goteborgs AIS
Degerfors IF	2	-	1	Malmo FF	Goteborg IFK	0 - 1	Elfsborg IF
Halmia IS	1	-	0	Orebro SK	Halmia IS	3 - 2	Jonkoping Sodra IF
Jonkoping Sodra IF	2	-	1	Goteborgs AIS	Norrkoping IFK	4 - 0	Landskrona BoIS
Landskrona BoIS	2	-	2	Elfsborg IF	Orebro SK	1 - 2	Helsingborgs IF
Norrkoping IFK	0	-	2	Helsingborgs IF	Solna AIK	3 - 0	Malmo FF
Solna AIK	0	-	3	Goteborg IFK	*May 6, 1949*		
September 26, 1948					Malmo FF	2 - 2	Helsingborgs IF
Goteborg IFK	5	-	2	Landskrona BoIS	*May 8, 1949*		
Halmia IS	1	-	1	Degerfors IF	Degerfors IF	4 - 2	Halmia IS
Helsingborgs IF	1	-	1	Malmo FF	Elfsborg IF	1 - 2	Orebro SK
Norrkoping IFK	5	-	0	Goteborgs AIS	Goteborgs AIS	2 - 0	Norrkoping IFK
Orebro SK	2	-	3	Elfsborg IF	Jonkoping Sodra IF	3 - 2	Solna AIK
Solna AIK	5	-	1	Jonkoping Sodra IF	Landskrona BoIS	0 - 1	Goteborg IFK
October 3, 1948					*May 15, 1949*		
Degerfors IF	2	-	1	Norrkoping IFK	Goteborg IFK	2 - 2	Jonkoping Sodra IF
Elfsborg IF	4	-	2	Solna AIK	Halmia IS	4 - 2	Landskrona BoIS
Goteborgs AIS	4	-	0	Helsingborgs IF	Helsingborgs IF	5 - 1	Goteborgs AIS
Jonkoping Sodra IF	0	-	2	Goteborg IFK	Norrkoping IFK	1 - 1	Degerfors IF
Landskrona BoIS	0	-	2	Halmia IS	Orebro SK	1 - 2	Malmo FF
Malmo FF	4	-	2	Orebro SK	Solna AIK	2 - 1	Elfsborg IF
October 17, 1948					*May 20, 1949*		
Goteborg IFK	1	-	3	Degerfors IF	Goteborgs AIS	0 - 0	Goteborg IFK
Halmia IS	1	-	1	Norrkoping IFK	*May 22, 1949*		
Helsingborgs IF	3	-	0	Elfsborg IF	Degerfors IF	3 - 3	Helsingborgs IF
Malmo FF	0	-	1	Goteborgs AIS	Halmia IS	2 - 2	Solna AIK
Orebro SK	2	-	2	Jonkoping Sodra IF	Jonkoping Sodra IF	2 - 0	Elfsborg IF
Solna AIK	0	-	1	Landskrona BoIS	Landskrona BoIS	0 - 6	Malmo FF
October 24, 1948					Norrkoping IFK	0 - 1	Orebro SK
Degerfors IF	0	-	1	Solna AIK	*May 26, 1949*		
Elfsborg IF	2	-	1	Malmo FF	Elfsborg IF	1 - 5	Goteborgs AIS
Goteborgs AIS	1	-	0	Halmia IS	Goteborg IFK	1 - 0	Halmia IS
Jonkoping Sodra IF	3	-	1	Helsingborgs IF	Helsingborgs IF	1 - 1	Landskrona BoIS
Landskrona BoIS	1	-	2	Orebro SK	Malmo FF	12 - 0	Jonkoping Sodra IF
Norrkoping IFK	4	-	2	Goteborg IFK	Orebro SK	1 - 4	Degerfors IF
October 31, 1948					Solna AIK	0 - 3	Norrkoping IFK
Degerfors IF	5	-	0	Elfsborg IF	*May 29, 1949*		
Goteborg IFK	4	-	1	Orebro SK	Degerfors IF	4 - 1	Goteborg IFK
Halmia IS	2	-	2	Helsingborgs IF	Elfsborg IF	0 - 3	Helsingborgs IF
Landskrona BoIS	1	-	1	Jonkoping Sodra IF	Goteborgs AIS	1 - 5	Malmo FF
Norrkoping IFK	2	-	2	Malmo FF	Jonkoping Sodra IF	1 - 1	Orebro SK
Solna AIK	0	-	2	Goteborgs AIS	Landskrona BoIS	2 - 3	Solna AIK
November 7, 1948					Norrkoping IFK	2 - 3	Halmia IS
Elfsborg IF	1	-	4	Norrkoping IFK	*June 6, 1949*		
Goteborgs AIS	6	-	0	Landskrona BoIS	Goteborg IFK	0 - 1	Norrkoping IFK
Helsingborgs IF	2	-	0	Goteborg IFK	Halmia IS	0 - 0	Goteborgs AIS
Jonkoping Sodra IF	2	-	2	Degerfors IF	Helsingborgs IF	5 - 0	Jonkoping Sodra IF
Malmo FF	6	-	0	Halmia IS	Malmo FF	4 - 0	Elfsborg IF
Orebro SK	0	-	2	Solna AIK	Orebro SK	2 - 2	Landskrona BoIS
					Solna AIK	4 - 2	Degerfors IF

Switzerland

Lugano ran away with the title, while Grasshopper were relegated along with newly promoted Urania

		Pld	W	D	L	F	A	GA	Pts
1	Lugano	26	18	4	4	41	18	2.28	40
2	Basel	26	13	7	6	58	37	1.57	33
3	La Chaux-de-Fonds	26	11	7	8	54	50	1.08	29
4	Servette Geneve	26	10	7	9	59	43	1.37	27
5	Zurich	26	10	7	9	65	59	1.10	27
6	Bellinzona	26	9	9	8	31	33	0.94	27
7	Locarno	26	10	7	9	32	40	0.80	27
8	Lausanne-Sports	26	11	4	11	52	41	1.27	26
9	Biel-Bienne	26	10	5	11	39	38	1.03	25
10	Grenchen	26	6	11	9	39	42	0.93	23
11	Chiasso	26	8	6	12	35	55	0.64	22
12	Young Fellows Zurich	26	8	5	13	45	66	0.68	21
13	Grasshopper Zurich	26	7	6	13	42	51	0.82	20
14	Urania Geneve Sport	26	4	9	13	32	51	0.63	17

Lugano	1 - 0 Basel	Lausanne-Sports	0 - 1 Lugano
Lugano	3 - 0 La Chaux-de-Fonds	Lausanne-Sports	2 - 0 Basel
Lugano	2 - 1 Servette Geneve	Lausanne-Sports	2 - 3 La Chaux-de-Fonds
Lugano	1 - 1 Zurich	Lausanne-Sports	4 - 3 Servette Geneve
Lugano	2 - 0 AC Bellinzona	Lausanne-Sports	1 - 3 Zurich
Lugano	3 - 0 Locarno	Lausanne-Sports	0 - 1 AC Bellinzona
Lugano	2 - 1 Lausanne-Sports	Lausanne-Sports	0 - 1 Locarno
Lugano	1 - 0 Biel-Bienne	Lausanne-Sports	1 - 0 Biel-Bienne
Lugano	0 - 0 Grenchen	Lausanne-Sports	1 - 1 Grenchen
Lugano	2 - 0 Chiasso	Lausanne-Sports	1 - 3 Chiasso
Lugano	2 - 0 Young Fellows Zurich	Lausanne-Sports	2 - 1 Young Fellows Zurich
Lugano	0 - 2 Grasshopper Zurich	Lausanne-Sports	4 - 1 Grasshopper Zurich
Lugano	1 - 1 Urania Geneve-Sports	Lausanne-Sports	1 - 1 Urania Geneve-Sports
Basel	0 - 1 Lugano	Biel-Bienne	4 - 2 Lugano
Basel	3 - 2 La Chaux-de-Fonds	Biel-Bienne	2 - 1 Basel
Basel	3 - 0 Servette Geneve	Biel-Bienne	3 - 2 La Chaux-de-Fonds
Basel	3 - 1 Zurich	Biel-Bienne	0 - 0 Servette Geneve
Basel	1 - 0 AC Bellinzona	Biel-Bienne	2 - 3 Zurich
Basel	4 - 1 Locarno	Biel-Bienne	4 - 0 AC Bellinzona
Basel	3 - 1 Lausanne-Sports	Biel-Bienne	1 - 1 Locarno
Basel	1 - 1 Biel-Bienne	Biel-Bienne	0 - 4 Lausanne-Sports
Basel	2 - 2 Grenchen	Biel-Bienne	2 - 0 Grenchen
Basel	4 - 0 Chiasso	Biel-Bienne	1 - 2 Chiasso
Basel	6 - 1 Young Fellows Zurich	Biel-Bienne	1 - 4 Young Fellows Zurich

Basel	2	-	0 Grasshopper Zurich	Biel-Bienne	5	-	2 Grasshopper Zurich
Basel	1	-	1 Urania Geneve-Sports	Biel-Bienne	2	-	1 Urania Geneve-Sports
La Chaux-de-Fonds	2	-	0 Lugano	Grenchen	0	-	1 Lugano
La Chaux-de-Fonds	2	-	4 Basel	Grenchen	2	-	3 Basel
La Chaux-de-Fonds	2	-	2 Servette Geneve	Grenchen	1	-	1 La Chaux-de-Fonds
La Chaux-de-Fonds	5	-	2 Zurich	Grenchen	2	-	4 Servette Geneve
La Chaux-de-Fonds	0	-	0 AC Bellinzona	Grenchen	2	-	2 Zurich
La Chaux-de-Fonds	1	-	1 Locarno	Grenchen	1	-	0 AC Bellinzona
La Chaux-de-Fonds	4	-	3 Lausanne-Sports	Grenchen	0	-	0 Locarno
La Chaux-de-Fonds	0	-	0 Biel-Bienne	Grenchen	4	-	5 Lausanne-Sports
La Chaux-de-Fonds	3	-	2 Grenchen	Grenchen	0	-	2 Biel-Bienne
La Chaux-de-Fonds	3	-	1 Chiasso	Grenchen	5	-	0 Chiasso
La Chaux-de-Fonds	3	-	4 Young Fellows Zurich	Grenchen	5	-	1 Young Fellows Zurich
La Chaux-de-Fonds	4	-	1 Grasshopper Zurich	Grenchen	2	-	1 Grasshopper Zurich
La Chaux-de-Fonds	3	-	0 Urania Geneve-Sports	Grenchen	1	-	0 Urania Geneve-Sports
Servette Geneve	0	-	3 Lugano	Chiasso	0	-	2 Lugano
Servette Geneve	1	-	1 Basel	Chiasso	2	-	1 Basel
Servette Geneve	0	-	3 La Chaux-de-Fonds	Chiasso	1	-	2 La Chaux-de-Fonds
Servette Geneve	4	-	3 Zurich	Chiasso	2	-	1 Servette Geneve
Servette Geneve	1	-	1 AC Bellinzona	Chiasso	1	-	2 Zurich
Servette Geneve	6	-	0 Locarno	Chiasso	2	-	2 AC Bellinzona
Servette Geneve	2	-	1 Lausanne-Sports	Chiasso	2	-	1 Locarno
Servette Geneve	2	-	0 Biel-Bienne	Chiasso	0	-	0 Lausanne-Sports
Servette Geneve	1	-	3 Grenchen	Chiasso	2	-	2 Biel-Bienne
Servette Geneve	1	-	0 Chiasso	Chiasso	4	-	0 Grenchen
Servette Geneve	8	-	2 Young Fellows Zurich	Chiasso	2	-	1 Young Fellows Zurich
Servette Geneve	5	-	0 Grasshopper Zurich	Chiasso	3	-	1 Grasshopper Zurich
Servette Geneve	6	-	1 Urania Geneve-Sports	Chiasso	1	-	1 Urania Geneve-Sports
Zurich	2	-	3 Lugano	Young Fellows Zurich	1	-	1 Lugano
Zurich	2	-	4 Basel	Young Fellows Zurich	3	-	3 Basel
Zurich	3	-	3 La Chaux-de-Fonds	Young Fellows Zurich	2	-	2 La Chaux-de-Fonds
Zurich	3	-	3 Servette Geneve	Young Fellows Zurich	0	-	5 Servette Geneve
Zurich	1	-	1 AC Bellinzona	Young Fellows Zurich	0	-	0 Zurich
Zurich	5	-	3 Locarno	Young Fellows Zurich	4	-	0 AC Bellinzona
Zurich	2	-	6 Lausanne-Sports	Young Fellows Zurich	4	-	0 Locarno
Zurich	2	-	1 Biel-Bienne	Young Fellows Zurich	0	-	4 Lausanne-Sports
Zurich	4	-	1 Grenchen	Young Fellows Zurich	1	-	0 Biel-Bienne
Zurich	5	-	1 Chiasso	Young Fellows Zurich	2	-	2 Grenchen
Zurich	5	-	0 Young Fellows Zurich	Young Fellows Zurich	4	-	2 Chiasso
Zurich	0	-	4 Grasshopper Zurich	Young Fellows Zurich	0	-	3 Grasshopper Zurich
Zurich	3	-	2 Urania Geneve-Sports	Young Fellows Zurich	6	-	1 Urania Geneve-Sports
AC Bellinzona	1	-	0 Lugano	Grasshopper Zurich	2	-	4 Lugano
AC Bellinzona	3	-	3 Basel	Grasshopper Zurich	2	-	2 Basel
AC Bellinzona	2	-	1 La Chaux-de-Fonds	Grasshopper Zurich	1	-	2 La Chaux-de-Fonds
AC Bellinzona	3	-	0 Servette Geneve	Grasshopper Zurich	2	-	2 Servette Geneve
AC Bellinzona	3	-	3 Zurich	Grasshopper Zurich	2	-	1 Zurich
AC Bellinzona	2	-	1 Locarno	Grasshopper Zurich	1	-	1 AC Bellinzona
AC Bellinzona	1	-	2 Lausanne-Sports	Grasshopper Zurich	1	-	1 Locarno
AC Bellinzona	1	-	0 Biel-Bienne	Grasshopper Zurich	0	-	3 Lausanne-Sports
AC Bellinzona	1	-	1 Grenchen	Grasshopper Zurich	4	-	3 Biel-Bienne
AC Bellinzona	2	-	0 Chiasso	Grasshopper Zurich	1	-	1 Grenchen
AC Bellinzona	2	-	1 Young Fellows Zurich	Grasshopper Zurich	7	-	0 Chiasso

AC Bellinzona	0 - 0	Grasshopper Zurich	Grasshopper Zurich	1 - 2	Young Fellows Zurich
AC Bellinzona	3 - 1	Urania Geneve-Sports	Grasshopper Zurich	2 - 0	Urania Geneve-Sports
Locarno	0 - 1	Lugano	Urania Geneve-Sports	0 - 2	Lugano
Locarno	2 - 0	Basel	Urania Geneve-Sports	2 - 3	Basel
Locarno	3 - 0	La Chaux-de-Fonds	Urania Geneve-Sports	6 - 1	La Chaux-de-Fonds
Locarno	1 - 0	Servette Geneve	Urania Geneve-Sports	1 - 1	Servette Geneve
Locarno	2 - 1	Zurich	Urania Geneve-Sports	1 - 6	Zurich
Locarno	2 - 1	AC Bellinzona	Urania Geneve-Sports	1 - 0	AC Bellinzona
Locarno	2 - 1	Lausanne-Sports	Urania Geneve-Sports	0 - 0	Locarno
Locarno	1 - 2	Biel-Bienne	Urania Geneve-Sports	2 - 2	Lausanne-Sports
Locarno	0 - 0	Grenchen	Urania Geneve-Sports	0 - 1	Biel-Bienne
Locarno	2 - 2	Chiasso	Urania Geneve-Sports	1 - 1	Grenchen
Locarno	2 - 1	Young Fellows Zurich	Urania Geneve-Sports	2 - 2	Chiasso
Locarno	3 - 1	Grasshopper Zurich	Urania Geneve-Sports	4 - 0	Young Fellows Zurich
Locarno	2 - 1	Urania Geneve-Sports	Urania Geneve-Sports	1 - 0	Grasshopper Zurich

Turkey

There was no 1948 Mille Kume – National league play-offs between teams from Istanbul, Ankara and Izmir, because of the Olympic Games (London 1948). There was nothing next year either.

USSR

CSKA played Dynamo in the final match of the league season needing a win to pass them by and win the crown – this they did with a 3-2 victory. Lokomotiv Kharkov won Division two play-off group and replace Zenit next season. Well that would have been the usual state of affairs, except that the top league is extended to 18 teams and Zenit are not relegated. However 2nd placed team in the finals group are not promoted, only the third best are. More in next issue.

	Division 1	Pld	W	D	L	F	A	GA	Pts
1	CSKA Moscow	26	19	3	4	82	30	2.73	41
2	Moscow Dynamo	26	18	4	4	85	28	3.04	40
3	Spartak Moscow	26	18	1	7	64	34	1.88	37
5	Dynamo Tbilisi	26	13	7	6	54	35	1.54	33
4	Torpedo Moscow	26	15	3	8	58	43	1.35	33
6	Leningrad Dynamo	26	10	5	11	42	47	0.89	25
7	Lokomotiv Moscow	26	10	4	12	38	64	0.59	24
8	Torpedo Stalingrad	26	7	7	12	28	44	0.64	21
9	VVS Moscow	26	9	3	14	33	52	0.63	21
10	Dynamo Kiev	26	7	6	13	32	50	0.64	20
11	Krylia S Kuibushev	26	5	9	12	22	40	0.55	19
12	Dynamo Minsk	26	5	8	13	38	62	0.61	18
13	Krylia S Moscow	26	5	5	16	32	60	0.53	15
14	Zenit Leningrad	26	4	9	13	29	48	0.60	11

May 2, 1948
CSKA Moscow   2 - 1 Spartak Moscow
Dynamo Kiev   3 - 2 Lokomotiv Moscow
Krylia S Kuibushev 3 - 2 VVS Moscow
May 5, 1948
Torpedo Moscow   2 - 1 Zenit Leningrad
May 6, 1948
Dynamo Tbilisi   2 - 0 Dynamo Minsk
May 9, 1948
Krylia S Moscow   0 - 2 CSKA Moscow
May 11, 1948
Torpedo Stalingrad 0 - 3 Spartak Moscow
May 12, 1948
VVS Moscow   2 - 0 Dynamo Kiev
May 16, 1948
Zenit Leningrad   0 - 0 Dynamo Kiev
Torpedo Stalingrad 0 - 4 CSKA Moscow

July 19, 1948
Zenit Leningrad   1 - 4 Spartak Moscow
Lokomotiv Moscow   2 - 0 Dynamo Minsk
Krylia S Moscow   0 - 1 VVS Moscow
July 20, 1948
Moscow Dynamo   2 - 2 CSKA Moscow
July 21, 1948
Dynamo Tbilisi   2 - 2 Torpedo Stalingrad
Torpedo Moscow   2 - 1 Dynamo Kiev
VVS Moscow   2 - 0 Leningrad Dynamo
July 23, 1948
Dynamo Minsk   1 - 1 Krylia S Moscow
July 25, 1948
Krylia S Kuibushev 1 - 0 Moscow Dynamo
Zenit Leningrad   1 - 1 Torpedo Moscow
July 26, 1948
Spartak Moscow   2 - 0 CSKA Moscow

Dynamo Tbilisi	1	-	1 Krylia S Moscow	Lokomotiv Moscow	1	-	0 Dynamo Kiev
Moscow Dynamo	2	-	2 Krylia S Kuibushev	July 27, 1948			
Dynamo Minsk	2	-	2 Lokomotiv Moscow	Dynamo Minsk	0	-	3 Dynamo Tbilisi
May 17, 1948				Krylia S Moscow	3	-	1 Torpedo Stalingrad
Leningrad Dynamo	1	-	1 VVS Moscow	July 29, 1948			
May 18, 1948				VVS Moscow	3	-	1 Krylia S Kuibushev
Spartak Moscow	4	-	1 Torpedo Moscow	Leningrad Dynamo	1	-	0 Zenit Leningrad
May 20, 1948				July 30, 1948			
Lokomotiv Moscow	1	-	5 Moscow Dynamo	Moscow Dynamo	3	-	0 Lokomotiv Moscow
May 21, 1948				July 31, 1948			
Dynamo Tbilisi	1	-	0 CSKA Moscow	CSKA Moscow	4	-	2 Dynamo Tbilisi
Zenit Leningrad	1	-	0 VVS Moscow	Dynamo Kiev	3	-	2 Krylia S Moscow
Torpedo Stalingrad	2	-	1 Krylia S Moscow	August 2, 1948			
May 22, 1948				Spartak Moscow	2	-	0 Torpedo Stalingrad
Leningrad Dynamo	3	-	1 Dynamo Kiev	Torpedo Moscow	5	-	1 Dynamo Minsk
May 23, 1948				Leningrad Dynamo	3	-	0 Krylia S Kuibushev
Spartak Moscow	7	-	1 Krylia S Kuibushev	August 3, 1948			
Dynamo Minsk	1	-	2 Torpedo Moscow	Zenit Leningrad	1	-	3 Moscow Dynamo
May 25, 1948				August 4, 1948			
Moscow Dynamo	3	-	0 Zenit Leningrad	Krylia S Moscow	0	-	1 Dynamo Tbilisi
May 26, 1948				Dynamo Kiev	5	-	1 VVS Moscow
Torpedo Stalingrad	1	-	2 Lokomotiv Moscow	August 5, 1948			
May 27, 1948				Dynamo Minsk	1	-	4 CSKA Moscow
Torpedo Moscow	2	-	2 Krylia S Kuibushev	Lokomotiv Moscow	1	-	1 Torpedo Stalingrad
Dynamo Minsk	4	-	3 Spartak Moscow	Torpedo Moscow	1	-	0 Spartak Moscow
May 28, 1948				August 7, 1948			
Krylia S Moscow	2	-	4 Dynamo Kiev	Zenit Leningrad	0	-	0 Krylia S Kuibushev
Dynamo Tbilisi	1	-	1 Leningrad Dynamo	August 8, 1948			
May 31, 1948				Leningrad Dynamo	1	-	5 Dynamo Tbilisi
Torpedo Moscow	3	-	1 VVS Moscow	Moscow Dynamo	0	-	0 Dynamo Kiev
June 1, 1948				August 9, 1948			
Krylia S Kuibushev	1	-	1 Zenit Leningrad	VVS Moscow	0	-	3 Torpedo Moscow
CSKA Moscow	2	-	2 Dynamo Minsk	Krylia S Moscow	3	-	1 Lokomotiv Moscow
June 2, 1948				August 10, 1948			
Dynamo Tbilisi	9	-	2 Lokomotiv Moscow	CSKA Moscow	4	-	2 Torpedo Stalingrad
Krylia S Moscow	0	-	3 Spartak Moscow	August 13, 1948			
Dynamo Kiev	0	-	4 Moscow Dynamo	Dynamo Minsk	0	-	2 VVS Moscow
June 3, 1948				Krylia S Kuibushev	0	-	1 Spartak Moscow
Torpedo Stalingrad	3	-	1 Leningrad Dynamo	Lokomotiv Moscow	1	-	0 Dynamo Tbilisi
June 5, 1948				Moscow Dynamo	1	-	2 Torpedo Moscow
VVS Moscow	1	-	4 Dynamo Minsk	Dynamo Kiev	1	-	1 Zenit Leningrad
June 6, 1948				August 14, 1948			
Dynamo Kiev	1	-	4 Torpedo Moscow	CSKA Moscow	7	-	0 Krylia S Moscow
Spartak Moscow	0	-	4 Zenit Leningrad	Leningrad Dynamo	1	-	2 Torpedo Stalingrad
June 7, 1948				August 17, 1948			

Lokomotiv Moscow	3	-	0	Krylia S Moscow	VVS Moscow	1 - 1	Zenit Leningrad
June 8, 1948					Lokomotiv Moscow	2 - 1	Torpedo Moscow
Krylia S Kuibushev	0	-	0	Torpedo Stalingrad	August 18, 1948		
Leningrad Dynamo	1	-	1	CSKA Moscow	Dynamo Kiev	1 - 1	Dynamo Minsk
Moscow Dynamo	4	-	2	Dynamo Tbilisi	Spartak Moscow	4 - 2	Krylia S Moscow
June 11, 1948					Dynamo Tbilisi	1 - 3	Moscow Dynamo
Krylia S Moscow	2	-	3	Dynamo Minsk	CSKA Moscow	2 - 1	Leningrad Dynamo
Dynamo Kiev	0	-	2	Spartak Moscow	August 19, 1948		
June 12, 1948					Torpedo Stalingrad	1 - 0	Krylia S Kuibushev
Zenit Leningrad	2	-	4	Leningrad Dynamo	August 22, 1948		
June 13, 1948					Zenit Leningrad	1 - 3	Lokomotiv Moscow
CSKA Moscow	0	-	3	VVS Moscow	VVS Moscow	0 - 3	CSKA Moscow
Torpedo Moscow	4	-	1	Lokomotiv Moscow	Dynamo Kiev	3 - 2	Leningrad Dynamo
Krylia S Kuibushev	0	-	0	Dynamo Tbilisi	Spartak Moscow	3 - 2	Dynamo Minsk
June 14, 1948					August 23, 1948		
Moscow Dynamo	4	-	3	Torpedo Stalingrad	Dynamo Tbilisi	2 - 0	Krylia S Kuibushev
June 17, 1948					Torpedo Stalingrad	1 - 5	Moscow Dynamo
CSKA Moscow	7	-	1	Lokomotiv Moscow	August 24, 1948		
Zenit Leningrad	1	-	1	Krylia S Moscow	Torpedo Moscow	3 - 3	Krylia S Moscow
June 18, 1948					August 26, 1948		
Dynamo Minsk	0	-	4	Moscow Dynamo	CSKA Moscow	6 - 1	Dynamo Kiev
Dynamo Kiev	1	-	0	Krylia S Kuibushev	August 27, 1948		
Spartak Moscow	1	-	1	Dynamo Tbilisi	Torpedo Stalingrad	0 - 1	VVS Moscow
Leningrad Dynamo	2	-	1	Torpedo Moscow	Dynamo Tbilisi	2 - 0	Spartak Moscow
June 20, 1948					Zenit Leningrad	3 - 3	Dynamo Minsk
VVS Moscow	1	-	0	Torpedo Stalingrad	Leningrad Dynamo	3 - 4	Lokomotiv Moscow
June 22, 1948					August 29, 1948		
Lokomotiv Moscow	1	-	5	Spartak Moscow	Krylia S Kuibushev	0 - 1	Torpedo Moscow
Leningrad Dynamo	4	-	1	Krylia S Moscow	Moscow Dynamo	4 - 2	Krylia S Moscow
June 23, 1948					August 31, 1948		
Zenit Leningrad	0	-	2	Torpedo Stalingrad	Lokomotiv Moscow	0 - 5	CSKA Moscow
Dynamo Minsk	4	-	2	Dynamo Kiev	Leningrad Dynamo	2 - 2	Dynamo Minsk
CSKA Moscow	5	-	1	Krylia S Kuibushev	September 2, 1948		
June 24, 1948					Torpedo Stalingrad	1 - 1	Zenit Leningrad
Torpedo Moscow	0	-	7	Moscow Dynamo	September 3, 1948		
June 25, 1948					Krylia S Kuibushev	1 - 0	Dynamo Kiev
VVS Moscow	1	-	2	Dynamo Tbilisi	Dynamo Tbilisi	4 - 1	VVS Moscow
June 27, 1948					Moscow Dynamo	5 - 1	Spartak Moscow
Dynamo Kiev	0	-	5	CSKA Moscow	September 5, 1948		
Lokomotiv Moscow	1	-	1	Krylia S Kuibushev	CSKA Moscow	4 - 3	Torpedo Moscow
Dynamo Minsk	1	-	2	Leningrad Dynamo	September 6, 1948		
June 29, 1948					Krylia S Moscow	2 - 0	Leningrad Dynamo
Zenit Leningrad	1	-	4	Dynamo Tbilisi	September 7, 1948		
Spartak Moscow	3	-	0	Moscow Dynamo	Krylia S Kuibushev	0 - 1	Lokomotiv Moscow
June 30, 1948					September 8, 1948		

Torpedo Stalingrad	0 - 2	Torpedo Moscow
VVS Moscow	6 - 0	Krylia S Moscow

July 4, 1948

Dynamo Minsk	2 - 0	Zenit Leningrad
VVS Moscow	0 - 2	Lokomotiv Moscow
Leningrad Dynamo	1 - 1	Moscow Dynamo

July 6, 1948

Krylia S Kuibushev	1 - 0	Krylia S Moscow
Dynamo Tbilisi	3 - 1	Torpedo Moscow

July 8, 1948

Lokomotiv Moscow	2 - 6	Zenit Leningrad

July 9, 1948

Spartak Moscow	2 - 1	Leningrad Dynamo
Torpedo Stalingrad	3 - 1	Dynamo Minsk

July 10, 1948

Moscow Dynamo	4 - 2	VVS Moscow

July 11, 1948

Krylia S Moscow	2 - 0	Torpedo Moscow
Dynamo Tbilisi	1 - 1	Dynamo Kiev
Spartak Moscow	3 - 0	VVS Moscow

July 12, 1948

CSKA Moscow	0 - 1	Zenit Leningrad

July 13, 1948

Lokomotiv Moscow	1 - 2	Leningrad Dynamo

July 14, 1948

Krylia S Kuibushev	3 - 0	Dynamo Minsk

July 15, 1948

Krylia S Moscow	0 - 3	Moscow Dynamo

July 16, 1948

Torpedo Moscow	2 - 3	CSKA Moscow
Torpedo Stalingrad	1 - 0	Dynamo Kiev

July 18, 1948

Krylia S Kuibushev	0 - 1	Leningrad Dynamo

Dynamo Minsk	1 - 1	Torpedo Stalingrad
Dynamo Tbilisi	2 - 1	Zenit Leningrad
Spartak Moscow	1 - 0	Dynamo Kiev

September 9, 1948

VVS Moscow	0 - 6	Moscow Dynamo

September 11, 1948

Krylia S Kuibushev	1 - 3	CSKA Moscow

September 12, 1948

Leningrad Dynamo	4 - 1	Spartak Moscow
Torpedo Moscow	3 - 0	Torpedo Stalingrad

September 13, 1948

Moscow Dynamo	5 - 0	Dynamo Minsk
Dynamo Kiev	3 - 1	Dynamo Tbilisi
Lokomotiv Moscow	0 - 0	VVS Moscow

September 16, 1948

Krylia S Moscow	1 - 1	Krylia S Kuibushev

September 17, 1948

Dynamo Kiev	1 - 1	Torpedo Stalingrad
VVS Moscow	1 - 6	Spartak Moscow

September 18, 1948

Zenit Leningrad	0 - 4	CSKA Moscow
Torpedo Moscow	6 - 2	Dynamo Tbilisi

September 19, 1948

Moscow Dynamo	5 - 0	Leningrad Dynamo
Dynamo Minsk	2 - 2	Krylia S Kuibushev

September 21, 1948

Spartak Moscow	2 - 1	Lokomotiv Moscow
Krylia S Moscow	3 - 0	Zenit Leningrad
Torpedo Stalingrad	0 - 0	Dynamo Tbilisi

September 22, 1948

Torpedo Moscow	3 - 0	Leningrad Dynamo

September 24, 1948

CSKA Moscow	3 - 2	Moscow Dynamo

Division 2 - Final	Pld	W	D	L	F	A	GA	Pts
1 Lokomotiv Kharkov	5	3	1	1	11	3	3.67	7
2 Metallurg Moscow	5	3	0	2	4	2	2.00	6
3 Dynamo Erevan	5	2	2	1	10	7	1.43	6
4 Dzerzhinets Chelyabinsk	5	3	0	2	9	8	1.13	6
5 Dynamo Kazan	5	1	2	2	4	6	0.67	4
6 DO Tashkent	5	0	1	4	7	19	0.37	1

Lokomotiv Kharkov	0 - 2	Metallurg Moscow
Lokomotiv Kharkov	0 - 0	Dynamo Erevan
Lokomotiv Kharkov	3 - 1	Dzerzhinets Chelyabinsk
Lokomotiv Kharkov	2 - 0	Dynamo Kazan
Lokomotiv Kharkov	6 - 0	DO Tashkent
Metallurg Moscow	1 - 0	Dynamo Erevan
Metallurg Moscow	0 - 1	Dzerzhinets Chelyabinsk
Metallurg Moscow	0 - 1	Dynamo Kazan
Metallurg Moscow	1 - 0	DO Tashkent
Dynamo Erevan	2 - 1	Dzerzhinets Chelyabinsk
Dynamo Erevan	2 - 2	Dynamo Kazan
Dynamo Erevan	6 - 3	DO Tashkent
Dzerzhinets Chelyabinsk	1 - 0	Dynamo Kazan
Dzerzhinets Chelyabinsk	5 - 3	DO Tashkent
Dynamo Kazan	1 - 1	DO Tashkent

Division 2 Central	Pld	W	D	L	F	A	GA	Pts
1 Metallurg Moscow	28	18	6	4	43	22	1.95	42
2 Dynamo Riga	28	17	4	7	57	27	2.11	38
3 MVO Moscow	28	16	6	6	52	28	1.86	38
4 Spartak Vilnius	28	15	6	7	54	30	1.80	36
5 Sudostroitel Leningrad	28	14	7	7	42	28	1.50	35
6 Trudovye reservy Moscow	28	13	6	9	41	33	1.24	32
7 Kalev Tallin	28	10	8	10	34	34	1.00	28
8 Daugava Riga	28	10	7	11	31	45	0.69	27
9 DO Leningrad	28	9	8	11	29	36	0.81	26
10 Spartak Minsk	28	9	6	13	38	37	1.03	24
11 VMS Moscow	28	9	5	14	44	59	0.75	23
12 Metro Moscow	28	4	11	13	27	39	0.69	19
13 DO Minsk	28	6	7	15	23	48	0.48	19
14 Spartak Leningrad	28	5	8	15	25	46	0.54	18
15 Dynamo Tallin	28	4	7	17	23	51	0.45	15

Metallurg Moscow 2 - 1 Dynamo Riga   DO Leningrad 1 - 0 Metallurg Moscow

Metallurg Moscow	0 -	0 MVO Moscow	DO Leningrad	2 -	1 Dynamo Riga
Metallurg Moscow	2 -	2 Spartak Vilnius	DO Leningrad	2 -	3 MVO Moscow
Metallurg Moscow	0 -	0 Sudostroitel Leningrad	DO Leningrad	0 -	0 Spartak Vilnius
Metallurg Moscow	4 -	1 Trudovye Moscow	DO Leningrad	1 -	4 Sudostroitel Leningrad
Metallurg Moscow	1 -	2 Kalev Tallin	DO Leningrad	2 -	0 Trudovye Moscow
Metallurg Moscow	3 -	1 Daugava Riga	DO Leningrad	0 -	0 Kalev Tallin
Metallurg Moscow	3 -	0 DO Leningrad	DO Leningrad	1 -	0 Daugava Riga
Metallurg Moscow	1 -	0 Spartak Minsk	DO Leningrad	1 -	1 Spartak Minsk
Metallurg Moscow	2 -	2 VMS Moscow	DO Leningrad	1 -	1 VMS Moscow
Metallurg Moscow	2 -	1 Metro Moscow	DO Leningrad	2 -	1 Metro Moscow
Metallurg Moscow	1 -	0 DO Minsk	DO Leningrad	2 -	1 DO Minsk
Metallurg Moscow	2 -	0 Spartak Leningrad	DO Leningrad	0 -	2 Spartak Leningrad
Metallurg Moscow	1 -	0 Dynamo Tallin	DO Leningrad	2 -	1 Dynamo Tallin
Dynamo Riga	0 -	1 Metallurg Moscow	Spartak Minsk	0 -	0 Metallurg Moscow
Dynamo Riga	3 -	2 MVO Moscow	Spartak Minsk	1 -	5 Dynamo Riga
Dynamo Riga	2 -	1 Spartak Vilnius	Spartak Minsk	0 -	2 MVO Moscow
Dynamo Riga	4 -	1 Sudostroitel Leningrad	Spartak Minsk	1 -	2 Spartak Vilnius
Dynamo Riga	2 -	1 Trudovye Moscow	Spartak Minsk	1 -	3 Sudostroitel Leningrad
Dynamo Riga	3 -	1 Kalev Tallin	Spartak Minsk	1 -	1 Trudovye Moscow
Dynamo Riga	5 -	0 Daugava Riga	Spartak Minsk	3 -	0 Kalev Tallin
Dynamo Riga	3 -	0 DO Leningrad	Spartak Minsk	0 -	0 Daugava Riga
Dynamo Riga	3 -	1 Spartak Minsk	Spartak Minsk	1 -	2 DO Leningrad
Dynamo Riga	2 -	4 VMS Moscow	Spartak Minsk	5 -	1 VMS Moscow
Dynamo Riga	2 -	2 Metro Moscow	Spartak Minsk	1 -	0 Metro Moscow
Dynamo Riga	0 -	1 DO Minsk	Spartak Minsk	2 -	1 DO Minsk
Dynamo Riga	0 -	0 Spartak Leningrad	Spartak Minsk	1 -	1 Spartak Leningrad
Dynamo Riga	5 -	0 Dynamo Tallin	Spartak Minsk	1 -	3 Dynamo Tallin
MVO Moscow	0 -	1 Metallurg Moscow	VMS Moscow	2 -	2 Metallurg Moscow
MVO Moscow	1 -	0 Dynamo Riga	VMS Moscow	0 -	0 Dynamo Riga
MVO Moscow	0 -	2 Spartak Vilnius	VMS Moscow	0 -	3 MVO Moscow
MVO Moscow	1 -	0 Sudostroitel Leningrad	VMS Moscow	1 -	3 Spartak Vilnius
MVO Moscow	1 -	1 Trudovye Moscow	VMS Moscow	0 -	0 Sudostroitel Leningrad
MVO Moscow	1 -	0 Kalev Tallin	VMS Moscow	0 -	1 Trudovye Moscow
MVO Moscow	3 -	1 Daugava Riga	VMS Moscow	0 -	4 Kalev Tallin
MVO Moscow	1 -	0 DO Leningrad	VMS Moscow	5 -	1 Daugava Riga
MVO Moscow	2 -	2 Spartak Minsk	VMS Moscow	0 -	5 DO Leningrad
MVO Moscow	4 -	0 VMS Moscow	VMS Moscow	3 -	1 Spartak Minsk
MVO Moscow	4 -	2 Metro Moscow	VMS Moscow	3 -	0 Metro Moscow
MVO Moscow	1 -	1 DO Minsk	VMS Moscow	1 -	2 DO Minsk
MVO Moscow	4 -	1 Spartak Leningrad	VMS Moscow	4 -	2 Spartak Leningrad
MVO Moscow	2 -	0 Dynamo Tallin	VMS Moscow	1 -	0 Dynamo Tallin
Spartak Vilnius	1 -	2 Metallurg Moscow	Metro Moscow	1 -	2 Metallurg Moscow
Spartak Vilnius	2 -	1 Dynamo Riga	Metro Moscow	0 -	2 Dynamo Riga
Spartak Vilnius	3 -	2 MVO Moscow	Metro Moscow	1 -	1 MVO Moscow
Spartak Vilnius	1 -	1 Sudostroitel Leningrad	Metro Moscow	0 -	0 Spartak Vilnius
Spartak Vilnius	0 -	3 Trudovye Moscow	Metro Moscow	2 -	2 Sudostroitel Leningrad
Spartak Vilnius	1 -	3 Kalev Tallin	Metro Moscow	0 -	0 Trudovye Moscow
Spartak Vilnius	4 -	0 Daugava Riga	Metro Moscow	1 -	1 Kalev Tallin
Spartak Vilnius	1 -	1 DO Leningrad	Metro Moscow	1 -	2 Daugava Riga
Spartak Vilnius	1 -	0 Spartak Minsk	Metro Moscow	0 -	0 DO Leningrad
Spartak Vilnius	4 -	1 VMS Moscow	Metro Moscow	2 -	1 Spartak Minsk
Spartak Vilnius	3 -	0 Metro Moscow	Metro Moscow	2 -	0 VMS Moscow

Spartak Vilnius	5 - 1	DO Minsk	Metro Moscow	3 - 0	DO Minsk
Spartak Vilnius	1 - 2	Spartak Leningrad	Metro Moscow	0 - 0	Spartak Leningrad
Spartak Vilnius	2 - 1	Dynamo Tallin	Metro Moscow	1 - 1	Dynamo Tallin
Sudostroitel Leningrad	0 - 2	Metallurg Moscow	DO Minsk	1 - 3	Metallurg Moscow
Sudostroitel Leningrad	1 - 3	Dynamo Riga	DO Minsk	0 - 1	Dynamo Riga
Sudostroitel Leningrad	3 - 1	MVO Moscow	DO Minsk	1 - 1	MVO Moscow
Sudostroitel Leningrad	1 - 2	Spartak Vilnius	DO Minsk	0 - 5	Spartak Vilnius
Sudostroitel Leningrad	1 - 2	Trudovye Moscow	DO Minsk	0 - 0	Sudostroitel Leningrad
Sudostroitel Leningrad	0 - 3	Kalev Tallin	DO Minsk	0 - 2	Trudovye Moscow
Sudostroitel Leningrad	0 - 0	Daugava Riga	DO Minsk	1 - 4	Kalev Tallin
Sudostroitel Leningrad	0 - 0	DO Leningrad	DO Minsk	1 - 1	Daugava Riga
Sudostroitel Leningrad	2 - 0	Spartak Minsk	DO Minsk	1 - 1	DO Leningrad
Sudostroitel Leningrad	4 - 0	VMS Moscow	DO Minsk	0 - 1	Spartak Minsk
Sudostroitel Leningrad	3 - 2	Metro Moscow	DO Minsk	0 - 4	VMS Moscow
Sudostroitel Leningrad	2 - 0	DO Minsk	DO Minsk	1 - 0	Metro Moscow
Sudostroitel Leningrad	1 - 0	Spartak Leningrad	DO Minsk	1 - 3	Spartak Leningrad
Sudostroitel Leningrad	2 - 1	Dynamo Tallin	DO Minsk	1 - 3	Dynamo Tallin
Trudovye Moscow	3 - 0	Metallurg Moscow	Spartak Leningrad	1 - 2	Metallurg Moscow
Trudovye Moscow	1 - 2	Dynamo Riga	Spartak Leningrad	0 - 2	Dynamo Riga
Trudovye Moscow	0 - 4	MVO Moscow	Spartak Leningrad	1 - 2	MVO Moscow
Trudovye Moscow	2 - 0	Spartak Vilnius	Spartak Leningrad	0 - 3	Spartak Vilnius
Trudovye Moscow	2 - 3	Sudostroitel Leningrad	Spartak Leningrad	0 - 2	Sudostroitel Leningrad
Trudovye Moscow	0 - 0	Kalev Tallin	Spartak Leningrad	0 - 2	Trudovye Moscow
Trudovye Moscow	1 - 2	Daugava Riga	Spartak Leningrad	1 - 1	Kalev Tallin
Trudovye Moscow	2 - 1	DO Leningrad	Spartak Leningrad	1 - 2	Daugava Riga
Trudovye Moscow	1 - 0	Spartak Minsk	Spartak Leningrad	2 - 1	DO Leningrad
Trudovye Moscow	4 - 2	VMS Moscow	Spartak Leningrad	0 - 3	Spartak Minsk
Trudovye Moscow	1 - 1	Metro Moscow	Spartak Leningrad	2 - 5	VMS Moscow
Trudovye Moscow	0 - 2	DO Minsk	Spartak Leningrad	0 - 1	Metro Moscow
Trudovye Moscow	4 - 1	Spartak Leningrad	Spartak Leningrad	0 - 0	DO Minsk
Trudovye Moscow	0 - 2	Dynamo Tallin	Spartak Leningrad	3 - 0	Dynamo Tallin
Kalev Tallin	0 - 2	Metallurg Moscow	Dynamo Tallin	0 - 2	Metallurg Moscow
Kalev Tallin	0 - 1	Dynamo Riga	Dynamo Tallin	1 - 3	Dynamo Riga
Kalev Tallin	0 - 3	MVO Moscow	Dynamo Tallin	1 - 2	MVO Moscow
Kalev Tallin	0 - 3	Spartak Vilnius	Dynamo Tallin	1 - 1	Spartak Vilnius
Kalev Tallin	0 - 1	Sudostroitel Leningrad	Dynamo Tallin	0 - 2	Sudostroitel Leningrad
Kalev Tallin	1 - 1	Trudovye Moscow	Dynamo Tallin	0 - 3	Trudovye Moscow
Kalev Tallin	2 - 1	Daugava Riga	Dynamo Tallin	0 - 0	Kalev Tallin
Kalev Tallin	2 - 0	DO Leningrad	Dynamo Tallin	1 - 1	Daugava Riga
Kalev Tallin	0 - 2	Spartak Minsk	Dynamo Tallin	2 - 0	DO Leningrad
Kalev Tallin	3 - 2	VMS Moscow	Dynamo Tallin	0 - 5	Spartak Minsk
Kalev Tallin	4 - 3	Metro Moscow	Dynamo Tallin	1 - 2	VMS Moscow
Kalev Tallin	0 - 1	DO Minsk	Dynamo Tallin	0 - 0	Metro Moscow
Kalev Tallin	0 - 0	Spartak Leningrad	Dynamo Tallin	0 - 3	DO Minsk
Kalev Tallin	1 - 1	Dynamo Tallin	Dynamo Tallin	2 - 2	Spartak Leningrad
Daugava Riga	2 - 0	Metallurg Moscow			
Daugava Riga	1 - 1	Dynamo Riga			
Daugava Riga	2 - 1	MVO Moscow			
Daugava Riga	2 - 1	Spartak Vilnius			
Daugava Riga	0 - 3	Sudostroitel Leningrad			
Daugava Riga	1 - 2	Trudovye Moscow			
Daugava Riga	1 - 2	Kalev Tallin			

Daugava Riga	3 - 1	DO Leningrad	
Daugava Riga	0 - 3	Spartak Minsk	
Daugava Riga	1 - 0	VMS Moscow	
Daugava Riga	1 - 0	Metro Moscow	
Daugava Riga	2 - 2	DO Minsk	
Daugava Riga	0 - 0	Spartak Leningrad	
Daugava Riga	3 - 1	Dynamo Tallin	

	Division 2 - Russia 1st zone	Pld	W	D	L	F	A	GA	Pts
1	Dynamo Kazan	26	20	3	3	71	18	3.94	43
2	Torpedo Gorkyi	26	18	3	5	81	31	2.61	39
3	Krasnoye znamya Ivanovo	26	18	3	5	64	31	2.06	39
4	Khimick Dzerzhinsk	26	17	3	6	60	32	1.88	37
5	Khimick Orekhovo Zuevo	26	14	7	5	58	26	2.23	35
6	Dynamo Moscow M reg	26	13	4	9	55	41	1.34	30
7	Zenith Kaliningrad M reg	26	9	9	8	45	39	1.15	27
8	Zenith Kovrov	26	5	10	11	38	54	0.70	20
9	Dzerzhinets Kolomna	26	7	4	15	36	48	0.75	18
10	Zenith Izhevsk	26	7	4	15	35	60	0.58	18
11	Dynamo Saratov	26	5	7	14	37	63	0.59	17
12	Spartak Ivanovo	26	4	8	14	33	66	0.50	16
13	Spartak Voronezh	26	4	5	17	19	70	0.27	13
14	Spartak Penza	26	3	6	17	39	92	0.42	12

Note – M Reg = Moscow Region.

Dynamo Kazan	2 - 1	Torpedo Gorkyi	Zenith Kovrov	1 - 2	Dynamo Kazan
Dynamo Kazan	0 - 3	Krasnoye Ivanovo	Zenith Kovrov	2 - 4	Torpedo Gorkyi
Dynamo Kazan	1 - 0	Khimick Dzerzhinsk	Zenith Kovrov	1 - 4	Krasnoye Ivanovo
Dynamo Kazan	1 - 1	Khimick Orekhovo	Zenith Kovrov	2 - 3	Khimick Dzerzhinsk
Dynamo Kazan	4 - 1	Dynamo Moscow reg.	Zenith Kovrov	1 - 0	Khimick Orekhovo
Dynamo Kazan	2 - 1	Zenith Kalinin reg	Zenith Kovrov	2 - 2	Dynamo Moscow reg.
Dynamo Kazan	4 - 0	Zenith Kovrov	Zenith Kovrov	0 - 4	Zenith Kalinin reg
Dynamo Kazan	3 - 0	Dzerzhinets Kolomna	Zenith Kovrov	4 - 2	Dzerzhinets Kolomna
Dynamo Kazan	3 - 0	Zenith Izhevsk	Zenith Kovrov	1 - 3	Zenith Izhevsk
Dynamo Kazan	2 - 0	Dynamo Saratov	Zenith Kovrov	2 - 0	Dynamo Saratov
Dynamo Kazan	9 - 2	Spartak Ivanovo	Zenith Kovrov	2 - 2	Spartak Ivanovo
Dynamo Kazan	0 - 0	Spartak Voronezh	Zenith Kovrov	0 - 2	Spartak Voronezh
Dynamo Kazan	7 - 0	Spartak Penza	Zenith Kovrov	2 - 2	Spartak Penza
Torpedo Gorkyi	3 - 2	Dynamo Kazan	Dzerzhinets Kolomna	1 - 0	Dynamo Kazan
Torpedo Gorkyi	7 - 2	Krasnoye Ivanovo	Dzerzhinets Kolomna	0 - 4	Torpedo Gorkyi
Torpedo Gorkyi	1 - 4	Khimick Dzerzhinsk	Dzerzhinets Kolomna	1 - 2	Krasnoye Ivanovo
Torpedo Gorkyi	1 - 1	Khimick Orekhovo	Dzerzhinets Kolomna	0 - 1	Khimick Dzerzhinsk
Torpedo Gorkyi	1 - 1	Dynamo Moscow reg.	Dzerzhinets Kolomna	w - o	Khimick Orekhovo
Torpedo Gorkyi	3 - 0	Zenith Kalinin reg	Dzerzhinets Kolomna	0 - 1	Dynamo Moscow reg.

Torpedo Gorkyi	4	1	Zenith Kovrov	Dzerzhinets Kolomna	0	-	3	Zenith Kalinin reg
Torpedo Gorkyi	5	0	Dzerzhinets Kolomna	Dzerzhinets Kolomna	3	-	3	Zenith Kovrov
Torpedo Gorkyi	3	2	Zenith Izhevsk	Dzerzhinets Kolomna	3	-	3	Zenith Izhevsk
Torpedo Gorkyi	4	0	Dynamo Saratov	Dzerzhinets Kolomna	0	-	3	Dynamo Saratov
Torpedo Gorkyi	2	1	Spartak Ivanovo	Dzerzhinets Kolomna	2	-	0	Spartak Ivanovo
Torpedo Gorkyi	6	0	Spartak Voronezh	Dzerzhinets Kolomna	2	-	2	Spartak Voronezh
Torpedo Gorkyi	6	0	Spartak Penza	Dzerzhinets Kolomna	4	-	0	Spartak Penza
Krasnoye Ivanovo	0	2	Dynamo Kazan	Zenith Izhevsk	1	-	3	Dynamo Kazan
Krasnoye Ivanovo	1	1	Torpedo Gorkyi	Zenith Izhevsk	0	-	4	Torpedo Gorkyi
Krasnoye Ivanovo	1	0	Khimick Dzerzhinsk	Zenith Izhevsk	0	-	5	Krasnoye Ivanovo
Krasnoye Ivanovo	2	2	Khimick Orekhovo	Zenith Izhevsk	0	-	1	Khimick Dzerzhinsk
Krasnoye Ivanovo	0	2	Dynamo Moscow reg.	Zenith Izhevsk	0	-	2	Khimick Orekhovo
Krasnoye Ivanovo	4	1	Zenith Kalinin reg	Zenith Izhevsk	5	-	2	Dynamo Moscow reg.
Krasnoye Ivanovo	1	0	Zenith Kovrov	Zenith Izhevsk	1	-	1	Zenith Kalinin reg
Krasnoye Ivanovo	4	1	Dzerzhinets Kolomna	Zenith Izhevsk	1	-	2	Zenith Kovrov
Krasnoye Ivanovo	4	2	Zenith Izhevsk	Zenith Izhevsk	w	-	o	Dzerzhinets Kolomna
Krasnoye Ivanovo	4	0	Dynamo Saratov	Zenith Izhevsk	0	-	2	Dynamo Saratov
Krasnoye Ivanovo	1	2	Spartak Ivanovo	Zenith Izhevsk	3	-	0	Spartak Ivanovo
Krasnoye Ivanovo	4	0	Spartak Voronezh	Zenith Izhevsk	1	-	0	Spartak Voronezh
Krasnoye Ivanovo	5	1	Spartak Penza	Zenith Izhevsk	0	-	3	Spartak Penza
Khimick Dzerzhinsk	0	3	Dynamo Kazan	Dynamo Saratov	0	-	4	Dynamo Kazan
Khimick Dzerzhinsk	2	1	Torpedo Gorkyi	Dynamo Saratov	2	-	6	Torpedo Gorkyi
Khimick Dzerzhinsk	1	3	Krasnoye Ivanovo	Dynamo Saratov	2	-	1	Krasnoye Ivanovo
Khimick Dzerzhinsk	0	2	Khimick Orekhovo	Dynamo Saratov	1	-	3	Khimick Dzerzhinsk
Khimick Dzerzhinsk	2	1	Dynamo Moscow reg.	Dynamo Saratov	3	-	1	Khimick Orekhovo
Khimick Dzerzhinsk	3	1	Zenith Kalinin reg	Dynamo Saratov	2	-	3	Dynamo Moscow reg.
Khimick Dzerzhinsk	1	1	Zenith Kovrov	Dynamo Saratov	1	-	1	Zenith Kalinin reg
Khimick Dzerzhinsk	0	3	Dzerzhinets Kolomna	Dynamo Saratov	2	-	2	Zenith Kovrov
Khimick Dzerzhinsk	2	0	Zenith Izhevsk	Dynamo Saratov	1	-	6	Dzerzhinets Kolomna
Khimick Dzerzhinsk	1	0	Dynamo Saratov	Dynamo Saratov	1	-	2	Zenith Izhevsk
Khimick Dzerzhinsk	5	0	Spartak Ivanovo	Dynamo Saratov	2	-	2	Spartak Ivanovo
Khimick Dzerzhinsk	7	0	Spartak Voronezh	Dynamo Saratov	1	-	1	Spartak Voronezh
Khimick Dzerzhinsk	3	2	Spartak Penza	Dynamo Saratov	1	-	5	Spartak Penza
Khimick Orekhovo	0	1	Dynamo Kazan	Spartak Ivanovo	0	-	2	Dynamo Kazan
Khimick Orekhovo	3	1	Torpedo Gorkyi	Spartak Ivanovo	0	-	2	Torpedo Gorkyi
Khimick Orekhovo	0	0	Krasnoye Ivanovo	Spartak Ivanovo	1	-	3	Krasnoye Ivanovo
Khimick Orekhovo	1	1	Khimick Dzerzhinsk	Spartak Ivanovo	1	-	3	Khimick Dzerzhinsk
Khimick Orekhovo	4	1	Dynamo Moscow reg.	Spartak Ivanovo	3	-	6	Khimick Orekhovo
Khimick Orekhovo	3	2	Zenith Kalinin reg	Spartak Ivanovo	2	-	1	Dynamo Moscow reg.
Khimick Orekhovo	2	2	Zenith Kovrov	Spartak Ivanovo	0	-	0	Zenith Kalinin reg
Khimick Orekhovo	2	1	Dzerzhinets Kolomna	Spartak Ivanovo	0	-	2	Zenith Kovrov
Khimick Orekhovo	4	1	Zenith Izhevsk	Spartak Ivanovo	1	-	1	Dzerzhinets Kolomna
Khimick Orekhovo	4	1	Dynamo Saratov	Spartak Ivanovo	2	-	2	Zenith Izhevsk
Khimick Orekhovo	5	1	Spartak Ivanovo	Spartak Ivanovo	2	-	2	Dynamo Saratov
Khimick Orekhovo	0	0	Spartak Voronezh	Spartak Ivanovo	0	-	0	Spartak Voronezh

Khimick Orekhovo	6		0 Spartak Penza	Spartak Ivanovo	2	-	2	Spartak Penza
Dynamo Moscow reg.	0		1 Dynamo Kazan	Spartak Voronezh	1	-	2	Dynamo Kazan
Dynamo Moscow reg.	1		0 Torpedo Gorkyi	Spartak Voronezh	1	-	4	Torpedo Gorkyi
Dynamo Moscow reg.	1		3 Krasnoye Ivanovo	Spartak Voronezh	0	-	1	Krasnoye Ivanovo
Dynamo Moscow reg.	2		5 Khimick Dzerzhinsk	Spartak Voronezh	1	-	4	Khimick Dzerzhinsk
Dynamo Moscow reg.	1		0 Khimick Orekhovo	Spartak Voronezh	0	-	5	Khimick Orekhovo
Dynamo Moscow reg.	0		0 Zenith Kalinin reg	Spartak Voronezh	0	-	1	Dynamo Moscow reg.
Dynamo Moscow reg.	2		2 Zenith Kovrov	Spartak Voronezh	0	-	3	Zenith Kalinin reg
Dynamo Moscow reg.	2		1 Dzerzhinets Kolomna	Spartak Voronezh	3	-	2	Zenith Kovrov
Dynamo Moscow reg.	4		0 Zenith Izhevsk	Spartak Voronezh	2	-	1	Dzerzhinets Kolomna
Dynamo Moscow reg.	2		0 Dynamo Saratov	Spartak Voronezh	3	-	4	Zenith Izhevsk
Dynamo Moscow reg.	5		1 Spartak Ivanovo	Spartak Voronezh	0	-	5	Dynamo Saratov
Dynamo Moscow reg.	7		1 Spartak Voronezh	Spartak Voronezh	0	-	3	Spartak Ivanovo
Dynamo Moscow reg.	5		2 Spartak Penza	Spartak Voronezh	2	-	1	Spartak Penza
Zenith Kalinin reg	1		1 Dynamo Kazan	Spartak Penza	1	-	10	Dynamo Kazan
Zenith Kalinin reg	3		4 Torpedo Gorkyi	Spartak Penza	0	-	3	Torpedo Gorkyi
Zenith Kalinin reg	1		2 Krasnoye Ivanovo	Spartak Penza	2	-	4	Krasnoye Ivanovo
Zenith Kalinin reg	3		3 Khimick Dzerzhinsk	Spartak Penza	1	-	5	Khimick Dzerzhinsk
Zenith Kalinin reg	1		2 Khimick Orekhovo	Spartak Penza	1	-	2	Khimick Orekhovo
Zenith Kalinin reg	3		2 Dynamo Moscow reg.	Spartak Penza	0	-	5	Dynamo Moscow reg.
Zenith Kalinin reg	0		0 Zenith Kovrov	Spartak Penza	3	-	3	Zenith Kalinin reg
Zenith Kalinin reg	1		0 Dzerzhinets Kolomna	Spartak Penza	1	-	1	Zenith Kovrov
Zenith Kalinin reg	2		1 Zenith Izhevsk	Spartak Penza	1	-	4	Dzerzhinets Kolomna
Zenith Kalinin reg	3	-	3 Dynamo Saratov	Spartak Penza	3	-	3	Zenith Izhevsk
Zenith Kalinin reg	3	-	1 Spartak Ivanovo	Spartak Penza	2	-	2	Dynamo Saratov
Zenith Kalinin reg	1	-	0 Spartak Voronezh	Spartak Penza	1	-	4	Spartak Ivanovo
Zenith Kalinin reg	3	-	0 Spartak Penza	Spartak Penza	5	-	0	Spartak Voronezh

Division 2 - Russia 2nd zone

#	Team	Pld	W	D	L	F	A	GA	Pts
1	Dzerzhinets Chelyabinsk	25	19	3	3	83	28	2.96	41
2	DO Novosibirsk	25	19	1	5	62	27	2.30	39
3	DO Sverdlovsk	24	12	6	6	56	25	2.24	30
4	Krylya Sovetov Molotov	24	12	6	6	54	30	1.80	30
5	Dynamo Sverdlovsk	24	11	5	8	51	44	1.16	27
6	Dzerzhinets Nizhni Tagil	24	11	5	8	32	32	1.00	27
7	Dynamo Chelyabinsk	24	9	6	9	39	39	1.00	24
8	Avangard Sverdlovsk	24	10	3	11	44	48	0.92	23
9	Baranov's traid Omsk	24	8	5	11	44	39	1.13	21
10	Khimick Kemerovo	24	8	5	11	42	45	0.93	21
11	Metallurg Magnitogorsk	24	7	1	16	34	66	0.52	15
12	Tsvetnye Metally Kamensk Uralski	24	4	2	18	33	91	0.36	10
13	Gornyak Kemerovo	24	1	4	19	20	80	0.25	6

Note – the table includes the championship play-off game between Dzerzhinets Chelyabinsk and DO Novosibirsk that ended 3-1 to Chelyabinsk who went through to the Division 2 finals. This was despite losing both regular season games to Novosibirsk.

Dz Chelyabinsk	3	-	1 DO Novosibirsk	Championship play-off				
Dz Chelyabinsk	1	-	2 DO Novosibirsk	Avangard Sverdlovsk	0	-	3	Dz Chelyabinsk
Dz Chelyabinsk	1	-	1 DO Sverdlovsk	Avangard Sverdlovsk	2	-	2	DO Novosibirsk
Dz Chelyabinsk	1	-	1 Krylya S Molotov	Avangard Sverdlovsk	0	-	6	DO Sverdlovsk
Dz Chelyabinsk	5	-	1 Dynamo Sverdlovsk	Avangard Sverdlovsk	0	-	2	Krylya S Molotov
Dz Chelyabinsk	3	-	0 Dzerzhinets Nizhni	Avangard Sverdlovsk	3	-	2	Dynamo Sverdlovsk
Dz Chelyabinsk	1	-	0 Dynamo Chelyabinsk	Avangard Sverdlovsk	2	-	0	Dzerzhinets Nizhni
Dz Chelyabinsk	5	-	0 Avangard Sverdlovsk	Avangard Sverdlovsk	1	-	3	Dynamo Chelyabinsk
Dz Chelyabinsk	4	-	3 Baranov's traid Omsk	Avangard Sverdlovsk	3	-	1	Baranov's traid Omsk
Dz Chelyabinsk	5	-	3 Khimick Kemerovo	Avangard Sverdlovsk	2	-	2	Khimick Kemerovo
Dz Chelyabinsk	6	-	2 Met Magnitogorsk	Avangard Sverdlovsk	0	-	2	Met Magnitogorsk
Dz Chelyabinsk	7	-	3 Tsvetnye Metally	Avangard Sverdlovsk	5	-	1	Tsvetnye Metally
Dz Chelyabinsk	4	-	3 Gornyak Kemerovo	Avangard Sverdlovsk	4	-	0	Gornyak Kemerovo
DO Novosibirsk	3	-	2 Dz Chelyabinsk	Baranov's traid Omsk	1	-	3	Dz Chelyabinsk
DO Novosibirsk	2	-	1 DO Sverdlovsk	Baranov's traid Omsk	o	-	w	DO Novosibirsk
DO Novosibirsk	2	-	1 Krylya S Molotov	Baranov's traid Omsk	1	-	3	DO Sverdlovsk
DO Novosibirsk	3	-	2 Dynamo Sverdlovsk	Baranov's traid Omsk	0	-	1	Krylya S Molotov
DO Novosibirsk	0	-	1 Dzerzhinets Nizhni	Baranov's traid Omsk	4	-	0	Dynamo Sverdlovsk
DO Novosibirsk	3	-	0 Dynamo Chelyabinsk	Baranov's traid Omsk	1	-	1	Dzerzhinets Nizhni
DO Novosibirsk	0	-	1 Avangard Sverdlovsk	Baranov's traid Omsk	2	-	3	Dynamo Chelyabinsk
DO Novosibirsk	2	-	1 Baranov's traid Omsk	Baranov's traid Omsk	5	-	1	Avangard Sverdlovsk
DO Novosibirsk	3	-	0 Khimick Kemerovo	Baranov's traid Omsk	0	-	3	Khimick Kemerovo
DO Novosibirsk	4	-	0 Met Magnitogorsk	Baranov's traid Omsk	3	-	0	Met Magnitogorsk
DO Novosibirsk	5	-	2 Tsvetnye Metally	Baranov's traid Omsk	3	-	4	Tsvetnye Metally
DO Novosibirsk	2	-	0 Gornyak Kemerovo	Baranov's traid Omsk	2	-	2	Gornyak Kemerovo
DO Novosibirsk	1	-	1 Dz Chelyabinsk	Khimick Kemerovo	0	-	2	Dz Chelyabinsk
DO Sverdlovsk	2	-	5 DO Novosibirsk	Khimick Kemerovo	0	-	2	DO Novosibirsk
DO Sverdlovsk	1	-	1 Krylya S Molotov	Khimick Kemerovo	3	-	0	DO Sverdlovsk
DO Sverdlovsk	3	-	1 Dynamo Sverdlovsk	Khimick Kemerovo	0	-	1	Krylya S Molotov
DO Sverdlovsk	o	-	w Dzerzhinets Nizhni	Khimick Kemerovo	1	-	3	Dynamo Sverdlovsk
DO Sverdlovsk	3	-	1 Dynamo Chelyabinsk	Khimick Kemerovo	1	-	2	Dzerzhinets Nizhni
DO Sverdlovsk	1	-	1 Avangard Sverdlovsk	Khimick Kemerovo	1	-	1	Dynamo Chelyabinsk
DO Sverdlovsk	1	-	1 Baranov's traid Omsk	Khimick Kemerovo	1	-	2	Avangard Sverdlovsk
DO Sverdlovsk	1	-	2 Khimick Kemerovo	Khimick Kemerovo	1	-	2	Baranov's traid Omsk
DO Sverdlovsk	3	-	0 Met Magnitogorsk	Khimick Kemerovo	4	-	0	Met Magnitogorsk
DO Sverdlovsk	3	-	0 Tsvetnye Metally	Khimick Kemerovo	4	-	2	Tsvetnye Metally
DO Sverdlovsk	6	-	0 Gornyak Kemerovo	Khimick Kemerovo	1	-	1	Gornyak Kemerovo
Krylya S Molotov	0	-	2 Dz Chelyabinsk	Met Magnitogorsk	0	-	6	Dz Chelyabinsk
Krylya S Molotov	0	-	4 DO Novosibirsk	Met Magnitogorsk	1	-	5	DO Novosibirsk
Krylya S Molotov	0	-	2 DO Sverdlovsk	Met Magnitogorsk	3	-	5	DO Sverdlovsk
Krylya S Molotov	1	-	1 Dynamo Sverdlovsk	Met Magnitogorsk	3	-	1	Krylya S Molotov
Krylya S Molotov	1	-	1 Dzerzhinets Nizhni	Met Magnitogorsk	0	-	4	Dynamo Sverdlovsk

Krylya S Molotov	5	-	1 Dynamo Chelyabinsk	Met Magnitogorsk	1	-	3 Dzerzhinets Nizhni
Krylya S Molotov	3	-	0 Avangard Sverdlovsk	Met Magnitogorsk	3	-	1 Dynamo Chelyabinsk
Krylya S Molotov	3	-	1 Baranov's traid Omsk	Met Magnitogorsk	0	-	3 Avangard Sverdlovsk
Krylya S Molotov	4	-	4 Khimick Kemerovo	Met Magnitogorsk	0	-	2 Baranov's traid Omsk
Krylya S Molotov	3	-	2 Met Magnitogorsk	Met Magnitogorsk	2	-	3 Khimick Kemerovo
Krylya S Molotov	4	-	0 Tsvetnye Metally	Met Magnitogorsk	1	-	1 Tsvetnye Metally
Krylya S Molotov	3	-	0 Gornyak Kemerovo	Met Magnitogorsk	0	-	1 Gornyak Kemerovo
Dynamo Sverdlovsk	1	-	0 Dz Chelyabinsk	Tsvetnye Metally	1	-	5 Dz Chelyabinsk
Dynamo Sverdlovsk	3	-	2 DO Novosibirsk	Tsvetnye Metally	0	-	1 DO Novosibirsk
Dynamo Sverdlovsk	1	-	1 DO Sverdlovsk	Tsvetnye Metally	1	-	0 DO Sverdlovsk
Dynamo Sverdlovsk	3	-	1 Krylya S Molotov	Tsvetnye Metally	0	-	11 Krylya S Molotov
Dynamo Sverdlovsk	2	-	2 Dzerzhinets Nizhni	Tsvetnye Metally	1	-	6 Dynamo Sverdlovsk
Dynamo Sverdlovsk	1	-	1 Dynamo Chelyabinsk	Tsvetnye Metally	0	-	3 Dzerzhinets Nizhni
Dynamo Sverdlovsk	5	-	2 Avangard Sverdlovsk	Tsvetnye Metally	1	-	8 Dynamo Chelyabinsk
Dynamo Sverdlovsk	1	-	1 Baranov's traid Omsk	Tsvetnye Metally	1	-	5 Avangard Sverdlovsk
Dynamo Sverdlovsk	2	-	0 Khimick Kemerovo	Tsvetnye Metally	1	-	3 Baranov's traid Omsk
Dynamo Sverdlovsk	2	-	3 Met Magnitogorsk	Tsvetnye Metally	4	-	4 Khimick Kemerovo
Dynamo Sverdlovsk	4	-	2 Tsvetnye Metally	Tsvetnye Metally	1	-	3 Met Magnitogorsk
Dynamo Sverdlovsk	3	-	0 Gornyak Kemerovo	Tsvetnye Metally	2	-	0 Gornyak Kemerovo
Dzerzhinets Nizhni	0	-	4 Dz Chelyabinsk	Gornyak Kemerovo	1	-	5 Dz Chelyabinsk
Dzerzhinets Nizhni	3	-	0 DO Novosibirsk	Gornyak Kemerovo	0	-	5 DO Novosibirsk
Dzerzhinets Nizhni	0	-	2 DO Sverdlovsk	Gornyak Kemerovo	0	-	8 DO Sverdlovsk
Dzerzhinets Nizhni	0	-	4 Krylya S Molotov	Gornyak Kemerovo	2	-	3 Krylya S Molotov
Dzerzhinets Nizhni	4	-	2 Dynamo Sverdlovsk	Gornyak Kemerovo	o	-	w Dynamo Sverdlovsk
Dzerzhinets Nizhni	0	-	0 Dynamo Chelyabinsk	Gornyak Kemerovo	1	-	2 Dzerzhinets Nizhni
Dzerzhinets Nizhni	1	-	0 Avangard Sverdlovsk	Gornyak Kemerovo	2	-	2 Dynamo Chelyabinsk
Dzerzhinets Nizhni	1	-	2 Baranov's traid Omsk	Gornyak Kemerovo	1	-	7 Avangard Sverdlovsk
Dzerzhinets Nizhni	3	-	0 Khimick Kemerovo	Gornyak Kemerovo	0	-	4 Baranov's traid Omsk
Dzerzhinets Nizhni	0	-	2 Met Magnitogorsk	Gornyak Kemerovo	1	-	3 Khimick Kemerovo
Dzerzhinets Nizhni	2	-	0 Tsvetnye Metally	Gornyak Kemerovo	1	-	5 Met Magnitogorsk
Dzerzhinets Nizhni	2	-	2 Gornyak Kemerovo	Gornyak Kemerovo	2	-	4 Tsvetnye Metally
Dynamo Chelyabinsk	0	-	4 Dz Chelyabinsk				
Dynamo Chelyabinsk	1	-	4 DO Novosibirsk				
Dynamo Chelyabinsk	0	-	2 DO Sverdlovsk				
Dynamo Chelyabinsk	0	-	0 Krylya S Molotov				
Dynamo Chelyabinsk	4	-	1 Dynamo Sverdlovsk				
Dynamo Chelyabinsk	2	-	1 Dzerzhinets Nizhni				
Dynamo Chelyabinsk	1	-	0 Avangard Sverdlovsk				
Dynamo Chelyabinsk	1	-	1 Baranov's traid Omsk				
Dynamo Chelyabinsk	0	-	1 Khimick Kemerovo				
Dynamo Chelyabinsk	4	-	1 Met Magnitogorsk				
Dynamo Chelyabinsk	2	-	1 Tsvetnye Metally				
Dynamo Chelyabinsk	3	-	0 Gornyak Kemerovo				

Division 2 - Ukraine - Final	Pld	W	D	L	F	A	GA	Pts
1 Lokomotiv Kharkov	4	3	1	0	10	3	3.33	7
2 Stal Dnepropetrovsk	4	2	1	1	6	5	1.20	5
3 DO Kiev	3	1	0	2	3	6	0.50	2
4 Bolshevik Mukachevo	3	0	0	3	1	6	0.17	0

Championship play-off

Lokomotiv Kharkov	3 - 1	Stal Dnepropetrovsk
Lokomotiv Kharkov	1 - 1	Stal Dnepropetrovsk
Lokomotiv Kharkov	4 - 1	DO Kiev
Lokomotiv Kharkov	2 - 0	Bolshevik Mukachevo
Stal Dnepropetrovsk	2 - 0	DO Kiev
Stal Dnepropetrovsk	2 - 1	Bolshevik Mukachevo
DO Kiev	2 - 0	Bolshevik Mukachevo

Division 2 - Ukraine - Group A	Pld	W	D	L	F	A	GA	Pts
1 Lokomotiv Kharkov	14	8	5	1	40	10	4.00	21
2 Stal Dnepropetrovsk	14	9	2	3	34	24	1.42	20
3 Shakhter Stalino	14	8	3	3	33	15	2.20	19
4 Dynamo Voroshilovgrad	14	4	6	4	30	29	1.03	14
5 Lokomotiv Zaporozhe	14	4	3	7	22	30	0.73	11
6 Avagard Kramatorsk	14	3	4	7	23	40	0.58	10
7 Dzerzhinets Kharkov	14	4	1	9	16	37	0.43	9
8 Shakhter Kadievka	14	3	2	9	16	29	0.55	8

Division 2 - Ukraine - Group B	Pld	W	D	L	F	A	GA	Pts
1 Bolshevik Mukachevo	14	10	2	2	35	16	2.19	22
2 DO Kiev	14	9	4	1	27	14	1.93	22
3 Spartak Lvov	14	6	5	3	26	22	1.18	17
4 Spartak Uzhgorod	14	7	2	5	33	19	1.74	16
5 Pischevik Odessa	14	5	5	4	19	18	1.06	15
6 Spartak Herson	14	5	3	6	18	22	0.82	13
7 Dynamo Chisinau	14	1	2	11	11	35	0.31	4
8 Sudostroitel Nikolaev	14	0	3	11	8	31	0.26	3

Group A

Lokomotiv Kharkov	3 - 1	Stal Dnepropetrovsk
Lokomotiv Kharkov	0 - 1	Shakhter Stalino
Lokomotiv Kharkov	1 - 1	D Voroshilovgrad
Lokomotiv Kharkov	2 - 0	Lokomotiv Zaporozhe
Lokomotiv Kharkov	9 - 0	Avagard Kramatorsk

Group B

Bol Mukachevo	1 - 1	DO Kiev
Bol Mukachevo	3 - 0	Spartak Lvov
Bol Mukachevo	2 - 1	Spartak Uzhgorod
Bol Mukachevo	5 - 1	Pischevik Odessa
Bol Mukachevo	2 - 1	Spartak Herson

Lokomotiv Kharkov	8	-	1 Dzerzhinets Kharkov	Bol Mukachevo	4	-	2 Dynamo Chisinau
Lokomotiv Kharkov	2	-	0 Shakhter Kadievka	Bol Mukachevo	5	-	1 Sud Nikolaev
Stal Dnepropetrovsk	0	-	6 Lokomotiv Kharkov	DO Kiev	2	-	2 Bol Mukachevo
Stal Dnepropetrovsk	2	-	1 Shakhter Stalino	DO Kiev	1	-	1 Spartak Lvov
Stal Dnepropetrovsk	4	-	1 D Voroshilovgrad	DO Kiev	3	-	1 Spartak Uzhgorod
Stal Dnepropetrovsk	4	-	2 Lokomotiv Zaporozhe	DO Kiev	2	-	0 Pischevik Odessa
Stal Dnepropetrovsk	5	-	3 Avagard Kramatorsk	DO Kiev	1	-	0 Spartak Herson
Stal Dnepropetrovsk	2	-	2 Dzerzhinets Kharkov	DO Kiev	3	-	0 Dynamo Chisinau
Stal Dnepropetrovsk	4	-	0 Shakhter Kadievka	DO Kiev	3	-	1 Sud Nikolaev
Shakhter Stalino	2	-	2 Lokomotiv Kharkov	Spartak Lvov	2	-	1 Bol Mukachevo
Shakhter Stalino	2	-	1 Stal Dnepropetrovsk	Spartak Lvov	1	-	2 DO Kiev
Shakhter Stalino	2	-	1 D Voroshilovgrad	Spartak Lvov	2	-	1 Spartak Uzhgorod
Shakhter Stalino	4	-	1 Lokomotiv Zaporozhe	Spartak Lvov	1	-	1 Pischevik Odessa
Shakhter Stalino	4	-	1 Avagard Kramatorsk	Spartak Lvov	5	-	2 Spartak Herson
Shakhter Stalino	6	-	0 Dzerzhinets Kharkov	Spartak Lvov	4	-	2 Dynamo Chisinau
Shakhter Stalino	3	-	0 Shakhter Kadievka	Spartak Lvov	2	-	2 Sud Nikolaev
D Voroshilovgrad	2	-	2 Lokomotiv Kharkov	Spartak Uzhgorod	2	-	4 Bol Mukachevo
D Voroshilovgrad	1	-	1 Stal Dnepropetrovsk	Spartak Uzhgorod	4	-	1 DO Kiev
D Voroshilovgrad	3	-	3 Shakhter Stalino	Spartak Uzhgorod	2	-	2 Spartak Lvov
D Voroshilovgrad	4	-	1 Lokomotiv Zaporozhe	Spartak Uzhgorod	1	-	1 Pischevik Odessa
D Voroshilovgrad	5	-	3 Avagard Kramatorsk	Spartak Uzhgorod	3	-	0 Spartak Herson
D Voroshilovgrad	2	-	1 Dzerzhinets Kharkov	Spartak Uzhgorod	6	-	0 Dynamo Chisinau
D Voroshilovgrad	4	-	1 Shakhter Kadievka	Spartak Uzhgorod	5	-	1 Sud Nikolaev
Lokomotiv Zaporozhe	1	-	1 Lokomotiv Kharkov	Pischevik Odessa	0	-	1 Bol Mukachevo
Lokomotiv Zaporozhe	0	-	1 Stal Dnepropetrovsk	Pischevik Odessa	0	-	0 DO Kiev
Lokomotiv Zaporozhe	2	-	1 Shakhter Stalino	Pischevik Odessa	2	-	0 Spartak Lvov
Lokomotiv Zaporozhe	5	-	2 D Voroshilovgrad	Pischevik Odessa	0	-	2 Spartak Uzhgorod
Lokomotiv Zaporozhe	1	-	1 Avagard Kramatorsk	Pischevik Odessa	2	-	2 Spartak Herson
Lokomotiv Zaporozhe	3	-	2 Dzerzhinets Kharkov	Pischevik Odessa	2	-	0 Dynamo Chisinau
Lokomotiv Zaporozhe	2	-	2 Shakhter Kadievka	Pischevik Odessa	3	-	0 Sud Nikolaev
Avagard Kramatorsk	1	-	1 Lokomotiv Kharkov	Spartak Herson	3	-	1 Bol Mukachevo
Avagard Kramatorsk	1	-	3 Stal Dnepropetrovsk	Spartak Herson	2	-	4 DO Kiev
Avagard Kramatorsk	1	-	1 Shakhter Stalino	Spartak Herson	0	-	1 Spartak Lvov
Avagard Kramatorsk	2	-	2 D Voroshilovgrad	Spartak Herson	2	-	1 Spartak Uzhgorod
Avagard Kramatorsk	3	-	2 Lokomotiv Zaporozhe	Spartak Herson	1	-	1 Pischevik Odessa
Avagard Kramatorsk	1	-	2 Dzerzhinets Kharkov	Spartak Herson	1	-	0 Dynamo Chisinau
Avagard Kramatorsk	3	-	1 Shakhter Kadievka	Spartak Herson	2	-	1 Sud Nikolaev
Dzerzhinets Kharkov	0	-	2 Lokomotiv Kharkov	Dynamo Chisinau	0	-	2 Bol Mukachevo
Dzerzhinets Kharkov	1	-	4 Stal Dnepropetrovsk	Dynamo Chisinau	0	-	2 DO Kiev
Dzerzhinets Kharkov	1	-	0 Shakhter Stalino	Dynamo Chisinau	3	-	3 Spartak Lvov
Dzerzhinets Kharkov	1	-	0 D Voroshilovgrad	Dynamo Chisinau	1	-	3 Spartak Uzhgorod
Dzerzhinets Kharkov	3	-	1 Lokomotiv Zaporozhe	Dynamo Chisinau	2	-	3 Pischevik Odessa
Dzerzhinets Kharkov	1	-	2 Avagard Kramatorsk	Dynamo Chisinau	0	-	2 Spartak Herson
Dzerzhinets Kharkov	1	-	4 Shakhter Kadievka	Dynamo Chisinau	1	-	0 Sud Nikolaev
Shakhter Kadievka	0	-	1 Lokomotiv Kharkov	Sud Nikolaev	0	-	2 Bol Mukachevo
Shakhter Kadievka	1	-	2 Stal Dnepropetrovsk	Sud Nikolaev	1	-	2 DO Kiev
Shakhter Kadievka	0	-	3 Shakhter Stalino	Sud Nikolaev	0	-	2 Spartak Lvov
Shakhter Kadievka	2	-	2 D Voroshilovgrad	Sud Nikolaev	0	-	1 Spartak Uzhgorod
Shakhter Kadievka	0	-	1 Lokomotiv Zaporozhe	Sud Nikolaev	1	-	3 Pischevik Odessa
Shakhter Kadievka	3	-	1 Avagard Kramatorsk	Sud Nikolaev	0	-	0 Spartak Herson
Shakhter Kadievka	2	-	0 Dzerzhinets Kharkov	Sud Nikolaev	0	-	0 Dynamo Chisinau

	Division 2 - South	Pld	W	D	L	F	A	GA	Pts
1	Dynamo Erevan	18	13	4	1	48	12	4.00	30
2	DO Tbilisi	18	12	5	1	40	16	2.50	29
3	Spartak Tbilisi	18	11	3	4	52	24	2.17	25
4	Neftyanick Baki	18	8	5	5	27	19	1.42	21
5	Lokomotiv Tbilisi	18	8	3	7	40	37	1.08	19
6	Dynamo Rostov-na-Donu	18	6	5	7	40	33	1.21	17
7	Dynamo Baki	18	7	2	9	26	28	0.93	16
8	Spartak Erevan	18	3	5	10	21	35	0.60	11
9	Traktor Taganrog	18	3	3	12	19	47	0.40	9
10	Pischevik Astrakhan	18	1	1	16	10	72	0.14	3

Dynamo Erevan	2 - 0	DO Tbilisi		Dynamo Rostov	1 - 1	Dynamo Erevan
Dynamo Erevan	3 - 2	Spartak Tbilisi		Dynamo Rostov	1 - 1	DO Tbilisi
Dynamo Erevan	1 - 1	Neftyanick Baki		Dynamo Rostov	1 - 1	Spartak Tbilisi
Dynamo Erevan	8 - 0	Lokomotiv Tbilisi		Dynamo Rostov	1 - 2	Neftyanick Baki
Dynamo Erevan	3 - 2	Dynamo Rostov		Dynamo Rostov	3 - 3	Lokomotiv Tbilisi
Dynamo Erevan	4 - 0	Dynamo Baki		Dynamo Rostov	4 - 1	Dynamo Baki
Dynamo Erevan	2 - 0	Spartak Erevan		Dynamo Rostov	0 - 1	Spartak Erevan
Dynamo Erevan	3 - 0	Traktor Taganrog		Dynamo Rostov	2 - 1	Traktor Taganrog
Dynamo Erevan	8 - 1	Pischevik Astrakhan		Dynamo Rostov	8 - 0	Pischevik Astrakhan
DO Tbilisi	1 - 0	Dynamo Erevan		Dynamo Baki	0 - 2	Dynamo Erevan
DO Tbilisi	3 - 0	Spartak Tbilisi		Dynamo Baki	2 - 2	DO Tbilisi
DO Tbilisi	3 - 1	Neftyanick Baki		Dynamo Baki	1 - 0	Spartak Tbilisi
DO Tbilisi	2 - 0	Lokomotiv Tbilisi		Dynamo Baki	0 - 1	Neftyanick Baki
DO Tbilisi	4 - 3	Dynamo Rostov		Dynamo Baki	4 - 0	Lokomotiv Tbilisi
DO Tbilisi	5 - 1	Dynamo Baki		Dynamo Baki	1 - 2	Dynamo Rostov
DO Tbilisi	1 - 1	Spartak Erevan		Dynamo Baki	1 - 0	Spartak Erevan
DO Tbilisi	3 - 2	Traktor Taganrog		Dynamo Baki	0 - 0	Traktor Taganrog
DO Tbilisi	3 - 0	Pischevik Astrakhan		Dynamo Baki	4 - 1	Pischevik Astrakhan
Spartak Tbilisi	1 - 1	Dynamo Erevan		Spartak Erevan	2 - 4	Dynamo Erevan
Spartak Tbilisi	0 - 2	DO Tbilisi		Spartak Erevan	1 - 1	DO Tbilisi
Spartak Tbilisi	2 - 0	Neftyanick Baki		Spartak Erevan	2 - 4	Spartak Tbilisi
Spartak Tbilisi	4 - 2	Lokomotiv Tbilisi		Spartak Erevan	1 - 0	Neftyanick Baki
Spartak Tbilisi	3 - 0	Dynamo Rostov		Spartak Erevan	2 - 3	Lokomotiv Tbilisi
Spartak Tbilisi	3 - 2	Dynamo Baki		Spartak Erevan	4 - 2	Dynamo Rostov
Spartak Tbilisi	3 - 1	Spartak Erevan		Spartak Erevan	0 - 3	Dynamo Baki
Spartak Tbilisi	6 - 1	Traktor Taganrog		Spartak Erevan	3 - 3	Traktor Taganrog
Spartak Tbilisi	7 - 0	Pischevik Astrakhan		Spartak Erevan	1 - 3	Pischevik Astrakhan
Neftyanick Baki	0 - 0	Dynamo Erevan		Traktor Taganrog	0 - 2	Dynamo Erevan
Neftyanick Baki	0 - 0	DO Tbilisi		Traktor Taganrog	1 - 4	DO Tbilisi
Neftyanick Baki	2 - 5	Spartak Tbilisi		Traktor Taganrog	2 - 4	Spartak Tbilisi
Neftyanick Baki	1 - 3	Lokomotiv Tbilisi		Traktor Taganrog	0 - 1	Neftyanick Baki
Neftyanick Baki	1 - 1	Dynamo Rostov		Traktor Taganrog	0 - 2	Lokomotiv Tbilisi
Neftyanick Baki	2 - 1	Dynamo Baki		Traktor Taganrog	2 - 3	Dynamo Rostov
Neftyanick Baki	0 - 0	Spartak Erevan		Traktor Taganrog	0 - 2	Dynamo Baki

Neftyanick Baki	8	-	0	Traktor Taganrog	Traktor Taganrog	2	-	1	Spartak Erevan
Neftyanick Baki	2	-	0	Pischevik Astrakhan	Traktor Taganrog	2	-	1	Pischevik Astrakhan
Lokomotiv Tbilisi	1	-	2	Dynamo Erevan	Pischevik Astrakhan	0	-	2	Dynamo Erevan
Lokomotiv Tbilisi	1	-	3	DO Tbilisi	Pischevik Astrakhan	0	-	2	DO Tbilisi
Lokomotiv Tbilisi	1	-	1	Spartak Tbilisi	Pischevik Astrakhan	0	-	6	Spartak Tbilisi
Lokomotiv Tbilisi	1	-	2	Neftyanick Baki	Pischevik Astrakhan	0	-	3	Neftyanick Baki
Lokomotiv Tbilisi	3	-	0	Dynamo Rostov	Pischevik Astrakhan	2	-	3	Lokomotiv Tbilisi
Lokomotiv Tbilisi	2	-	1	Dynamo Baki	Pischevik Astrakhan	1	-	6	Dynamo Rostov
Lokomotiv Tbilisi	3	-	1	Spartak Erevan	Pischevik Astrakhan	0	-	2	Dynamo Baki
Lokomotiv Tbilisi	1	-	1	Traktor Taganrog	Pischevik Astrakhan	0	-	0	Spartak Erevan
Lokomotiv Tbilisi	11	-	0	Pischevik Astrakhan	Pischevik Astrakhan	1	-	2	Traktor Taganrog

	Division 2 - Middle East	Pld	W	D	L	F	A	GA	Pts
1	DO Tashkent	12	8	2	2	37	9	4.11	18
2	Dynamo Alma Ata	12	7	3	2	22	9	2.44	17
3	Lokomotiv Ashhabad	12	5	3	4	21	13	1.62	13
4	Zenith Frunse	12	4	3	5	12	21	0.57	11
5	Dynamo Tashkent	12	4	1	7	16	25	0.64	9
6	Dynamo Stalinabad	12	3	3	6	13	21	0.62	9
7	Spartak Alma Ata	12	3	1	8	15	38	0.39	7

DO Tashkent	1	-	1	Dynamo Alma Ata	Dynamo Tashkent	0	-	3	DO Tashkent
DO Tashkent	1	-	0	Lokomotiv Ashhabad	Dynamo Tashkent	1	-	0	Dynamo Alma Ata
DO Tashkent	6	-	0	Zenith Frunse	Dynamo Tashkent	2	-	3	Lokomotiv Ashhabad
DO Tashkent	3	-	1	Dynamo Tashkent	Dynamo Tashkent	3	-	1	Zenith Frunse
DO Tashkent	1	-	2	Dynamo Stalinabad	Dynamo Tashkent	4	-	3	Dynamo Stalinabad
DO Tashkent	8	-	1	Spartak Alma Ata	Dynamo Tashkent	2	-	3	Spartak Alma Ata
Dynamo Alma Ata	4	-	0	DO Tashkent	Dynamo Stalinabad	0	-	2	DO Tashkent
Dynamo Alma Ata	1	-	1	Lokomotiv Ashhabad	Dynamo Stalinabad	2	-	1	Dynamo Alma Ata
Dynamo Alma Ata	4	-	1	Zenith Frunse	Dynamo Stalinabad	2	-	2	Lokomotiv Ashhabad
Dynamo Alma Ata	2	-	0	Dynamo Tashkent	Dynamo Stalinabad	1	-	2	Zenith Frunse
Dynamo Alma Ata	1	-	0	Dynamo Stalinabad	Dynamo Stalinabad	1	-	0	Dynamo Tashkent
Dynamo Alma Ata	3	-	0	Spartak Alma Ata	Dynamo Stalinabad	2	-	2	Spartak Alma Ata
Lokomotiv Ashhabad	0	-	0	DO Tashkent	Spartak Alma Ata	0	-	10	DO Tashkent
Lokomotiv Ashhabad	1	-	2	Dynamo Alma Ata	Spartak Alma Ata	1	-	2	Dynamo Alma Ata
Lokomotiv Ashhabad	3	-	1	Zenith Frunse	Spartak Alma Ata	0	-	2	Lokomotiv Ashhabad
Lokomotiv Ashhabad	0	-	2	Dynamo Tashkent	Spartak Alma Ata	0	-	1	Zenith Frunse
Lokomotiv Ashhabad	4	-	0	Dynamo Stalinabad	Spartak Alma Ata	5	-	0	Dynamo Tashkent
Lokomotiv Ashhabad	5	-	1	Spartak Alma Ata	Spartak Alma Ata	2	-	0	Dynamo Stalinabad
Zenith Frunse	0	-	2	DO Tashkent					
Zenith Frunse	1	-	1	Dynamo Alma Ata					
Zenith Frunse	1	-	0	Lokomotiv Ashhabad					
Zenith Frunse	1	-	1	Dynamo Tashkent					
Zenith Frunse	0	-	0	Dynamo Stalinabad					
Zenith Frunse	3	-	0	Spartak Alma Ata					

Yugoslavia

Partizan only dropped one point against Red Star and Hajduk and that basically won them the title. Novi Sad and Trst were both relegated. From next year, Yugoslavia will switch to a Spring-Autumn season.

		Pld	W	D	L	F	A	GA	Pts
1	Partizan Beograd	18	14	1	3	39	14	2.79	29
2	Crvena zvezda Beograd	18	11	4	3	37	19	1.95	26
3	Hajduk Split	18	10	5	3	41	20	2.05	25
4	Dinamo Zagreb	18	7	5	6	29	25	1.16	19
5	Nasa Krila Zemun	18	6	4	8	32	28	1.14	16
6	Buducnost Titograd	18	6	4	8	29	36	0.81	16
7	Metalac Beograd	18	5	4	9	31	34	0.91	14
8	Lokomotiva Zagreb	18	6	1	11	23	38	0.61	13
9	Sloga Novi Sad	18	5	2	11	17	31	0.55	12
10	Ponziana Trst	18	3	4	11	12	45	0.27	10

Partizan Beograd	1 - 0	Crvena zvezda	Buducnost Titograd	2 - 0	Partizan Beograd
Partizan Beograd	3 - 1	Hajduk Split	Buducnost Titograd	2 - 3	Crvena zvezda
Partizan Beograd	3 - 1	Dinamo Zagreb	Buducnost Titograd	2 - 5	Hajduk Split
Partizan Beograd	1 - 0	Nasa Krila Zemun	Buducnost Titograd	1 - 1	Dinamo Zagreb
Partizan Beograd	2 - 1	Buducnost Titograd	Buducnost Titograd	3 - 1	Nasa Krila Zemun
Partizan Beograd	3 - 1	Metalac Beograd	Buducnost Titograd	2 - 1	Metalac Beograd
Partizan Beograd	2 - 0	Lokomotiva Zagreb	Buducnost Titograd	3 - 0	Lokomotiva Zagreb
Partizan Beograd	2 - 0	Sloga Novi Sad	Buducnost Titograd	1 - 0	Sloga Novi Sad
Partizan Beograd	4 - 0	Ponziana Trst	Buducnost Titograd	1 - 1	Ponziana Trst
Crvena zvezda	2 - 2	Partizan Beograd	Metalac Beograd	0 - 3	Partizan Beograd
Crvena zvezda	1 - 1	Hajduk Split	Metalac Beograd	0 - 3	Crvena zvezda
Crvena zvezda	2 - 1	Dinamo Zagreb	Metalac Beograd	0 - 3	Hajduk Split
Crvena zvezda	0 - 0	Nasa Krila Zemun	Metalac Beograd	1 - 1	Dinamo Zagreb
Crvena zvezda	1 - 1	Buducnost Titograd	Metalac Beograd	1 - 5	Nasa Krila Zemun
Crvena zvezda	4 - 1	Metalac Beograd	Metalac Beograd	7 - 0	Buducnost Titograd
Crvena zvezda	2 - 1	Lokomotiva Zagreb	Metalac Beograd	8 - 2	Lokomotiva Zagreb
Crvena zvezda	3 - 1	Sloga Novi Sad	Metalac Beograd	2 - 0	Sloga Novi Sad
Crvena zvezda	3 - 0	Ponziana Trst	Metalac Beograd	2 - 0	Ponziana Trst
Hajduk Split	0 - 2	Partizan Beograd	Lokomotiva Zagreb	0 - 3	Partizan Beograd
Hajduk Split	3 - 2	Crvena zvezda	Lokomotiva Zagreb	0 - 2	Crvena zvezda
Hajduk Split	1 - 1	Dinamo Zagreb	Lokomotiva Zagreb	1 - 1	Hajduk Split
Hajduk Split	1 - 1	Nasa Krila Zemun	Lokomotiva Zagreb	1 - 3	Dinamo Zagreb
Hajduk Split	2 - 1	Buducnost Titograd	Lokomotiva Zagreb	4 - 0	Nasa Krila Zemun
Hajduk Split	4 - 0	Metalac Beograd	Lokomotiva Zagreb	2 - 1	Buducnost Titograd
Hajduk Split	4 - 1	Lokomotiva Zagreb	Lokomotiva Zagreb	1 - 0	Metalac Beograd
Hajduk Split	3 - 0	Sloga Novi Sad	Lokomotiva Zagreb	4 - 1	Sloga Novi Sad
Hajduk Split	3 - 0	Ponziana Trst	Lokomotiva Zagreb	4 - 0	Ponziana Trst
Dinamo Zagreb	2 - 1	Partizan Beograd	Sloga Novi Sad	1 - 0	Partizan Beograd

Dinamo Zagreb	1 - 3	Crvena zvezda	Sloga Novi Sad	1 - 2	Crvena zvezda
Dinamo Zagreb	2 - 1	Hajduk Split	Sloga Novi Sad	1 - 2	Hajduk Split
Dinamo Zagreb	0 - 2	Nasa Krila Zemun	Sloga Novi Sad	1 - 0	Dinamo Zagreb
Dinamo Zagreb	5 - 3	Buducnost Titograd	Sloga Novi Sad	2 - 1	Nasa Krila Zemun
Dinamo Zagreb	2 - 2	Metalac Beograd	Sloga Novi Sad	2 - 4	Buducnost Titograd
Dinamo Zagreb	3 - 0	Lokomotiva Zagreb	Sloga Novi Sad	1 - 1	Metalac Beograd
Dinamo Zagreb	3 - 1	Sloga Novi Sad	Sloga Novi Sad	1 - 0	Lokomotiva Zagreb
Dinamo Zagreb	3 - 0	Ponziana Trst	Sloga Novi Sad	0 - 0	Ponziana Trst
Nasa Krila Zemun	2 - 3	Partizan Beograd	Ponziana Trst	1 - 4	Partizan Beograd
Nasa Krila Zemun	1 - 3	Crvena zvezda	Ponziana Trst	2 - 1	Crvena zvezda
Nasa Krila Zemun	1 - 1	Hajduk Split	Ponziana Trst	1 - 5	Hajduk Split
Nasa Krila Zemun	2 - 0	Dinamo Zagreb	Ponziana Trst	0 - 0	Dinamo Zagreb
Nasa Krila Zemun	3 - 1	Buducnost Titograd	Ponziana Trst	3 - 2	Nasa Krila Zemun
Nasa Krila Zemun	0 - 0	Metalac Beograd	Ponziana Trst	0 - 0	Buducnost Titograd
Nasa Krila Zemun	4 - 0	Lokomotiva Zagreb	Ponziana Trst	0 - 4	Metalac Beograd
Nasa Krila Zemun	1 - 3	Sloga Novi Sad	Ponziana Trst	0 - 2	Lokomotiva Zagreb
Nasa Krila Zemun	6 - 2	Ponziana Trst	Ponziana Trst	2 - 1	Sloga Novi Sad

Wales

No national league in Wales for nearly the next 50 years. All the best Welsh teams compete in the English Football League. Of course there is the Welsh Cup, which is recorded in the following section

Cup Competitions

International

This season the Latin Cup was begun – the champions of Italy, Spain, France and Portugal played a knockout tournament in Spain. Victory to Barca, though Torino's team was totally different to that which won the Italian title for 4 years. In addition the cross border end of season tournament between teams from Northern Ireland and the Republic of Ireland was played again – the Republic providing both finalists this year, the green & white Shamrock's winning.

Latin Cup Semi Final
Sporting Lisboa	3 - 1 Torino	at Barcelona
Barcelona CF	5 - 0 Stade de Reims	at Madrid

Latin Cup 3rd place
Torino	5 - 3 Stade de Reims	at Barcelona

Latin Cup Final
July 3, 1949
Barcelona CF	2 - 1 Sporting Lisboa	at Madrid

Intercity Cup 1st Round
April 6, 1949
Drumcondra 3 - 0 Cliftonville
April 7, 1949
Derry City 5 - 1 Limerick
April 25, 1949
Shelbourne 1 - 2 Lisburn Distillery
April 29, 1949
Glentoran 1 - 1 Shamrock Rovers   Both clubs to quarter finals

Intercity Cup Quarter Final
May 5, 1949
Bohemians Dublin 1 - 0 Glentoran
Lisburn Distillery 1 - 3 Dundalk
May 6, 1949
Ballymena United 0 - 4 Drumcondra
May 7, 1949
Shamrock Rovers 2 - 0 Derry City

Intercity Cup Semi Final
May 11, 1949
Bohemians Dublin 1 - 1 Dundalk

May 14, 1949
Shamrock Rovers   2 - 1 Drumcondra

Intercity Cup Semi Final replay
May 16, 1949
Dundalk   3 - 1 Bohemians Dublin

Intercity Cup Final
May 18, 1949
Shamrock Rovers   3 - 0 Dundalk

Domestic
Austria

The last Austrian Cup until 1958-59 – to enable a qualifier for the start of the European Cup Winners Cup – was won by Austria Wien. Regional Cup winners qualified to the main event – which meant only one Viennese team as usual, and Austria Wien duly completed the double.

Wien Last 32
November 20, 1948

HSV	2	- 1	Floridsdorfer AC
Austria Wien	13	- 1	Graphia
Sparta	0	- 0	Auto

November 21, 1948

Rapid Wien	4	- 1	Feuerwehr
Wacker Wien	2	- 1	Wiener Sportclub
FC Wien	5	- 2	Rapid Oberlaa
First Vienna	5	- 0	Liesing
Favoritner AC Wien	3	- 12	Admira Wien
Rasenspieler Hochstadt	2	- 2	Telegraphia
Gaswerk	2	- 2	VorwartsXI
Wien AC	6	- 2	Unilever
Simmering	11	- 2	Bally
Slovan	3	- 3	1 Schwechater SC
Ostbahn X	1	- 8	Favoritner SK Blau Weiss
Hakoah	6	- 2	Rennweg
Alt Ottakring	0	- 4	Nova

Replay
December 4, 1948

Telegraphia   0 - 6 Rasenspieler

				Hochstadt	
	December 5, 1948				
Auto		3	-	1	Sparta	
Vorwarts X1		0	-	0	Gaswerk	
Schwechater SC		3	-	4	Slovan	
	December 12, 1948				
Gaswerk		2	-	1	VorwartsXI	

Last 16

	December 11, 1948				
Admira Wien		8	-	1	Nova	
	December 12, 1948				
First Vienna		5	-	1	Hakoah	
Simmering		3	-	1	Auto	
Rasenspieler Hochstadt		1	-	2	Wien AC	
Favoritner SK Blau Weiss		0	-	8	Wacker Wien	FSKBW Known as Ankerbrot until Dec 3rd
FC Wien		1	-	2	Gaswerk	
	January 23, 1949				
Rapid Wien		1	-	1	Austria Wien	
Slovan		2	-	1	Heiligenstadter SV	

Replay

	February 19, 1949				
Austria Wien		3	-	2	Rapid Wien

Quarter Final

	February 15, 1949				
Wacker Wien		0	-	3	Wien AC	awarded 0-3 due to non-arrival of Wacker
	February 19, 1949				
Simmering		0	-	1	Gaswerk	
	February 20, 1949				
First Vienna		5	-	1	Admira Wien	
	March 2, 1949				
Slovan		1	-	4	Austria Wien	

Semi Final

	March 23, 1949				
Wien AC		2	-	4	Austria Wien
	March 24, 1949				
First Vienna		3	-	2	Gaswerk

Wien Final

	April 30, 1949				
Austria Wien		3	-	1	First Vienna

Niederosterreich Final
April 10, 1948
SV Siebenhirten 3 - 1 Zistersdorf

Burgenland Final
April 10, 1949
SV Oberwart 1 - 1 SV Siegendorf in Eisenstadt
Replay
April 24, 1949
SV Oberwart 5 - 1 SV Siegendorf in Pinkafeld

Oberosterreich Final
May 8, 1949
Vorwarts Steyr 3 - 1 LASK in Steyr

Salzburg Final
August 29, 1948
UFC Salzburg 4 - 2 SAK 1914

Tirol Tyrolia
No cup played 1948/49
Innsbrucker AC w - o bye Autumn 48 halfway champion qualified

Vorarlberg Final
December 12, 1948
Admira Dornbirn 6 - 1 FC Lustenau

Steiermark Final
March 27, 1949
Austria Graz 2 - 2 Sturm Graz at Sturm Platz
Replay
April 21, 1949
Sturm Graz 0 - 0 Austria Graz at Sturm Platz
2nd Replay
April 30, 1949
Austria Graz 2 - 2 Sturm Graz at Sturm Platz
Replay
May 4, 1949
Sturm Graz 3 - 1 Austria Graz at Sturm Platz

Karnten Final
May 1, 1949
ASK Klagenfurt 3 - 0 Post Klagenfurt

Last 16

	April 30, 1949				
SV Siebenhirten		3	-	1	SV Oberwart

Quarter Final

	May 26, 1949				
ASK Klagenfurt		2	-	3	Austria Wien
Admira Dornbirn		1	-	5	UFC Salzburg
	June 6, 1949				
Vorwarts Steyr		3	-	2	Sturm Graz
	June 12, 1949				
Innsbrucker AC		2	-	3	SV Siebenhirten

Semi Final

	June 25, 1949				
Austria Wien		8	-	1	SV Siebenhirten
	June 26, 1949				
Vorwarts Steyr		3	-	0	UFC Salzburg

	July 3, 1949				

Final

| Austria Wien | | 5 | - | 2 | Vorwarts Steyr |

Bulgaria

Levski completed the double over CSKA

Last 16
Levski Sofia	4 - 1	Spartak Pazardzhik
Minyor Pernik	2 - 1	Cherno more Varna
Slavia Sofia	0 - 0	Marek Dupnitsa
CSKA Sofia	4 - 0	Partizanin Yambol
Spartak Sofia	1 - 0	Spartak Varna
Septemvri Pleven	2 - 1	Lokomotiv Plovdiv
Botev Burgas	2 - 1	Lokomotiv Sofia

Replay
Marek Dupnitsa	0 - 2	Slavia Sofia

Quarter Final
Levski Sofia	7 - 0	Minyor Pernik
Slavia Sofia	4 - 0	Benkovski Vidin
CSKA Sofia	1 - 1	Spartak Sofia
Septemvri Pleven	3 - 1	Botev Burgas

Replay
Spartak Sofia	2 - 3	CSKA Sofia

Semi Final
Levski Sofia	1 - 0	Slavia Sofia
CSKA Sofia	6 - 4	Septemvri Pleven

Final
May 8, 1949
Levski Sofia	1 - 1	CSKA Sofia

Replay
May 16, 1949
Levski Sofia	2 - 2	CSKA Sofia

2nd Replay
May 17, 1949
Levski Sofia	2 - 1	CSKA Sofia

Cyprus

After complete chaos in the league programme, Anorthosis beat the previously unbeatbale APOEL 3-0 in the cup final.

Quarter Final
Anorthosis Famagusta   3 - 0 POL Larnaca
APOEL Nicosia   3 - 0 Olympiakos Nicosia
Chetin Kaya   5 - 1 EPA Larnaca
AEL Limassol   4 - 1 AIMA

Semi Final
APOEL Nicosia   3 - 2 AEL Limassol
Anorthosis Famagusta   5 - 1 Chetin Kaya

Final
    April 3, 1949
APOEL Nicosia   3 - 2 Anorthosis Famagusta   abandoned in 87' due to fights in
                                                           crowd and between players
Final Replay
    June 19, 1949
Anorthosis Famagusta   3 - 0 APOEL Nicosia

England

Portsmouth gained favourable home draws throughout, and drew second division Leicester in the semi final and their dream of the double and a repeat match up of the 1939 final was on. Until that is the team struggling to avoid relegation to the third division. Of course this is the FA Cup, and the underdogs won 3-1. Wolves beat Manchester United 1-0 and finished off the upstarts in the final.

FA Cup 1st Round
Crewe Alexandra	5 - 0	Billingham
Crystal Palace	0 - 1	Bristol City
Dartford	2 - 3	Leyton Orient
Gainsborough Trinity	1 - 0	Witton Albion
Gateshead	3 - 0	Netherfield
Hartlepool United	1 - 3	Chester City
Hull City	3 - 1	Accrington Stanley
Kidderminster Harriers	0 - 3	Hereford United
Mansfield Town	4 - 0	Gloucester City
Milwall	1 - 0	Tooting & Mitcham
New Brighton	1 - 0	Carlisle United
Newport County	3 - 1	Brighton & Hove Albion
Northampton Town	2 - 1	Dulwich Hamlet
Norwich City	1 - 0	Wellington
Notts County	2 - 1	Port Vale
Peterborough United	0 - 1	Torquay United
Rochdale	1 - 1	Barrow
Southport	2 - 1	Horden
Tranmere Rovers	1 - 3	Darlington
Walsall	2 - 1	Bristol Rovers
Walthamstow	3 - 2	Cambridge United
Weymouth	2 - 1	Chelmsford City
Workington	0 - 3	Stockport County
Wrexham	0 - 3	Oldham Athletic
Yeovil Town	4 - 0	Romford
York City	2 - 1	Runcorn

December 4, 1948
Barnet	2 - 6	Exeter City
Bradford City	4 - 3	Doncaster Rovers
Colchester United	2 - 4	Reading
Halifax Town	0 - 0	Scunthorpe United
Ipswich Town	0 - 3	Aldershot
Leytonstone	2 - 1	Watford
Rhyl	0 - 2	Scarborough
Southend United	1 - 2	Swansea Town

Replay

December 4, 1948
Barrow   2 - 0 Rochdale
December 6, 1948
Scunthorpe United   1 - 0 Halifax Town

FA Cup 2nd Round
December 11, 1948
Aldershot   1 - 0 Chester City
Bradford City   0 - 0 New Brighton
Bristol City   3 - 1 Swansea Town
Crewe Alexandra   3 - 2 Milwall
Darlington   1 - 0 Leyton Orient
Exeter City   2 - 1 Hereford United
Gateshead   3 - 0 Scarborough
Hull City   0 - 0 Reading
Leytonstone   3 - 4 Newport County
Mansfield Town   2 - 1 Northampton Town
Notts County   3 - 2 Barrow
Scunthorpe United   0 - 1 Stockport County
Southport   2 - 2 York City
Torquay United   3 - 1 Norwich City
Walsall   4 - 3 Gainsborough Trinity
Walthamstow   2 - 2 Oldham Athletic
Weymouth   0 - 4 Yeovil Town

FA Cup 2nd Round replay
December 18, 1948
New Brighton   1 - 0 Bradford City
Oldham Athletic   3 - 1 Walthamstow
Reading   1 - 2 Hull City
York City   0 - 2 Southport

FA Cup 3rd Round
January 8, 1949
Arsenal   3 - 0 Tottenham Hotspur
Aston Villa   1 - 1 Bolton Wanderers
Barnsley   0 - 1 Blackpool
Blackburn Rovers   1 - 2 Hull City
Brentford   3 - 2 Middlesbrough
Bristol City   1 - 3 Chelsea
Burnley   2 - 1 Charlton Athletic
Crewe Alexandra   0 - 2 Sunderland
Derby County   4 - 1 Southport
Everton   1 - 0 Manchester City
Fulham   0 - 1 Walsall
Gateshead   3 - 1 Aldershot

Grimsby Town	2 - 1	Exeter City
Leeds United	1 - 3	Newport County
Leicester City	1 - 1	Birmingham City
Lincoln City	0 - 1	West Bromwich Albion
Luton Town	3 - 1	West Ham United
Manchester United	6 - 0	Bournemouth & BA
Newcastle United	0 - 2	Bradford Park Avenue
Nottingham Forest	2 - 2	Liverpool
Oldham Athletic	2 - 3	Cardiff City
Plymouth Argyle	0 - 1	Notts County
Portsmouth	7 - 0	Stockport County
Preston North End	2 - 1	Mansfield Town
Queens Park Rangers	0 - 0	Huddersfield Town
Rotherham United	4 - 2	Darlington
Sheffield United	5 - 2	New Brighton
Sheffield Wednesday	2 - 1	Southampton
Swindon Town	1 - 3	Stoke City
Torquay United	1 - 0	Coventry City
Wolverhampton Wanderers	6 - 0	Chesterfield
Yeovil Town	3 - 1	Bury

FA Cup 3rd Round replay
January 15, 1949

Birmingham City	1 - 1	Leicester City
Bolton Wanderers	0 - 0	Aston Villa
Huddersfield Town	5 - 0	Queens Park Rangers
Liverpool	4 - 0	Nottingham Forest

January 17, 1949

Aston Villa	2 - 1	Bolton Wanderers
Birmingham City	1 - 2	Leicester City

FA Cup 4th Round
January 29, 1949

Aston Villa	1 - 2	Cardiff City
Brentford	1 - 0	Torquay United
Chelsea	2 - 0	Everton
Derby County	1 - 0	Arsenal
Gateshead	1 - 3	West Bromwich Albion
Grimsby Town	2 - 3	Hull City
Leicester City	2 - 0	Preston North End
Liverpool	1 - 0	Notts County
Luton Town	4 - 0	Walsall
Manchester United	1 - 1	Bradford Park Avenue
Newport County	3 - 3	Huddersfield Town
Portsmouth	2 - 1	Sheffield Wednesday
Rotherham United	0 - 1	Burnley

Sheffield United	0 - 3	Wolverhampton Wanderers
Stoke City	1 - 1	Blackpool
Yeovil Town	2 - 1	Sunderland

FA Cup 4th Round replay
February 5, 1949

Blackpool	0 - 1	Stoke City
Bradford Park Avenue	1 - 1	Manchester United
Huddersfield Town	1 - 3	Newport County

FA Cup 4th Round 2nd replay
February 7, 1949

Bradford Park Avenue	0 - 5	Manchester United

FA Cup 5th Round
February 12, 1949

Brentford	4 - 2	Burnley
Derby County	2 - 1	Cardiff City
Luton Town	5 - 5	Leicester City
Manchester United	8 - 0	Yeovil Town
Portsmouth	3 - 2	Newport County
Stoke City	0 - 2	Hull City
West Bromwich Albion	3 - 0	Chelsea
Wolverhampton Wanderers	3 - 1	Liverpool

FA Cup 5th Round replay
February 19, 1949

Leicester City	5 - 3	Luton Town

FA Cup Quarter Final
February 26, 1949

Brentford	0 - 2	Leicester City
Hull City	0 - 1	Manchester United
Portsmouth	2 - 1	Derby County
Wolverhampton Wanderers	1 - 0	West Bromwich Albion

FA Cup Semi Final
March 26, 1949

Leicester City	3 - 1	Portsmouth	at Arsenal
Manchester United	1 - 1	Wolverhampton Wanderers	at Hillsborough

FA Cup Semi Final replay
April 2, 1949

Manchester United	0 - 1	Wolverhampton Wanderers	at Everton

FA Cup Final
April 30, 1949

Leicester City	1 - 3	Wolverhampton Wanderers	at Wembley

France

Paris RC upset Lille in the final to leave Lille runners-up in both domestic events.

Last 32
                January 30, 1949

Arras RC	3 - 0 Chartrain VS	at Rouen
Le Havre AC	2 - 0 Dolois FC	at Toulouse
Olympique SC de Lille Metropole	6 - 0 Sedan-Torcy UA	at Reims
Metz FC	3 - 1 Douaisien SA	at Charleville
Nice Olympique	4 - 1 Ponot CA	at Montpellier
Nimes Olympique	2 - 1 St Etienne AS	at Marseille
Paris RC	3 - 1 Stade Malherbe Caennais	at Le Havre
Stade Francais/Red Star	3 - 2 Roubaix-Tourcoing CO	at Strasbourg
Quevillaise US	1 - 0 Colmar SR	at Nancy
Stade de Reims	2 - 1 Sochaux-Montbeliard FC	at Paris
Stade Rennais FC	3 - 1 Vitry CA	at Nantes
Rouen FC	4 - 1 Nantes Atlantique FC	at Bordeaux
St Malo US	1 - 0 Stade Bethunois	at Angers
Sete FC	5 - 0 Mulhouse 1893 FC	at Lyon
Troyes ESTAC	5 - 0 Seynoise US	at Villefranche
Valenciennes FC	4 - 1 Olympique Saint Quentinois	at Lille

Last 16
                February 27, 1949

Arras RC	2 - 1 Valenciennes FC	at Lens
Olympique SC de Lille Metropole	1 - 1 Rouen FC	at Lyon
Metz FC	4 - 2 Stade Rennais FC	at Paris
Nice Olympique	3 - 0 Stade de Reims	at Marseille
Nimes Olympique	4 - 0 St Malo US	at Saint Ouen
Paris RC	2 - 0 Quevillaise US	at Rennes
Stade Francais/Red Star	3 - 0 Troyes ESTAC	at Metz
Sete FC	3 - 1 Le Havre AC	at Bordeaux

Replay
                March 3, 1949

Olympique SC de Lille Metropole	2 - 1 Rouen FC	at Paris

Quarter Final
                March 20, 1949

Olympique SC de Lille Metropole	2 - 1 Nice Olympique	at Paris
Metz FC	6 - 0 Arras RC	at Lille
Paris RC	2 - 1 Nimes Olympique	at Lyon
Stade Francais/Red Star	3 - 1 Sete FC	at Marseille

Semi Final
April 10, 1949
Paris RC 2 - 2 Metz FC at Paris
Olympique SC de Lille Metropole 1 - 0 Stade Francais/Red Star at Lyon
Replay
April 19, 1930
Paris RC 2 - 0 Metz FC at Paris

Final
May 8, 1949
Paris RC 5 - 2 Olympique SC de Lille Metropole at Paris

Greece

Aek were not even second best in the Athens area through the season, but they beat the bational champions in the cup final after a replay.

Quarter-Final
PAOK Salonika 2 - 1 Iraklis Thessalonikis
Panathinaikos 4 - 1 Apollon Athinas
Iraklis Kavalas 1 - 4 AEK Athens
Olympiakos Piraeus 3 - 3 APO Fostiras
Replay
APO Fostiras 1 - 4 Olympiakos Piraeus

Semi Final
AEK Athens 2 - 1 Olympiakos Piraeus
Panathinaikos 1 - 0 PAOK Salonika

Final
June 19, 1949
AEK Athens 0 - 0 Panathinaikos
Replay
July 3, 1949
AEK Athens 2 - 1 Panathinaikos

Republic of Ireland

League winners Drumcondra overcame City Cup winners Dundalk in one semi while Shield winners Shelbourne beat Watreford in the other. However Dundal stopped a double for Drumcondra with a 2-1 win. The President's Cup & Leinster cup went to Shamrock while Limerick won the Munster.

FAI Cup 1st Round
    February 19, 1949
Shamrock Rovers   1 - 1 St Patrick's Athletic Dublin
    February 20, 1949
Dundalk   4 - 1 Cork Athletic   Athletic replaced Cork United after Oct 10th

Freebooters Cork   0 - 3 Shelbourne
Transport Bray   2 - 0 Sligo Rovers
Waterford   4 - 1 Bohemians Dublin
FAI Cup 1st Round replay
    February 23, 1949
St Patrick's Athletic Dublin   2 - 1 Shamrock Rovers

FAI Cup Quarter Final
    March 6, 1949
St Patrick's Athletic Dublin   0 - 1 Shelbourne
    March 9, 1949
Drumcondra   4 - 0 Transport Bray

FAI Cup Semi Final
    March 26, 1949
Drumcondra   2 - 2 Dundalk
    March 27, 1949
Shelbourne   3 - 1 Waterford
FAI Cup Semi Final replay
    March 30, 1949
Dundalk   2 - 1 Drumcondra

FAI Cup Final
    April 10, 1949
Dundalk   3 - 0 Shelbourne

Leinster Cup Quarter Final
    October 13, 1948
Shamrock Rovers   2 - 1 Dundalk
    October 14, 1948
Drumcondra   3 - 0 W & R Jacobs Dublin
    October 20, 1948

Transport Bray   1 - 1 St Patrick's Athletic Dublin
    October 27, 1948
Bohemians Dublin   2 - 3 Shelbourne
Leinster Cup Quarter Final replay
    November 3, 1948
St Patrick's Athletic Dublin   1 - 0 Transport Bray

Leinster Cup Semi Final
    November 20, 1948
Shamrock Rovers   1 - 0 St Patrick's Athletic Dublin
    November 21, 1948
Shelbourne   2 - 1 Drumcondra

Leinster Cup Final
    December 26, 1948
Shelbourne   5 - 2 Shamrock Rovers

Munster Cup Semi Final
    November 21, 1948
Freebooters Cork   1 - 6 Waterford

Munster Cup Final
    December 26, 1948
Limerick   1 - 1 Waterford
Munster Cup Final replay
    March 17, 1949
Limerick   2 - 1 Waterford

President's Cup
    August 15, 1948
Shamrock Rovers   3 - 2 Drumcondra

Luxembourg

Eventual champions Spora went out in the Last 32, winners Stade Dudelange were drawn away from home in every round.

Last 32

    September 26, 1948

Progres Niederkorn	3	2	Spora Luxemburg
Union Luxemburg	3	1	Egalite Weimerskirch
Fola Esch	3	1	CS Obercorn
US Dudelange	5	2	CS Petange
Sporting Bettemburg	4	1	Rapid Neudorf
Jeunesse Wasserbillig	2	2	Red Black Pfaffenthal
Jeunesse 07 Kayl	0	1	The National Schifflange
Racing Rodange	3	0	Alliance Dudelange

Replay

    October 17, 1948

Red Black Pfaffenthal	4	5	Jeunesse Wasserbillig

Last 16

    November 7, 1948

US Dudelange	1	2	Fola Esch
The National Schifflange	1	5	Red Boys Differdange
Racing Rodange	4	2	Progres Niederkorn
Sporting Bettemburg	3	2	SC Tetange
US Rumelange	0	8	Stade Dudelange
Red Star Merl	0	3	CS Grevenmacher
Union Luxemburg	4	3	Chiers Rodange
Jeunesse Esch	1	0	Jeunesse Wasserbillig

Quarter Final

    January 2, 1949

Fola Esch	3	1	Red Boys Differdange
Sporting Bettemburg	0	3	Racing Rodange
Union Luxemburg	1	2	Stade Dudelange
CS Grevenmacher	4	3	Jeunesse Esch

Semi Final

    February 27, 1949

CS Grevenmacher	2	5	Stade Dudelange
Racing Rodange	1	0	Fola Esch

Final

    April 10, 1949

Stade Dudelange	1	0	Racing Rodange

Malta

Champions Sliema could not have expected a 5-1 thrashing at the hands of Floriana, having beaten them twice in the league.

Semi Final
June 9, 1949
Sliema Wanderers   8 - 3 Valletta

Final
June 16, 1949
Floriana Valletta   5 - 1 Sliema Wanderers

Netherlands

The Dutch cup final again went to penaties.
Final
Quick Nijmegen   1 - 1 Helmondia   Nijmegen won 2-1 on penalties

Northern Ireland

The best two teams in the Irish league were both knocked out in the Last 16. Derry eventually got to play and beat Glentoran in the final after Glentoran took three games to beat Portadown.

Last 16
Linfield	0 - 2	Glentoran Belfast
Dundela	4 - 4	Glenavon Lurgan
Ballyclare Comrades	0 - 1	Cliftonville
Brantwood	1 - 3	Derry City
Ballymena United	1 - 2	Coleraine
Ards	0 - 3	Bangor
Distillery Belfast	2 - 1	Coleraine
Portadown	1 - 0	Belfast Celtic

Replay
Glenavon Lurgan	4 - 0	Dundela

Quarter Final
Cliftonville	1 - 3	Glentoran Belfast
Derry City	1 - 1	Bangor
Distillery Belfast	2 - 1	Coleraine
Portadown	3 - 1	Glenavon

Replay
Bangor	3 - 3	Derry City

2nd replay
Derry City	1 - 1	Bangor

3rd replay
Bangor	1 - 0	Derry City

Semi Final
Derry City	2 - 0	Distillery Belfast	at Belfast Celtic
Glentoran Belfast	2 - 2	Portadown	

Replay
Glentoran Belfast	1 - 1	Portadown

2nd replay
Glentoran Belfast	3 - 0	Portadown

Final
Derry City	3 - 1	Glentoran Belfast	at Windsor Park

Norway

Fredrikstad's charge for a double was foiled at the final hurdle by Sarpsborg.

Last 32
    August 15, 1948
Sarpsborg FK	2	- 1	Solberg SV
Skeid Oslo	4	- 2	Aalesunds FK
Frigg SK Oslo	0	- 1	Storms BK Skien
Drammens BK	1	- 2	Lyn Oslo
Mjondalen IF	3	- 1	Rakkestad IF
Orn FK Horten	3	- 1	Jevnaker IF
Sandefjord BK	2	- 3	Odds BK Skien
Pors IF Porsgrunn	3	- 1	Sandaker SFK Oslo
Herkules IF Skien	1	- 3	Fredrikstad FK
Skiens-Grane	2	- 3	Sparta IL Sarpsborg
Viking Stavanger	3	- 1	Arstad IL Bergen
Brann Bergen	1	- 1	Vard SK Haugesund
Djerv 1919 Haugesund	1	- 1	Stavanger IF
Kristiansund FK	0	- 2	Kvik Trondheim
Freidig SK Trondheim	3	- 0	Neset FK Frosta
Ranheim IL	3	- 2	Clausenengen FK Kristiansund

Replay
    August 19, 1948
Vard SK Haugesund	0	- 2	Brann Bergen
Stavanger IF	5	- 1	Djerv 1919 Haugesund

Last 16
    August 19, 1948
Sparta IL Sarpsborg	2	- 1	Pors IF Porsgrunn
Fredrikstad FK	4	- 0	Orn FK Horten
Lyn Oslo	1	- 2	Ranheim IL
Mjondalen IF	2	- 2	Brann Bergen
Storms BK Skien	0	- 3	Viking Stavanger
Odds BK Skien	1	- 3	Freidig SK Trondheim
Stavanger IF	0	- 3	Sarpsborg FK
Kvik Trondheim	5	- 1	Skeid Oslo

Replay
Brann Bergen	1	- 4	Mjondalen IF

Quarter Final
    September 26, 1948
Fredrikstad FK	2	- 1	Sparta IL Sarpsborg
Sarpsborg FK	2	- 1	Ranheim IL
Freidig SK Trondheim	1	- 0	Kvik Trondheim
Mjondalen IF	0	- 1	Viking Stavanger

Semi Final
    October 3, 1948
Sarpsborg FK	3 - 1	Viking Stavanger
Fredrikstad FK	3 - 1	Freidig SK Trondheim

Final
    October 17, 1948
Sarpsborg FK	1 - 0	Fredrikstad FK

Portugal

Sporting lost to Tirsense in the last 32, while Benfica bagged a baker's dozen against Viseu enroute to defeating Atletico Lisboa in the final.

Last 32
Academico Viseu	2 - 1	O Elvas
Almada	1 - 2	Porto FC
Atletico Lisboa	2 - 1	Barreirense FC
Beja	2 - 3	Sporting Covilha
Belenenses Lisboa	4 - 1	Oriental Lisboa
Benfica Lisboa	7 - 1	Boavista Porto
FC Famalicao	2 - 1	Oliveirense
Lusitano Algarve	7 - 0	Silves FC
Os Leoes	1 - 3	Academica Coimbra
Sanjoanense	0 - 1	CUF Barreiro
Sporting Braga	1 - 0	Olhanense SC
Tirsense	2 - 1	Sporting Lisboa
Vitoria Guimaraes	3 - 2	Estoril Praia
Vitoria Setubal	3 - 1	Portimonense SC

Last 16
Atletico Lisboa	2 - 1	FC Famalicao
Benfica Lisboa	13 - 1	Academico Viseu
Lusitano Algarve	5 - 1	Tirsense
Sporting Braga	1 - 0	Belenenses Lisboa
Sporting Covilha	4 - 1	CUF Barreiro
Vitoria Guimaraes	1 - 4	Porto FC
Vitoria Setubal	8 - 1	Academica Coimbra

Quarter Final
Atletico Lisboa	6 - 2	Lusitano Algarve
Benfica Lisboa	9 - 3	Maritimo Funchal Madeira
Sporting Covilha	3 - 1	Sporting Braga

Vitoria Setubal 1 - 0 Porto FC

Semi Final
Sporting Covilha 0 - 1 Atletico Lisboa
Vitoria Setubal 0 - 5 Benfica Lisboa

Final
      June 12, 1949
Benfica Lisboa 2 - 1 Atletico Lisboa

Scotland

And the winners are ….. Glasgow Rangers, who won all 3 major domestic trophies in the one season.

SFA Cup 1st Round
      January 22, 1949
Alloa Athletic	8 - 3	Montrose
Arbroath	3 - 4	Partick Thistle
Ayr United	2 - 1	Queen's Park Glasgow
Clyde	2 - 0	Fraserburgh
Cowdenbeath	6 - 2	Keith
Dumbarton	5 - 2	Kilmarnock
Dundee	5 - 1	Perth St Johnstone
Dundee United	4 - 3	Glasgow Celtic
East Fife	2 - 1	Falkirk
Forfar Athletic	0 - 4	Hibernians Edinburgh
Hamilton Academicals	1 - 2	Albion Rovers
Heart of Midlothian	4 - 1	Airdrieonians
Inverness Caledonians	2 - 2	Greenock Morton
Leith Athletic	0 - 1	Raith Rovers
Motherwell	3 - 0	Stranraer
Queen of the South Dumfries	2 - 0	East Stirlingshire
Glasgow Rangers	6 - 1	Elgin City
St Mirren	2 - 0	Stirling Albion
Stenhousemuir	2 - 0	Dunfermline Athletic
Third Lanark	2 - 1	Aberdeen

SFA Cup 1st Round replay
      January 26, 1949
Greenock Morton 2 - 0 Inverness Caledonians

SFA Cup 2nd Round
      February 5, 1949
Alloa Athletic 1 - 3 Clyde
Ayr United 0 - 2 Greenock Morton

Cowdenbeath	1 - 2	East Fife
Dumbarton	1 - 1	Dundee United
Dundee	0 - 0	St Mirren
Heart of Midlothian	3 - 1	Third Lanark
Hibernians Edinburgh	1 - 1	Raith Rovers
Motherwell	0 - 3	Glasgow Rangers
Partick Thistle	3 - 0	Queen of the South Dumfries
Stenhousemuir	5 - 1	Albion Rovers

SFA Cup 2nd Round replay
   February 8, 1949

St Mirren	1 - 2	Dundee

   February 9, 1949

Dundee United	1 - 3	Dumbarton
Raith Rovers	3 - 4	Hibernians Edinburgh

SFA Cup 3rd Round
   February 19, 1949

Heart of Midlothian	3 - 0	Dumbarton
Greenock Morton	0 - 2	Clyde

SFA Cup Quarter Final
   March 5, 1949

Heart of Midlothian	2 - 4	Dundee
Hibernians Edinburgh	0 - 2	East Fife
Glasgow Rangers	4 - 0	Partick Thistle
Stenhousemuir	0 - 1	Clyde

SFA Cup Semi Final
   March 26, 1949

Clyde	2 - 2	Dundee	at Easter Road
Glasgow Rangers	3 - 0	East Fife	at Hampden Park

SFA Cup Semi Final replay
   April 4, 1949

Clyde	2 - 1	Dundee	at Hampden Park

SFA Cup The Final
   April 23, 1949

Glasgow Rangers	4 - 1	Clyde	at Hampden Park

Scottish League Cup Group Stage
   September 11, 1948

Aberdeen	3 - 1	St Mirren Paisley	Division 1 Section D
Airdrieonians	8 - 1	Dumbarton	Division 2 Section D
Ayr United	4 - 2	Arbroath	Division 2 Section D

Dundee	2 - 1	Albion Rovers	Division 1 Section B
Dunfermline Athletic	1 - 1	Stirling Albion	Division 2 Section A
East Stirlingshire	2 - 1	Kilmarnock	Division 2 Section B
Glasgow Celtic	1 - 0	Hibernians Edinburgh	Division 1 Section A
Glasgow Rangers	1 - 1	Clyde	Division 1 Section A
Greenock Morton	2 - 1	Third Lanark	Division 1 Section D
Hearts of Midlothian	2 - 2	Partick Thistle	Division 1 Section C
Motherwell	1 - 0	Falkirk	Division 1 Section B
Queen of the South Dumries	0 - 4	East Fife	Division 1 Section C
Queen's Park Glasgow	4 - 1	Alloa Athletic	Division 2 Section B
Raith Rovers	3 - 3	Cowdenbeath	Division 2 Section A
Perth St Johnstone	1 - 1	Dundee United	Division 2 Section C
Stenhousemuir	1 - 1	Hamilton Academicals	Division 2 Section C

September 18, 1948

Albion Rovers	0 - 1	Motherwell	Division 1 Section B
Alloa Athletic	1 - 0	East Stirlingshire	Division 2 Section B
Arbroath	2 - 3	Airdrieonians	Division 2 Section D
Clyde	0 - 2	Glasgow Celtic	Division 1 Section A
Cowdenbeath	0 - 2	Dunfermline Athletic	Division 2 Section A
Dumbarton	1 - 2	Ayr United	Division 2 Section D
Dundee United	4 - 2	Stenhousemuir	Division 2 Section C
East Fife	4 - 0	Hearts of Midlothian	Division 1 Section C
Falkirk	2 - 3	Dundee	Division 1 Section B
Hamilton Academicals	2 - 2	Perth St Johnstone	Division 2 Section C
Hibernians Edinburgh	0 - 0	Glasgow Rangers	Division 1 Section A
Kilmarnock	3 - 3	Queen's Park Glasgow	Division 2 Section B
Partick Thistle	9 - 0	Queen of the South Dumries	Division 1 Section C
St Mirren Paisley	1 - 1	Greenock Morton	Division 1 Section D
Third Lanark	1 - 1	Aberdeen	Division 1 Section D

September 25, 1948

Aberdeen	3 - 1	Greenock Morton	Division 1 Section D
Airdrieonians	6 - 1	Ayr United	Division 2 Section D
Arbroath	4 - 2	Dumbarton	Division 2 Section D
Cowdenbeath	3 - 3	Stirling Albion	Division 2 Section A
Dundee United	1 - 2	Hamilton Academicals	Division 2 Section C
Falkirk	2 - 1	Albion Rovers	Division 1 Section B
Glasgow Celtic	3 - 1	Glasgow Rangers	Division 1 Section A
Hibernians Edinburgh	4 - 0	Clyde	Division 1 Section A
Kilmarnock	4 - 3	Alloa Athletic	Division 2 Section B
Motherwell	0 - 1	Dundee	Division 1 Section B
Partick Thistle	2 - 5	East Fife	Division 1 Section C
Queen of the South Dumries	2 - 3	Hearts of Midlothian	Division 1 Section C
Queen's Park Glasgow	2 - 0	East Stirlingshire	Division 2 Section B
Raith Rovers	2 - 1	Dunfermline Athletic	Division 2 Section A
Perth St Johnstone	2 - 1	Stenhousemuir	Division 2 Section C

St Mirren Paisley	4 - 0 Third Lanark	Division 1 Section D
October 2, 1948		
Albion Rovers	2 - 3 Dundee	Division 1 Section B
Alloa Athletic	1 - 0 Queen's Park Glasgow	Division 2 Section B
Arbroath	1 - 1 Ayr United	Division 2 Section D
Clyde	1 - 3 Glasgow Rangers	Division 1 Section A
Cowdenbeath	0 - 6 Raith Rovers	Division 2 Section A
Dumbarton	5 - 0 Airdrieonians	Division 2 Section D
Dundee United	4 - 2 Perth St Johnstone	Division 2 Section C
East Fife	3 - 1 Queen of the South Dumries	Division 1 Section C
Falkirk	1 - 0 Motherwell	Division 1 Section B
Hamilton Academicals	3 - 0 Stenhousemuir	Division 2 Section C
Hibernians Edinburgh	4 - 2 Glasgow Celtic	Division 1 Section A
Kilmarnock	4 - 1 East Stirlingshire	Division 2 Section B
Partick Thistle	3 - 1 Hearts of Midlothian	Division 1 Section C
St Mirren Paisley	1 - 1 Aberdeen	Division 1 Section D
Stirling Albion	4 - 3 Dunfermline Athletic	Division 2 Section A
Third Lanark	2 - 2 Greenock Morton	Division 1 Section D
October 9, 1948		
Aberdeen	2 - 4 Third Lanark	Division 1 Section D
Airdrieonians	3 - 2 Arbroath	Division 2 Section D
Ayr United	2 - 1 Dumbarton	Division 2 Section D
Dundee	4 - 2 Falkirk	Division 1 Section B
Dunfermline Athletic	3 - 2 Cowdenbeath	Division 2 Section A
East Stirlingshire	1 - 3 Alloa Athletic	Division 2 Section B
Glasgow Celtic	3 - 6 Clyde	Division 1 Section A
Glasgow Rangers	1 - 0 Hibernians Edinburgh	Division 1 Section A
Greenock Morton	0 - 3 St Mirren Paisley	Division 1 Section D
Hearts of Midlothian	6 - 1 East Fife	Division 1 Section C
Motherwell	8 - 3 Albion Rovers	Division 1 Section B
Queen of the South Dumries	3 - 2 Partick Thistle	Division 1 Section C
Queen's Park Glasgow	2 - 2 Kilmarnock	Division 2 Section B
Raith Rovers	6 - 2 Stirling Albion	Division 2 Section A
Perth St Johnstone	0 - 0 Hamilton Academicals	Division 2 Section C
Stenhousemuir	2 - 1 Dundee United	Division 2 Section C
Stirling Albion	1 - 7 Raith Rovers	Division 2 Section A
October 16, 1948		
Albion Rovers	2 - 1 Falkirk	Division 1 Section B
Alloa Athletic	2 - 0 Kilmarnock	Division 2 Section B
Ayr United	1 - 4 Airdrieonians	Division 2 Section D
Clyde	1 - 4 Hibernians Edinburgh	Division 1 Section A
Dumbarton	1 - 1 Arbroath	Division 2 Section D
Dundee	0 - 1 Motherwell	Division 1 Section B
Dunfermline Athletic	1 - 0 Raith Rovers	Division 2 Section A
East Fife	3 - 0 Partick Thistle	Division 1 Section C

East Stirlingshire	1 - 1 Queen's Park Glasgow	Division 2 Section B
Glasgow Rangers	2 - 1 Glasgow Celtic	Division 1 Section A
Greenock Morton	3 - 1 Aberdeen	Division 1 Section D
Hamilton Academicals	6 - 3 Dundee United	Division 2 Section C
Hearts of Midlothian	4 - 0 Queen of the South Dumries	Division 1 Section C
Stenhousemuir	3 - 4 Perth St Johnstone	Division 2 Section C
Stirling Albion	5 - 2 Cowdenbeath	Division 2 Section A
Third Lanark	4 - 2 St Mirren Paisley	Division 1 Section D

Quarter Final
        October 30, 1948

Dundee	1 - 1 Alloa Athletic	
Glasgow Rangers	1 - 0 St Mirren Paisley	
Hamilton Academicals	1 - 1 Airdrieonians	
Raith Rovers	5 - 3 East Fife	

Quarter Final replay
        November 3, 1948

Airdrieonians	1 - 1 Hamilton Academicals	
Alloa Athletic	1 - 3 Dundee	

Quarter Final 2nd replay
        November 8, 1948

Hamilton Academicals	1 - 0 Airdrieonians	at Celtic Park

Semi Final
        November 20, 1948

Glasgow Rangers	4 - 1 Dundee	at Hampden Park
Raith Rovers	2 - 0 Hamilton Academicals	at Celtic Park

Final
        March 12, 1949

Glasgow Rangers	2 - 0 Raith Rovers	at Hampden Park

Spain

Valencia well deserved their cup win having ko'd Barcelona in the semi, while Real's conqueror Atletico Bilbao were the other finalists.

Last 64
January 1, 1949
Sabadell	2 - 4	Gerona
Badalona CF	0 - 2	Mallorca RCD
Hercules Alicante	3 - 2	Segarra V Uxo

January 2, 1949
Deportivo La Coruna	3 - 0	Ferrol
Real Aviles	1 - 2	Sporting Gijon
Barakaldo CF	3 - 0	Santander
Real Sociedad	1 - 0	Osasuna Pamplona
Arenas Zaragoza	2 - 1	Castellon
Malaga CD	6 - 1	SD Ceuta
Salamanca	6 - 1	Levante Valencia
Valencia CF Mestalla	1 - 2	Alcoyano
Real Murcia CF	2 - 3	Albacete Balompie
Tomelloso	0 - 1	Granada CF
RCD Cordoba	0 - 3	Sevilla FC

January 6, 1949
Gimn Lucense Lugo	1 - 2	Celta de Vigo
Atletico Bilbao	8 - 2	Arenas de Guecho

Last 32
March 13, 1949
Celta de Vigo	6 - 3	Salamanca
Barakaldo CF	0 - 3	Real Sociedad S Sebastian
Gerona	4 - 2	Mallorca RCD
Albacete Balompie	1 - 0	Alcoyano
Granada CF	2 - 1	Hercules Alicante
Sevilla FC	5 - 2	Malaga CD

March 27, 1949
Sporting Gijon	2 - 3	Deportivo La Coruna
Atletico Bilbao	7 - 0	Arenas Zaragoza

Last 16
April 21, 1949
Tarragona CG	5 - 1	Albacete Balompie
Espanyol Barcelona	3 - 1	Celta de Vigo

April 24, 1949
Deportivo La Coruna	0 - 1	Valencia CF
Real Sociedad San Sebastian	4 - 0	Real Oviedo

Barcelona CF	9 - 0	Gerona
Granada CF	4 - 1	Real Valladolid
Real Madrid CF	2 - 2	Athletic Bilbao
Atletico de Madrid	2 - 1	Sevilla FC

Last 16 2nd leg

Celta de Vigo	1 - 0	Espanyol Barcelona
Albacete Balompie	3 - 0	Gimnastico Tarragona

Replay
April 27, 1949

Athletic Bilbao	3 - 1	Real Madrid CF	at Barcelona

Quarter Final 1st Leg
May 1, 1949

Espanyol Barcelona	6 - 1	Atletico de Madrid
Athletic Bilbao	3 - 0	Tarragona CG
Granada CF	2 - 2	Barcelona CF
Valencia CF	3 - 2	Real Sociedad San Sebastian

Quarter Final 2nd Leg
May 8, 1949

Atletico de Madrid	5 - 1	Espanyol Barcelona
Tarragona CG	2 - 0	Athletic Bilbao
Barcelona CF	5 - 0	Granada CF
Real Sociedad San Sebastian	1 - 2	Valencia CF

Semi Final 1st Leg
May 15, 1949

Espanyol Barcelona	1 - 2	Atletico Bilbao
Valencia CF	3 - 1	Barcelona CF

Semi Final 2nd Leg

Athletic Bilbao	6 - 2	Espanyol Barcelona
Barcelona CF	3 - 2	Valencia CF

Final
May 29, 1949

Valencia CF	1 - 0	Athletic Bilbao	at Madrid

Sweden

None of the top division teams entered the cup, and it was left to two level three teams to fight for the trophy – back to normal next season.

Last 32
        June 27, 1948
Friska Viljor IF   3 - 0   Ostersund IKK
Hoganas BK   1 - 2   Karlstads BIK
Kalmar AIK   2 - 3   Vasteras IFK
Kenty BK   3 - 1   Fagerviks GF
Raa IF   2 - 1   Landskrona BoIS
Sundsvall GIF   4 - 5   Kramfors IF
Surahammars IF   2 - 1   Holmsund IFK
Viken IF   1 - 2   Sandvikens IF

Last 16
        July 4, 1948
Vasteras IFK   3 - 2   Sleipner IK
Kramfors IF   2 - 4   Kenty BK
Reymersholms IK   5 - 2   Atvidabergs FF
Wifsta/Ostrands IF   4 - 3   Ludvika
Raa IF   3 - 2   Sandvikens IF
Sandvikens AIK   2 - 3   Tidaholms GIF
Karlstads BIK   2 - 5   Friska Viljor IF
Sandviks IK   2 - 3   Surahammars IF

Quarter Final
        July 11, 1948
Surahammars IF   2 - 5   Raa IF
Tidaholms GIF   8 - 4   Wifsta/Ostrands IF
Kenty BK   3 - 2   Reymersholms IK
Friska Viljor IF   2 - 0   Vasteras IFK

Semi Final
        July 18, 1948
Raa IF   9 - 1   Friska Viljor IF
Kenty BK   1 - 0   Tidaholms GIF

Final
        July 25, 1948
Raa IF   6 - 0   Kenty BK

Switzerland

It was not a good Christmas for champions to be Lugano, they lost in the Last 32 round to soon to be relegated Grasshopper. Servette stopped Grasshopper's run in the final with a 3-0 win.

Last 64
    November 14, 1948

Urania Geneve-Sport	3 - 1	Helvetia Bern
Gardy-Jonction GE	1 - 1	Bern
Moutier	1 - 0	Stade Lausanne
Thun	1 - 1	BSC Old Boys Basel
Allschwil	0 - 5	Chiasso
AC Bellinzona	2 - 0	Red Star ZH
Biel-Bienne	2 - 0	Stade Nyonnais
Monthey	1 - 3	Servette Geneve
Birsfelden	4 - 0	SC Bruhl St.Gallen
Lengnau	2 - 1	Young Fellows Zurich
Lausanne-Sports	8 - 0	Ambrosiana Lausanne
Etoile Sp. Chaux-de-Fonds	0 - 1	La Chaux-de-Fonds
Fribourg	3 - 0	US Bienne-Boujean
Vevey-Sports	5 - 2	Solothurn
St.Gallen	2 - 0	Schaffhausen
Nordstern Basel	3 - 1	SC Kleinhuningen
Aarau	1 - 1	Altstetten ZH
SC Zug	3 - 1	SV Ceresio Schaffhausen
Zurich	6 - 3	Wil
SC Schoftland	4 - 2	Mendrisiostar
Grasshopper Zurich	8 - 0	Emmenbrucke
Lugano	5 - 1	Uster
Concordia Basel	5 - 3	SC Zofingen
Winterthur	1 - 2	Basel
SV Hongg ZH	1 - 3	Contone
Yverdon-Sport	2 - 1	CS International GE
ES Malley	2 - 1	Grenchen
Cantonal Neuchatel	1 - 0	Racing Lausanne
BSC Young Boys Bern	3 - 1	Montreux-Sports
Locarno	2 - 1	Blue Stars Zurich
Kreuzlingen	4 - 1	Wettingen

    December 5, 1948

SC Derendingen	1 - 1	Luzern

Replay
    December 5, 1948

Bern	0 - 1	Gardy-Jonction GE
BSC Old Boys Basel	1 - 5	Thun
Altstetten ZH	0 - 1	Aarau

December 26, 1948
Luzern   1 - 1 SC Derendingen   SC Derendingen qualified on coin toss

Last 32
      December 5, 1948
Fribourg   3 - 2 Vevey-Sports
St.Gallen   0 - 2 Nordstern Basel
      December 26, 1948
Urania Geneve Sport   4 - 0 Jonction-Gardy GE
Moutier   0 - 0 Thun
Chiasso   2 - 1 AC Bellinzona
Biel-Bienne   1 - 2 Servette Geneve
Birsfelden   1 - 3 Lengnau
Lausanne-Sports   4 - 0 La Chaux-de-Fonds
Aarau   1 - 0 SC Zug
Zurich   5 - 1 SC Schoftland
Grasshopper   2 - 1 Lugano
Concordia Basel   0 - 1 Basel
Yverdon-Sport   0 - 1 ES Malley
Cantonal Neuchatel   3 - 1 BSC Young Boys Bern
Locarno   3 - 0 Kreuzlingen
      January 2, 1949
SC Derendingen   5 - 1 Contone
Replay
      January 2, 1949
Thun   3 - 1 Moutier

Last 16
      January 9, 1949
Urania Geneve Sport   5 - 0 Thun
Lengnau   0 - 5 Lausanne-Sports
Fribourg   3 - 0 Nordstern Basel
Aarau   2 - 2 Zurich
Grasshopper   1 - 1 Basel
Derendingen   0 - 1 ES Malley
Cantonal Neuchatel   0 - 1 Locarno
      January 23, 1949
Chiasso   1 - 3 Servette Geneve
Replay
      January 23, 1949
Zurich   4 - 0 Aarau
Basel   1 - 2 Grasshopper

Quarter Final
      January 16, 1949

Lausanne-Sports 1 - 0 Fribourg
  February 13, 1949
Urania Geneve Sport 0 - 1 Servette Geneve
Zurich 0 - 6 Grasshopper
ES Malley 2 - 0 Locarno

Semi Final
  March 13, 1949
Grasshopper 3 - 0 ES Malley
  March 27, 1949
Servette Geneve 5 - 1 Lausanne-Sports

Final
  April 18, 1949
Servette Geneve 3 - 0 Grasshopper Zurich   at Bern

USSR

CSKA did the double with a 1-0 win over Spartak, having beaten league runners-up Dynamo in the semi final.

Last 32
    September 25, 1948
Dynamo Leningrad	2 - 1	Krylya Sovetov Kuibyshev
Dynamo Kiev	2 - 1	Dynamo Erevan
Torpedo Moscow	5 - 1	Torpedo Stalingrad
Zenit Leningrad	0 - 0	Dynamo Kazan

    September 26, 1948
Zenit Leningrad	4 - 1	Dynamo Kazan

Last 16
    September 29, 1948
Lokomotiv Moscow	0 - 1	Dynamo Tbilisi
VVS Moscow	2 - 1	Metallurg Moscow
Spartak Moscow	3 - 0	Dzerzhinets Chelyabinsk
Dynamo Kiev	2 - 1	Dynamo Leningrad
Torpedo Moscow	3 - 1	Zenit Leningrad
CSKA Moscow	3 - 0	Dynamo Minsk
Krylia Sovetov Moscow	0 - 1	Lokomotiv Kharkov
Dynamo Moscow	3 - 0	DO Toshkent

Quarter Final
    October 4, 1948
VVS Moscow	1 - 2	Dynamo Tbilisi
Spartak Moscow	1 - 0	Dynamo Kiev
CSKA Moscow	w o	Torpedo Moscow
Dynamo Moscow	7 - 1	Lokomotiv Kharkov

    October 6, 1948
CSKA Moscow	3 - 1	Torpedo Moscow

Semi Final
    October 17, 1948
Spartak Moscow	1 - 0	Dynamo Tbilisi
CSKA Moscow	0 - 0	Dynamo Moscow

    October 18, 1948
CSKA Moscow	1 - 0	Dynamo Moscow

Final
    October 24, 1948
CSKA Moscow	3 - 0	Spartak Moscow

Wales

Merthyr Tydfil defeated the more illustrious clubs Cardiff City in the semi and Swansea in the final as well as famous wartime team Lovell's in an earlier round.

Last 16
Bangor City	0 - 2	Rhyl
Chester	0 - 6	Wrexham
Pwllheli & District	4 - 1	Johnstown United
South Liverpool	7 - 4	Flint Town United
Lovell's Athletic	1 - 0	Shrewsbury Town
Milford United	2 - 0	Newport County
Cardiff City	3 - 1	Troedyrhiw
Merthyr Tydfil	6 - 4	Haverfordwest Athletic
Barry Town	1 - 7	Swansea Town

Intermediate round
Lovell's Athletic	2 - 3	Merthyr Tydfil

Quarter Final
Swansea Town	9 - 1	South Liverpool
Rhyl	1 - 0	Wrexham
Milford United	1 - 2	Cardiff City
Merthyr Tydfil	4 - 0	Pwllheli & District

Semi Final
Swansea Town	3 - 0	Rhyl	at Wrexham
Cardiff City	1 - 3	Merthyr Tydfil	at Swansea

Final
May 5, 1949
Merthyr Tydfil	2 - 0	Swansea Town

Yugoslavia

Red Star (Crvena Zvezda) beat champions Partizan in the final.

Last 32
    November 7, 1948

Buducnost Titograd	3 - 0	Sar Tetovo
Dinamo Pancevo	0 - 2	Metalac Beograd
Garnizon JNA Nis	2 - 4	Metalac Zagreb
Jedinstvo Zemun	2 - 4	Napredak Krusevac
Kvarner Rijeka	2 - 3	Ponciana Triëst
Lokomotiva Zagreb	4 - 0	Garnizon JNA Radovljica
Nasa Krila Zemun	2 - 1	Enotnost Ljubljana
Proleter Osijek	5 - 1	Dinamo Skopje
Rudar Trbovlje	0 - 0	Zagreb after extra time lots drawn
Sarajevo	2 - 1	Mornar Split
Sloga Novi Sad	5 - 2	Podrinje Sabac
Spartak Subotica	2 - 1	Vardar Skopje

Last 16
    November 14, 1948

Crvena Zvezda	5 - 1	Spartak Subotica
Hajduk Split	0 - 2	Buducnost Titograd
Metalac Beograd	1 - 1	Metalac Zagreb after extra time lots drawn
Napredak Krusevac	1 - 1	Ponciana Triëst after extra time lots drawn
Proleter Osijek	2 - 3	Partizan Beograd
Sarajevo	0 - 0	Lokomotiva Zagreb after extra time lots drawn
Sloga Novi Sad	4 - 8	Nasa Krila Zemun
Zagreb	3 - 4	Dinamo Zagreb

Quarter Final
    November 21, 1948

Lokomotiva Zagreb	0 - 2	Partizan Beograd
Metalac Zagreb	1 - 5	Dinamo Zagreb
Napredak Krusevac	1 - 4	Crvena Zvezda
Nasa Krila Zemun	4 - 1	Buducnost Titograd

Semi Final
    November 28, 1948

Crvena Zvezda	4 - 3	Nasa Krila Zemun
Partizan Beograd	3 - 3	Dinamo Zagreb after extra time lots drawn

Final
    November 29, 1948

Crvena Zvezda	3 - 0	Partizan Beograd

Errors & Omissions
Iceland

Results from 1946 and 1947 seasons – Fram won them both, unbeaten.

1946

		Pld	W	D	L	F	A	GA	Pts
1	Fram Reykjavik	5	4	1	0	17	10	1.70	9
2	KR Reykjavik	5	3	1	1	16	9	1.78	7
3	Valur Reykjavik	5	3	1	1	11	7	1.57	7
4	Vikingur Reykjavik	5	0	3	2	11	15	0.73	3
5	IA Akranes	5	0	2	3	6	13	0.46	2
6	IB Akureyri	5	0	2	3	6	13	0.46	2

Fram Reykjavik	3 -	1	KR Reykjavik
Fram Reykjavik	2 -	1	Valur Reykjavik
Fram Reykjavik	5 -	5	Vikingur Reykjavik
Fram Reykjavik	4 -	1	IA Akranes
Fram Reykjavik	3 -	2	IB Akureyri
KR Reykjavik	3 -	3	Valur Reykjavik
KR Reykjavik	4 -	1	Vikingur Reykjavik
KR Reykjavik	4 -	1	IA Akranes
KR Reykjavik	4 -	1	IB Akureyri
Valur Reykjavik	2 -	1	Vikingur Reykjavik
Valur Reykjavik	2 -	1	IA Akranes
Valur Reykjavik	3 -	0	IB Akureyri
Vikingur Reykjavik	2 -	2	IA Akranes
Vikingur Reykjavik	2 -	2	IB Akureyri
IA Akranes	1 -	1	IB Akureyri

1947

		Pld	W	D	L	F	A	GA	Pts
1	Fram Reykjavik	4	3	1	0	7	4	1.75	7
2	Valur Reykjavik	4	3	0	1	8	2	4.00	6
3	KR Reykjavik	4	2	1	1	8	6	1.33	5
4	Vikingur Reykjavik	4	0	1	3	4	7	0.57	1
5	IA Akranes	4	0	1	3	3	11	0.27	1

Fram Reykjavik	1 -	0	Valur Reykjavik
Fram Reykjavik	2 -	2	KR Reykjavik
Fram Reykjavik	2 -	1	Vikingur Reykjavik
Fram Reykjavik	2 -	1	IA Akranes
Valur Reykjavik	2 -	0	KR Reykjavik
Valur Reykjavik	2 -	1	Vikingur Reykjavik
Valur Reykjavik	4 -	0	IA Akranes
KR Reykjavik	2 -	1	Vikingur Reykjavik
KR Reykjavik	4 -	1	IA Akranes
Vikingur Reykjavik	1 -	1	IA Akranes